C🌼OKIES
CAKES & PIES

Taste of Home BOOKS

RDA ENTHUSIAST BRANDS, LLC
MILWAUKEE, WI

Taste of Home

EDITORIAL

Editor-in-Chief Catherine Cassidy
Vice President, Content Operations Kerri Balliet
Creative Director: Howard Greenberg

Managing Editor, Print & Digital Books: Mark Hagen
Associate Creative Director: Edwin Robles Jr.

Editor: Amy Glander
Associate Editors: Julie Kuczynski, Molly Jasinski
Art Director: Maggie Conners
Layout Designer: Courtney Lovetere
Editorial Production Manager: Dena Ahlers
Editorial Production Coordinator: Jill Banks
Copy Chief: Deb Warlaumont Mulvey
Copy Editor: Chris McLaughlin
Contributing Copy Editors: Michael Juley, Valerie Phillips
Business Architect, Publishing Technologies: Amanda Harmatys
Solutions Architect, Publishing Technologies: John Mosey
Junior Business Analyst: Shannon Stroud
Editorial Services Administrator: Marie Brannon

Content Director: Julie Blume Benedict
Food Editors: Gina Nistico; James Schend;
Peggy Woodward, RDN
Recipe Editors: Sue Ryon (lead), Mary King, Irene Yeh

Test Kitchen & Food Styling Manager: Sarah Thompson
Test Cooks: Nicholas Iverson (lead), Matthew Hass,
Lauren Knoelke
Food Stylists: Kathryn Conrad (lead), Leah Rekau,
Shannon Roum
Prep Cooks: Bethany Van Jacobson (lead), Melissa Hansen,
Aria C. Thornton
Culinary Team Assistant: Megan Behr

Photography Director: Stephanie Marchese
Photographers: Dan Roberts, Jim Wieland
Photographer/Set Stylist: Grace Natoli Sheldon
Set Stylists: Melissa Franco (lead), Stacey Genaw, Dee Dee Jacq
Set Stylist Assistant: Stephanie Chojnacki

Editorial Business Manager: Kristy Martin
Rights & Permissions Associate: Samantha Lea Stoeger
Editorial Business Associate: Andrea Heeg Polzin

BUSINESS

Vice President, Group Publisher: Kirsten Marchioli
Publisher: Donna Lindskog
Business Development Director, Taste of Home Live: Laurel Osman
Promotional Partnerships Manager, Taste of Home Live:
Jamie Piette Andrzejewski

TRUSTED MEDIA BRANDS, INC.

President and Chief Executive Officer: Bonnie Kintzer
Chief Financial Officer: Dean Durbin
Chief Marketing Officer: C. Alec Casey
Chief Revenue Officer: Richard Sutton
Chief Digital Officer: Vince Errico
Senior Vice President, Global HR & Communications:
Phyllis E. Gebhardt, SPHR; SHRM-SCP
General Counsel: Mark Sirota
Vice President, Magazine Marketing: Christopher Gaydos
Vice President, Operations: Michael Garzone
Vice President, Consumer Marketing Planning: Jim Woods
Vice President, Digital Content & Audience Development:
Diane Dragan
Vice President, Financial Planning & Analysis: William Houston
Publishing Director, Books: Debra Polansky

For other Taste of Home books and products,
visit us at tasteofhome.com.

International Standard Book Number: 978-1-61765-531-9
Library of Congress Control Number: 2016940430

Printed in China.
1 3 5 7 9 10 8 6 4 2

Pictured on front cover: Best-Ever Sugar Cookies, page 54;
Mocha Hazelnut Torte, page 125; Red Velvet Whoopie Pies,
page 70; Go Bananas Whoopie Pies, page 60; Gingerbread
Whoopie Pies, page 61; Chocolate Dream Whoopie Pies,
page 70; and Berry Patch Pie, page 218.
Pictured on back cover: Marvelous Marble Cake, page 131;
Cinnamon-Candy Cookies, page 16; and Grasshopper Pie,
page 274.
Pictured on page 1: Chocolate Butterscotch Haystacks, page 98;
Rainbow Sherbet Angel Food Cake, page 141; and Cherry Cream
Pie, page 245.

GET SOCIAL WITH US

LIKE US
facebook.com/tasteofhome

FOLLOW US
@tasteofhome

PIN US
pinterest.com/taste_of_home

TWEET US
twitter.com/tasteofhome

To find a recipe
tasteofhome.com

To submit a recipe
tasteofhome.com/submit

To find out about other
Taste of Home **products**
shoptasteofhome.com

Chocolate Mint Wafers, page 60

Rainbow Cake with Clouds, page 154

Contents

It's a 3-in-1 Cookbook!

Bake up the perfect treat for any occasion with *Taste of Home Cookies, Cakes & Pies*. Divided into three sections, this handy cookbook is truly like having three cookbooks in one. Need a recipe for your Christmas cookie exchange? See the chapter Cookies: Christmas Classics. Want to make a showstopping cake for your next birthday celebration? Turn to Cakes: Layered Cakes & Tortes. Have a bounty of raspberries? Look through the chapter Pies: Fruit Pies. Plus, in the next six pages read top tips on getting your cookies just right, baking the best cake ever and preparing a pie crust that looks as good as it tastes.

Caramel-Apple Skillet Buckle, page 300

HANDY ICONS: **⑤INGREDIENTS** With the exception of water, salt, pepper, oils and optional ingredients, you only need a few items for these recipes.

FREEZE IT With a little planning, you can stash these sweets in the freezer for last-minute fun! What could be easier?

BIG BATCH All these desserts are real crowd pleasers, perfect for potluck dinners, parties and classroom treats.

Deluxe
Sugar
Cookies,
page 50

COOKIES 101

Whether you like them crisp and buttery or soft and chewy, there's no denying the crowd-pleasing appeal of cookies. Here are some tips to make sure you bake up a batch that turns out just right.

Before You Begin

Read the entire recipe and check to see that you have all the required ingredients. Also, make sure you understand the cooking techniques.

Preheat the oven for 10 to 15 minutes before baking. Use an oven thermometer to verify the accuracy of your oven. If the set oven temperature and the oven thermometer do not agree, adjust the oven temperature accordingly.

Get the Oven Ready

Position the oven rack so the baking pan will be in the center of the oven, unless the recipe directs otherwise.

Mixing It Up

Always prepare the ingredients before you start mixing. Let the butter soften, toast the coconut, chop the nuts, etc. Measure the ingredients correctly.

Prepare the recipe according to directions.

Avoid overmixing the cookie dough. If it's handled too much, the cookies will be tough. For even baking, always make cookies the same size and thickness.

The Right Pan

Use heavy-gauge dull aluminum baking sheets with low sides for cookies. Pans with high sides can deflect heat and make it more difficult to remove the cookies once they are baked. It's best to use the size of pan called for in the recipe.

When a recipe calls for greased baking sheets or pans, grease them with shortening or cooking spray. For easy removal, line the bottom of the pan with parchment paper and grease the paper.

Unless the recipe directs otherwise, place cookie dough 2 to 3 inches apart on a cool baking sheet.

While Baking

Leave at least 2 inches between the baking sheet or pan and the oven walls for good heat circulation. For best results, bake only one sheet of cookies at a time. If you need to bake two sheets at once, switch the position of the baking sheets halfway through the baking time.

Unless otherwise directed, let cookies cool for 1 minute on the baking sheet before removing to a wire rack to cool completely.

Let baking sheet cool before placing the next batch on it. Otherwise, the heat will soften the dough and cause it to spread.

Storing Cookies

Cookies tend to change texture after storing—soft cookies get hard and crisp cookies get soft. Check out these tips to keep morsels at peak freshness.

- Allow cookies and bars to cool completely before storing. Cut crisp bar cookies while slightly warm. Allow icing on cookies to dry completely before storing.

- Store soft and crisp cookies in separate airtight containers. If stored together, the moisture from the soft cookies will soften the crisp cookies. Flavors can also blend during storage, so don't store strong-flavored cookies with delicate-flavored cookies.

- Arrange cookies in an airtight container with waxed paper placed between layers.

- Store cookies in a cool, dry place. Cookies with a cream cheese frosting should be covered and stored in the refrigerator.

- If your crisp cookies became soft during storage, crisp them up easily by heating them in a 300° oven for 5 minutes.

- For longer storage, freeze cookies for up to 3 months.

- Wrap unfrosted cookies in plastic wrap, stack them in an airtight container, seal and freeze.

- Thaw the wrapped cookies at room temperature before frosting and serving.

Cherry Biscochitos, page 53

Problem-Solving Pointers

Cookies Spread Too Much
- ☐ Place cookies on a cool baking sheet.
- ☐ Replace part of the butter in the recipe with shortening.
- ☐ If using margarine, check label and make sure it contains 80% vegetable oil.

Cookies Don't Spread Enough
- ☐ Use all butter instead of shortening or margarine.
- ☐ Add 1 to 2 tablespoons of liquid, such as milk or water.
- ☐ Let dough stand at room temperature before baking.

Cookies Are Tough
- ☐ The dough was overhandled or overmixed; use a light touch when mixing.
- ☐ Too much flour was worked into the dough.
- ☐ Add 1 or 2 tablespoons more shortening or butter or sugar.

Cookies Are Too Brown
- ☐ Check the oven temperature with an oven thermometer.
- ☐ Use heavy-gauge dull aluminum baking sheets. Dark baking sheets will cause the cookies to become overly brown.

Cookies Are Too Pale
- ☐ Check the oven temperature with an oven thermometer.
- ☐ Use heavy-gauge dull aluminum baking sheets. Insulated baking sheets cause cookies to be pale in color.
- ☐ Use butter, not shortening or margarine.

Lemon-Blueberry Pound Cake, page 165

CAKES 101

Are you ready to create gorgeous bakery-quality cakes at home? Follow the pointers here to ensure baking success every time. Then just grab an apron and get started!

4 Tips for Baking Success

1. Select and Prep Pans
Use and grease the type of pan and the size of pan stated in the recipe. In general, baking pans are filled two-thirds to three-fourths full.

2. Mix It Up
Follow the mixing directions as they are written. Altering the method may affect how the final baked good looks and/or tastes.

3. Check Doneness
Check for doneness at the shortest time given in the recipe using the stated doneness test. If the baked good does not test done, continue baking and check again.

4. Take Time To Cool
Cakes need to rest for 10 minutes in their pans. The resting time helps prevent them from crumbling when they are removed. Angel food cakes and chiffon cakes baked in tube pans are cooled completely in their pans. Some baked goods are delicious warm, but others should cool completely for frosting or easy slicing.

1. Grease the pan as the recipe directs with shortening or cooking spray.

2. Cream until light and fluffy.

3. A cake is done when it bounces back to touch.

4. Cool most baked goods for 10 minutes before removing from the pan.

Mixing Methods

Have you ever been unsure about the meaning of a term in a recipe? After all, when it comes to baking, there is more to mixing ingredients than you might think! This brief list may help when whipping up your next batch of baked goodies:

- **Beat:** To make a mixture smooth by rapidly mixing with an electric mixer, fork, spoon or wire whisk.

- **Combine:** To place several ingredients in a single bowl or container and thoroughly mix.

- **Cream:** To beat butter, margarine or shortening alone or with sugar using a spoon or mixer until light and fluffy.

- **Moisten:** To add enough liquid to dry ingredients while stirring to make a wet but not runny mixture.

- **Soft peaks:** To beat cream or egg whites until soft, rounded peaks form when the beaters are lifted.

- **Whip:** To beat rapidly by hand or with an electric mixer to add air and increase volume.

STIFF PEAKS

To beat egg whites until stiff, pointed peaks form when beaters are lifted.

Choosing Bakeware

Baking pans are made of metal. Aluminum pans with dull finishes give the best overall results. Pans with dark finishes often cook and brown foods more quickly. If you use pans with dark finishes, you may need to adjust the baking time and cover tops of baked goods with foil to prevent overbrowning. Insulated pans and pans with shiny finishes generally take longer to bake and brown foods.

Baking dishes are made of ovenproof glass or ceramic. If you substitute a glass baking dish in a recipe calling for a metal pan, reduce the oven temperature by 25° to avoid overbaking.

To determine your bakeware's measurements, use a ruler to measure from one inside top edge to the opposite inside top edge. To measure height, place a ruler on the outside of the dish and measure from the bottom to a top edge. For volume, fill the pan or dish to the rim with measured water.

For best results, use the pan size called for in the recipe. However, the chart below offers some practical substitutions.

If you don't have this pan(s):	Use this pan(s) instead:
One 9x5-in. loaf pan	Three 5¾x3x2-in. loaf pans
One 8x4-in. loaf pan	Two 5¾x3x2-in. loaf pans
One 9-in. round baking pan	One 8-in. square baking dish
Two 9-in. round baking pans	One 13x9-in. baking pan
One 10-in. fluted tube pan	One 10-in. tube pan or two 9x5-in. loaf pans
One 13x9-in. baking pan	Two 9-in. round baking pans or two 8-in. square baking dishes

Tart Cherry Lattice Pie, page 231

PIES 101

Nothing beats a pie made from scratch. Prepare a pie with a homemade crust and create a beautiful dessert that looks just as good as it tastes. You'll be blue-ribbon bound in no time!

Making and Shaping Single- and Double-Crust Pie Pastry

1. Accurately measure the flour and salt and combine in a bowl. Using a pastry blender or two knives, cut in the shortening until the mixture resembles coarse crumbs (the size of small peas).

2. Sprinkle 1 tablespoon of cold water over the mixture and toss gently with a fork. Repeat until the dry ingredients are moist and the dough holds together. Use only as much water as necessary.

3. Shape into a ball. (For a double-crust pie, divide pastry in half so that one ball is slightly larger than the other.) On a floured surface or a floured pastry cloth, flatten the ball (the larger one if making a double-crust pie) into a neat circle, pressing together any cracks or breaks.

4. Roll the dough with a floured rolling pin from the center of the pastry to the edges, forming a circle 2 inches larger than the pie plate. The pastry should be about $\frac{1}{8}$ inch thick.

5. To move pastry to the pie plate, roll up onto the rolling pin. Position over the edge of the pie plate and unroll. Let the pastry ease into the plate. Do not stretch the pastry to fit. For a single-crust pie, trim the pastry with kitchen scissors to $\frac{1}{2}$ inch beyond the plate edge; turn under and flute as in step 8. Either bake the shell or fill according to the recipe's directions. For a double-crust pie, trim the pastry even with the edge of the plate. For a lattice crust, trim pastry to 1 inch beyond the plate edge.

6. For a double-crust pie, roll out the second ball into a 12-inch circle, about $\frac{1}{8}$ inch thick. Roll up pastry onto rolling pin; position over filling. With a knife, cut slits in top to allow steam to escape while baking.

7. With scissors, trim top pastry to 1 inch beyond the plate edge. Fold the top pastry over the bottom pastry.

8. To flute the edge, position your thumb and index finger on the inside of the crust. Place your index finger or knuckle of your other hand on the outside edge and pinch pastry around it to form a V-shape and seal the dough together. Continue around the edge. Bake according to recipe directions.

Pie Pastry Pointers

Whether you're a beginner or well-seasoned baker, you'll appreciate these practical pointers for creating homemade pastry for pies and tarts.

Starting from Scratch

- Classic pie pastry recipes are prepared with solid shortening. Lard or butter-flavored shortening can be substituted for plain shortening if desired.

- Measure all ingredients accurately. Combine the flour and salt thoroughly before adding the shortening and water. Be sure to use ice-cold water. Add an ice cube to water and measure before adding it to the flour mixture.

- To produce a flaky crust, avoid overmixing when adding the water to the flour and shortening mixture. Overmixing develops gluten in the flour, causing the pastry to become tough. Chill pie pastry dough for 30 minutes before rolling to make it easier to handle.

- A floured surface is essential to prevent sticking when rolling out pastry. A pastry cloth and rolling pin cover are good investments—they will keep the pastry from sticking and minimize the amount of flour used. The less flour you add while rolling, the flakier and lighter the pie pastry will be.

- Choose dull-finish aluminum or glass pie plates for crisp, golden crusts. Shiny pans can produce soggy crusts. Because of the high fat content in a pastry, do not grease the pie plate unless the recipe directs.

- Use dried uncooked beans or rice atop heavy-duty foil to weigh down a crust when it's prebaked. The beans or rice prevent the sides of the pie crust from shrinking and slipping down the pie plate during baking. Note: Do not eat the beans or rice.

Decorative Pie Crusts

A fold here, a twist there—with some simple but snappy finger work, you can turn out a pie or tart that's as yummy to look at as it is to eat.

An eye-catching, well-woven lattice top gives a pie a fancy finishing touch. And although it may look difficult, you'll find it's a cinch to complete.

To help unravel the mystery behind making this appealing crust, we've compiled simple-to-follow instructions here so you can create your own at home.

Lattice Top Crust

A lattice top crust is suitable for a double-crust pie. Line bottom of a 9-in. pie plate with half the pastry and add the filling. Roll the remaining dough into an 11-in. circle. Cut 1-in.-wide strips using a knife, pizza cutter or clean pinking shears for a scalloped edge. Lay half the strips across the pie, about 1 inch apart.

Fold back every other strip about halfway. Lay a strip of dough across center of pie at a right angle to the other strips. Unfold strips over the center strip.

Fold back the alternate strips; place second cross strip in place. Continue to add strips until the entire pie is covered with lattice.

Trim all but 1 inch of the overlapping dough; fold the edges under bottom crust. Pinch dough around edge of pie to form a decorative edge.

Cinnamon-Candy
Cookies, page 16

Jumbo Brownie
Cookies, page 40

Roll-Out Cookies, page 57

Almond Bonbon Cookies, page 110

Cookies

YOU DON'T NEED TO WAIT FOR THE WEEKEND OR A SPECIAL OCCASION TO WHIP UP SOME TREATS! WITH EASY SLICE-AND-BAKE AND EVEN DROP-COOKIE OPTIONS, YOU CAN HAVE A BATCH DONE IN NO TIME. YOU'LL ALSO FIND EXCELLENT CHOICES FOR LARGE YIELDS THAT ARE PERFECT FOR BAKE SALES AND POTLUCKS AS WELL AS A VARIETY OF TRADITIONAL HOLIDAY FAVORITES THAT ALMOST LOOK TOO GOOD TO EAT!

PISTACHIO CREAM CHEESE COOKIES *PAGE 26*

Slice & Bake

PLEASE A CROWD WITH THESE ALL-TIME CLASSIC COOKIES! MAKE THE DOUGH AHEAD OF TIME, THEN SLICE THEM UP AND BAKE AS NEEDED. WHAT COULD BE EASIER? TRY THESE NUT- AND CITRUS-FLAVORED FAVORITES AS WELL AS ICEBOX TREATS, SWIRLED DELIGHTS AND OTHERS.

DOUBLE BUTTERSCOTCH COOKIES
PAGE 15

NEAPOLITAN COOKIES
PAGE 20

BITE-SIZE CINNAMON ROLL COOKIES *PAGE 22*

Black Walnut Cookies

BIG BATCH
Black Walnut Cookies

Black walnuts have a more distinctive flavor than traditional English walnuts. They have a short shelf life, so it's best to store them in the freezer. Use regular walnuts if you can't find black ones.

—**DOUG BLACK** CONOVER, NC

PREP: 20 MIN. + CHILLING • **BAKE:** 15 MIN./BATCH
MAKES: 10 DOZEN

- 1 **cup butter, softened**
- 2 **cups packed brown sugar**
- 2 **large eggs**
- 1 **teaspoon vanilla extract**
- 3½ **cups all-purpose flour**
- 1 **teaspoon baking soda**
- ¼ **teaspoon salt**
- 2 **cups chopped black walnuts or walnuts, divided**

1. In a large bowl, cream butter and brown sugar until light and fluffy. Beat in eggs, vanilla. Combine flour, baking soda and salt; gradually add to creamed mixture. Stir in 1¼ cups walnuts. Finely chop remaining nuts.
2. Shape dough into two 15-in. rolls. Roll in chopped nuts, pressing gently. Wrap each in plastic wrap. Refrigerate for 2 hours or until firm.
3. Unwrap dough; cut into ¼-in. slices. Place 2 in. apart on greased baking sheets. Bake at 300° for 12 minutes or until lightly browned. Remove to wire racks to cool.

TOP TIP
Make the Perfect Cut

How do you slice cookies and keep their nice round shape? The answer is dental floss! Slide a piece (about 1 foot long) under a roll of dough, crisscross the ends above the dough and pull until you've cut through the dough. This also works well when cutting cakes into layers.

—**G.W.** FAIRPORT, NY

Double Butterscotch Cookies

I've made this old-fashioned recipe for years. It also can be made with miniature chocolate chips or coconut in place of the toffee bits.

—BEVERLY DUNCAN LAKEVILLE, OH

PREP: 20 MIN. + CHILLING
BAKE: 10 MIN./BATCH + COOLING
MAKES: ABOUT 7 DOZEN

- ½ cup butter, softened
- ½ cup shortening
- 4 cups packed brown sugar
- 4 large eggs
- 1 tablespoon vanilla extract
- 6 cups all-purpose flour
- 3 teaspoons baking soda
- 3 teaspoons cream of tartar
- 1 teaspoon salt
- 1 package English toffee bits (10 ounces) or almond brickle chips (7½ ounces)
- 1 cup finely chopped pecans

1. In a large bowl, beat the butter, shortening and brown sugar for 2 minutes or until mixture resembles wet sand. Add the eggs, one at a time, beating well after each addition. Beat in vanilla. Combine the flour, baking soda, cream of tartar and salt; gradually add to the brown sugar mixture and mix well. Stir in toffee bits and pecans.
2. Shape into three 14-in. rolls (mixture will be slightly crumbly); wrap each in plastic wrap. Refrigerate for 4 hours or until firm.
3. Unwrap and cut into ½-in. slices. Place 2 in. apart on greased baking sheets. Bake at 375° for 9-11 minutes or until lightly browned. Cool for 1-2 minutes before removing from pans to wire racks to cool completely.

Chocolate Orange Rounds

Chocolate Orange Rounds

To give a gift from the Sunshine State, I make orange-flavored cookies and ship them across the country to my family and friends.

—GEORDYTH SULLIVAN CUTLER BAY, FL

PREP: 40 MIN. + CHILLING **• BAKE:** 5 MIN./BATCH
MAKES: ABOUT 6½ DOZEN

- 1 cup butter, softened
- 1½ cups sugar
- 1 large egg
- 1 teaspoon orange extract
- 2½ cups all-purpose flour
- 1½ teaspoons baking powder
- ¼ teaspoon salt
- 2½ teaspoons grated orange peel
- 2 ounces unsweetened chocolate, melted

1. In a large bowl, cream butter and sugar until light and fluffy. Beat in egg and extract. In another bowl, whisk flour, baking powder and salt; gradually beat into creamed mixture. Divide dough in half. Add orange peel to one half; add melted chocolate to the other half.
2. Shape each portion into two 10x1-in. rolls; wrap each in plastic wrap. Refrigerate 3 hours or overnight.
3. Preheat oven to 375°. Cut each roll down the center lengthwise. Reassemble rolls, alternating chocolate and orange halves. Wrap and chill until firm enough to slice if necessary.
4. Cut dough into ¼-in. slices. Place 2 in. apart on ungreased baking sheets. Bake cookies 5-6 minutes or until set. Remove from pans to wire racks to cool.

Caramel Swirls

Caramel Swirls

Nothing beats a couple of cookies when I crave something sweet. With a crisp outside and a chewy caramel filling, these swirls are one of my favorite ways to satisfy my sweet tooth.

—**JAN SMITH** STAR, TX

PREP: 25 MIN. + CHILLING • **BAKE:** 15 MIN./BATCH
MAKES: 6½ DOZEN

- 1 **cup butter, softened**
- 4 **ounces cream cheese, softened**
- 1 **cup packed brown sugar**
- 1 **large egg yolk**
- 1 **teaspoon maple flavoring**
- 2¾ **cups all-purpose flour**

FILLING

- 30 **caramels**
- 6 **ounces cream cheese, softened**

1. In a large bowl, cream butter, cream cheese and brown sugar until light and fluffy. Beat in egg yolk and flavoring. Gradually beat flour into creamed mixture. Refrigerate 2 hours or until easy to handle.
2. In a microwave-safe bowl, melt caramels; stir until smooth. Stir in cream cheese until blended; set aside. Divide dough in half. Roll each portion between two pieces of waxed paper to ¼-in. thickness. Spread caramel mixture over dough to within ½ in. of edges.
3. Roll up tightly jelly-roll style, starting with a long side. Wrap rolls in plastic wrap; refrigerate 4 hours or until firm.
4. Preheat oven to 350°. Unwrap and cut dough crosswise into ¼-in. slices. Place 1 in. apart on greased baking sheets. Bake 12-14 minutes or until golden brown. Remove from pans to wire racks to cool.

Cinnamon-Candy Cookies

I was trying to make a unique Christmas cookie inspired by my brother's love of Red Hots. I used the candies in these lace-like cookies for cinnamon flavor.

—**WENDY RUSCH** TREGO, WI

PREP: 20 MIN. + CHILLING • **BAKE:** 10 MIN./BATCH
MAKES: ABOUT 5 DOZEN

- ⅔ **cup Red Hots**
- 2⅓ **cups all-purpose flour**
- 1 **cup butter, softened**
- 1 **cup sugar**
- 1 **teaspoon vanilla extract**

FROSTING

- 2 **cups confectioners' sugar**
- ½ **cup butter, softened**
- ½ **teaspoon vanilla or cinnamon extract**
- ⅛ **teaspoon salt**
- 4 **to 6 tablespoons 2% milk**

1. Place Red Hots in a food processor; process until fine and powdery. Add flour; pulse to combine.
2. In a large bowl, cream butter and sugar until light and fluffy. Beat in the vanilla. Gradually beat flour mixture into creamed mixture.
3. Shape into two 8-in. rolls; wrap each roll in plastic wrap. Refrigerate 1 hour or until firm.
4. Preheat oven to 350°. Unwrap and cut into ¼-in. slices. Place 2 in. apart on ungreased baking sheets. Bake for 7-9 minutes or until edges are just light brown. Cool on pans 2 minutes before removing the cookies to wire racks to cool completely.
5. For frosting, in a small bowl, beat confectioners' sugar, butter, extract, salt and enough milk to reach a desired consistency. Decorate the cookies in a crisscross pattern or as desired.
FREEZE OPTION *Place wrapped logs in resealable plastic freezer bags; return to freezer. To use, unwrap frozen logs and cut into slices. If necessary, let dough stand a few minutes at room temperature before cutting. Prepare, bake and decorate cookies as directed.*

Cinnamon-Candy
Cookies

BIG BATCH

Aunt Ione's Icebox Cookies

Whenever we visited my Aunt Ione in south Georgia, her icebox cookies were our favorite treat.

—**JENNY HILL** MERIDIANVILLE, AL

PREP: 20 MIN. + CHILLING
BAKE: 10 MIN./BATCH
MAKES: ABOUT 17 DOZEN

Aunt Ione's
Icebox Cookies

- 6 cups all-purpose flour
- 1½ teaspoons baking powder
- 1 teaspoon baking soda
- 1 teaspoon ground nutmeg
- 1 teaspoon ground cinnamon
- 2 cups butter, softened
- 1 cup sugar
- 1 cup packed brown sugar
- 3 large eggs
- 1 teaspoon vanilla extract
- 1 teaspoon lemon extract
- 2 cups chopped nuts

1. Sift together the first five ingredients; set aside. In a bowl, cream butter and sugars. Add eggs, vanilla and lemon extract; beat well. Add dry ingredients; mix well. Stir in nuts.

2. Divide dough into four parts and shape into 11x1½-in. rolls. Wrap in foil and chill overnight. Slice cookies ⅜ in. thick.

3. Bake on greased baking sheets at 350° for about 10 minutes.

Lemon Lover's Cookies

These light cookies will melt in your mouth. They're sure to be a hit wherever you serve them—mine always are!

—**VIRGINIA DILLARD** WHITMIRE, SC

PREP: 20 MIN. + CHILLING
BAKE: 10 MIN./BATCH + COOLING
MAKES: ABOUT 3½ DOZEN

- ¾ cup butter, softened
- ⅓ cup confectioners' sugar
- 2 teaspoons lemon juice
- 1 cup all-purpose flour
- ½ cup cornstarch
- 1 teaspoon grated lemon peel

LEMON FROSTING

- ¼ cup butter, softened
- 1 cup confectioners' sugar
- 2 teaspoons lemon juice
- 1 teaspoon grated lemon peel

GARNISH

- Additional grated lemon peel, optional

1. In a small bowl, cream butter and sugar until light and fluffy, about 5 minutes. Beat in lemon juice. Combine the flour, cornstarch and lemon peel; gradually add to the creamed mixture and mix well.
2. Shape into a 1½-in. roll; wrap in plastic wrap. Refrigerate 1 hour or until firm. Unwrap and cut into ¼-in. slices. Place 2 in. apart on greased baking sheets.
3. Bake at 350° for 10-12 minutes or until edges are golden brown. Gently remove to wire racks to cool completely.
4. In a small bowl, beat butter until fluffy. Add the confectioners' sugar, lemon juice and peel; beat until smooth. Spread over cooled cookies; sprinkle with additional lemon peel if desired. Let stand until set. Store the cookies in an airtight container.

Grandma Krauses' Coconut Cookies

FREEZE IT *BIG BATCH*

Grandma Krauses' Coconut Cookies

When my two daughters were young, their great-grandma made them cookies with oats and coconut. Thankfully, she shared the recipe.

—**DEBRA DORN** HOMOSASSA, FL

PREP: 40 MIN. + FREEZING • **BAKE:** 10 MIN./BATCH
MAKES: ABOUT 4 DOZEN

- 1 cup shortening
- 1 cup sugar
- 1 cup packed brown sugar
- 2 large eggs
- 1 teaspoon vanilla extract
- 2 cups all-purpose flour
- 1 teaspoon baking powder
- 1 teaspoon baking soda
- ¼ teaspoon salt
- 1 cup old-fashioned oats
- 1 cup flaked coconut

1. In a large bowl, beat shortening and sugars until blended. Beat in eggs and vanilla. In another bowl, whisk flour, baking powder, baking soda and salt; gradually beat into sugar mixture. Stir in oats and coconut.
2. Divide dough into four portions. On a lightly floured surface, shape each into a 6-in.-long roll. Wrap in plastic wrap; freeze 2 hours or until firm.
3. Preheat oven to 350°. Unwrap and cut dough crosswise into ½-in. slices, reshaping as needed. Place 2 in. apart on ungreased baking sheets. Bake for 10-12 minutes or until golden brown. Cool on pans 5 minutes. Remove to wire racks to cool.
FREEZE OPTION *Place wrapped logs in resealable plastic freezer bag; return to freezer. To use, unwrap frozen logs and cut into slices. If necessary, let dough stand a few minutes at room temperature before cutting. Prepare and bake as directed.*

BIG BATCH
Chocolate-Dipped Cookies

Tender almond sugar cookies are made even better when hand-dipped completely in chocolate and then drizzled beautifully with a contrasting candy coating.
—*TASTE OF HOME* TEST KITCHEN

PREP: 25 MIN. + CHILLING
BAKE: 10 MIN./BATCH + COOLING
MAKES: 4½ DOZEN

- ½ **cup butter, softened**
- ¾ **cup sugar**
- 1 **large egg**
- 1 **teaspoon vanilla extract**
- 1 **cup all-purpose flour**
- ⅓ **cup baking cocoa**
- ½ **teaspoon baking soda**
- ¼ **teaspoon salt**
- ½ **cup chopped almonds**
- ½ **cup miniature semisweet chocolate chips**
- 12 **ounces white candy coating disks, melted**
- 12 **ounces dark chocolate candy coating disks, melted**
- 2 **ounces milk chocolate candy coating disks, melted**

1. In a large bowl, cream butter and sugar. Beat in egg and vanilla. Combine the flour, cocoa, baking soda and salt; gradually add to the creamed mixture. Stir in almonds and chocolate chips. Cover and refrigerate for 2 hours. Divide dough in half. Shape into two 8-in. rolls; wrap each in plastic wrap. Refrigerate for 3 hours or until firm.
2. Unwrap, cut into ¼-in. slices. Place 2 in. apart on greased baking sheets. Bake at 350° for 8-10 minutes or until set. Remove to wire racks to cool.
3. Dip half of the total cookies in white coating; allow excess to drip off. Place on waxed paper. Repeat with remaining cookies in dark chocolate coating.
4. Place the milk chocolate coating in a resealable plastic bag; cut a small hole in one corner of bag. Pipe designs on cookies. Let stand for 30 minutes or until set.

Neapolitan Cookies

BIG BATCH
Neapolitan Cookies

My sister shared the recipe for these tricolor treats several years ago. The crisp cookies are fun to eat one section at a time or with all three in one bite!
—**JAN MALLO** WHITE PIGEON, MI

PREP: 20 MIN. + CHILLING • **BAKE:** 10 MIN./BATCH
MAKES: ABOUT 11 DOZEN

- 1 **cup butter, softened**
- 1½ **cups sugar**
- 1 **large egg**
- 1 **teaspoon vanilla extract**
- 2½ **cups all-purpose flour**
- 1½ **teaspoons baking powder**
- ½ **teaspoon salt**
- ½ **teaspoon almond extract**
- 6 **drops red food coloring**
- ½ **cup chopped walnuts**
- 1 **ounce unsweetened chocolate, melted**

1. Line a 9x5-in. loaf pan with waxed paper, letting ends extend up the sides. In a large bowl, cream butter and sugar until light and fluffy. Beat in egg and vanilla. In another bowl, whisk flour, baking powder and salt; gradually beat into creamed mixture.
2. Divide dough into three portions. Mix almond extract and food coloring into one portion; spread evenly into prepared pan. Mix walnuts into another portion; spread evenly over first layer. Mix melted chocolate into remaining portion; spread over top. Refrigerate, covered, overnight.
3. Preheat oven to 350°. Lifting with waxed paper, remove dough from pan. Cut lengthwise in half; cut each half crosswise into ⅛-in. slices.
4. Place 1 in. apart on ungreased baking sheets. Bake 10-12 minutes or until edges are firm. Remove from pans to wire racks to cool.

BIG BATCH
Orange Pistachio Cookies

I had never tried pistachios until I visited a friend who served me these cookies. I was in love! I made the recipe my own, and now my family can't get enough of them.
—**LORRAINE CALAND** SHUNIAH, ON

PREP: 20 MIN. + CHILLING • **BAKE:** 10 MIN./BATCH
MAKES: ABOUT 4½ DOZEN

- ¾ cup butter, softened
- 1 cup sugar
- 1 large egg
- 1 tablespoon grated orange peel
- 1 teaspoon vanilla extract
- 2 cups all-purpose flour
- ¼ cup cornstarch
- ½ cup pistachios, toasted and finely chopped

ICING
- 2¼ cups confectioners' sugar
- ¼ cup orange juice
- 1 tablespoon butter, melted
  Additional pistachios, toasted and finely chopped, optional

1. In a large bowl, cream butter and sugar until light and fluffy. Beat in egg, orange peel and vanilla. In another bowl, whisk flour and cornstarch; gradually beat into creamed mixture.

2. Divide dough in half. Roughly shape each portion into a 7-in. roll along the long end of a 14x8-in. sheet of waxed paper. Tightly roll waxed paper over dough, using the waxed paper to mold the dough into a smooth roll. Securely wrap waxed paper-covered roll in plastic wrap; freeze 30 minutes or until firm, or refrigerate overnight.

3. Preheat oven to 350°. Place the pistachios in a shallow bowl. Unwrap and roll each roll of dough in pistachios. Cut dough crosswise into ¼-in. slices. Place slices ½ in. apart onto parchment paper-lined baking sheets. Bake for 6-8 minutes or until bottoms are light brown. Cool slightly on pan. Transfer to wire racks to cool completely.

4. In a small bowl, combine confectioners' sugar, orange juice and butter until smooth. Spread over cookies. Sprinkle with pistachios if desired. Let stand until set.

NOTE *To toast nuts, bake in a shallow pan in a 350° oven for 5-10 minutes or cook in a skillet over low heat until lightly browned, stirring occasionally.*

BIG BATCH
Icebox Sugar Cookies

I've been making light, buttery and easily portable Icebox Sugar Cookies since I was a little girl.
—**LOUISE WORSHAM** KALAMAZOO, MI

PREP: 20 MIN. + CHILLING • **BAKE:** 10 MIN.
MAKES: ABOUT 8 DOZEN

- 1 cup butter, softened
- 2 cups sugar
- 2 large eggs
- 1 teaspoon vanilla extract
- 3½ cups all-purpose flour
- 1 teaspoon baking soda
- ½ teaspoon salt

1. In a bowl, cream butter and sugar. Beat in eggs and vanilla. Combine flour, baking soda and salt; gradually add to creamed mixture. On a lightly floured surface, shape dough into three 10-in. long rolls. Tightly wrap each roll in waxed paper. Chill for 1 hour or until firm.

2. Cut into ⅜-in. slices; place on greased baking sheets. Sprinkle with sugar. Bake at 375° for 8-10 minutes or until lightly browned. Cool on wire racks.

Orange Pistachio Cookies

Slice 'n' Bake Lemon Gems

BIG BATCH

Bite-Size Cinnamon Roll Cookies

If you love cinnamon rolls and spiced cookies, try this recipe that combines the best of both. Genius!

—**JASMINE SHETH** NEW YORK, NY

PREP: 1 HOUR + CHILLING • **BAKE:** 10 MIN./BATCH
MAKES: 6 DOZEN

- ½ cup packed brown sugar
- 4 teaspoons ground cinnamon
- 1¼ cups butter, softened
- 4 ounces cream cheese, softened
- 1½ cups sugar
- 2 eggs
- 2 teaspoons vanilla extract
- 2 teaspoons grated orange peel
- 4¼ cups all-purpose flour
- 1 teaspoon baking powder
- 1 teaspoon active dry yeast
- ½ teaspoon salt

GLAZE
- 1 cup confectioners' sugar
- 2 tablespoons 2% milk
- 1 teaspoon vanilla extract

1. In a small bowl, mix brown sugar and cinnamon until blended. In a large bowl, cream butter, cream cheese and sugar until light and fluffy. Beat in eggs, vanilla and orange peel. In another bowl, whisk flour, baking powder, yeast and salt; gradually beat into creamed mixture.
2. Divide dough into four portions. On a lightly floured surface, roll each into an 8x6-in. rectangle; sprinkle with about 2 tablespoons brown sugar mixture. Roll up tightly jelly-roll style, starting with a long side. Wrap in plastic wrap. Refrigerate 1 hour or until firm.
3. Preheat oven to 350°. Cut dough crosswise into ⅜-in. slices. Place 1 in. apart on greased baking sheets. Bake 8-10 minutes or until bottoms are light brown. Remove from pans to wire racks to cool completely.
4. In a small bowl, whisk glaze ingredients. Dip tops of cookies in glaze. Let stand until set. Store in an airtight container.

Slice 'n' Bake Lemon Gems

Cookies are meant to brighten someone's day. I like to make a lot of these lemony treats so I can fill the dessert tray with morsels of happiness.

—**DELORES EDGECOMB** ATLANTA, NY

PREP: 25 MIN. + CHILLING
BAKE: 10 MIN./BATCH + COOLING
MAKES: ABOUT 2 DOZEN

- ¾ cup butter, softened
- ½ cup confectioners' sugar
- 1 tablespoon grated lemon peel
- 1 cup all-purpose flour
- ½ cup cornstarch
- ¼ cup colored sugar or nonpareils

ICING
- 1 cup confectioners' sugar
- ½ teaspoon grated lemon peel
- 2 tablespoons lemon juice

1. In a small bowl, cream butter and confectioners' sugar until light and fluffy. Beat in lemon peel. In another bowl, whisk flour and cornstarch; gradually beat into creamed mixture. Refrigerate, covered, 1 hour or until easy to handle.
2. Shape into a 7-in.-long roll (about 1¾-in. diameter); roll in colored sugar or nonpareils. Wrap in plastic wrap; refrigerate 2-3 hours or until firm.
3. Preheat oven to 375°. Unwrap and cut dough crosswise into ¼-in. slices. Place 1 in. apart on ungreased baking sheets. Bake 9-11 minutes or until set and edges are light brown. Cool on pans 1 minute. Remove to wire racks to cool completely.
4. In a small bowl, mix icing ingredients; spread over cookies. Let stand until set.

BIG BATCH

Cran-Orange Cookies

When my family ranked our favorite Christmas sweets, this cranberry, orange and pecan cookie was at the top of the list.

—NANCY ROLLAG KEWASKUM, WI

PREP: 30 MIN. + CHILLING • **BAKE:** 10 MIN./BATCH
MAKES: ABOUT 5 DOZEN

- 1 **cup butter, softened**
- 1 **cup sugar**
- 1 **large egg**
- 2 **tablespoons 2% milk**
- 1 **teaspoon vanilla extract**
- 3 **cups all-purpose flour**
- 1½ **teaspoons baking powder**
- 2 **teaspoons grated orange peel**
- ⅔ **cup chopped dried cranberries**
- ¼ **cup chopped pecans**
- 8 **to 10 drops red food coloring, optional**

1. In a large bowl, cream butter and sugar until light and fluffy. Beat in the egg, milk and vanilla. Combine flour and baking powder; gradually add to creamed mixture and mix well.
2. Transfer 1 cup dough to a small bowl; stir in orange peel and set aside. Add the cranberries, pecans and, if desired, food coloring; divide in half.
3. Line an 8x4-in. loaf pan with waxed paper. Press one portion of cranberry dough evenly into pan; top with orange dough, then remaining cranberry dough. Cover, refrigerate for 2 hours or until firm.
4. Remove dough from pan; cut in half lengthwise. Cut each portion into ¼-in. slices. Place 1 in. apart on lightly greased baking sheets.
5. Bake at 375° for 8-10 minutes or until the edges begin to brown. Remove to wire racks. Store cookies in an airtight container.

Cran-Orange Cookies

Basic Chocolate
Pinwheel Cookies

BIG BATCH
Basic Chocolate Pinwheel Cookies

Evolved from several different recipes that I combined into one, these cookies are absolutely delish. I've never received so many compliments on my baking.
—**DENISE HUFFORD** MIDLAND, MI

PREP: 15 MIN. + CHILLING • **BAKE:** 10 MIN./BATCH
MAKES: 6 DOZEN

- 1 **cup butter, softened**
- 2 **cups sugar**
- ½ **cup packed brown sugar**
- 2 **large eggs**
- 3 **teaspoons vanilla extract**
- 3¾ **cups all-purpose flour**
- 2 **teaspoons baking powder**
- ⅛ **teaspoon salt**
- ¼ **cup baking cocoa**

1. In a large bowl, cream butter and sugars until light and fluffy. Add the eggs, one at a time, beating well after each. Beat in vanilla. Combine the flour, baking powder and salt; gradually add to the creamed mixture and mix well.
2. Divide dough in half; add cocoa to one portion. Divide each portion in half. On a baking sheet, roll out each portion between waxed paper into a 12x10-in. rectangle. Refrigerate for 30 minutes.
3. Remove waxed paper. Place one chocolate rectangle over a plain rectangle. Roll up tightly, jelly-roll style, starting with a long side; wrap in plastic wrap. Repeat with remaining dough. Refrigerate for 2 hours or until firm. Unwrap and cut into ¼-in. slices.
4. Place 2 in. apart onto lightly greased baking sheets. Bake cookies at 350° for 10-12 minutes or until set. Remove to wire racks to cool.

Jeweled Cookie Slices

Jeweled Cookie Slices

I mark recipes with "G" for good or "VG" for very good. This favorite is marked "VVG"! I usually double the recipe.
—**ROSELLA PETERS** GULL LAKE, SK

PREP: 20 MIN. + CHILLING • **BAKE:** 10 MIN./BATCH
MAKES: ABOUT 2½ DOZEN

- ⅓ **cup butter, melted**
- ⅓ **cup sugar**
- ¼ **cup packed brown sugar**
- 1 **large egg**
- ½ **teaspoon vanilla extract**
- 1½ **cups all-purpose flour**
- 1 **teaspoon baking powder**
- ⅛ **teaspoon baking soda**
- ⅛ **teaspoon ground nutmeg**
- ½ **cup red and green candied cherries or chopped candied pineapple**
- 2 **tablespoons chopped blanched almonds**

1. Line an 8x4-in. loaf pan with plastic wrap. In a large bowl, beat melted butter and sugars until blended. Beat in egg and vanilla. In a small bowl, whisk flour, baking powder, baking soda and nutmeg; gradually beat into butter mixture. Stir in cherries or pineapple and almonds. Transfer to prepared pan. Refrigerate, covered, at least 2 hours or until firm.
2. Preheat oven to 350°. Invert dough onto a cutting board; remove plastic wrap. Cut dough crosswise into ¼-in. slices. Place 2 in. apart on greased baking sheets. Bake for 10-12 minutes or until light brown. Remove from pans to wire racks to cool.

Pistachio Cream Cheese Cookies

Pecan Swirls

I can't recommend these attractive nutty spirals highly enough. Cream cheese makes the cookies rich and tender, and the sweet filling showcases chopped pecans.

—**WANDA RASCOE** SHREVEPORT, LA

PREP: 25 MIN. + CHILLING
BAKE: 10 MIN. + COOLING
MAKES: 7 DOZEN

- 2 cups butter, softened
- 2 packages (8 ounces each) cream cheese, softened
- 2 teaspoons vanilla extract
- 4 cups all-purpose flour
- ½ teaspoon salt
- 2¼ cups finely chopped pecans
- 1⅓ cups sugar

1. In a large bowl, cream butter and cream cheese until light and fluffy. Beat in vanilla. Combine flour and salt; gradually add to creamed mixture and mix well. Divide into three portions. Wrap each in plastic wrap; refrigerate for 2 hours or until easy to handle.
2. On a lightly floured surface, roll each portion into a 16x9-in. rectangle. Combine pecans and sugar; sprinkle over dough to within ½ in. of edges. Roll up each rectangle tightly, jelly-roll style, starting with a long side. Wrap in plastic wrap; refrigerate for 2 hours.
3. Unwrap and cut into ⅜-in. slices. Place 2 in. apart on lightly greased baking sheets. Bake at 400° for 12-14 minutes or until lightly browned. Remove to wire racks to cool.

"These swirls have to be my very favorite cookies. They are well worth the effort."

—**KARBAUER**
FROM TASTEOFHOME.COM

Pistachio Cream Cheese Cookies

My son-in-law is a big fan of pistachios. He looks forward to these buttery cookies at holiday time, but I make them for him more than just once a year.

—**LILY JULOW** LAWRENCEVILLE, GA

PREP: 30 MIN. + CHILLING • **BAKE:** 10 MIN./BATCH
MAKES: 5 DOZEN

- ½ cup butter, softened
- 3 ounces cream cheese, softened
- 1½ cups confectioners' sugar
- 1 large egg
- 3 teaspoons grated lemon peel
- 1½ teaspoons vanilla extract
- 1 to 2 drops green food coloring
- 2½ cups all-purpose flour
- ½ teaspoon baking powder
- ½ teaspoon salt
- ½ cup finely chopped pistachios
- 60 shelled pistachios (about ⅓ cup)

1. In a large bowl, beat butter, cream cheese and confectioners' sugar until blended. Beat in egg, lemon peel, vanilla and food coloring. In another bowl, whisk flour, baking powder and salt; gradually beat into creamed mixture.
2. Divide dough in half; shape each into a 7½-in.-long roll. Roll in chopped pistachios. Wrap in plastic wrap. Refrigerate 2 hours or until firm.
3. Preheat oven to 375°. Unwrap and cut crosswise into ¼-in. slices. Place 1 in. apart on ungreased baking sheets. Press a whole pistachio into the center of each cookie.
4. Bake 7-9 minutes or until edges are lightly browned. Remove from pans to wire racks to cool.

BIG BATCH
Cranberry Icebox Cookies

I serve these cranberry-studded cookies at Christmas with a cup of hot tea or coffee. They're so convenient.

—GLORIA ANDERSON PASO ROBLES, CA

PREP: 15 MIN. + CHILLING
BAKE: 10 MIN./BATCH
MAKES: 5½ DOZEN

- 1¼ cups butter, softened
- 1 cup packed brown sugar
- ⅔ cup sugar
- 2 large eggs
- 1 teaspoon vanilla extract
- ¼ teaspoon almond extract
- 3¼ cups all-purpose flour
- 1 teaspoon baking powder
- ½ teaspoon salt
- ¼ teaspoon baking soda
- 1 cup chopped walnuts
- 2 cups chopped fresh or frozen cranberries

1. In a bowl, cream butter and sugars. Add eggs, one at a time, beating well after each addition. Beat in extracts. Combine the flour, baking powder, salt and baking soda; gradually add to creamed mixture. Stir in walnuts. Carefully stir in cranberries. Shape into three 7-in. rolls; wrap each roll in plastic wrap and refrigerate for 4 hours or overnight.

2. Unwrap and cut into ¼-in. slices and place 1 in. apart onto ungreased baking sheets. Bake cookies at 375° for 10-12 minutes or until golden brown. Cool on wire racks.

Cranberry Icebox Cookies

SOFT BLUEBERRY BUTTON COOKIES *PAGE 43*

Drop Cookies

FILL YOUR COOKIE JAR WITH SWEETS—AND FILL YOUR KITCHEN WITH SMILES! FROM AUNT MYRTLE'S COCONUT OAT COOKIES TO STAINED GLASS CHERRY MACAROONS, THESE ARE QUITE POSSIBLY THE EASIEST COOKIES TO WHIP UP! DID SOMEONE SAY, "YUM?"

CHOCOLATE-DIPPED SPUMONI COOKIES *PAGE 33*

STAINED GLASS CHERRY MACAROONS *PAGE 37*

SNOW DAY COOKIES *PAGE 34*

Old-Fashioned Oatmeal Raisin Cookies

Pumpkin Cookies with Cream Cheese Frosting

A classic cream cheese frosting tops these pleasantly spiced pumpkin cookies. Everyone enjoys the soft, cake-like texture.

—**LISA CHERNETSKY** LUZERNE, PA

PREP: 30 MIN. • **BAKE:** 10 MIN./BATCH + COOLING
MAKES: 4 DOZEN

- 1 cup butter, softened
- ⅔ cup packed brown sugar
- ⅓ cup sugar
- 1 large egg
- 1 teaspoon vanilla extract
- 1 cup canned pumpkin
- 2 cups all-purpose flour
- 1½ teaspoons ground cinnamon
- 1 teaspoon baking soda
- ½ teaspoon salt
- ¼ teaspoon baking powder
- 1 cup chopped walnuts

FROSTING

- ¼ cup butter, softened
- 4 ounces cream cheese, softened
- 2 cups confectioners' sugar
- 1½ teaspoons vanilla extract

1. In a large bowl, cream butter and sugars until light and fluffy. Beat in egg and vanilla. Add pumpkin; mix well. Combine the flour, cinnamon, baking soda, salt and baking powder; gradually add to creamed mixture and mix well. Stir in walnuts.

2. Drop by rounded tablespoonfuls 2 in. apart onto greased baking sheets. Bake at 350° for 8-10 minutes or until edges are lightly browned. Remove to wire racks to cool completely.

3. In a small bowl, beat the frosting ingredients until light and fluffy. Frost cookies. Store in an airtight container in the refrigerator.

Old-Fashioned Oatmeal Raisin Cookies

I've been making these cookies for nearly 30 years. They're an all-time favorite with my family. The spice cake mix provides a delicious backdrop to the oat and raisins.

—**NANCY HORTON** GREENBRIER, TN

PREP: 10 MIN. • **BAKE:** 10 MIN./BATCH
MAKES: 7 DOZEN

- ¾ cup canola oil
- ¼ cup packed brown sugar
- 2 large eggs
- ½ cup 2% milk
- 1 package spice cake mix (regular size)
- 2 cups old-fashioned oats
- 2½ cups raisins
- 1 cup chopped pecans

1. In a large bowl, beat oil and brown sugar until blended. Beat in eggs, then milk. Combine the cake mix and oats; gradually add to brown sugar mixture and mix well. Fold in raisins and pecans.

2. Drop by tablespoonfuls 2 in. apart onto greased baking sheets. Bake at 350° for 10-12 minutes or until golden brown. Cool for 1 minute before removing to wire racks.

❝Fantastic! So easy and full of flavor! Definite keeper!❞

—**ASNUNEZ**
FROM TASTEOFHOME.COM

Pumpkin Cookies with
Cream Cheese Frosting

Macadamia-Coffee Bean Cookies

(5)INGREDIENTS
Macadamia-Coffee Bean Cookies

Anyone who loves coffee will love this java-flavored cookie! If you had to play matchmaker with these treats, what hot beverage would you pair them with? There's only one answer.
—**KATHY SPECHT** CLINTON, MT

PREP: 20 MIN. • **BAKE:** 10 MIN./BATCH
MAKES: ABOUT 2½ DOZEN

1 package (17½ ounces) double chocolate chunk cookie mix
1 large egg
¼ cup canola oil
2 tablespoons water
1½ cups chocolate-covered coffee beans, finely chopped
1 cup macadamia nuts, chopped

1. In a large bowl, beat the cookie mix, egg, oil and water until blended. Stir in coffee beans and nuts.
2. Drop by tablespoonfuls 2 in. apart onto greased baking sheets. Bake at 375° for 8-10 minutes or until set. Remove to wire racks to cool. Store in an airtight container.

TOP TIP

Storage Savvy

Flavors of different cookies can blend during storage, so don't partner strong-flavored cookies with delicate-flavored ones in a container. When layering cookies, separate each layer with waxed paper, and make sure to allow cookies to cool completely before storing.

BIG BATCH

Chocolate-Dipped Spumoni Cookies

I combined my favorite cookie and ice cream into one dessert. With so many delicious flavors going on, it's hard to eat just one of these cookies.

—**ERICA INGRAM** LAKEWOOD, OH

PREP: 20 MIN. • **BAKE:** 10 MIN./BATCH + COOLING
MAKES: ABOUT 6 DOZEN

- 1 cup butter, softened
- ¾ cup sugar
- ¾ cup packed brown sugar
- 2 large eggs
- 1 tablespoon vanilla extract
- 2½ cups all-purpose flour
- ½ cup Dutch-processed cocoa
- 1 teaspoon baking soda
- ½ teaspoon salt
- 1⅓ cups finely chopped pistachios, divided
- 1⅓ cups finely chopped dried cherries, divided
- 1¾ cups semisweet chocolate chips
- 1 tablespoon shortening

1. Preheat oven to 350°. In a large bowl, cream butter and sugars until light and fluffy. Beat in eggs and vanilla. In another bowl, whisk flour, cocoa, baking soda and salt; gradually beat into creamed mixture. Stir in 1 cup each pistachios and cherries.

2. Drop by tablespoonfuls 2 in. apart onto ungreased baking sheets. Bake 10-12 minutes or until set. Cool on pans for 2 minutes. Remove to wire racks to cool completely.

3. In a microwave, melt the chocolate chips and shortening; stir until smooth. Dip each cookie halfway into chocolate, allowing excess to drip off; sprinkle with remaining pistachios and cherries. Place on waxed paper; let stand until set.

Grandma Brubaker's Orange Cookies

BIG BATCH

Grandma Brubaker's Orange Cookies

At least two generations of my family have enjoyed the recipe for these light, delicate, orange-flavored cookies.

—**SHERI DEBOLT** HUNTINGTON, IN

START TO FINISH: 30 MIN.
MAKES: ABOUT 6 DOZEN

- 1 cup shortening
- 2 cups sugar
- 2 large eggs, separated
- 1 cup buttermilk
- 5 cups all-purpose flour
- 2 teaspoons baking powder
- 2 teaspoons baking soda
  Pinch salt
  Juice and grated peel of 2 medium navel oranges

ICING

- 2 cups confectioners' sugar
- ¼ cup orange juice
- 1 tablespoon butter
- 1 tablespoon grated orange peel

1. In a bowl, cream shortening and sugar. Beat in egg yolks and buttermilk. Sift together flour, baking powder, baking soda and salt; add alternately with orange juice and peel to creamed mixture. Add egg whites and beat until smooth.

2. Drop by rounded teaspoonfuls onto greased cookie sheets. Bake at 325° for 10 minutes.

3. For icing, combine all ingredients and beat until smooth. Frost the cookies when they are cool.

Jelly Bean Cookies

½ teaspoon salt
1½ cups coarsely crushed potato chips
1½ cups coarsely crushed pretzels
1 cup (6 ounces) semisweet chocolate chips
¾ cup milk chocolate M&M's

1. Preheat oven to 350°. In a large bowl, cream butter and brown sugar until light and fluffy. Beat in eggs, vanilla and milk. In another bowl, whisk oats, flour, baking soda and salt; gradually beat into creamed mixture. Stir in potato chips, pretzels, chocolate chips and M&M's.
2. Drop dough by scant ¼ cupfuls 2 in. apart onto ungreased baking sheets; flatten slightly. Bake 14-16 minutes or until edges are golden brown (centers will be light). Cool on pans for 2 minutes. Remove to wire racks to cool.

(5) INGREDIENTS

Pecan Butterscotch Cookies
I come back to this recipe often. These are the quickest, tastiest cookies I've ever made. Change the pudding flavor or nuts for a twist.
—**TRISHA KRUSE** EAGLE, ID

START TO FINISH: 25 MIN.
MAKES: ABOUT 1½ DOZEN

1 cup complete buttermilk pancake mix
1 package (3.4 ounces) instant butterscotch pudding mix
⅓ cup butter, melted
1 large egg
½ cup chopped pecans, toasted

1. In a large bowl, beat the pancake mix, dry pudding mix, butter and egg until blended. Stir in pecans.
2. Roll into 1½-in. balls. Place cookies 2 in. apart on greased baking sheets. Flatten with the bottom of a glass. Bake at 350° for 8-10 minutes or until edges begin to brown. Remove to wire racks to cool.
NOTE *You may substitute regular biscuit/baking mix for the complete buttermilk pancake mix.*

Jelly Bean Cookies
It's a family tradition for my grandmother and me to make these colorful cookies every year for the holidays.
—**CHEYENNE FINK** PLEASANTVILLE, PA

PREP: 15 MIN. • **BAKE:** 10 MIN./BATCH
MAKES: ABOUT 2½ DOZEN

½ cup shortening
¾ cup sugar
1 large egg
2 tablespoons 2% milk
1 teaspoon vanilla extract
1½ cups all-purpose flour
1¼ teaspoons baking powder
½ teaspoon salt
¾ cup small jelly beans

1. Preheat oven to 350°. In a large bowl, cream shortening and sugar until blended. Beat in egg, milk and vanilla. In another bowl, whisk flour, baking powder and salt; gradually beat into creamed mixture. Stir in jelly beans.

2. Drop dough by tablespoonfuls 1½ in. apart onto greased baking sheets. Bake 8-10 minutes or until edges are light golden brown. Cool on pans for 2 minutes. Remove to wire racks to cool.

Snow Day Cookies
To make these chocolate chip cookies loaded with goodies, you'll clear your pantry. I add oats, M&M's, pretzels and even potato chips.
—**BRITTNEY MUSGROVE** DALLAS, GA

PREP: 25 MIN. • **BAKE:** 15 MIN./BATCH
MAKES: ABOUT 2½ DOZEN

1 cup butter, softened
1¼ cups packed brown sugar
2 large eggs
3 teaspoons vanilla extract
2 teaspoons 2% milk
2 cups old-fashioned oats
1¾ cups all-purpose flour
1 teaspoon baking soda

Chewy Good Oatmeal Cookies

Here's a great oatmeal cookie with all my favorite extras: dried cherries, white chocolate chips and macadamia nuts.

—SANDY HARZ GRAND HAVEN, MI

PREP: 20 MIN. • **BAKE:** 10 MIN./BATCH
MAKES: 3½ DOZEN

- 1 **cup butter, softened**
- 1 **cup packed brown sugar**
- ½ **cup sugar**
- 2 **large eggs**
- 1 **tablespoon honey**
- 2 **teaspoons vanilla extract**
- 2½ **cups quick-cooking oats**
- 1½ **cups all-purpose flour**
- 1 **teaspoon baking soda**
- ½ **teaspoon salt**
- ½ **teaspoon ground cinnamon**
- 1⅓ **cups dried cherries**
- 1 **cup white baking chips**
- 1 **cup (4 ounces) chopped macadamia nuts**

1. Preheat oven to 350°. In a large bowl, cream butter and sugars until light and fluffy. Beat in the eggs, honey and vanilla. In another bowl, mix the oats, flour, baking soda, salt and cinnamon; gradually beat into creamed mixture. Stir in the remaining ingredients.

2. Drop dough by rounded tablespoonfuls 2 in. apart onto greased baking sheets. Bake 10-12 minutes or until golden brown. Cool on pan for 2 minutes; remove to wire racks to cool.

Chewy Good Oatmeal Cookies

BIG BATCH
Toffee Coffee Cookies

My favorite ice cream has coffee and toffee flavors, so I created a cookie recipe with them for my wedding reception. It's so good that everyone wants it.

—JOANNE WRIGHT NILES, MI

PREP: 30 MIN. • **BAKE:** 20 MIN./BATCH
MAKES: 4 DOZEN

- 3 **tablespoons instant coffee granules**
- 1 **tablespoon hot water**
- ½ **cup butter, softened**
- ½ **cup shortening**
- ¾ **cup sugar**
- ¾ **cup packed brown sugar**
- 2 **large eggs**
- 2 **ounces semisweet chocolate, melted**
- 1 **teaspoon vanilla extract**
- 3¼ **cups all-purpose flour**
- 1 **teaspoon baking soda**
- ½ **teaspoon salt**
- 1 **cup milk chocolate English toffee bits**
- 1 **cup (6 ounces) 60% cacao bittersweet chocolate baking chips**

1. Preheat oven to 350°. In a small bowl, dissolve coffee granules in hot water.
2. In a large bowl, cream the butter, shortening and sugars until light and fluffy. Beat in eggs, melted chocolate, vanilla and coffee mixture. In another bowl, whisk flour, baking soda and salt; gradually beat into creamed mixture. Stir in toffee bits and baking chips.
3. Drop by rounded tablespoonfuls 2 in. apart onto greased baking sheets. Bake 16-18 minutes or until edges are lightly browned. Cool on pans for 2 minutes. Remove to wire racks to cool.

Chocolate Fudge Peanut Butter Cookies

(5) INGREDIENTS
Chocolate Fudge Peanut Butter Cookies

Five ingredients are all you'll need to whip up a batch of these dense, rich goodies. They go over big with kids and make a nice pick-me-up for adults when it's time for a coffee break.

—ELAINE STEPHENS CARMEL, IN

PREP: 20 MIN. • **BAKE:** 10 MIN./BATCH + COOLING
MAKES: 3½ DOZEN

- 2 **cans (16 ounces each) chocolate fudge frosting, divided**
- 1 **large egg**
- 1 **cup chunky peanut butter**
- 1½ **cups all-purpose flour**
  Granulated sugar

1. Preheat oven to 375°. Reserve one can plus ⅓ cup frosting for topping cookies. In a large bowl, mix egg, peanut butter and remaining frosting until blended. Stir in flour just until moistened.
2. Drop by rounded tablespoonfuls 2 in. apart onto greased baking sheets. Flatten each drop with a fork dipped in sugar.
3. Bake 8-11 minutes or until cookies are set. Remove from pans to wire racks to cool completely. Spread with reserved frosting.

> **"I cannot say enough about these wonderful cookies. I turn to them every time I get a chocolate craving, and they always satisfy."**
> **—KATEJUDY311**
> FROM TASTEOFHOME.COM

Stained Glass Cherry Macaroons

Macaroons have been around for ages. I wanted to keep the true cookie but add a neat addition to a family favorite. Make sure the eggs are at room temperature and whisk them.

—JAMIE JONES MADISON, GA

PREP: 45 MIN. • **BAKE:** 15 MIN./BATCH
MAKES: ABOUT 7 DOZEN

- 6 **large egg whites**
- ¾ **teaspoon vanilla extract**
- ½ **teaspoon salt**
- ¾ **cup sugar**
- 8 **cups flaked coconut (22 ounces)**
- ¾ **cup finely chopped green candied cherries**
- ¾ **cup finely chopped red candied cherries**
- ⅓ **cup all-purpose flour**

1. Place egg whites in a large bowl; let stand at room temperature for 30 minutes. Preheat oven to 325°. Add vanilla and salt to egg whites; beat on medium speed until foamy. Gradually add sugar, 1 tablespoon at a time, beating on high after each addition until sugar is dissolved. Continue beating until stiff glossy peaks form. In another bowl, combine coconut, candied cherries and flour; stir into egg white mixture.

2. Drop by tablespoonfuls 1 in. apart onto parchment paper-lined baking sheets. Bake 14-16 minutes or until edges are golden. Cool on pans for 2 minutes. Remove to wire racks to cool. Store in an airtight container.

FREEZE OPTION *Freeze cookies, layered between waxed paper, in freezer containers. To use, thaw in covered containers.*

Frosted Red Velvet Cookies

I worked in a bakery during my college years, so I like to make these when I want to remember the good ol' times. They are special treats!

—CHRISTINA PETRI ALEXANDRIA, MN

PREP: 20 MIN. • **BAKE:** 10 MIN./BATCH
MAKES: 5 DOZEN

- 2 **ounces unsweetened chocolate, chopped**
- ½ **cup butter, softened**
- ⅔ **cup packed brown sugar**
- ⅓ **cup sugar**
- 1 **large egg**
- 1 **tablespoon red food coloring**
- 1 **teaspoon vanilla extract**
- 2 **cups all-purpose flour**
- ½ **teaspoon baking soda**
- ½ **teaspoon salt**
- 1 **cup sour cream**
- 1 **cup (6 ounces) semisweet chocolate chips**
- 1 **can (16 ounces) cream cheese frosting**

1. In a microwave, melt unsweetened chocolate; stir until smooth. Cool.

2. In a large bowl, cream butter and sugars until light and fluffy. Beat in the egg, food coloring and vanilla. Add cooled chocolate; beat until blended. In another bowl, mix the flour, baking soda and salt; add to creamed mixture alternately with sour cream, beating well after each addition. Stir in the chocolate chips.

3. Drop by tablespoonfuls 2 in. apart onto parchment paper-lined baking sheets. Bake at 375° for 6-9 minutes or until set. Remove to wire racks to cool completely. Spread with frosting.

Stained Glass Cherry Macaroons

Cranberry Cookies with
Browned Butter Glaze

BIG BATCH
Cranberry Cookies with Browned Butter Glaze

I won a baking contest with these soft glazed cookies, which are so easy to make that just about anyone can pull them off. What makes them special? Fresh cranberries.
—**LAURIE CORNETT** CHARLEVOIX, MI

PREP: 40 MIN. • **BAKE:** 10 MIN./BATCH + COOLING
MAKES: ABOUT 4½ DOZEN

- ½ cup butter, softened
- 1 cup sugar
- ¾ cup packed brown sugar
- 1 large egg
- 2 tablespoons orange juice
- 3 cups all-purpose flour
- 1 teaspoon baking powder
- ½ teaspoon salt
- ¼ teaspoon baking soda
- ¼ cup 2% milk
- 2½ cups coarsely chopped fresh cranberries
- 1 cup white baking chips
- 1 cup chopped pecans or walnuts

GLAZE
- ⅓ cup butter, cubed
- 2 cups confectioners' sugar
- 1½ teaspoons vanilla extract
- 3 to 4 tablespoons water

1. Preheat oven to 375°. In a large bowl, cream butter and sugars until light and fluffy. Beat in egg and orange juice. In another bowl, whisk flour, baking powder, salt and baking soda; add to creamed mixture alternately with milk. Stir in cranberries, baking chips and pecans.
2. Drop dough by level tablespoonfuls 1 in. apart onto greased baking sheets. Bake 10-12 minutes or until light brown. Remove to wire racks to cool completely.
3. For glaze, in a small heavy saucepan, melt butter over medium heat. Heat 5-7 minutes or until golden brown, stirring constantly. Remove from heat. Stir in confectioners' sugar, vanilla and water to reach a drizzling consistency. Drizzle over cookies. Let stand until set.

Super Chunky Cookies

BIG BATCH
Super Chunky Cookies

Chocolate lovers will go crazy over these cookies that feature four kinds of chocolate! When friends ask me to make "those cookies," I know exactly what recipe they mean.
—**REBECCA JENDRY** SPRING BRANCH, TX

PREP: 15 MIN. • **BAKE:** 10 MIN./BATCH
MAKES: 6½ DOZEN

- ½ cup butter-flavored shortening
- ½ cup butter, softened
- 1 cup packed brown sugar
- ¾ cup sugar
- 2 large eggs
- 2 teaspoons vanilla extract
- 2½ cups all-purpose flour
- 1 teaspoon baking soda
- ⅛ teaspoon salt
- 1 cup miniature semisweet chocolate chips
- 1 cup milk chocolate chips
- 1 cup vanilla or white chips
- 4 ounces bittersweet chocolate, coarsely chopped
- ¾ cup English toffee bits or almond brickle chips
- ½ cup chopped pecans

1. In a large bowl, cream the shortening, butter and sugars until light and fluffy. Add eggs, one at a time, beating well after each addition. Beat in vanilla. Combine the flour, baking soda and salt; gradually add to the creamed mixture and mix well. Stir in remaining ingredients.
2. Drop by tablespoonfuls 3 in. apart onto ungreased baking sheets. Bake at 350° for 10-12 minutes or until lightly browned. Cool for 2-3 minutes before removing to wire racks to cool completely.

Jumbo Brownie Cookies

Jumbo Brownie Cookies

Bring these deeply fudgy cookies to a party and you're sure to make a friend. A little espresso powder in the dough makes them even more over-the-top.

—**REBECCA CABABA** LAS VEGAS, NV

PREP: 20 MIN. • **BAKE:** 15 MIN./BATCH
MAKES: ABOUT 1½ DOZEN

- 2⅔ cups (16 ounces) 60% cacao bittersweet chocolate baking chips
- ½ cup unsalted butter, cubed
- 4 large eggs
- 1½ cups sugar
- 4 teaspoons vanilla extract
- 2 teaspoons instant espresso powder, optional
- ⅔ cup all-purpose flour
- ½ teaspoon baking powder
- ¼ teaspoon salt
- 1 package (11½ ounces) semisweet chocolate chunks

1. Preheat oven to 350°. In a large saucepan, melt chocolate chips and butter over low heat, stirring until smooth. Remove from heat; cool until mixture is warm.

2. In a small bowl, whisk the eggs, sugar, vanilla and, if desired, espresso powder until blended. Whisk into chocolate mixture. In another bowl, mix the flour, baking powder and salt; add to chocolate mixture, mixing well. Fold in chocolate chunks; let stand 10 minutes or until mixture thickens slightly.

3. Drop by ¼ cupfuls 3 in. apart onto parchment paper-lined baking sheets. Bake 12-14 minutes or until set. Cool on pans for 1-2 minutes. Remove to wire racks to cool.

NOTE *This recipe was tested with Ghirardelli 60% Cacao Bittersweet Chocolate Baking Chips; results may vary when using a different product.*

BIG BATCH
Rhubarb Cookies

We have two prolific rhubarb plants, so I'm always looking for new ways to use the harvest. A friend gave me the recipe for these soft, delicious cookies that are also flavored with coconut.

—**SHAUNA SCHNEYDER** IDAHO FALLS, ID

PREP: 30 MIN. • **BAKE:** 10 MIN./BATCH + COOLING
MAKES: 4 DOZEN

- 1 cup shortening
- 1½ cups packed brown sugar
- 2 large eggs
- 3 cups all-purpose flour
- 1 teaspoon baking soda
- ½ teaspoon salt
- 1½ cups diced fresh or frozen rhubarb
- ¾ cup flaked coconut

FROSTING
- 1 package (3 ounces) cream cheese, softened
- 1 tablespoon butter, softened
- 1½ cups confectioners' sugar
- 3 teaspoons vanilla extract

1. In a large bowl, cream shortening and brown sugar until light and fluffy. Beat in eggs. Combine the flour, baking soda and salt; gradually add to creamed mixture and mix well. Fold in rhubarb and coconut.

2. Drop by rounded tablespoonfuls 2 in. apart onto greased baking sheets. Bake at 350° for 10-14 minutes or until golden brown. Cool for 1 minute before removing to wire racks to cool completely.

3. For frosting, in a small bowl, beat cream cheese and butter until fluffy. Beat in the confectioners' sugar and vanilla. Spread over cookies.

NOTE *If using frozen rhubarb, measure rhubarb while still frozen, then thaw completely. Drain in a colander, but do not press liquid out.*

BIG BATCH

Aunt Myrtle's Coconut Oat Cookies

These cookies are the stuff of happy memories. Coconut and oatmeal give them rich flavor and texture. Store them in your best cookie jar.

—CATHERINE CASSIDY MILWAUKEE, WI

PREP: 30 MIN. • **BAKE:** 10 MIN./BATCH
MAKES: ABOUT 5 DOZEN

- 1 **cup butter, softened**
- 1 **cup packed brown sugar**
- 2 **large eggs**
- 2 **teaspoons vanilla extract**
- 2⅓ **cups all-purpose flour**
- 1 **teaspoon salt**
- 1 **teaspoon baking soda**
- ¾ **teaspoon baking powder**
- 2 **cups flaked coconut**
- 1 **cup old-fashioned or quick-cooking oats**
- ¾ **cup chopped walnuts, toasted**

1. Preheat oven to 375°. In a large bowl, cream butter and brown sugar until light and fluffy. Beat in eggs and vanilla. In another bowl, whisk flour, salt, baking soda and baking powder; gradually beat into creamed mixture. Stir in coconut, oats and walnuts.

2. Drop dough by tablespoonfuls 2 in. apart onto ungreased baking sheets. Bake 8-10 minutes or until light brown. Remove from pans to wire racks to cool.

NOTE *To toast nuts, bake in a shallow pan in a 350° oven for 5-10 minutes or cook in a skillet over low heat until lightly browned, stirring occasionally.*

Aunt Myrtle's Coconut Oat Cookies

"The whole family loved these. They are the perfect soft and slightly chewy texture."

—SHANNONDOBOS
FROM TASTEOFHOME.COM

Coffeehouse Caramel-Dark Chocolate-Latte Cookie

These taste like my favorite coffeehouse drink in cookie form. They're crispy outside but soft in the middle.
—**ANGELA SPENGLER** TAMPA, FL

PREP: 20 MIN. • **BAKE:** 10 MIN./BATCH
MAKES: ABOUT 3 DOZEN

- 6 **tablespoons butter, softened**
- ⅓ **cup shortening**
- ½ **cup packed brown sugar**
- ⅓ **cup sugar**
- 1 **large egg**
- 2 **tablespoons hot caramel ice cream topping**
- 1 **teaspoon vanilla extract**
- 1½ **cups all-purpose flour**
- 4 **teaspoons dark roast instant coffee granules**
- ½ **teaspoon baking soda**
- ½ **teaspoon salt**
- 1½ **cups (9 ounces) dark chocolate chips**

1. Preheat oven to 350°. In a large bowl, cream butter, shortening and sugars until light and fluffy. Beat in egg, ice cream topping and vanilla. In another bowl, whisk flour, coffee granules, baking soda and salt; gradually beat into creamed mixture. Fold in chocolate chips.

2. Drop dough by rounded tablespoonfuls 2 in. apart onto ungreased baking sheets. Bake 8-10 minutes or until set. Cool on pans for 2 minutes. Remove to wire racks to cool.

FREEZE OPTION *Drop dough by rounded tablespoonfuls onto waxed paper-lined baking sheets; freeze until firm. Transfer to resealable plastic freezer bags; return to freezer. To use, bake frozen cookies as directed, increasing time by 1-2 minutes.*

Coffeehouse Caramel-Dark Chocolate-Latte Cookie

Orange & Lemon Wafer Cookies

Soft Blueberry Button Cookies

I have fond memories of picking blueberries and enjoying icy cold lemonade at my aunt's house. This cookie is an attempt to marry those two flavors and memories.
—**RENEE MURBY** JOHNSTON, RI

PREP: 30 MIN. • **BAKE:** 15 MIN./BATCH
MAKES: ABOUT 2½ DOZEN

- ½ cup butter, softened
- ½ cup sugar
- ½ cup packed brown sugar
- 1½ teaspoons grated lemon peel
- 1 large egg
- ½ cup fat-free lemon Greek yogurt
- ⅓ cup blueberry juice cocktail
- 1 teaspoon almond extract
- 2 cups all-purpose flour
- 1½ teaspoons ground cinnamon
- 1 teaspoon baking powder
- ¼ teaspoon salt
- ¼ teaspoon baking soda
- 1 to 1½ cups fresh blueberries

GLAZE

- 1 cup confectioners' sugar
- 2 tablespoons blueberry juice cocktail
- 1 tablespoon butter, melted

1. Preheat oven to 350°. In a large bowl, cream butter, sugars and lemon peel until light and fluffy. Beat in egg. Beat in yogurt, juice and extract until blended. In another bowl, whisk flour, cinnamon, baking powder, salt and baking soda; gradually beat into creamed mixture.
2. Drop dough by rounded tablespoonfuls 2 in. apart onto ungreased baking sheets. Press four blueberries into each cookie to resemble a button.
3. Bake 13-15 minutes or until edges begin to brown. Remove from pans to wire racks to cool slightly.
4. In a small bowl, mix the glaze ingredients until smooth. Spoon glaze over warm cookies. Let stand until set. Store in an airtight container.

Orange & Lemon Wafer Cookies

These light citrus cookies go so well with a cup of coffee or tea after a heavy meal. They are fanciful, yet simple to make. You'll find that they are both sweet and tart.
—**PATRICIA SWART** GALLOWAY, NJ

PREP: 25 MIN. • **BAKE:** 10 MIN./BATCH
MAKES: ABOUT 4 DOZEN

- ½ cup unsalted butter, softened
- ¾ cup sugar
- 1 large egg
- 2 teaspoons grated orange peel
- 1 teaspoon grated lemon peel
- 1 teaspoon vanilla extract
- 1 teaspoon orange extract
- 1 cup all-purpose flour
- 5 teaspoons cornstarch
- ¼ teaspoon baking soda
- ¼ teaspoon salt
- Thin orange or lemon peel strips, optional

1. Preheat oven to 350°. In a large bowl, cream butter and sugar until light and fluffy. Beat in egg, orange peel, lemon peel and extracts. In another bowl, mix flour, cornstarch, baking soda and salt; gradually beat into creamed mixture.
2. Drop by rounded teaspoonfuls 2 in. apart onto parchment paper-lined baking sheets. If desired, top with orange or lemon peel strips.
3. Bake 6-8 minutes or until edges are golden brown. Remove from pans to wire racks to cool.

CHERRY BISCOCHITOS
PAGE 53

Cutout Treats

WHO DOESN'T LIKE TO GET OUT A FEW COOKIE CUTTERS AND BAKE UP A LITTLE FUN? TURN TO THESE CUTE CUTOUTS WHEN YOU NEED AN EYE-APPEALING TREAT. FROM BAKE-SALE STANDOUTS TO CHRISTMAS COOKIE DELIGHTS, YOU'LL FIND OLD AND NEW FAVORITES RIGHT HERE!

CRISP BUTTER COOKIES
PAGE 48

CHOCOLATE MARSHMALLOW CUTOUTS *PAGE 48*

ROLL-OUT COOKIES
PAGE 57

Melt-In-Your-Mouth
Lemon Cutouts

Melt-In-Your-Mouth Lemon Cutouts

Full of lemony flavor, these cookies are nice dainties for any time of the year. They're always popular with family and friends.

—PATRICIA QUINN OMAHA, NE

PREP: 35 MIN. • **BAKE:** 10 MIN./BATCH + COOLING
MAKES: 5 DOZEN

- 1 cup shortening
- 1½ cups sugar
- 2 large eggs
- 1½ teaspoons lemon extract
- ½ teaspoon vanilla extract
- 3½ cups all-purpose flour
- 2 teaspoons baking powder
- ½ teaspoon salt

FROSTING

- 1 package (8 ounces) cream cheese, softened
- ½ cup shortening
- 1 teaspoon lemon extract
- 1 teaspoon vanilla extract
- 2 cups confectioners' sugar
   Yellow colored sugar

1. In a large bowl, cream shortening and the sugar until light and fluffy. Beat in eggs and extracts. In another bowl, whisk flour, baking powder and salt; gradually beat into the creamed mixture.

2. Preheat oven to 375°. Divide dough in half. On a lightly floured surface, roll each portion to ⅛-in. thickness. Cut with a floured 3-in. flower-shaped cookie cutter. Place 1 in. apart on greased baking sheets.

3. Bake 6-8 minutes or until edges are light brown. Cool on pans for 2 minutes. Remove to wire racks to cool completely.

4. For frosting, in a bowl, beat cream cheese, shortening and extracts until blended. Gradually beat in confectioners' sugar until smooth. Spread over cookies; sprinkle with colored sugar. Let stand until set. Store in airtight containers in the refrigerator.

Ghost Shortbread Cookies

Ghost Shortbread Cookies

Pac-Man was my favorite video game when I was growing up. For a party, I decided to get creative and shape my go-to sugar cookies into the ghosts from the game.

—JAMIE S. REGINA, SK

PREP: 45 MIN. • **BAKE:** 5 MIN./BATCH
MAKES: 2½ DOZEN

- 1 cup butter, softened
- 1 cup confectioners' sugar
- ½ cup cornstarch
- 2 cups all-purpose flour
   Orange and blue food coloring, optional

FROSTING

- 1⅓ cups confectioners' sugar
- ¼ cup butter, softened
- 2½ teaspoons 2% milk
- 60 miniature semisweet chocolate chips

1. Preheat oven to 325°. In a large bowl, beat butter, confectioners' sugar and cornstarch until blended. Gradually beat in flour. If desired, divide the dough in half; tint one portion orange and the other blue. On a lightly floured surface, roll each portion of dough to ¼-in. thickness. Cut with a floured 2-in. tulip-shaped cookie cutter.

2. Place 2 in. apart on greased baking sheets. Bake for 7-9 minutes or until bottoms are light brown. Remove from pans to wire racks to cool completely.

3. For frosting, in a small bowl, combine confectioners' sugar, butter and milk; beat until smooth. Pipe the eyes onto each ghost with the frosting mixture; top with the chocolate chips. Let stand until set.

Chocolate Marshmallow Cutouts

Crisp Butter Cookies

With just six everyday ingredients plus colored sugar, you can bake dozens of from-scratch cutouts. Bring a plate of the goodies to your next get-together.
—**TAMMY MACKIE** SEWARD, NE

PREP: 20 MIN. • **BAKE:** 10 MIN./BATCH
MAKES: 2½ DOZEN

- ½ cup butter, softened
- 1 cup sugar
- 5 large egg yolks
- 1½ teaspoons vanilla extract
- 2 cups all-purpose flour
- ⅛ teaspoon salt
- Colored sugar

1. In a large bowl, cream butter and sugar until light and fluffy. Beat in egg yolks and vanilla. In a small bowl, combine flour and salt; gradually beat into creamed mixture, mixing well (dough will be very stiff).
2. On a well-floured surface, roll out the dough to ⅛-in. thickness. With a sharp knife or pastry wheel, cut dough into 2½-in. squares, rectangles or diamonds. Place 1 in. apart on ungreased baking sheets. Sprinkle with colored sugar.
3. Bake at 375° for 7-8 minutes or until lightly browned. (Watch carefully as cookies will brown quickly.) Remove to wire racks to cool. Store in an airtight container.

FREEZE IT

Chocolate Marshmallow Cutouts

I make rich, fudgy cookies that taste like brownies with a marshmallow filling. I usually use heart-shaped cutters, but I've also left them uncut and filled with pink marshmallow creme.
—**KELLY WARD** STRATFORD, ON

PREP: 35 MIN. + CHILLING
BAKE: 10 MIN./BATCH + COOLING
MAKES: ABOUT 2 DOZEN

- 1¼ cups butter, softened
- 2 cups sugar
- 2 large eggs
- 2 teaspoons vanilla extract
- 2 cups all-purpose flour
- ¾ cup baking cocoa
- 1 teaspoon baking soda
- ½ teaspoon salt
- 1 jar (7 ounces) marshmallow creme

1. In a large bowl, cream butter and sugar until light and fluffy. Beat in eggs and vanilla. In another bowl, whisk flour, cocoa, baking soda and salt; gradually beat into creamed mixture. Refrigerate, covered, 1 hour or until firm enough to shape.
2. Preheat oven to 350°. Shape level tablespoons of dough into balls; place 2 in. apart on ungreased baking sheets. Bake 6-8 minutes or until cookies are set. Using a 1¼-in. heart-shaped cookie cutter, score center of half of the cookies. Cool completely on pans on wire racks.
3. Using the same heart-shaped cookie cutter, gently cut scored cookie tops and remove the center of each. Spread marshmallow creme over the bottom of the solid cookies; cover with remaining cookies.
FREEZE OPTION *Freeze shaped balls of dough on baking sheets until firm. Transfer to resealable plastic freezer bags; return to the freezer. To use, bake cookies as directed.*

TOP TIP

Sticky Situation: Marshmallow Creme

To easily remove marshmallow creme from a jar, place the jar in a pan of hot water. Repeat this once or twice, and then spoon out the creme with a wooden spoon.
—**MARY FRENCH** PORT ORANGE, FL

Gingerbread Cookies with Buttercream Icing

When it's time to start the cookie baking season, this recipe is always the first one I use. My mother-in-law originally shared the recipie with me, but it is too good to keep to myself! You can tint the buttery icing a cheery pink or green and pipe it on with a decorating tip.

—ANN SCHERZER ANACORTES, WA

PREP: 30 MIN. + CHILLING
BAKE: 10 MIN./BATCH + COOLING
MAKES: 1½ DOZEN

- ⅔ **cup shortening**
- 1 **cup sugar**
- 1 **large egg**
- ¼ **cup molasses**
- 2 **cups all-purpose flour**
- 1 **teaspoon baking soda**
- 1 **teaspoon salt**
- 1 **teaspoon each ground cinnamon, cloves and ginger**

ICING
- 3 **cups confectioners' sugar**
- ⅓ **cup butter, softened**
- 1 **teaspoon vanilla extract**
- ¼ **teaspoon lemon extract**
- ¼ **teaspoon butter flavoring**
- 3 **to 4 tablespoons milk**

1. In a large bowl, cream shortening and sugar until light and fluffy. Beat in egg and molasses. Combine flour, baking soda, salt and spices; gradually add to the creamed mixture and mix well. Refrigerate for 2 hours or overnight.
2. On a lightly floured surface, roll dough to ¼-in. thickness. Cut with a floured 3½-in. cookie cutter into desired shapes. Place 2 in. apart on ungreased baking sheets. Bake at 350° for 8-10 minutes or until edges begin to brown. Remove from pans to cool on wire racks.
3. For icing, beat confectioners' sugar, butter, extracts and flavoring in a bowl. Gradually stir in enough milk to achieve desired consistency. Frost cookies as desired. Let stand until set.

Gingerbread Cookies with Buttercream Icing

Deluxe Sugar Cookies

BIG BATCH

Deluxe Sugar Cookies

Christmas cutouts signal the start of the holidays. For variety, sprinkle half of the cookies with colored sugar before baking, and frost the rest after they've cooled.

—DAWN FAGERSTROM WARREN, MN

PREP: 20 MIN. + CHILLING
BAKE: 10 MIN./BATCH
MAKES: 5 DOZEN (2-INCH COOKIES)

- 1 cup butter, softened
- 1½ cups confectioners' sugar
- 1 large egg, beaten
- 1 teaspoon vanilla extract
- ½ teaspoon almond extract
- 2½ cups all-purpose flour
- 1 teaspoon baking soda
- 1 teaspoon cream of tartar

1. In a large bowl, cream butter and sugar until light and fluffy. Beat in egg and extracts. Combine flour, baking soda and cream of tartar; gradually add to the creamed mixture and mix well. Chill for at least 1 hour or until dough is easy to handle.

2. Divide the dough into four sections. On a surface lightly sprinkled with confectioners' sugar, roll out one section to ⅛-in. thickness. Cut into desired shapes. Place on ungreased baking sheets. Repeat with the remaining dough. Bake at 350° for 7-8 minutes, or until edges begin to brown. Remove to wire racks to cool.

NOTE *Cookies may be sprinkled with colored sugar before baking or frosted after being baked and cooled.*

Lemon-Lime Butter Cookies

I was looking for a light cookie that would freeze and travel well, but I couldn't find one, so I created these. They are so good you won't be able to eat just one.

—BRENDA BROOKS BOWIE, MD

PREP: 20 MIN. + CHILLING • **BAKE:** 20 MIN./BATCH
MAKES: 3½ DOZEN

- ¾ cup butter, softened
- 1 cup confectioners' sugar
- 3 tablespoons grated lime peel
- 1 tablespoon grated lemon peel
- ¼ cup lemon juice
- 2 cups all-purpose flour

1. In a small bowl, beat butter and confectioners' sugar until blended. Beat in citrus peels and lemon juice. Gradually beat in flour.
2. Shape into a disk; wrap in plastic wrap. Refrigerate 2 hours or until firm enough to roll.
3. Preheat oven to 325°. On a lightly floured surface, roll dough to ⅛-in. thickness. Cut with a floured 2-in. round cookie cutter. Place cookies 1 in. apart on ungreased baking sheets.
4. Bake 16-19 minutes or until edges are light brown. Remove from pans to wire racks to cool.

BIG BATCH
Caramel Pecan Shortbread

My grandchildren look for Grandma's "candy bar cookies" every Christmas. I recommend doubling the recipe for these sweet treats because they go fast.

—DOROTHY BUITER WORTH, IL

PREP: 30 MIN. + CHILLING
BAKE: 15 MIN./BATCH + COOLING
MAKES: ABOUT 4 DOZEN

- ¾ cup butter, softened
- ¾ cup confectioners' sugar
- 2 tablespoons evaporated milk
- 1 teaspoon vanilla extract
- 2 cups all-purpose flour
- ¼ teaspoon salt

FILLING
- 28 caramels
- 6 tablespoons evaporated milk
- 2 tablespoons butter
- ½ cup confectioners' sugar
- ¾ cup finely chopped pecans

ICING
- 1 cup (6 ounces) semisweet chocolate chips
- 3 tablespoons evaporated milk
- 2 tablespoons butter
- ½ cup confectioners' sugar
- ½ teaspoon vanilla extract
  Pecan halves

1. In a large bowl, cream butter and confectioners' sugar until light and fluffy. Beat in milk and vanilla. Combine flour and salt; gradually add to creamed mixture. Cover and refrigerate for 1 hour or until easy to handle.
2. On a lightly floured surface, roll out the dough to ¼-in. thickness. Cut into 2x1-in. strips. Place 1 in. apart on greased baking sheets.
3. Bake at 325° for 12-14 minutes or until lightly browned. Remove to wire racks to cool.
4. For filling, combine caramels and milk in a large saucepan. Cook and stir over medium-low heat until caramels are melted and smooth. Remove from the heat; stir in the butter, confectioners' sugar and pecans. Cool for 5 minutes. Spread 1 teaspoon over each cookie.
5. For icing, in a microwave-safe bowl, melt chips and milk; stir until smooth. Stir in the butter, confectioners' sugar and vanilla until smooth. Cool for 5 minutes.
6. Spread 1 teaspoon of icing on each cookie; top each with a pecan half. Let stand until set. Store in an airtight container.

Lemon-Lime Butter Cookies

Pistachio-Walnut Cookies

Pistachio-Walnut Cookies

I've had this cookie in my rotation for many years, and it never fails to please. I prefer pistachio nuts and black walnuts on top, but use whatever nuts you prefer.
—**LORRAINE CALAND** SHUNIAH, ON

PREP: 35 MIN. + CHILLING
BAKE: 10 MIN./BATCH + COOLING
MAKES: 4 DOZEN

- ¾ **cup butter, softened**
- ¾ **cup sugar**
- 1 **large egg**
- 1 **teaspoon vanilla extract**
- 2 **cups all-purpose flour**
- 1½ **teaspoons baking powder**
- ¼ **teaspoon ground nutmeg**

TOPPINGS
- 1 **large egg white**
- 1 **teaspoon water**
- ⅔ **cup chopped pistachios**
- ⅔ **cup chopped black walnuts**
  Melted dark chocolate chips, optional

1. In a large bowl, cream butter and sugar until light and fluffy. Beat in egg and vanilla. In another bowl, whisk flour, baking powder and nutmeg; gradually beat into creamed mixture.

2. Divide dough in half. Shape each into a disk; wrap in plastic wrap. Refrigerate 2 hours or until firm enough to roll.

3. Preheat oven to 375°. On a lightly floured surface, roll each portion of dough to ⅛-in. thickness. Cut with a floured 2½-in. flower-shaped cookie cutter. Using a floured 1-in. flower-shaped cookie cutter, cut and remove the center of each. Reroll removed centers and scraps. Place cookies 1 in. apart on greased baking sheets.

4. In a small bowl, whisk egg white and water until blended; brush lightly over tops. Sprinkle with nuts.

5. Bake 8-10 minutes or until edges are golden brown. Cool on pans for 2 minutes. Remove to wire racks to cool completely.

6. If desired, drizzle tops with melted chocolate. Let stand until set.

FREEZE IT *BIG BATCH*

Cherry Biscochitos

I discovered the wonderful anise flavor of biscochitos, which are traditional cookies of New Mexico. I created my own version with maraschino cherries and fresh cranberries.
—**MARY SHIVERS** ADA, OK

PREP: 45 MIN. • **BAKE:** 10 MIN./BATCH
MAKES: 11 DOZEN

- 1 **cup shortening**
- 1 **cup sugar**
- 1 **large egg**
- ¼ **cup maraschino cherry juice**
- ¼ **teaspoon anise extract**
- 3¾ **cups all-purpose flour**
- 1½ **teaspoons baking powder**
- ¼ **teaspoon salt**
- 1 **cup fresh or frozen cranberries, finely chopped**
- ¼ **cup maraschino cherries, well-drained and finely chopped**
- ¼ **cup confectioners' sugar**

1. Preheat oven to 375°. In a large bowl, cream shortening and sugar until light and fluffy. Beat in egg, cherry juice and anise extract. In another bowl, whisk flour, baking powder and salt; gradually beat into creamed mixture. Stir in cranberries and cherries.
2. Divide dough in half; shape each into a disk. On a lightly floured surface, roll each portion of dough to ¼-in. thickness. Cut with a floured 2-in. star-shaped cookie cutter. Place 1 in. apart on ungreased baking sheets.
3. Bake for 7-9 minutes or until edges begin to brown. Remove from oven and immediately dust cookies with confectioners' sugar. Remove from pans to wire racks to cool.
FREEZE OPTION *Freeze cookies, layered between waxed paper, in freezer containers. To use, thaw before serving or, if desired, reheat on a baking sheet in a preheated 350° oven until warmed.*

Apricot-Filled Triangles

BIG BATCH

Apricot-Filled Triangles

It's a good thing this recipe makes a big batch because it seems no one can stop eating these! The crisp, buttery cookies truly do melt in your mouth.
—**MILDRED LORENCE** CARLISLE, PA

PREP: 1¼ HOURS + CHILLING
BAKE: 10 MIN./BATCH + COOLING
MAKES: 6 DOZEN

- 1 **pound dried apricots (2½ cups)**
- 1½ **cups water**
- ½ **cup sugar**

DOUGH

- ⅔ **cup shortening**
- 3 **tablespoons 2% milk**
- 1⅓ **cups sugar**
- 2 **large eggs**
- 1 **teaspoon lemon extract**
- 4 **cups cake flour**
- 2 **teaspoons baking powder**
- 1 **teaspoon salt**

1. In a small saucepan, cook apricots and water over low heat for 45 minutes or until the water is absorbed and apricots are soft. Cool slightly; transfer to a blender. Cover and process until smooth. Add sugar; cover and process until blended. Set aside.
2. In a large saucepan over low heat, melt shortening and milk. Remove from heat; stir in sugar. Add eggs, one at a time, whisking well after each addition. Stir in extract. Combine the flour, baking powder and salt; gradually add to the saucepan and mix well. Cover and refrigerate for 4 hours or until easy to handle.
3. On a lightly floured surface, roll out dough to ⅛-in. thickness. Cut with a floured 3-in. round cookie cutter. Place 1 teaspoon apricot filling in the center of each. Bring three edges together over filling, overlapping slightly (a small portion of filling will show in the center); pinch edges gently. Place 1 in. apart on ungreased baking sheets.
4. Bake at 400° for 8-10 minutes or until golden brown. Remove to wire racks to cool.

Best-Ever Sugar Cookies

What makes these cookies the best ever? Delicious dough flavored with cream cheese, vanilla, almond and a hint of nutmeg that's wonderfully easy to work with. The adorable decorations don't hurt, either!

—CHRISTY HINRICHS SPARKVILLE, MO

PREP: 30 MIN. + CHILLING
BAKE: 10 MIN./BATCH + COOLING
MAKES: ABOUT 4 DOZEN

- 1 **cup butter, softened**
- 3 **ounces cream cheese, softened**
- 1 **cup sugar**
- 1 **large egg yolk**
- ½ **teaspoon vanilla extract**
- ¼ **teaspoon almond extract**
- 2¼ **cups all-purpose flour**
- ½ **teaspoon salt**
- ¼ **teaspoon baking soda**
- ⅛ **teaspoon ground nutmeg**
- **ICING**
- 3¾ **cups confectioners' sugar**
- ⅓ **cup water**
- 4 **teaspoons meringue powder**
  Assorted colors of liquid food coloring

1. In a large bowl, cream the butter, cream cheese and sugar until light and fluffy. Beat in egg yolk and extracts. Combine the flour, salt, baking soda and nutmeg; gradually add to creamed mixture. Cover and refrigerate for 3 hours or until easy to handle.
2. On a lightly floured surface, roll out dough to ⅛-in. thickness. Cut with floured 2½-in. cookie cutters.
3. Place 1 in. apart on ungreased baking sheets. Bake at 375° for 8-10 minutes or until edges begin to brown. Cool for 2 minutes before removing from pans to wire racks to cool completely.
4. For icing, in a small bowl, combine the confectioners' sugar, water and meringue powder; beat on low speed just until combined. Beat on high for 4 minutes or until soft peaks form. Cover icing with damp paper towels or plastic wrap between uses.

5. Working quickly, spread or pipe icing over the cookies; let dry at room temperature for several hours or until firm. Use small new paintbrushes or toothpicks and food coloring to make designs on the cookies. Let stand until set. Store in an airtight container.

Brown Sugar Cutout Cookies

Brown Sugar Cutout Cookies

My neighbor made these for me when I was little, and now I make them for my kids, grandkids and for school children. Serve them with milk for the kids and tea for the grown-ups.

—NANCY LYNCH SOMERSET, PA

PREP: 55 MIN. + CHILLING
BAKE: 10 MIN./BATCH + COOLING
MAKES: 7½ DOZEN

- 1 **cup butter, softened**
- 2 **cups packed dark brown sugar**
- 3 **large eggs**
- 6 **tablespoons cold water**
- 3 **tablespoons canola oil**
- 1 **teaspoon vanilla extract**
- 6 **cups all-purpose flour**
- 1 **teaspoon cream of tartar**
- 1 **teaspoon baking soda**
- ½ **teaspoon salt**
- **ICING**
- 1 **cup butter, softened**
- 4 **teaspoons meringue powder**
- 3 **teaspoons cream of tartar**
- ½ **teaspoon salt**
- 4 **cups confectioners' sugar**
- 4 **to 6 tablespoons water**

1. In a large bowl, cream butter and brown sugar until light and fluffy. Beat in eggs, water, oil and vanilla. In another bowl, whisk flour, cream of tartar, baking soda and salt; gradually beat into creamed mixture.
2. Divide dough into four portions. Shape each into a disk; wrap in plastic wrap. Refrigerate 2 hours or until firm enough to roll.
3. Preheat oven to 350°. On a lightly floured surface, roll each portion of dough to ⅛-in. thickness. Cut with a floured 2¼-in. fluted square cookie cutter. Place 1 in. apart on greased baking sheets.
4. Bake 7-9 minutes or until bottoms are light brown. Remove from pans to wire racks to cool completely.
5. For icing, in a small bowl, beat butter, meringue powder, cream of tartar and salt until blended. Beat in confectioners' sugar alternately with enough water to reach a spreading consistency. Spread over cookies. Let stand until set.
NOTE *Meringue powder is available from Wilton Industries. Call 800-794-5866 or visit wilton.com.*

FREEZE IT

Chocolate-Glazed Doughnut Cookies

My little nieces love to help decorate these doughnut-shaped cookies. They top them with sprinkles or chopped pecans.
—**JOLIE STINSON** MARION, IN

PREP: 35 MIN. + CHILLING
BAKE: 15 MIN./BATCH + STANDING
MAKES: 1½ DOZEN

- 1½ cups butter, softened
- 1 cup sugar
- 1 teaspoon vanilla extract
- 3½ cups all-purpose flour
- 1 teaspoon ground cinnamon
- ¼ teaspoon salt

GLAZE
- ½ cup butter, cubed
- ¼ cup half-and-half cream
- 1 tablespoon light corn syrup
- 2 teaspoons vanilla extract
- 4 ounces bittersweet chocolate, chopped
- 2 cups confectioners' sugar
  Sprinkles or chopped nuts, optional

1. In a large bowl, cream butter and sugar until light and fluffy. Beat in vanilla. In another bowl, whisk flour, cinnamon and salt; gradually beat into creamed mixture.

2. Divide dough in half. Shape each into a disk; wrap in plastic wrap. Refrigerate 30 minutes or until firm enough to roll.

3. Preheat oven to 350°. On a lightly floured surface, roll each portion of dough to ½-in. thickness. Cut with a floured 3-in. doughnut-shaped cookie cutter. Place 1 in. apart on ungreased baking sheets.

4. Bake 12-14 minutes or until edges begin to brown. Cool on pans for 2 minutes. Remove to wire racks to cool completely.

5. For glaze, in a small saucepan, melt butter over medium heat. Stir in cream, corn syrup and vanilla. Reduce heat to low. Add chocolate; whisk until blended. Transfer to a large bowl. Gradually beat in confectioners' sugar until smooth. Dip tops of cookies into glaze.

Decorate as desired with sprinkles or chopped nuts. Let stand 30 minutes or until set.

FREEZE OPTION *Place wrapped disks in resealable plastic freezer bag; freeze. To use, thaw disks in refrigerator until soft enough to roll. Prepare, bake and decorate cookies as directed.*

BIG BATCH

Granny's Spice Cookies

No one can compete with Granny's cooking, but these spice cookies come pretty close!
—**VALERIE HUDSON** MASON CITY, IA

PREP: 20 MIN. + CHILLING • **BAKE:** 10 MIN.
MAKES: 4 DOZEN

- 1 cup butter, softened
- 1½ cups sugar
- 1 large egg, lightly beaten
- 2 tablespoons light corn syrup
- 2 tablespoons grated orange peel
- 1 tablespoon cold water
- 3¼ cups all-purpose flour
- 2 teaspoons baking soda
- 2 teaspoons ground cinnamon
- 1 teaspoon ground ginger
- ½ teaspoon ground cloves
  Red Hot candies, nonpareils and/or sprinkles

1. Cream butter and sugar until light and fluffy. Beat in egg, corn syrup, orange peel and cold water. In another bowl, whisk together flour, baking soda, cinnamon, ginger and cloves; gradually beat into creamed mixture. Divide dough in half. Shape each into a disk; wrap in plastic. Refrigerate at least 1 hour or until firm enough to roll.

2. Preheat oven to 375°. On a lightly floured surface, roll each portion of dough to ⅛-in. thickness. Cut into desired shapes with a cookie cutter. Place 1 in. apart on greased baking sheets. Decorate as desired. Bake until lightly browned, 6-8 minutes. Remove from pans to wire racks to cool.

Chocolate-Glazed Doughnut Cookies

Mint-Chocolate Dipped
Shortbread Cookies

FREEZE IT BIG BATCH
Mint-Chocolate Dipped Shortbread Cookies

A delicious little festive morsel. The cookie is crisp, buttery and not too sweet, which complements the chocolate and candy perfectly.
—**DAHLIA ABRAMS** DETROIT, MI

PREP: 40 MIN. + CHILLING
BAKE: 15 MIN./BATCH + COOLING
MAKES: ABOUT 6 DOZEN

- 2 **cups butter, softened**
- 1 **cup confectioners' sugar**
- ½ **cup sugar**
- 4 **teaspoons vanilla extract**
- 4 **cups all-purpose flour**
- 1 **teaspoon salt**
- 4 **cups (24 ounces) semisweet chocolate chips**
- 2 **tablespoons shortening**
- 2 **teaspoons peppermint extract**
- ½ **cup crushed candy canes (about 5 regular size)**

1. In a large bowl, cream butter and sugars until light and fluffy. Beat in vanilla. In another bowl, whisk flour and salt; gradually beat into creamed mixture. Divide dough in half. Shape each into a disk; wrap in plastic wrap. Refrigerate 30 minutes or until firm enough to roll.
2. Preheat oven to 350°. On a lightly floured surface, roll each portion of dough to ¼-in. thickness. Cut with a floured 2-in. round cookie cutter. Place 2 in. apart on ungreased baking sheets.
3. Bake 12-15 minutes or until edges begin to brown. Remove from pans to wire racks to cool completely.
4. In top of a double boiler or a metal bowl over barely simmering water, melt chocolate chips and shortening; stir until smooth. Stir in extract. Dip each cookie halfway into chocolate mixture; shake off excess. Place on waxed paper; sprinkle with candies. Place on waxed paper-lined baking sheets; refrigerate until set.
FREEZE OPTION *Freeze decorated cookies, layered between waxed paper, in freezer containers. To use, thaw in covered containers.*

BIG BATCH
Star Anise-Honey Cookies

When I was growing up, my mother made many desserts and pastries with anise. Today, I continue the tradition with these cookies, which are flavorful and great for decorating in a variety of ways.
—**DARLENE BRENDEN** SALEM, OR

PREP: 25 MIN. • **BAKE:** 5 MIN./BATCH
MAKES: 6 DOZEN

- 1 **cup sugar**
- 1 **cup honey**
- 3 **large eggs**
- 5 **cups all-purpose flour**
- 2½ **teaspoons baking soda**
- 1 **teaspoon ground star anise**

1. Preheat oven to 350°. In a large bowl, beat sugar and honey until blended. Beat in eggs. In another bowl, whisk flour, baking soda and star anise; gradually beat into sugar mixture.
2. Divide dough in half. On a lightly floured surface, roll each portion of dough to ¼-in. thickness. Cut with a floured 1½-in. star-shaped cookie cutter. Place 1 in. apart on greased baking sheets.
3. Bake 4-6 minutes or until edges are light brown. Remove from pans to wire racks to cool.
NOTE *To make 1 teaspoon ground star anise, grind 2-3 whole star anise (or 2 teaspoons broken star anise points) using a spice grinder or a mortar and pestle until fine.*

> ❝The Roll-Out is my favorite sugar/cutout cookie! Easy to make and fast. No chilling time. Winner!❞
> —**SPICERJOAN**
> FROM TASTEOFHOME.COM

Roll-Out Cookies

I collect cookie cutters (I have more than 5,000!), so a good cutout recipe is a must. These cookies are crisp and buttery-tasting with just a hint of lemon. The dough handles nicely.

—**BONNIE PRICE** YELM, WA

PREP: 25 MIN. • **BAKE:** 10 MIN./BATCH
MAKES: ABOUT 6 DOZEN (2¼ INCH COOKIES)

- 1 **cup butter, softened**
- 1 **cup sugar**
- 1 **large egg**
- 1 **teaspoon vanilla extract**
- ½ **teaspoon lemon extract**
- 3 **cups all-purpose flour**
- 2 **teaspoons baking powder**

GLAZE
- 1 **cup confectioners' sugar**
- 2 **tablespoons water**
- 1 **tablespoon light corn syrup**
  Food coloring, optional

1. In a bowl, cream butter and sugar. Add egg and extracts. Combine flour and baking powder; gradually add to creamed mixture and mix well. (Dough will be very stiff. If necessary, stir in the last cup of flour mixture by hand. Do not chill.) On a lightly floured surface, roll the dough to ⅛-in. thickness. Cut out cookies into desired shapes. Place 2 in. apart on ungreased baking sheets.

2. Bake at 400° for 6-7 minutes or until edges are lightly browned. Cool for 2 minutes before removing to wire racks; cool completely. For glaze, combine the confectioners' sugar, water and corn syrup until smooth. Tint with food coloring if desired. Using a small brush and stirring glaze often, brush on cookies as desired.

**Roll-Out
Cookies**

BERRY-FILLED BUTTER RIBBONS *PAGE 69*

Sweet Sandwiches

COOKIES ARE MEANT TO BE FUN, RIGHT? SO IF YOU'VE NEVER MADE SANDWICHES WITH THEM, NOW'S THE TIME! THEY'RE OH-SO CUTE, AND THE CHOICES FOR COOKIE-FILLING COMBINATIONS ARE ENDLESS. CONSIDER THE STACKED SNACKS FOUND HERE OR TRY CREATING YOUR OWN!

**PEANUT BUTTER
SANDWICH COOKIES** *PAGE 62*

WHOOPIE PIES
PAGE 67

**CHOCOLATE-CHERRY
SANDWICH COOKIES** *PAGE 66*

Chocolate Mint Wafers

Go Bananas Whoopie Pies

I love anything with peanut butter, so this recipe for soft banana cookies with a yummy peanut butter filling is perfect. Using a cookie scoop keeps them nicely rounded and all the same size.
—**JESSIE SARRAZIN** LIVINGSTON, MT

PREP: 30 MIN. • **BAKE:** 15 MIN./BATCH + COOLING
MAKES: ABOUT 2 DOZEN

- ½ cup butter, softened
- ¾ cup sugar
- ¼ cup packed brown sugar
- 1 large egg
- 1 teaspoon vanilla extract
- ½ cup mashed ripe banana
- ½ cup buttermilk
- 2 cups all-purpose flour
- ½ teaspoon salt
- ½ teaspoon baking powder
- ½ teaspoon baking soda

FILLING

- 8 ounces cream cheese, softened
- 1 cup creamy peanut butter
- 3 tablespoons butter, softened
- 1 cup confectioners' sugar
- 1 teaspoon vanilla extract
  Additional confectioners' sugar

1. In a large bowl, cream butter and sugars until light and fluffy. Beat in egg and vanilla. In a small bowl, combine banana and buttermilk. Combine the flour, salt, baking powder and baking soda; gradually add to creamed mixture alternately with banana mixture.
2. Drop by tablespoonfuls 2 in. apart onto parchment paper-lined baking sheets. Bake at 350° for 12-15 minutes or until set. Cool for 2 minutes before removing from pans to wire racks to cool completely.
3. For filling, in a large bowl, beat the cream cheese, peanut butter and butter until fluffy. Beat in confectioners' sugar and vanilla until smooth. Spread filling on the bottoms of half of the cookies, about 1 tablespoon on each; top with remaining cookies. Dust with additional confectioners' sugar. Store in the refrigerator.

BIG BATCH

Chocolate Mint Wafers

I guarantee a batch of these chocolaty treats with cool mint filling won't last long around your house. They're so pretty piled high on a glass plate.
—**ANNETTE ESAU** DURHAM, ON

PREP: 30 MIN. + CHILLING
BAKE: 5 MIN./BATCH + COOLING
MAKES: ABOUT 7½ DOZEN

- ⅔ cup butter, softened
- ½ cup sugar
- ½ cup packed brown sugar
- ¼ cup whole milk
- 1 large egg
- 2 cups all-purpose flour
- ¾ cup baking cocoa
- 1 teaspoon baking powder
- ½ teaspoon baking soda
- ¼ teaspoon salt

FILLING

- 2¾ cups confectioners' sugar
- ¼ cup half-and-half cream
- ¼ teaspoon peppermint extract
- ¼ teaspoon salt
  Green food coloring

1. In a large bowl, cream butter and sugars until light and fluffy. Beat in milk and egg. Combine the flour, cocoa, baking powder, baking soda and salt; gradually add to creamed mixture and mix well. Cover and refrigerate for 2 hours or until firm.
2. On a lightly floured surface, roll out dough to ⅛-in. thickness. Cut with a 1½-in. cookie cutter and place 1 in. apart on greased baking sheets. Bake at 375° for 5-6 minutes or until edges are lightly browned. Remove to wire racks to cool completely.
3. Combine filling ingredients; spread on bottom of half of the cookies and top with remaining cookies.

Gingerbread Whoopie Pies

These little delights are spiced just right. They combine two popular flavors into one. Roll the chewy cookies in sugar before baking for a bit of crunch.

—JAMIE JONES MADISON, GA

PREP: 25 MIN. + CHILLING
BAKE: 10 MIN./BATCH + COOLING
MAKES: ABOUT 2 DOZEN

- ¾ cup butter, softened
- ¾ cup packed brown sugar
- ½ cup molasses
- 1 large egg
- 3 cups all-purpose flour
- 2 teaspoons ground ginger
- 1 teaspoon ground cinnamon
- 1 teaspoon baking soda
- ¼ teaspoon salt
- ½ cup sugar

FILLING
- ¾ cup butter, softened
- ¾ cup marshmallow creme
- 1½ cups confectioners' sugar
- ¾ teaspoon lemon extract

1. In a large bowl, cream butter and brown sugar until light and fluffy. Beat in molasses and egg. Combine flour, ginger, cinnamon, baking soda and salt; gradually add to creamed mixture and mix well. Cover and refrigerate at least 3 hours.

2. Preheat oven to 350°. Shape the dough into 1-in. balls; roll in sugar. Place 3 in. apart on ungreased baking sheets. Flatten to ½-in. thickness with a glass dipped in sugar. Bake 8-10 minutes or until set. Cool for 2 minutes before removing from pans to wire racks to cool completely.

3. For filling, in a small bowl, beat butter and marshmallow creme until light and fluffy. Gradually beat in confectioners' sugar and extract.

4. Spread filling on the bottoms of half of the cookies, about 1 tablespoon on each; top with remaining cookies.

Blue Ribbon Carrot Cake Cookies

BIG BATCH

Blue Ribbon Carrot Cake Cookies

I created this recipe because I just love carrot cake and wanted to be able to take it with me anywhere. I entered my recipe in the Los Angeles County Fair, and the cookies not only won first place, but also were named Best of Division.

—MARINA CASTLE CANYON COUNTRY, CA

PREP: 50 MIN. **BAKE:** 10 MIN./BATCH + COOLING
MAKES: 4 DOZEN

- 1 cup butter, softened
- 1 cup packed brown sugar
- ¾ cup sugar
- 2 large eggs
- 1½ teaspoons vanilla extract
- ½ teaspoon rum extract
- 3 cups all-purpose flour
- ½ cup old-fashioned oats
- 1½ teaspoons ground cinnamon
- ¾ teaspoon salt
- ¾ teaspoon baking soda
- ½ teaspoon ground ginger
- ½ teaspoon ground nutmeg
- 1 cup chopped walnuts, toasted
- ¾ cup shredded carrots
- ¾ cup raisins

FILLING
- 1 package (8 ounces) cream cheese, softened
- ½ cup butter, softened
- 1¼ cups confectioners' sugar
- 1 teaspoon vanilla extract
- ½ cup chopped walnuts, toasted
- 2 tablespoons crushed pineapple
  Additional confectioners' sugar

1. In a large bowl, cream butter and sugars until light and fluffy. Beat in the eggs and extracts. Combine the flour, oats, cinnamon, salt, baking soda, ginger and nutmeg; gradually add to creamed mixture and mix well. Stir in the walnuts, carrots and raisins.

2. Drop by rounded teaspoonfuls 2 in. apart onto greased baking sheets. Flatten with a glass dipped in sugar. Bake at 350° for 9-11 minutes or until lightly browned. Remove to wire racks to cool completely.

3. In a small bowl, beat the cream cheese, butter, confectioners' sugar and vanilla until light and fluffy. Stir in walnuts and pineapple. Spread over the bottoms of half of the cookies; top with remaining cookies. Sprinkle both sides with additional confectioners' sugar. Store in the refrigerator.

TO MAKE AHEAD *Package cookies in an airtight container, separating layers with waxed paper, and freeze for up to 1 month. Thaw in a single layer before filling.*

Raspberry Coconut Cookies

Peanut Butter Sandwich Cookies

I'm a busy mother of two young children. I work in our school office and help my husband on our hog and cattle farm. When I find time to bake a treat, I like it to be a special one like this. The creamy filling gives traditional peanut butter cookies a nice twist.

—**DEBBIE KOKES** TABOR, SD

PREP: 20 MIN. • **BAKE:** 10 MIN./BATCH + COOLING
MAKES: 44 SANDWICH COOKIES

- 1 **cup butter-flavored shortening**
- 1 **cup creamy peanut butter**
- 1 **cup sugar**
- 1 **cup packed brown sugar**
- 3 **large eggs**
- 1 **teaspoon vanilla extract**
- 3 **cups all-purpose flour**
- 2 **teaspoons baking soda**
- ¼ **teaspoon salt**

FILLING

- ½ **cup creamy peanut butter**
- 3 **cups confectioners' sugar**
- 1 **teaspoon vanilla extract**
- 5 **to 6 tablespoons milk**

1. In a large bowl, cream the shortening, peanut butter and sugars until light and fluffy, about 4 minutes. Beat in eggs and vanilla. Combine the flour, baking soda and salt; add to creamed mixture and mix well.
2. Shape into 1-in. balls and place 2 in. apart on ungreased baking sheets. Flatten to ⅜-in. thickness with fork. Bake at 375° for 7-8 minutes or until golden. Remove to wire racks to cool.
3. For filling, in a large bowl, beat the peanut butter, confectioners' sugar, vanilla and enough milk to achieve spreading consistency. Spread on half of the cookies and top each with another cookie.

Raspberry Coconut Cookies

My mother gave me the recipe for these rich, buttery cookies. The raspberry preserves and a cream filling make them doubly delicious.

—**JUNE BROWN** VENETA, OR

PREP: 20 MIN. • **BAKE:** 15 MIN./BATCH + COOLING
MAKES: 2½ DOZEN

- ¾ **cup butter, softened**
- ½ **cup sugar**
- 1 **large egg**
- 1 **teaspoon vanilla extract**
- 2 **cups all-purpose flour**
- ½ **cup flaked coconut**
- 1½ **teaspoons baking powder**
- ¼ **teaspoon salt**

FILLING

- ¼ **cup butter, softened**
- ¾ **cup confectioners' sugar**
- 2 **teaspoons 2% milk**
- ½ **teaspoon vanilla extract**
- ½ **cup raspberry preserves**

1. In a large bowl, cream butter and sugar until light and fluffy. Beat in egg and vanilla. Combine the flour, coconut, baking powder and salt; gradually add to the creamed mixture and mix well.
2. Shape into 1-in. balls. Place cookies 1½ in. apart on ungreased baking sheets; flatten with a glass dipped in flour.
3. Bake at 350° for 12-14 minutes or until edges begin to brown. Cool on wire racks.
4. In a small bowl, beat the butter, confectioners' sugar, milk and vanilla until smooth. Place ½ teaspoon of preserves and a scant teaspoon of filling on bottom of half of the cookies; top with remaining cookies. Store in airtight container in refrigerator.

**Chocolate Chip
Red Velvet
Whoopie Pies**

Chocolate Chip Red Velvet Whoopie Pies

Baking a fun treat is a must when my four grandchildren come for "Grandma Camp." This year I'll recruit the oldest, Henry, to help pipe the cake batter.
—**LINDA SCHEND** KENOSHA, WI

PREP: 45 MIN.
BAKE: 10 MIN./BATCH + COOLING
MAKES: ABOUT 2 DOZEN

- 1 **package red velvet cake mix (regular size)**
- 3 **large eggs**
- ½ **cup canola oil**
- 2 **teaspoons vanilla extract**

FILLING
- 1 **package (8 ounces) cream cheese, softened**
- ½ **cup butter, softened**
- 2 **cups confectioners' sugar**
- 1 **cup (6 ounces) miniature semisweet chocolate chips**

1. Preheat oven to 350°. In a large bowl, combine cake mix, eggs, oil and extract; beat on low speed 30 seconds. Beat on medium 2 minutes.
2. Cut a ½-in. hole in the tip of a pastry bag or in a corner of a food-safe plastic bag. Transfer dough to bag. Pipe 1½x1-in. hearts onto parchment paper-lined baking sheets, spacing hearts 1 in. apart.
3. Bake 6-8 minutes or until edges are set. Cool on pans for 2 minutes. Remove to wire racks to cool completely.
4. For filling, in a large bowl, beat cream cheese and butter until blended. Gradually beat in confectioners' sugar until smooth. Stir in chocolate chips. Spread filling on bottoms of half of the cookies. Top with remaining cookies. Refrigerate leftovers.

"These cookies are so good and you can vary the filling. Kids love them, and they don't last long at our house!"

—RENA 55
FROM TASTEOFHOME.COM

Peppermint Patty Sandwich Cookies

Peppermint Patty Sandwich Cookies

These cookies are a hit with kids and adults at my annual holiday party. For extra flair, mix food coloring or crushed candy canes into the filling.

—AMY MARTIN VANCOUVER, WA

PREP: 30 MIN. • **BAKE:** 10 MIN./BATCH + COOLING
MAKES: 3 DOZEN

- 2 packages devil's food cake mix (regular size)
- 4 large eggs
- ⅔ cup canola oil
  Granulated sugar

FILLING
- 1 package (8 ounces) cream cheese, softened
- ½ cup butter, softened
- 1 teaspoon peppermint extract
- 4 cups confectioners' sugar

1. Preheat oven to 350°. In a large bowl, combine cake mixes, eggs and oil; beat until well blended. Shape into 1-in. balls; place 2 in. apart on greased baking sheets. Flatten with bottom of a glass dipped in granulated sugar.
2. Bake for 7-9 minutes or until tops are cracked. Cool for 2 minutes before removing cookies to wire racks to cool completely.
3. In a large bowl, beat cream cheese, butter and extract until blended. Gradually beat in confectioners' sugar until smooth.
4. Spread filling on bottoms of half of the cookies; cover with remaining cookies. Refrigerate the leftovers in an airtight container.

TOP TIP

Choppy Choices

If the word "chopped" comes before the ingredient when listed in a recipe, then chop the ingredient before measuring. If the word "chopped" comes after the ingredient, then chop after measuring.

Caramel Creams

Caramel Creams

These cookies are delicious plain, but I like to make them into sandwich cookies with a browned butter filling. In a pinch, use canned frosting instead of making your own from scratch.

—BARBARA YOUNGERS KINGMAN, KS

PREP: 20 MIN. + CHILLING
BAKE: 15 MIN./BATCH + COOLING
MAKES: ABOUT 3 DOZEN

- 1 cup butter, softened
- ⅔ cup packed brown sugar
- 2 large egg yolks
- ½ teaspoon vanilla extract
- 2½ cups all-purpose flour
- ⅓ cup finely chopped pecans
- ¼ teaspoon salt

FILLING
- 2 tablespoons plus 1½ teaspoons butter
- 1½ cups confectioners' sugar
- ½ teaspoon vanilla extract
- 2 to 3 tablespoons heavy whipping cream

1. In a large bowl, cream butter and brown sugar until light and fluffy. Beat in egg yolks and vanilla. Combine the flour, pecans and salt; gradually add to the creamed mixture and beat well. Shape into two 10-in. rolls; wrap each in plastic wrap. Refrigerate for 1-2 hours.
2. Unwrap and cut into ¼-in. slices. Place 2 in. apart on ungreased baking sheets. Bake at 350° for 11-13 minutes or until golden brown. Remove to wire racks to cool.
3. For filling, in a small saucepan cook butter over medium heat until golden brown. Pour into a large bowl, beat in the confectioners' sugar, vanilla and enough cream to achieve spreading consistency. Spread on the bottom of half of the cookies; top with remaining cookies.

Mocha Sandwich Cookies

I've had cookies that melted in my mouth, but not as much as these do! I've made several versions, but I like to make them as sandwiches with an almond-mocha filling.
—**AMY KALTENMARK** MERCHANTVILLE, NJ

PREP: 20 MIN. + CHILLING
BAKE: 10 MIN./BATCH + COOLING
MAKES: 2 DOZEN

- ¾ cup butter, softened
- ½ cup confectioners' sugar
- 1 teaspoon vanilla extract
- 1 cup all-purpose flour
- ½ cup cornstarch

FILLING
- 2 tablespoons butter, softened
- ⅔ cup confectioners' sugar
- 1½ teaspoons heavy whipping cream
- ¼ teaspoon almond extract
- 2 tablespoons baking cocoa
- ½ teaspoon instant coffee granules
- 1 to 2 tablespoons boiling water
- 2 tablespoons sliced almonds, toasted and finely chopped

1. In a large bowl, cream butter and confectioners' sugar until light and fluffy. Beat in vanilla. Combine flour and cornstarch; gradually add to creamed mixture and mix well. Cover and refrigerate for 1 hour.
2. Shape dough into ¾-in. balls; press lightly to flatten. Place 1 in. apart on ungreased baking sheets. Bake at 375° for 10-12 minutes. Cool on wire racks.
3. For filling, in a small bowl, cream butter and confectioners' sugar. Beat in cream and extract. In a small bowl, combine the cocoa, coffee and boiling water; stir to dissolve coffee granules. Add to creamed mixture and mix well. Fold in almonds. Cover and refrigerate for 30 minutes.
4. Spread filling over the bottom of half of the cookies; top with remaining cookies. Store in the refrigerator.

Chocolate-Cherry
Sandwich Cookies

Chocolate-Cherry Sandwich Cookies

I make these often at Christmastime, but they're also great for summer parties. Chilling the cookies before you dip them in chocolate is important because it firms up the filling.
—**AMY SAUERWALT** COLUMBIA, MD

PREP: 35 MIN. + CHILLING
MAKES: 3½ DOZEN

- 4 ounces cream cheese, softened
- ½ cup confectioners' sugar
- ½ cup finely chopped maraschino cherries, drained
- ¼ teaspoon almond extract
- 1 package (12 ounces) vanilla wafers
- 18 ounces milk chocolate candy coating, melted
   Red nonpareils or red colored sugar

1. In a small bowl, beat cream cheese and confectioners' sugar until smooth; stir in cherries and extract. Spread 1 teaspoon cream cheese mixture on bottoms of half of the wafers; cover with remaining wafers. Refrigerate 1 hour or until filling is firm.
2. Dip sandwiches in candy coating; allow excess to drip off. Place on waxed paper; sprinkle with nonpareils. Let stand until set. Store in an airtight container in the refrigerator.

BIG BATCH

Coconut-Pecan Shortbread Cookies

Similar to linzer cookies, these shortbread treats have a luscious caramel filling. They take a little bit of time to make but are well worth it.

—CATHY GRUBELNIK RATON, NM

PREP: 35 MIN. + CHILLING
BAKE: 10 MIN./BATCH + STANDING
MAKES: 4 DOZEN

- 1 cup butter, softened
- ½ cup sugar
- 1 teaspoon vanilla extract
- 2 cups all-purpose flour
- ½ teaspoon salt
- ½ cup flaked coconut
- ½ cup chopped pecans

FILLING
- ⅔ cup sugar
- 3 tablespoons water
- 1 teaspoon light corn syrup
- 3 tablespoons heavy whipping cream
- 2 tablespoons butter

1. In a large bowl, cream butter and sugar until light and fluffy. Beat in vanilla. Combine flour and salt; gradually add to creamed mixture and mix well. Stir in the coconut and pecans. Divide dough into two portions. Cover and refrigerate for 30 minutes or until the dough is easy to handle.
2. On a floured surface, roll each portion to ⅛-in. thickness. Cut with a 1-in round cookie cutter. Place 1 in. apart on greased baking sheets. Bake at 350° for 10-12 minutes or until lightly browned. Cool for 1 minute before removing from pans to wire racks to cool completely.
3. Meanwhile, for filling, in a large heavy saucepan, bring sugar and water to a boil. Add corn syrup; cook until syrup turns golden, about 5 minutes (do not stir). Gradually stir in cream and butter.
4. Spread a scant ½ teaspoon caramel filling on the bottoms of half of the cookies; top with remaining cookies. Let stand for 2 hours or until set.

Whoopie Pies

These soft cupcake-like treats have been a favorite of mine for many years. They're especially fun to assemble with kids.

—RUTH ANN STELFOX RAYMOND, AB

PREP: 15 MIN. • **BAKE:** 5 MIN./BATCH + COOLING
MAKES: 1½ DOZEN

- 1 cup butter, softened
- 1½ cups sugar
- 2 large eggs
- 2 teaspoons vanilla extract
- 4 cups all-purpose flour
- ¾ cup baking cocoa
- 2 teaspoons baking soda
- ½ teaspoon salt
- 1 cup water
- 1 cup buttermilk

FILLING
- 2 cups confectioners' sugar
- 2 cups marshmallow creme
- ½ cup butter, softened
- 2 teaspoons vanilla extract

1. In a large bowl, cream butter and sugar until light and fluffy. Beat in eggs and vanilla. Combine the flour, cocoa, baking soda and salt; add to creamed mixture alternately with water and buttermilk, beating well after each addition.
2. Drop by tablespoonfuls 2 in. apart onto greased baking sheets. Bake at 375° for 5-7 minutes or until set. Remove to wire racks to cool completely.
3. In a small bowl, beat filling ingredients until fluffy. Spread on bottoms of half of the cookies; top with remaining cookies.

Coconut-Pecan Shortbread Cookies

Chocolate Linzer Cookies

Root Beer Float Cookies

A hint of good old-fashioned root beer flavors these chewy-soft cookies. They're great with ice cream!

—**JIM GORDON** BEECHER, IL

PREP: 45 MIN. • **BAKE:** 10 MIN./BATCH + COOLING
MAKES: 2½ DOZEN

- ½ cup butter, softened
- 1 cup packed brown sugar
- 1 large egg
- 1 teaspoon root beer concentrate
- 1¾ cups all-purpose flour
- ½ teaspoon salt
- ½ teaspoon baking soda

FILLING
- ¼ cup butter, softened
- 1⅓ cups confectioners' sugar
- 1 teaspoon water
- 1 teaspoon root beer concentrate

1. In a large bowl, cream butter and brown sugar until light and fluffy. Beat in egg and root beer concentrate. Combine the flour, salt and baking soda; gradually add to creamed mixture and mix well.

2. Shape dough into ¾-in. balls. Place 2 in. apart on ungreased baking sheets. Bake at 375° for 6-8 minutes or until lightly browned. Remove to wire racks to cool completely.

3. In a small bowl, beat the filling ingredients until smooth. Spread on the bottoms of half of the cookies; top with remaining cookies.

TO MAKE AHEAD *Package cookies in an airtight container, separating layers with waxed paper, and freeze for up to 1 month. Thaw in a single layer before filling.*

NOTE *This recipe was tested with McCormick root beer concentrate.*

Chocolate Linzer Cookies

Living in the town of North Pole, it's no surprise that I enjoy Christmas baking! My mom and I used to make these cookies together. Now that I am married and living in Alaska, I love to bake them for my own family. They remind me of home.

—**HEATHER PETERS** NORTH POLE, AK

PREP: 30 MIN. + CHILLING
BAKE: 10 MIN./BATCH + COOLING
MAKES: 2 DOZEN

- ¾ cup butter, softened
- 1 cup sugar
- 2 large eggs
- ½ teaspoon almond extract
- 2⅓ cups all-purpose flour
- 1 teaspoon baking powder
- ½ teaspoon salt
- ½ teaspoon ground cinnamon
- 1 cup (6 ounces) semisweet chocolate chips, melted
  Confectioners' sugar
- 6 tablespoons seedless raspberry jam

1. In a small bowl, cream butter and sugar until light and fluffy. Add eggs, one at a time, beating well after each addition. Beat in extract. Combine the flour, baking powder, salt and cinnamon; gradually add to creamed mixture and mix well. Refrigerate dough for 1 hour or until easy to handle.

2. Divide dough in half. On a lightly floured surface, roll out one portion to ⅛-in. thickness; cut with a floured 2½-in. round cookie cutter. Roll out remaining dough; cut with a 2½-in. floured doughnut cutter so the center is cut out of each cookie.

3. Place 1 in. apart on ungreased baking sheets. Bake at 350° for 8-10 minutes or until edges are lightly browned. Remove to wire racks to cool.

4. Spread melted chocolate over the bottoms of solid cookies. Place cookies with cutout centers over chocolate. Sprinkle with confectioners' sugar. Spoon ½ teaspoon jam in center of each cookie.

FREEZE IT

Berry-Filled Butter Ribbons

Tangy boysenberry is an unusual flavor for a cookie, but it goes well with chocolate. I change the sprinkles and even the type of chocolate to suit the season.

—**AMY SAUERWALT** COLUMBIA, MD

PREP: 45 MIN. • **BAKE:** 10 MIN./BATCH + COOLING
MAKES: ABOUT 2½ DOZEN

- 1 **cup butter, softened**
- ¾ **cup sugar**
- 1 **large egg**
- 1 **teaspoon vanilla extract**
- 2¼ **cups all-purpose flour**
- ½ **teaspoon salt**
- ¼ **teaspoon baking powder**
- ¾ **cup boysenberry preserves**
- 1 **package (12 ounces) dark chocolate candy coating, melted**
  Assorted jimmies or sprinkles

1. Preheat oven to 375°. In a large bowl, cream butter and sugar until light and fluffy. Beat in egg and vanilla. In another bowl, whisk flour, salt and baking powder; gradually beat into creamed mixture.
2. Using a cookie press fitted with a ribbon disk, press long strips of dough onto ungreased baking sheets; cut ends to release from disk. Cut each strip into 2-in. lengths (no need to separate them).
3. Bake 6-8 minutes or until set (do not brown). Recut cookies if necessary. Remove from pans to wire racks to cool completely.
4. Spread preserves on bottoms of half of the cookies; cover with remaining cookies. Dip each cookie halfway in candy coating; allow excess to drip off. Sprinkle with jimmies. Place on waxed paper; let stand until set.
FREEZE OPTION *Wrap dough in plastic wrap; place in a resealable plastic freezer bag, and freeze. To use, thaw dough in refrigerator overnight or until dough is soft enough to shape with a cookie press. Proceed as directed.*

**Berry-Filled
Butter Ribbons**

Chocolate Dream Whoopie Pies

Chocolate lovers will find these cute triple-chocolate goodies irresistible. Two luscious cookies, a yummy mousse-like filling and mini semisweet chips make them memorable.

—JILL PAPKE OCONOMOWOC, WI

PREP: 40 MIN. • **BAKE:** 15 MIN./BATCH + COOLING
MAKES: 1 DOZEN

- 1 package chocolate cake mix (regular size)
- 3 large eggs
- ½ cup canola oil
- 1 teaspoon vanilla extract

FILLING

- ⅔ cup sugar
- 2 tablespoons all-purpose flour
- ⅛ teaspoon salt
- 1 cup 2% milk
- ½ cup milk chocolate chips
- ⅔ cup shortening
- ⅓ cup butter, softened
- ¾ teaspoon vanilla extract

GARNISH

- 1 cup miniature semisweet chocolate chips

1. In a large bowl, combine the cake mix, eggs, oil and vanilla; beat on low speed for 30 seconds. Beat on medium speed for 2 minutes (mixture will be sticky).

2. Drop by 2 tablespoonfuls 2 in. apart onto greased baking sheets. Bake at 350° for 9-11 minutes or until edges are set. Cool for 2 minutes before removing to wire racks to cool completely.

3. For filling, in a small saucepan, combine the sugar, flour and salt. Gradually add milk. Bring to a boil; cook and stir for 1-2 minutes or until thickened. Stir in chocolate chips until melted. Transfer to a small bowl; cover and refrigerate until chilled, about 1 hour.

4. In a large bowl, beat the shortening and butter until fluffy. Beat in chocolate mixture and vanilla.

5. Spread chocolate filling on the bottoms of half of the cookies, about 2 tablespoons on each; top with remaining cookies. Roll sides in miniature chocolate chips for garnish. Store in the refrigerator.

FREEZE IT

Red Velvet Whoopie Pies

Everyone gets a kick out of this fun take on the trendy cake. Take a shortcut and use packaged cream cheese frosting for the filling.

—JUDI DEXHEIMER STURGEON BAY, WI

PREP: 40 MIN.
BAKE: 10 MIN./BATCH + COOLING
MAKES: ABOUT 2 DOZEN

- ¾ cup butter, softened
- 1 cup sugar
- 2 large eggs
- ½ cup sour cream
- 1 tablespoon red food coloring
- 1½ teaspoons white vinegar
- 1 teaspoon clear vanilla extract
- 2¼ cups all-purpose flour
- ¼ cup baking cocoa
- 2 teaspoons baking powder
- ½ teaspoon salt
- ¼ teaspoon baking soda
- 2 ounces semisweet chocolate, melted and cooled

FILLING

- 1 package (8 ounces) cream cheese, softened

Red Velvet Whoopie Pies

- ½ cup butter, softened
- 2½ cups confectioners' sugar
- 2 teaspoons clear vanilla extract

TOPPINGS

- White baking chips, melted
- Finely chopped pecans

1. Preheat the oven to 375°. In a large bowl, cream butter and sugar until light and fluffy. Beat in eggs, sour cream, food coloring, vinegar and vanilla. In another bowl, whisk flour, cocoa, baking powder, salt and baking soda; gradually beat into creamed mixture. Stir in cooled chocolate.

2. Drop dough by tablespoonfuls 2 in. apart onto parchment paper-lined baking sheets. Bake 8-10 minutes or until edges are set. Cool on pans for 2 minutes. Remove to wire racks to cool completely.

3. For filling, in a large bowl, beat cream cheese and butter until fluffy. Beat in confectioners' sugar and vanilla until smooth. Spread filling on the bottom of half of the cookies; cover with the remaining cookies.

4. Drizzle with melted baking chips; sprinkle with pecans. Refrigerate until serving.

FREEZE OPTION *Freeze cookies in freezer containers. To use, thaw cookies in covered containers. Fill and decorate as directed.*

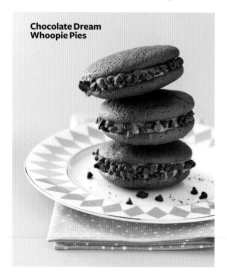

Chocolate Dream Whoopie Pies

Oatmeal Sandwich Cremes

Whenever I take these hearty cookies to a family get-together or church bake sale, they appeal to many palates. They're worth the little extra effort.

—LESLEY MANSFIELD MONROE, NC

PREP: 20 MIN. • **BAKE:** 15 MIN./BATCH + COOLING
MAKES: 3 DOZEN

- ¾ cup shortening
- 1 cup sugar
- 1 cup packed brown sugar
- 1 large egg
- ¼ cup water
- 1 teaspoon vanilla extract
- 1½ cups self-rising flour
- 1 teaspoon baking soda
- 1 teaspoon ground cinnamon
- 3 cups quick-cooking oats
- ¾ cup raisins

FILLING
- ½ cup butter, softened
- ½ cup shortening
- 3¾ cups confectioners' sugar
- 2 tablespoons 2% milk
- 1 teaspoon vanilla extract
  Dash salt

1. In a large bowl, cream shortening and sugars until light and fluffy. Beat in the egg, water and vanilla. Combine the flour, baking soda and cinnamon; gradually add to creamed mixture and mix well. Stir in oats and raisins.
2. Drop dough by tablespoonfuls 3 in. apart onto ungreased baking sheets. Flatten with a glass. Bake at 325° for 13-14 minutes or until lightly browned. Remove to wire racks to cool.
3. In a large bowl, combine filling ingredients; beat until smooth. Spread on the bottoms of half of the cookies; top with remaining cookies.
NOTE *As a substitute for each cup of self-rising flour, place 1½ teaspoons baking powder and ½ teaspoon salt in a measuring cup. Add all-purpose flour to measure 1 cup.*

Nutty Pie Crust Cookies

FREEZE IT
Nutty Pie Crust Cookies

I like Italian cream cake, so I used it as inspiration for this cookie recipe. The splash of orange liqueur in the filling makes it special.

—SONJI MCCARTY-ONEZINE BEAUMONT, TX

PREP: 15 MIN. + CHILLING
BAKE: 10 MIN./BATCH + COOLING
MAKES: ABOUT 3 DOZEN

- 1 cup butter, softened
- 1¾ cups all-purpose flour
- ¼ cup confectioners' sugar
- ⅛ teaspoon salt
- ⅓ cup heavy whipping cream

FILLING
- ½ cup finely chopped pecans, toasted
- ½ cup flaked coconut, toasted
- ½ cup butter, softened
- ½ cup cream cheese, softened
- ⅛ teaspoon salt
- 2 teaspoons orange liqueur, optional
- ¾ cup confectioners' sugar

1. In a large bowl, beat butter, flour, confectioners' sugar and salt until crumbly. Beat in cream. Divide dough in half. Shape each into a disk; wrap in plastic wrap. Refrigerate dough for 30 minutes or until firm enough to roll.
2. Preheat oven to 350°. On a lightly floured surface, roll each portion of dough to ¼-in. thickness. Cut with floured 1½-in. round cookie cutter. Place 1 in. apart on ungreased baking sheets.
3. Bake for 10-12 minutes or until edges begin to brown. Cool on pans for 2 minutes. Remove to wire racks to cool completely.
4. Place pecans and coconut in a small bowl; toss to combine. Reserve ½ cup coconut mixture. In another bowl, beat butter, cream cheese, salt and, if desired, liqueur until creamy. Gradually beat in confectioners' sugar until smooth. Fold in remaining coconut mixture. Spread over bottoms of half of the cookies; cover with remaining cookies. Place reserved coconut mixture in a shallow bowl. Roll sides of cookies in coconut mixture.
FREEZE OPTION *Transfer wrapped disks to a resealable plastic freezer bag; freeze. To use, thaw dough in refrigerator until soft enough to roll. Prepare, bake and fill cookies as directed.*

APRICOT-PECAN THUMBPRINT COOKIES *PAGE 87*

Shaped Sensations

THESE SHAPED GOODIES WILL SURE GO FAST AT ANY GET-TOGETHER OR BAKE SALE. WHETHER YOU ARE LOOKING TO BAKE THUMBPRINTS, SPRITZ, CRESCENTS OR TASSIES, WE'VE GOT YOU COVERED HERE! KIDS AND GROWN-UP KIDS ALIKE WILL ENJOY THESE DELICIOUS COOKIES.

TRAIL MIX COOKIE CUPS
PAGE 77

SPRITZ COOKIES
PAGE 82

RASPBERRY-ALMOND CRESCENT COOKIES *PAGE 85*

Salted Caramel Cookie Cups

Salted Caramel Cookie Cups

When I brought these salty sweet cookies to a potluck, I overheard people talking about how wonderful they were. I'm not sure if it was the cookie, the caramel or the chocolate that they loved best.

—**PRISCILLA YEE** CONCORD, CA

PREP: 30 MIN. • **BAKE:** 10 MIN./BATCH + COOLING
MAKES: 3 DOZEN

- 1 **package (17½ ounces) sugar cookie mix**
- 2 **tablespoons all-purpose flour**
- ⅓ **cup butter, softened**
- 1 **large egg**

FILLING

- 6 **ounces cream cheese, softened**
- ½ **cup semisweet chocolate chips, melted**
- ⅓ **cup confectioners' sugar**
- 36 **caramels**
- 2 **teaspoons coarse sea salt**
- 36 **pecan halves, toasted**

1. Preheat oven to 375°. In a large bowl, combine cookie mix and flour. Beat in butter and egg until blended. Shape dough into 1¼-in. balls; press onto bottom and up sides of greased mini-muffin cups.

2. In a small bowl, combine the cream cheese, chocolate chips and confectioners' sugar. Place a rounded teaspoon of filling in each cup. Press one caramel into the filling in each cup. Bake 9-11 minutes or until edges are golden brown and caramel is melted. Sprinkle with sea salt; top with a pecan half. Cool completely in pan on wire racks.

❝The anise cookies have a beautiful texture and flavor! This is one of my favorite recipes.❞

—**FAMILYBAKERLISA**
FROM TASTEOFHOME.COM

Anise Cookies

My aunt would make these cookies for dessert. I can remember walking into the house and I'd almost swoon when I smelled them baking.

—**ESTHER PEREA** VAN NUYS, CA

PREP: 25 MIN. • **BAKE:** 30 MIN. + COOLING
MAKES: 3½ DOZEN

- 2½ cups all-purpose flour
- 3 teaspoons baking powder
- 1½ teaspoons crushed aniseed
- ¾ teaspoon salt
- ¼ teaspoon ground cinnamon
- ¼ teaspoon ground nutmeg
- ½ cup butter, softened
- 1 cup sugar, divided
- 1¼ teaspoons vanilla extract
- 2 large eggs
- 1 cup blanched almonds, toasted and finely chopped
- 2 teaspoons milk

1. Line a baking pan with foil; set aside. In a large bowl, combine the flour, baking powder, aniseed, salt, cinnamon and nutmeg; set aside.
2. In a large bowl, cream butter and ¾ cup sugar until light and fluffy. Beat in vanilla and eggs. Stir in almonds and reserved flour mixture.
3. Divide dough in half. Shape each into a 12x2-in. rectangle on the prepared baking pan. Smooth the surface of each rectangle; brush with milk and sprinkle with remaining sugar.
4. Bake at 375° for 20 minutes or until golden brown and firm to the touch. Remove from the oven and reduce heat to 300°.
5. Transfer rectangles with foil to a wire rack; cool for 15 minutes. Place rectangles on a cutting board; cut diagonally into ½-in. slices. Place slices, cut side down, on baking pans.
6. Bake 10-12 minutes longer. Turn oven off, leaving cookies in oven to cool with door ajar. Store cookies in airtight containers.

Cherry
Almond
Delights

Cherry Almond Delights

A tender cream cheese dough filled with homemade almond paste and then topped with maraschino cherries makes an elegant cookie tart fit for a party.

—**GILDA LESTER** MILLSBORO, DE

PREP: 35 MIN. + CHILLING
BAKE: 20 MIN. + COOLING
MAKES: ABOUT 2 DOZEN

- ½ cup butter, softened
- 3 ounces cream cheese, softened
- 1 large egg
- 1 package (17½ ounces) sugar cookie mix

FILLING

- 1½ cups slivered almonds
- ¾ cup sugar
- 2 large eggs
- ¼ cup butter, softened
- 2 teaspoons vanilla extract
- 24 maraschino cherries, well drained
  Confectioners' sugar

1. In a large bowl, beat butter and cream cheese until smooth. Beat in egg. Add cookie mix; mix well (dough will be sticky). Shape the dough into a disk; wrap in plastic wrap. Refrigerate 1 hour or until firm enough to handle.
2. Place almonds and sugar in a food processor; pulse until almonds are finely chopped. Add eggs; process until mixture forms a paste. Add butter and vanilla; process until blended.
3. Preheat oven to 350°. Shape dough into 1¼-in. balls; press onto bottom and up the sides of greased mini-muffin cups.
4. Place 1 tablespoon of filling in each cup. Top each with a cherry. Bake for 16-18 minutes or until edges are golden and filling is set. Cool in pans 10 minutes. Remove to wire racks to cool completely. Dust tops with confectioners' sugar before serving.

Cranberry Tea Cookies

Chocolate-Almond Thumbprints

With a piped chocolate center, these special-looking thumbprints are almost too pretty to eat.

—**JESSIE APFEL** BERKELEY, CA

PREP: 45 MIN. • **BAKE:** 10 MIN./BATCH + COOLING
MAKES: ABOUT 5½ DOZEN

- 1½ cups butter, softened
- ½ cup sugar
- ½ cup packed brown sugar
- 2 large eggs
- 1 teaspoon almond extract
- 2½ cups all-purpose flour
- ½ cup baking cocoa
- ½ teaspoon salt
- 1 cup ground almonds

FILLING

- 6 ounces semisweet chocolate, chopped
- ¾ cup almond paste
- 2 cups confectioners' sugar
- ¼ cup water
- 4 teaspoons meringue powder

1. In a large bowl, cream butter and sugars until light and fluffy. Beat in the eggs and extract. Combine the flour, cocoa and salt; gradually add to creamed mixture and mix well.

2. Place almonds in a shallow bowl. Roll dough into 1-in. balls; roll in almonds. Place 2 in. apart on greased baking sheets. Using the end of a wooden spoon handle, make an indentation in center of each. Bake at 350° for 10-12 minutes or until firm. Remove to wire racks to cool completely.

3. In a small microwave-safe bowl, melt chocolate; stir until smooth. Cool slightly. Add almond paste and beat until crumbly. Beat in the confectioners' sugar, water and meringue powder until smooth. Pipe filling into cookies, about 1¼ teaspoons in each. Store in airtight container.

NOTE *Meringue powder is available from Wilton Industries. Call 800-794-5866 or visit wilton.com.*

Cranberry Tea Cookies

I usually have to make a double batch of these delicate cookies because they disappear so fast. They make a great hostess gift and look gorgeous set out on a silver platter. I use real butter for the best flavor.

—**TRISHA KRUSE** EAGLE, ID

PREP: 40 MIN. + CHILLING.
BAKE: 20 MIN./BATCH + COOLING
MAKES: 50 COOKIES

- ½ cup butter, softened
- 4 ounces cream cheese, softened
- ⅓ cup plus ½ cup sugar, divided
- ¼ teaspoon salt
- 1¼ cups all-purpose flour
- 1¼ cups dried cranberries, chopped
- 1 teaspoon grated orange peel
- ½ cup orange juice
  Confectioners' sugar

1. In a large bowl, beat butter, cream cheese, ⅓ cup sugar and salt until blended. Gradually beat in flour. Divide dough in half. Shape each into a disk; wrap in plastic wrap. Refrigerate 1 hour or until firm enough to roll.

2. In a small heavy saucepan, combine cranberries, orange peel, orange juice and remaining sugar. Bring to a boil. Reduce heat; simmer, uncovered, 8-10 minutes or until liquid is almost absorbed, stirring occasionally. Cool completely.

3. Preheat oven to 325°. On a floured surface, roll each portion of the dough to a 10-in. square. Cut each into twenty-five 2-in. squares. Place 1 teaspoon of the cranberry mixture in the center of each square. Bring the two opposite corners of each square to the center; pinch firmly to seal. Place 1 in. apart on greased baking sheets.

4. Bake 18-20 minutes or until edges are golden brown. Remove from pans to wire racks to cool completely. Dust tops with confectioners' sugar.

⑤ INGREDIENTS

Trail Mix Cookie Cups

My granddaughter helped create these cookie cups for the first time by using ingredients from my pantry and fridge. We used trail mix to jazz them up.
—**PAMELA SHANK** PARKERSBURG, WV

PREP: 20 MIN. • **BAKE:** 15 MIN. + COOLING
MAKES: 2 DOZEN

- 1 tube (16½ ounces) refrigerated peanut butter cookie dough
- ½ cup Nutella
- ½ cup creamy peanut butter
- 1½ cups trail mix

1. Preheat oven to 350°. Shape peanut butter cookie dough into twenty-four balls (about 1¼ in.). Press each evenly onto bottom and up sides of greased mini-muffin cups.

2. Bake for 12-14 minutes or until golden brown. Using the end of a wooden spoon handle, reshape cups as necessary. Cool in pans 15 minutes. Remove to wire racks to cool completely.

3. Fill each with 1 teaspoon each Nutella and peanut butter. Top with trail mix.

**Trail Mix
Cookie Cups**

Pretzel Cookies

It's easy to shape this shortbread-like dough into a fun pretzel-shaped cookie. You also can sprinkle them with colored sugar or sprinkles.

—**JOHNNA JOHNSON** SCOTTSDALE, AZ

PREP: 45 MIN. + CHILLING • **BAKE:** 10 MIN./BATCH
MAKES: 4 DOZEN

- 1 **cup butter, softened**
- 1¼ **cups confectioners' sugar**
- 1 **large egg**
- ½ **cup sour cream**
- ½ **teaspoon almond extract**
- ½ **teaspoon vanilla extract**
- 3 **cups all-purpose flour**
- ½ **teaspoon baking soda**
- ¼ **cup sliced almonds, chopped**
- ¼ **cup coarse sugar**

EGG WASH

- 1 **large egg**
- 1 **tablespoon water**

1. In a large bowl, cream butter and confectioners' sugar until light and fluffy. Beat in the egg, sour cream and extracts. Combine flour and baking soda; gradually add to creamed mixture and mix well. Cover and refrigerate for 2 hours or until firm.

2. Divide the dough into fourths; shape each portion into a 6-in. roll. Cut rolls into ½-in. slices; roll each into a 10-in. rope. Shape into a pretzel; place 2 in. apart on greased baking sheets.

3. In a small bowl, combine almonds and sugar. In another bowl, whisk egg and water. Brush each cookie with egg wash; sprinkle with almond mixture. Bake at 400° for 8-10 minutes or until firm. Cool for 1 minute before removing to wire racks.

TO MAKE AHEAD *Dough can be made 2 days in advance. Wrap in plastic wrap and place in a resealable bag. Store in the refrigerator.*

Rocky Road Cookie Cups

Rocky Road Cookie Cups

Traditional Rocky Road ice cream has nuts, marshmallows and chocolate. Using prepared cookie dough makes it easy to put the flavors together in these fast, kid-friendly cups.

—**CHARLOTTE MCDANIEL** JACKSONVILLE, AL

PREP: 20 MIN. • **BAKE:** 15 MIN. + COOLING
MAKES: 2 DOZEN

- 1 **tube (16½ ounces) refrigerated chocolate chip cookie dough**
- ¾ **cup miniature marshmallows**
- 2 **tablespoons miniature semisweet chocolate chips**
- ¼ **cup sliced almonds, toasted**

1. Preheat oven to 350°. Shape dough into 1¼-in. balls; press evenly onto bottom and up sides of 24 greased mini-muffin cups.

2. Bake 10-12 minutes or until edges are golden. Using the back of a measuring teaspoon, make an indentation in each cup. Immediately place 3 marshmallows and ¼ teaspoon chocolate chips in each cup; sprinkle with almonds. Return to oven; bake 1 minute longer. Cool completely in pans on wire racks.

NOTE *To toast nuts, spread them in a 15x10x1-in. baking pan. Bake at 350° for 5-10 minutes or until lightly browned, stirring occasionally. Or, place in a dry nonstick skillet and heat over low heat until lightly browned, stirring occasionally.*

Mini-Chip Crescent Cookies

These are an absolute necessity on any Christmas platter I put together. They're the only cookie my family wants for Christmas, so I don't make cutout cookies anymore.
—**NORENE LAESSIG** STRATFORD, WI

PREP: 40 MIN. + CHILLING
BAKE: 10 MIN./BATCH + CHILLING
MAKES: ABOUT 6 DOZEN

- 1 cup butter, softened
- 1 package (8 ounces) cream cheese, softened
- 2 cups sugar
- 1 large egg
- 1 teaspoon vanilla extract
- ¼ teaspoon almond extract
- ¼ teaspoon coconut extract, optional
- 3½ cups all-purpose flour
- 1 teaspoon baking powder
- 1½ cups miniature semisweet chocolate chips
- 2 cups (12 ounces) semisweet chocolate chips
- 2 tablespoons shortening
  Optional toppings: toasted coconut, sprinkles and toasted chopped almonds

1. In a large bowl, beat butter, cream cheese and sugar until blended. Beat in egg and extracts. In another bowl, whisk flour and baking powder; gradually beat into butter mixture. Stir in miniature chocolate chips. Refrigerate, covered, 1 hour or until firm enough to shape.

2. Preheat oven to 375°. Shape level tablespoons of dough into crescent shapes. Place 1 in. apart on greased baking sheets. Bake 10-12 minutes or until light brown. Remove from pans to wire racks to cool completely.

3. In a microwave, melt 2 cups chocolate chips and shortening; stir until smooth. Dip each cookie halfway into chocolate mixture; allow excess to drip off. Place on waxed paper-lined baking sheets. If desired, sprinkle with toppings. Refrigerate 30 minutes or until set.

NOTE *To toast nuts and coconut, bake in separate shallow pans in a 350° oven for 5-10 minutes or until golden brown, stirring occasionally.*

Mini-Chip Crescent Cookies

Buttery Nut Cookies

Make these wonderful cookies for the holidays as gifts for friends. They'll end up asking for the recipe.
—**STACY DUFFY** CHICAGO, IL

PREP: 15 MIN. + CHILLING • **BAKE:** 15 MIN./BATCH
MAKES: 4 DOZEN

- 1 cup butter, softened
- ½ cup sugar
- 1 large egg yolk
- 1 teaspoon vanilla extract
- ¼ teaspoon salt
- 2¼ cups all-purpose flour
- 1 cup ground pecans
  Confectioners' sugar, optional
- 2 ounces semisweet chocolate, melted, optional

1. In a bowl, cream butter, sugar, egg yolk, vanilla and salt until light and fluffy. Combine flour and pecans; gradually add to creamed mixture. Cover and refrigerate for 1 hour or up to 2 days.

2. Shape into 1-in. balls. Place 1½-in. apart on ungreased baking sheets. Bake at 350° for 12-15 minutes or until firm.

3. If desired, immediately roll the warm cookies in confectioners' sugar; or cool the cookies and drizzle them with melted chocolate.

Lemon & Rosemary
Butter Cookies

FREEZE IT
Lemon & Rosemary Butter Cookies

Cooling lemon and aromatic rosemary make these butter cookies stand out. I use them to punch up cookie trays for potlucks or give them as gifts.
—**ELIZABETH HOKANSON** ARBORG, MB

PREP: 20 MIN. • **BAKE:** 15 MIN.
MAKES: ABOUT 2 DOZEN

- 1¼ cups sugar, divided
- 4 teaspoons grated lemon peel, divided
- 1 cup butter, softened
- 2 large egg yolks
- ¾ teaspoon dried rosemary, crushed
- 2½ cups all-purpose flour
- 1 teaspoon baking soda
- ¼ teaspoon salt

1. Preheat oven to 350°. In a small bowl, combine ¼ cup sugar and 1 teaspoon lemon peel. In a large bowl, beat butter and remaining sugar until light and fluffy. Beat in egg yolks, rosemary and remaining lemon peel. In another bowl, whisk flour, baking soda and salt; gradually beat into creamed mixture.

2. Shape dough into 1¼-in. balls; roll in sugar mixture. Place 2 in. apart on parchment paper-lined baking sheets. Flatten to ¼-in. thickness with bottom of a glass. Sprinkle tops of cookies with remaining sugar mixture. Bake 12-15 minutes or until edges are golden brown. Cool on pans for 2 minutes. Remove to wire racks to cool.

FREEZE OPTION *Freeze shaped balls of dough on baking sheets until firm. Transfer to resealable plastic freezer bags; return to freezer. Prepare and bake cookies as directed.*

Italian Honey Clusters

Italian Honey Clusters

My mother made these treats flavored with cinnamon and anise for neighbors, teachers and anyone who stopped by. Make sure the honey doesn't boil longer than a minute or it could burn.
—**SARAH KNOBLOCK** HYDE PARK, IN

PREP: 45 MIN. + STANDING • **COOK:** 5 MIN./BATCH
MAKES: ABOUT 2 DOZEN

- 3 cups all-purpose flour
- ½ teaspoon ground cinnamon
- ½ teaspoon aniseed, crushed
- ⅛ teaspoon salt
- 4 large eggs, lightly beaten
- ⅓ cup 2% milk
  Oil for deep-fat frying
- 1 cup honey
- ¼ cup sugar
- ½ cup pine nuts, toasted
  Nonpareils, optional

1. Line 24 muffin cups with paper or foil liners. In a large bowl, whisk flour, cinnamon, aniseed and salt. Stir in eggs and milk. Turn dough onto a floured surface; knead until smooth and elastic, about 6-8 minutes. Shape into a disk; wrap in plastic wrap. Let stand 1 hour.

2. Divide dough into six portions. Roll each portion into ½-in.-thick ropes; cut crosswise into ½-in. pieces. In an electric skillet or deep-fat fryer, heat oil to 350°. Fry pieces, a few at a time, for 2-3 minutes on each side or until golden brown. Drain on paper towels. Place dough pieces in a large heatproof bowl and keep warm in a 200° oven.

3. In a large heavy saucepan, combine honey and sugar. Bring to a boil over medium heat; boil 1 minute. Immediately remove from heat and drizzle over dough pieces. Stir to coat. Immediately spoon into prepared cups. Sprinkle with pine nuts and, if desired, nonpareils.

Chocolate Covered Cherry Thumbprints

Chocolate Covered Cherry Thumbprints

When I dig out my best cookie recipes, they remind me of baking when my kids were young. These thumbprints with cherries elicit sweet memories.

—**DEBORAH PUETTE** LILBURN, GA

PREP: 30 MIN. + CHILLING
BAKE: 15 MIN. + COOLING
MAKES: 2 DOZEN

- ¼ cup butter, softened
- ¼ cup shortening
- ¼ cup packed brown sugar
- ¼ teaspoon salt
- 1 large egg, separated
- ½ teaspoon vanilla extract
- 1 cup all-purpose flour
- 1 cup finely chopped salted roasted almonds

FILLING
- ⅓ cup confectioners' sugar
- 1 tablespoon maraschino cherry juice
- 2 teaspoons butter, softened
- 1 teaspoon 2% milk

TOPPINGS
- 24 maraschino cherries
- 4 ounces milk chocolate candy coating, melted

1. Preheat oven to 350°. In a large bowl, cream butter, shortening, brown sugar and salt until light and fluffy. Beat in egg yolk and vanilla. Gradually beat flour into creamed mixture. Refrigerate, covered, 30 minutes or until easy to handle.

2. Preheat oven to 350°. Shape dough into 1¼-in. balls. In a shallow bowl, whisk egg white until foamy. Place almonds in a separate shallow bowl. Dip balls in egg white; roll in almonds.

3. Place balls 2 in. apart on ungreased baking sheets. Press a deep indentation in center of each with your thumb. Bake 10-12 minutes or until edges are light brown. Remove from pans to wire racks.

4. In a small bowl, beat confectioners' sugar, cherry juice, butter and milk until smooth. Fill each cookie with ¼ teaspoon of filling; top each with one cherry. Drizzle with candy coating. Let stand until set.

BIG BATCH
Spritz Cookies

It was a tradition to make these cookies with my grandmother every Christmas. Now my two daughters help me make them for the holidays.

—**SHARON CLAUSSEN** WHEAT RIDGE, CO

PREP: 25 MIN. • **BAKE:** 15 MIN.
MAKES: 11 DOZEN

- 2 cups butter, softened
- 1 cup sugar
- 2 large eggs
- 2 teaspoons vanilla extract
- 4 cups all-purpose flour
- 1 teaspoon baking powder
- ½ cup light corn syrup
- Colored sugar

1. In a large bowl, cream butter and sugar until light and fluffy. Add the eggs, one at a time, beating well after each addition. Beat in vanilla. Combine flour and baking powder; add to creamed mixture and mix well.

2. Using a cookie press fitted with the disk of your choice, press dough 2 in. apart onto ungreased baking sheets. Bake at 325° for 11-12 minutes or until set (do not brown). Remove to wire racks to cool.

3. Microwave corn syrup for 6-8 seconds or until thinned. Working with a few cookies at a time, brush corn syrup over the surface and dip into sugar. Reheat corn syrup as necessary. Let cookies stand until set.

BIG BATCH
Greek Butter Crescents

I had to bake something regarding my heritage for school. I made these little drops of heaven called kourabiedes.
—**REBECCA SPRAGUE** ST LOUIS, MO

PREP: 45 MIN. • **BAKE:** 15 MIN./BATCH + COOLING
MAKES: ABOUT 5 DOZEN

- 1 **pound butter, melted and cooled**
- 3½ **cups confectioners' sugar, divided**
- 1 **large egg yolk**
- 1 **teaspoon vanilla extract**
- 6 **cups all-purpose flour**
- ¼ **teaspoon baking powder**

1. Preheat oven to 400°. In a large bowl, beat butter and ½ cup confectioners' sugar until blended. Beat in egg yolk and vanilla. In another bowl, whisk flour and baking powder; gradually stir into creamed mixture until blended (mixture will be crumbly). Shape heaping tablespoons of dough into crescents. Place 1-in. apart on ungreased baking sheets. Bake 12-15 minutes or until edges are lightly browned. Remove from pans to wire racks to cool 15 minutes.
2. Place remaining confectioners' sugar in a small bowl. Toss slightly cooled cookies in sugar; return cookies to wire rack to cool completely. Toss cookies in sugar once more before serving. Store in an airtight container, adding any remaining sugar to cover cookies.

TOP TIP
The Perfect Crescent

To get just the right crescent shape for your cookie tray, roll a heaping tablespoon of dough into a small 2½-in. log first between the palms of your hands, and then bend the log slightly to form a crescent.

Greek Butter
Crescents

FREEZE IT

Cranberry Pecan Tassies

A traditional pecan tassie is a small tart with nuts. This Thanksgiving version adds cranberries. It's festive!

—**PEGGY WEST** GEORGETOWN, DE

PREP: 25 MIN. + CHILLING
BAKE: 20 MIN. + COOLING
MAKES: 2 DOZEN

- ½ **cup butter, softened**
- 3 **ounces cream cheese, softened**
- 1 **cup all-purpose flour**
- 1 **large egg**
- ⅔ **cup packed brown sugar**
- 1 **tablespoon butter, melted**
- 1 **teaspoon grated orange peel**
- ½ **cup chopped pecans**
- ½ **cup fresh or frozen cranberries, thawed**

1. In a small bowl, beat butter and cream cheese until smooth; gradually beat in flour. Refrigerate, covered, 30 minutes or until firm enough to shape.

2. Preheat oven to 325°. Shape dough into 1-in. balls; place in greased mini-muffin cups. Press evenly onto bottoms and up sides of cups.

3. In a small bowl, beat the egg, brown sugar, melted butter and the orange peel until blended. Stir in pecans. Spoon 1½ teaspoons of this mixture into each cup; top with cranberries.

4. Bake 20-25 minutes or until crust is golden and filling is set. Cool in pans for 2 minutes. Remove to wire racks to cool.

FREEZE OPTION *Freeze cookies, layered between waxed paper, in freezer containers. To use, thaw before serving.*

Cranberry Pecan Tassies

BIG BATCH
Raspberry-Almond Crescent Cookies

My flaky, two-bite crescent cookies are sensational treats. Filled with raspberry preserves, coconut and almonds, they might remind you of rugelach.
—KELLY WILLIAMS FORKED RIVER, NJ

PREP: 45 MIN. + CHILLING • **BAKE:** 15 MIN./BATCH
MAKES: 4 DOZEN

- **2 cups all-purpose flour**
- **1 cup cold butter, cubed**
- **1 large egg yolk**
- **½ cup sour cream**
- **1 teaspoon vanilla extract**

FILLING
- **1 cup seedless raspberry jam**
- **¾ cup flaked coconut**
- **⅓ cup finely chopped almonds**
- **¼ teaspoon almond extract**
- **1 large egg white, lightly beaten**
  Coarse sugar

1. Place the flour in a large bowl; cut in butter until mixture resembles coarse crumbs. In another bowl, whisk egg yolk, sour cream and vanilla until smooth; stir into flour mixture.
2. Divide dough into four portions. Shape each into a disk; wrap in plastic wrap. Refrigerate for 30 minutes or until firm.
3. Preheat oven to 350°. In a small bowl, mix raspberry jam, coconut, almonds and almond extract until blended. On a well-sugared surface, roll each portion of dough into a 10-in. circle. Spread about ⅓ cup filling over circles. Cut each into 12 wedges. Roll up wedges from the wide ends. Place 1 in. apart on parchment paper-lined baking sheets, point side down; curve to form crescents. Brush with egg white; sprinkle with coarse sugar.
4. Bake 15-18 minutes or until set (do not brown). Remove from pans to wire racks to cool.

Dipped Chocolate Logs

Dipped Chocolate Logs

When my sister and I were little, we used to beg my mother and grandmother to make these buttery cookies during the holidays. Now, as moms ourselves, we get together every year to make Christmas cookies and the chocolate logs are always on the top of our list.
—DEANNA MARKOS WESTERN SPRINGS, IL

PREP: 1 HOUR • **BAKE:** 20 MIN./BATCH + COOLING
MAKES: 3 DOZEN

- **6 tablespoons baking cocoa**
- **¼ cup hot water**
- **1 cup butter, softened**
- **½ cup confectioners' sugar**
- **½ cup sugar**
- **2 large egg yolks**
- **1½ teaspoons vanilla extract**
- **2½ cups all-purpose flour**
- **¼ teaspoon baking soda**

GLAZE
- **3 tablespoons baking cocoa**
- **2 tablespoons hot water**
- **2 tablespoons butter, softened**
- **2 tablespoons 2% milk**
- **½ teaspoon vanilla extract**
- **2 cups confectioners' sugar**
- **¼ cup finely ground pecans**
- **1 tablespoon red nonpareils**

1. Preheat oven to 350°. In a small bowl, mix cocoa and hot water until smooth; cool slightly.
2. In a large bowl, cream butter and sugars until light and fluffy. Beat in egg yolks, vanilla and cocoa mixture. In another bowl, whisk the flour and baking soda; gradually beat into the creamed mixture (dough will be stiff).
3. Cut a large hole in the tip of a pastry bag; insert #829 or other open star pastry tip. Working in batches, pipe dough to form 2½-in.-long logs, 2 in. apart, onto ungreased baking sheets.
4. Bake 18-22 minutes or until firm. Remove from pans to wire racks to cool completely.
5. For glaze, in a small bowl, mix cocoa and hot water until smooth; stir in butter, milk and vanilla. Gradually add confectioners' sugar, mixing until smooth.
6. Dip each cookie halfway into warm glaze, holding cookie at a slight angle; allow excess to drip off. Place on waxed paper. Immediately sprinkle with pecans and nonpareils. Let stand until set.

Big & Buttery Chocolate Chip Cookies

My version of this classic cookie is based on a recipe from a bakery in California called Hungry Bear. The cookie is big, thick and chewy—perfect for dunking.

—IRENE YEH MEQUON, WI

PREP: 35 MIN. + CHILLING • **BAKE:** 10 MIN./BATCH
MAKES: ABOUT 2 DOZEN

- 1 cup butter, softened
- 1 cup packed brown sugar
- ¾ cup sugar
- 2 large eggs
- 1½ teaspoons vanilla extract
- 2⅔ cups all-purpose flour
- 1¼ teaspoons baking soda
- 1 teaspoon salt
- 1 package (12 ounces) semisweet chocolate chips
- 2 cups coarsely chopped walnuts, toasted

1. In a large bowl, beat butter and sugars until blended. Beat in eggs and vanilla. In a small bowl, whisk flour, baking soda and salt; gradually beat into butter mixture. Stir in chocolate chips and walnuts.
2. Shape ¼ cupfuls of dough into balls. Flatten each to ¾-in. thickness (2½-in. diameter), smoothing edges as necessary. Place in an airtight container, separating layers with waxed or parchment paper; refrigerate, covered, overnight.
3. To bake, place dough portions 2 in. apart on parchment paper-lined baking sheets; let stand at room temperature 30 minutes before baking. Preheat oven to 400°.
4. Bake 10-12 minutes or until edges are golden brown (centers will be light). Cool on pans for 2 minutes. Remove to wire racks to cool.
NOTE *To toast nuts, bake in a shallow pan in a 350° oven for 5-10 minutes or cook in a skillet over low heat until lightly browned, stirring occasionally.*

Gingerbread Cookie Bites

Gingerbread Cookie Bites

I transformed store-bought cookie mix into mini tarts similar to gingerbread brownies. For garnish, try chopped crystalized ginger or a sprinkle of cinnamon and nutmeg.

—SHENAE PULLIAM SWANSEA, SC

PREP: 30 MIN. • **BAKE:** 10 MIN. + COOLING
MAKES: ABOUT 3 DOZEN

- 1 package (14½ ounces) gingerbread cake/cookie mix
- ½ cup butter, softened
- ¼ cup sugar
- 1 large egg
- 2 tablespoons all-purpose flour
- 1 tablespoon water
- ¼ teaspoon ground ginger, optional

FILLING
- 4 ounces cream cheese, softened
- ¼ cup butter, softened
- ½ teaspoon vanilla extract
- 1¾ cups confectioners' sugar
  Ground cinnamon and nutmeg
  Crystallized ginger, chopped, optional

1. In a large bowl, beat cake/cookie mix, butter, sugar, egg, flour, water and, if desired, ginger until blended. Refrigerate 30 minutes or until firm.
2. Preheat oven to 350°. Shape dough into 1-in. balls; place in ungreased mini-muffin cups. Press evenly onto bottoms and up the sides of cups. Bake 10-12 minutes or until edges are lightly golden. Cool in pans for 2 minutes. Remove to wire racks to cool completely.
3. For filling, in a large bowl, beat cream cheese, butter and vanilla until blended. Gradually beat in confectioners' sugar until smooth. Pipe into cookie cups; sprinkle with cinnamon, nutmeg and, if desired, crystallized ginger. Refrigerate in an airtight container.

FREEZE IT **BIG BATCH**

Apricot-Pecan Thumbprint Cookies

The past few years I have experimented using cake mixes to make favorite or new cookie recipes. This is one of those that has met approval with many.
—**NANCY JOHNSON** LAVERNE, OK

PREP: 30 MIN. • **BAKE:** 15 MIN./BATCH + COOLING
MAKES: ABOUT 7 DOZEN

- 2 **packages yellow cake mix (regular size)**
- ½ **cup all-purpose flour**
- 1 **cup canola oil**
- 6 **large eggs**
- 1 **teaspoon ground cinnamon**
- ½ **teaspoon ground ginger**
- 3 **tablespoons water**
- 4 **cups finely chopped pecans, divided**
- ⅔ **cup apricot preserves**

ICING

- 2 **cups confectioners' sugar**
- 3 **to 5 tablespoons water**

1. Preheat oven to 350°. In a large bowl, beat cake mix, flour, oil, 4 eggs, cinnamon and ginger until well blended.
2. In a shallow bowl, whisk water and remaining eggs. Place half of the pecans in another shallow bowl. Shape dough into 1-in. balls. Dip in egg mixture, then coat with pecans, adding remaining pecans to bowl as needed. Place cookies 2 in. apart on greased baking sheets.
3. Press a deep indentation in center of each cookie with the end of a wooden spoon handle. Fill each with preserves. Bake 12-14 minutes or until golden brown. Remove from pans to wire racks to cool completely.
4. In a small bowl, combine the confectioners' sugar and enough water to achieve a drizzling consistency. Drizzle over cookies. Let stand until set.
FREEZE OPTION *Freeze drizzled cookies, layered between waxed paper, in freezer containers. To use, thaw in covered containers.*

BIG BATCH

Lacy Brandy Snaps

These captivating, fluff-filled crisps are the perfect "little something sweet" that guests crave at the end of a filling meal.
—**NATALIE BREMSON** PLANTATION, FL

PREP: 30 MIN. • **BAKE:** 10 MIN./BATCH + COOLING
MAKES: 4 DOZEN

- 6 **tablespoons unsalted butter, cubed**
- ⅓ **cup sugar**
- 3 **tablespoons light corn syrup**
- ⅔ **cup all-purpose flour**
- 2 **teaspoons brandy**
- 1 **teaspoon ground ginger**

FILLING

- 4 **cups heavy whipping cream**
- 1¾ **cups confectioners' sugar**
- ½ **cup brandy**
  Grated chocolate, optional

1. In a small saucepan, combine butter, sugar and corn syrup. Cook and stir over medium heat until butter is melted. Remove from the heat. Stir in the flour, brandy and ginger.
2. Drop by teaspoonfuls, three at a time, 3 in. apart onto parchment paper-lined baking sheet. Bake at 350° for 7-8 minutes or until golden brown.
3. Cool for 30-45 seconds. Working quickly, loosen each cookie and curl around a thick wooden spoon handle. (If cookies become to cool to shape, return to oven for 1 minute to soften.) Remove to wire rack to cool completely.
4. For filling, in a large bowl, beat cream until it begins to thicken. Add confectioners' sugar and brandy; beat until stiff peaks form. Just before serving, pipe cream mixture into cookies. Sprinkle ends with chocolate if desired.

Apricot-Pecan Thumbprint Cookies

Caramel
Apple
Bites

Mexican Crinkle Cookies

When it's baking time, my family lobbies for these Mexican crinkle cookies. You can replace 1 oz. unsweetened chocolate with 3 Tbsp. cocoa powder plus 1 Tbsp. shortening, butter or oil.
—**KIM KENYON** GREENWOOD, MO

PREP: 25 MIN. + CHILLING • **BAKE:** 10 MIN./BATCH
MAKES: ABOUT 2 DOZEN

- ¾ cup butter, cubed
- 2 ounces unsweetened chocolate, chopped
- 1 cup packed brown sugar
- ¼ cup light corn syrup
- 1 large egg
- 2 cups all-purpose flour
- 2 teaspoons baking soda
- 1½ teaspoons ground cinnamon, divided
- ¼ teaspoon salt
- ½ cup confectioners' sugar

1. In a large microwave-safe bowl, melt butter and chocolate; stir until smooth. Beat in brown sugar and corn syrup until blended. Beat in egg. In another bowl, whisk flour, baking soda, 1 teaspoon cinnamon and salt; gradually beat into brown sugar mixture. Refrigerate, covered, 1 hour or until firm.
2. Preheat oven to 350°. In a shallow bowl, mix confectioners' sugar and remaining cinnamon. Shape dough into 1½-in. balls; roll in confectioners' sugar mixture. Place 2 in. apart on greased baking sheets.
3. Bake 10-12 minutes or until set and tops are cracked. Cool on pans for 2 minutes. Remove to wire racks to cool.

Caramel Apple Bites

Kids find this recipe especially appealing. They can help out by dipping the baked cookies in caramel and nuts—and also by eating the treats! These bites just disappear at my house.
—**DARLENE BRENDEN** SALEM, OR

PREP: 25 MIN. + STANDING
BAKE: 15 MIN. + COOLING
MAKES: ABOUT 3 DOZEN

FILLING
- ⅓ cup finely chopped unpeeled apple
- ⅓ cup evaporated milk
- ⅓ cup sugar
- ⅓ cup chopped walnuts

DOUGH
- ½ cup butter, softened
- ¼ cup confectioners' sugar
- ¼ cup packed brown sugar
- 1 large egg
- 1 teaspoon vanilla extract
- 2 cups all-purpose flour
- ¼ teaspoon salt

TOPPING
- 1 package (14 ounces) caramels
- ⅔ cup evaporated milk
  Green toothpicks
- 1 cup chopped walnuts

1. In a small saucepan, combine filling ingredients. Cook and stir over medium heat until thickened; set aside to cool.
2. In a large bowl, cream the butter and sugars until light and fluffy. Beat in egg. Beat in vanilla. Combine flour and salt. Gradually add to creamed mixture and mix well.
3. Shape dough into 1-in. balls. Flatten and place ¼ teaspoon filling in center of each. Fold dough over filling and reshape into balls. Place 1 in. apart on greased baking sheets.
4. Bake at 350° for 12-15 minutes or until lightly browned. Remove to wire racks to cool.
5. In a small saucepan over low heat, cook caramels and evaporated milk until caramels are melted; stir until smooth. Insert a toothpick into each cookie and dip into caramel until completely coated; allow excess to drip off. Dip bottoms into nuts. Place on wire racks to set.

❝The apple bites were a home run! I followed the directions exactly and they came out great.❞
—**ORACLEROGUE**
FROM TASTEOFHOME.COM

Mexican
Crinkle
Cookies

EASY MINT THINS
PAGE 94

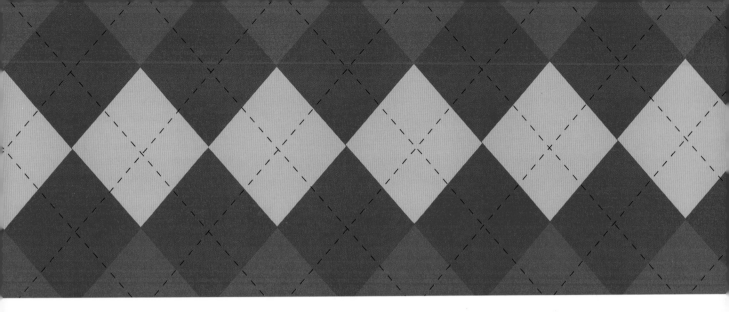

No-Bake Delights

DESSERT IN A FLASH! DO YOU HEAR THE CHEERING ALREADY? WHIP TOGETHER THESE TASTY TREATS WITHOUT OPENING THE OVEN DOOR. WHEN YOU NEED A LAST-MINUTE DISH TO BRING TO A PARTY, ONE OF THESE RECIPES WILL FIT THE BILL; MAYBE PLAN ON MAKING A DOUBLE BATCH!

WHITE ALMOND NO-BAKE COOKIES *PAGE 95*

CANNOLI WAFER SANDWICHES *PAGE 99*

BUTTERY LEMON SANDWICH COOKIES *PAGE 98*

Texas Tumbleweeds

occasionally. Stir a small amount into the egg, then return all to pan. Cook and stir over low heat for 2 minutes. Pour into a bowl; let cool for 15 minutes. Gently stir in marshmallows and nuts. Chill for 30 minutes.

2. On a sheet of waxed paper, shape the dough into a 1½-in.-diameter log. Place the coconut on another sheet of waxed paper. Gently roll the log over coconut to coat sides. Wrap up tightly, twisting ends to seal.

3. Freeze for 4 hours or overnight. Remove the waxed paper. Cut the log into ¼-in. slices. Store in an airtight container in the refrigerator.

BIG BATCH

Mocha Pecan Balls

Dust six-ingredient sweets with either confectioners' sugar or cocoa powder to get truffle-like treats. No baking required!
—**LORRAINE DAROCHA** MOUNTAIN CITY, TN

START TO FINISH: 25 MIN.
MAKES: 4 DOZEN

- 2½ **cups crushed vanilla wafers (about 65 wafers)**
- 2 **cups plus ¼ cup confectioners' sugar, divided**
- ⅔ **cup finely chopped pecans, toasted**
- 2 **tablespoons baking cocoa**
- ¼ **cup reduced-fat evaporated milk**
- ¼ **cup cold strong brewed coffee Additional baking cocoa, optional**

1. In a large bowl, combine the wafer crumbs, 2 cups of confectioners' sugar, pecans and cocoa. Stir in the milk and coffee (mixture will be sticky).

2. Dust hands in confectioners' sugar and shape the dough into ¾-in. balls; roll in remaining confectioners' sugar or additional baking cocoa if desired. Store in an airtight container.

---

⑤ **INGREDIENTS** *BIG BATCH*

Texas Tumbleweeds

Tumbleweeds blow across the roads in some parts of Texas, and I think these cute stacks looks like them. For years my sister and I have been making these sweet treats.
—**KAREN LEMAY** SEABROOK, TX

PREP: 20 MIN. + CHILLING
MAKES: ABOUT 4 DOZEN

- 1 **cup (6 ounces) butterscotch chips**
- 1 **cup creamy peanut butter**
- 1 **can (9 ounces) potato sticks (about 6 cups)**

1. In a microwave, melt butterscotch chips and peanut butter; stir until smooth. Stir in potato sticks.

2. Drop by rounded tablespoonfuls onto waxed paper-lined baking sheets. Refrigerate 10-15 minutes or until set.

BIG BATCH

Cathedral Cookies

Children love the colorful marshmallows in these no-bake slices, which mimic the look of stained glass. They really light up the cookie tray at our parties.
—**CAROL SHAFFER** CAPE GIRARDEAU, MO

PREP: 10 MIN. + FREEZING
COOK: 10 MIN. + COOLING
MAKES: ABOUT 5 DOZEN

- 1 **cup (6 ounces) semisweet chocolate chips**
- 2 **tablespoons butter**
- 1 **large egg, lightly beaten**
- 3 **cups pastel miniature marshmallows**
- ½ **cup chopped pecans or walnuts**
- 1 **cup flaked coconut**

1. In a heavy saucepan, melt chocolate chips and butter over low heat, stirring

---

FREEZE IT *BIG BATCH*

Dutch Waffle Cookies

My mom taught me how to make these waffle iron cookies. Now I have my friends bring their waffle irons to the house, and we make big batches.
—**RACHEL SETALA** SURREY, BC

PREP: 40 MIN. • **COOK:** 5 MIN./BATCH
MAKES: ABOUT 6 DOZEN

- 1 **cup butter, softened**
- 1 **cup sugar**
- 2 **large eggs**
- ½ **cup 2% milk**
- 1 **tablespoon vanilla extract**
- 4 **cups all-purpose flour**
- 1¾ **teaspoons baking powder**
- ¾ **teaspoon baking soda**
  Confectioners' sugar, optional

1. In large bowl, beat butter and sugar until blended. Beat in eggs, milk and vanilla. In another bowl, whisk flour, baking powder and baking soda; gradually beat into butter mixture.
2. Shape level tablespoons of dough into balls; place 2 in. apart on a preheated waffle iron coated with cooking spray. Bake on medium heat 3-4 minutes or until cookies are golden brown. Remove to wire racks to cool. If desired, dust with confectioners' sugar.
FREEZE OPTION *Freeze cookies layered between waxed paper in freezer containers. To use, thaw in covered containers. If desired, dust with additional confectioners' sugar.*

TOP TIP

Smart Spritzing

I prefer not to use commercial nonstick cooking spray. So I went to the kitchenware area of a department store and bought a spray bottle made just for cooking oil. I fill it with a favorite oil and use it whenever nonstick cooking spray is called for in a recipe.
—**ELIZABETH M.** ALBERT BRIDGE, NS

Dutch Waffle
Cookies

⑤INGREDIENTS *BIG BATCH*

Easy Mint Thins

My friends often try to guess the ingredients in these cookies, but I never tell them how simple they are to make. They taste just like the Girl Scout cookie, and they're perfect for Christmas and bake sales.

—JENNIFER SETSER
MORGANTOWN, IN

PREP: 40 MIN. + STANDING
MAKES: 5 DOZEN

- 24 **ounces milk or dark chocolate candy coating**
- 1½ **teaspoons peppermint extract**
- 60 **Ritz crackers**
- 2 **ounces white candy coating, melted**
  Optional decorations: chopped Andes candies, crushed spearmint candies and green colored sugar

1. In a microwave, melt chocolate candy coating; stir until smooth. Stir in extract.

2. Dip crackers in chocolate candy coating; allow excess to drip off. Place on waxed paper; let stand until set.

3. Drizzle tops of cookies with white candy coating; decorate as desired. Let stand until set. Store in airtight containers.

Easy Mint Thins

BIG BATCH
Browned Butter Cereal Bars

Crispy rice treats were one of the first recipes I ever made as a kid. For a new version, I wanted to make something similar but more special. Friends and family think using Cap'n Crunch and browned butter is genius, but I just call them delicious.

—**KELLY KRAUSS** LEBANON, NJ

PREP: 15 MIN. + FREEZING
COOK: 20 MIN. + COOLING
MAKES: 5 DOZEN

- 4 cups white fudge-covered miniature pretzels
- 1 package (10½ ounces) miniature marshmallows
- 1 package (10 to 12 ounces) white baking chips
- 2 cups butter, cubed
- 3 packages (10 ounces each) large marshmallows
- 2 teaspoons vanilla extract
- 1 teaspoon salt
- 8 cups Cap'n Crunch

1. Line a 15x10x1-in. pan with parchment paper, letting ends extend over sides; set aside. Freeze pretzels, miniature marshmallows and baking chips for 1 hour.
2. Remove pretzels, marshmallows and baking chips from the freezer; combine in a large bowl. In a Dutch oven, melt butter over medium heat. Heat 10-13 minutes or until golden brown, stirring constantly. Add large marshmallows; cook and stir until blended. Remove from heat; stir in vanilla and salt.
3. Stir in cereal until coated. Stir in pretzel mixture; transfer to prepared pan, pressing evenly with a buttered spatula. Cool completely.
4. Lifting with the parchment paper, remove cereal mixture from pan. Cut into bars. Store in airtight containers.

Browned Butter Cereal Bars

White Almond No-Bake Cookies

My daughter and I like to try new recipes. We were out of chocolate chips one day, so we came up with a different cookie by using white chips.

—**DEBBIE JOHNSON** WINONA LAKE, IN

PREP: 25 MIN. • **COOK:** 5 MIN. + CHILLING
MAKES: ABOUT 3½ DOZEN

- 2 cups sugar
- ½ cup butter, cubed
- ½ cup 2% milk
- 1 cup white baking chips
- ½ teaspoon almond extract
- 3 cups old-fashioned oats
- 1 cup dried cherries or dried cranberries, optional

1. In a large saucepan, combine sugar, butter and milk. Cook and stir over medium heat until butter is melted and sugar is dissolved. Remove from heat. Stir in baking chips and extract until smooth. Add oats and, if desired, cherries or cranberries; stir until coated.
2. Drop by rounded tablespoonfuls onto waxed paper-lined baking sheets. Refrigerate until set, about 30 minutes. Store in an airtight container in the refrigerator.

Easy
Cinnamon
Thins

Gooey Caramel-Topped Gingersnaps

Making these cookies is therapeutic for me. I often watch a movie while I put them together. I take a lot of cookies to fundraisers, and these gingersnaps are quite popular. You can make variations by changing the cookie base or by varying the nuts.
—**DEIRDRE COX** KANSAS CITY, MO

PREP: 30 MIN. + STANDING
MAKES: 3½ DOZEN

- 42 **gingersnap cookies**
- 1 **package (14 ounces) caramels**
- ¼ **cup 2% milk or heavy whipping cream**
- 1 **cup chopped honey-roasted peanuts**
- 12 **ounces white or dark chocolate candy coating, melted**
  Chocolate jimmies or finely chopped honey-roasted peanuts

1. Arrange cookies in a single layer on waxed paper-lined baking sheets. In a microwave, melt the caramels with the milk; stir until smooth. Stir in 1 cup chopped peanuts. Spoon about 1 teaspoon of caramel mixture over each cookie; refrigerate until set.
2. Dip each cookie halfway into the candy coating; allow excess to drip off. Return to baking sheet; sprinkle with jimmies. Refrigerate until set.

(5) INGREDIENTS
Easy Cinnamon Thins

When a co-worker's husband came home from Iraq, we had a potluck for him. Tasty cookies with coarse red sugar matched our patriotic theme.
—**JANET WHITTINGTON** HEATH, OH

PREP: 20 MIN. + STANDING
MAKES: 2½ DOZEN

- 12 **ounces white candy coating, chopped**
- 1 **teaspoon cinnamon extract**
- 30 **Ritz crackers**
- 12 **finely crushed cinnamon hard candies**
  Red colored sugar

1. In a microwave, melt candy coating; stir until smooth. Stir in extract.
2. Dip crackers in the candy coating mixture; allow excess to drip off. Place on waxed paper. Decorate with candies and colored sugar as desired. Let stand until set.

TOP TIP

Dipping Just Right

Before you start dipping cookies in chocolate—or any other candy coating—transfer the chocolate first to a narrow container. Dip cookie into chocolate and scrape the bottom of the cookie across the edge of the container to remove any excess. When chocolate is running low, spoon it over the cookies on waxed paper-lined baking sheets.

Gooey
Caramel-Topped
Gingersnaps

Frosty Orange Cream Cheese Cups

These bite-sized frozen treats are sure to cool you down during the dog days of summer.

—ROXANNE CHAN ALBANY, CA

PREP: 35 MIN. + FREEZING
MAKES: 2 DOZEN

- 1¼ cups crushed gingersnap cookies (about 25 cookies)
- 5 tablespoons butter, melted
- 4 ounces cream cheese, softened
- 2 tablespoons confectioners' sugar
- 2 tablespoons plus ½ cup heavy whipping cream, divided
- ½ cup orange marmalade
- 4 ounces white baking chocolate, chopped
- ⅓ cup salted pistachios, chopped

1. In a small bowl, mix cookie crumbs and butter; press onto bottoms and up sides of ungreased mini-muffin cups. Freeze 20 minutes.

2. In a small bowl, beat cream cheese, confectioners' sugar and 2 tablespoons cream until smooth. Stir in marmalade; drop by scant tablespoonfuls into cups. Freeze 2 hours or until set.

3. In a double boiler or metal bowl over hot water, melt chocolate with remaining cream; stir until smooth. Cool slightly. Spoon or drizzle over cups. Sprinkle with pistachios. Freeze, covered, overnight or until firm. Serve frozen.

Frosty Orange Cream Cheese Cups

Chocolate Butterscotch Haystacks

(5) INGREDIENTS

Chocolate Butterscotch Haystacks

My grandmother often made haystacks for my cousin Vonnie and me when our parents didn't want us to have any more sweets. I love this simple recipe!

—CHRISTINE SCHWESTER DIVIDE, CO

PREP: 25 MIN. + CHILLING
MAKES: 3 DOZEN

- 2 cups (12 ounces) semisweet chocolate chips
- 1 package (10 to 11 ounces) butterscotch chips
- 4 cups crispy chow mein noodles

1. In a microwave, melt the chocolate chips and butterscotch chips; stir until smooth. Add the noodles; toss to coat.

2. Drop by rounded tablespoonfuls onto waxed paper-lined baking sheets. Refrigerate 10-15 minutes or until set.

(5) INGREDIENTS

Buttery Lemon Sandwich Cookies

My grandson approves of these lemony sandwich cookies made with crackers and prepared frosting. Decorate with whatever sprinkles you like.

—NANCY FOUST STONEBORO, PA

START TO FINISH: 20 MIN.
MAKES: 2½ DOZEN

- ¾ cup lemon frosting
- 60 Ritz crackers
- 24 ounces white candy coating, melted
  Nonpareils, jimmies or sprinkles, optional

Spread frosting on bottoms of half of the crackers; cover with remaining crackers. Dip sandwiches in melted candy coating; allow excess to drip off. Place on waxed paper; decorate as desired. Let stand until set. Store in an airtight container in the refrigerator.

BIG BATCH

Salted Butterscotch & Pecan No-Bakes

When I was deciding what type of cookie to make for a Christmas swap, I decided to make something with coconut, pudding mix and salted caramel. For a special touch, I like to drizzle caramel over the tops of the cookies before serving. Put them in pretty boxes and give as gifts.
—**STACEY RITZ** SUDBURY, ON

PREP: 25 MIN. + CHILLING
MAKES: 4 DOZEN

- 1¾ cups pecans, toasted
- 1½ teaspoons kosher salt
- 1 can (14 ounces) sweetened condensed milk
- 1½ cups finely shredded unsweetened coconut
- 1 package (3.4 ounces) instant butterscotch pudding mix
- ½ cup sugar
- 48 pecan halves, toasted

1. Place 1¾ cups of pecans and the salt in a food processor; pulse until pecans are finely ground. Transfer to a large bowl. Stir in milk, coconut and pudding mix until blended. Refrigerate, covered, for 30 minutes or until mixture is firm enough to roll.

2. Shape mixture into forty-eight 1-in. balls; roll in sugar. Top each with a pecan half, flattening slightly. Store in airtight containers in the refrigerator.

NOTES *To toast nuts, spread in a 15x10x1-in. baking pan. Bake at 350° for 5-10 minutes or until lightly browned, stirring occasionally. Or, spread in a dry nonstick skillet and heat over low heat until lightly browned, stirring occasionally. Look for unsweetened coconut in the baking or health food section.*

Cannoli Wafer Sandwiches

My family loves to visit a local Italian restaurant that has a wonderful dessert buffet. The cannolis are among our favorites, so I just had to come up with a recipe of my own. They are best served the same day they are made so the wafers remain crisp.
—**NICHI LARSON** SHAWNEE, KS

PREP: 35 MIN. + STANDING
MAKES: 3½ DOZEN

- 1 cup whole-milk ricotta cheese
- ¼ cup confectioners' sugar
- 1 tablespoon sugar
- ¼ teaspoon vanilla extract
- 1 package (12 ounces) vanilla wafers
- 12 ounces white candy coating, melted
- ½ cup miniature semisweet chocolate chips
  Additional confectioners' sugar

1. In a small bowl, mix ricotta cheese, confectioners' sugar, sugar and vanilla until blended. Spread 1 scant teaspoon filling on bottoms of half of the wafers; cover with remaining wafers.

2. Dip each sandwich cookie halfway into candy coating; allow excess to drip off. Place on waxed paper; sprinkle with the chocolate chips. Let stand until set, about 10 minutes.

3. Serve within 2 hours or refrigerate until serving. Dust with additional confectioners' sugar just before serving.

Salted Butterscotch & Pecan No-Bakes

Cherry-Coconut
Slices

Cherry-Coconut Slices

My mother got this recipe from a woman named Emmie Oddie, a well-known home economist in Canada who had a column in a farming newspaper. She would test reader recipes in her own kitchen and write about them. These tasty sweets are so rich that you only need a small piece.

—JUDY OLSON WHITECOURT, AB

PREP: 15 MIN. + CHILLING
COOK: 5 MIN. + COOLING
MAKES: 32 BARS

- 3 cups graham cracker crumbs
- 1½ cups miniature marshmallows
- 1 cup finely shredded unsweetened coconut
- ½ cup chopped maraschino cherries
- 1 can (14 ounces) sweetened condensed milk
- 1 teaspoon maple flavoring

FROSTING

- 1 cup packed brown sugar
- ⅓ cup butter, cubed
- ¼ cup 2% milk
- 1 cup confectioners' sugar

1. In a large bowl, mix the cracker crumbs, marshmallows, coconut and cherries; stir in condensed milk and flavoring. Press into a greased 8-in. square baking pan.

2. For frosting, in a small saucepan, combine the brown sugar, butter and milk. Bring to a boil, stirring constantly; cook and stir for 3 minutes. Transfer to a small bowl; cool until lukewarm, about 15 minutes. Stir in confectioners' sugar until smooth. Spread the frosting over crumb mixture; refrigerate until set, about 1½ hours.

3. Cut into bars. Store in an airtight container in the refrigerator.

NOTE *Look for unsweetened coconut in the baking or health food section.*

No-Bake Fudgy Coconut Cookies

No-Bake Fudgy Coconut Cookies

My daughter works at a summer camp, so I send treats. Instead of a cookie jar we use a coffee can and call it the Wrangler Feeding Trough. Everyone asks for this cookie.

—SUE KLEMM RHINELANDER, WI

PREP: 30 MIN. + CHILLING
MAKES: 3½ DOZEN

- 1½ cups sugar
- ⅔ cup 2% milk
- ½ cup baking cocoa
- ½ cup butter, cubed
- ½ teaspoon salt
- ⅓ cup creamy peanut butter
- 1 teaspoon vanilla extract
- 2 cups quick-cooking oats
- 1 cup flaked coconut
- ½ cup white baking chips
- 1 teaspoon shortening

1. In a large saucepan, combine the first five ingredients. Bring to a boil, stirring constantly. Cook and stir 3 minutes.

2. Remove from heat; stir in peanut butter and vanilla until blended. Stir in oats and coconut. Drop mixture by tablespoonfuls onto waxed paper-lined baking sheets.

3. In a microwave, melt baking chips and shortening; stir until smooth. Drizzle over cookies; refrigerate until set. Store in airtight containers.

ALMOND BONBON COOKIES *PAGE 110*

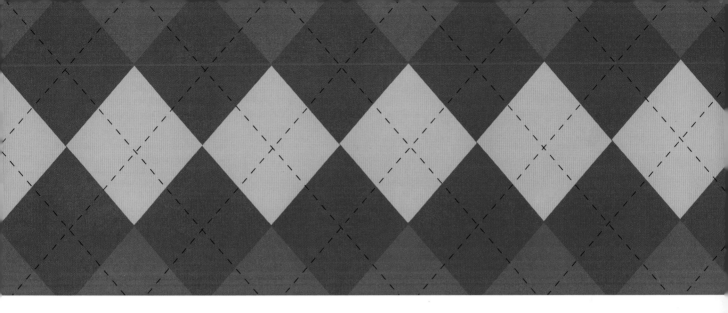

Christmas Classics

SPREAD A LITTLE JOY THIS SEASON WITH A GIFT FROM THE KITCHEN. TAKE A LOOK AT THE RECIPES HERE AND FIND A NEW TRADITION TO MAKE AND SHARE WITH FAMILY AND FRIENDS. THERE'S NO OTHER HOLIDAY QUITE LIKE CHRISTMAS, SO BAKE UP SOME MAGIC TODAY!

RED VELVET PEPPERMINT THUMBPRINTS *PAGE 110*

SANTA CLAUS SUGAR COOKIES *PAGE 107*

HOLIDAY CUTOUT COOKIES *PAGE 111*

Mint Chocolate Wafers

Holly Berry Cookies

What would Christmas be without overflowing tins of cookies? These festive filled cookies are all-time favorites of my family. Back when our children were small, we began baking them the day after Halloween.

—AUDREY THIBODEAU GILBERT, AZ

PREP: 30 MIN. + CHILLING
BAKE: 10 MIN. + COOLING
MAKES: 2 DOZEN

- 2 cups all-purpose flour
- 1 cup sugar
- 1 teaspoon ground cinnamon
- ¾ teaspoon baking powder
- ¼ teaspoon salt
- ½ cup cold butter, cubed
- 1 large egg
- ¼ cup 2% milk
- ⅔ cup seedless raspberry jam

GLAZE

- 2 cups confectioners' sugar
- 2 tablespoons 2% milk
- ½ teaspoon vanilla extract
  Red Hots
  Green food coloring

1. In a large bowl, combine the first five ingredients. Cut in butter until mixture resembles coarse crumbs. In a small bowl, beat egg and milk. Add to crumb mixture just until moistened. Cover and refrigerate for 1 hour or until dough is easy to handle.
2. On a lightly floured surface, roll out dough to ⅛-in. thickness. Cut with a 2-in. round cookie cutter. Place on ungreased baking sheets. Bake at 375° for 8-10 minutes or until edges are lightly browned. Cool on wire racks. Spread jam on half of the cookies; top each with another cookie.
3. In a small bowl, combine sugar, milk and vanilla until smooth; spread over cookies. Decorate with Red Hots before glaze is set. Let dry. Using a small new paintbrush and green food coloring, paint holly leaves on cookies.

BIG BATCH

Mint Chocolate Wafers

My grandmother gave me a cookbook that is loaded with terrific recipes. This is a slight twist on one of the first recipes I made from the book, and it is by far one of the best. Make sure to store these in the refrigerator.

—MARY MURPHY EVANSVILLE, IN

PREP: 1 HOUR + CHILLING
BAKE: 10 MIN./BATCH + COOLING
MAKES: 10 DOZEN

- 1 large egg
- ⅓ cup water
- 3 tablespoons canola oil
- 1 package chocolate fudge cake mix (regular size)
- ½ cup cake flour

COATING

- 4 cups (24 ounces) semisweet chocolate chips
- ¼ cup shortening
- ½ teaspoon peppermint extract
  Sprinkles

1. In a large bowl, beat egg, water and oil until blended. Gradually beat in cake mix and flour.
2. Divide dough in half. Shape each into a disk; wrap in plastic wrap. Refrigerate 2 hours or until firm enough to roll.
3. Preheat oven to 350°. On a lightly floured surface, roll each portion of dough to ⅛-in. thickness. Cut with a floured 1½-in. round cookie cutter. Place the cookies 1 in. apart on greased baking sheets.
4. Bake 8-10 minutes or until firm. Remove from pans to wire racks to cool completely.
5. In top of a double boiler or a metal bowl over hot water, melt chocolate chips and shortening; stir until smooth. Stir in extract. Spread cookies with chocolate mixture. Place on waxed paper-lined baking sheets. Decorate with sprinkles. Refrigerate until set.
NOTE *This recipe was tested with a Betty Crocker chocolate fudge cake mix (regular size).*

FREEZE IT

JoJo's Ginger Cookies

It's so much fun to decorate cookies with children's help. We created these gingery moose-shaped cookies to go with a book made especially for my niece's third-grade class. The crispy golden brown cookies stole the show.

—**JENET CATTAR** NEPTUNE BEACH, FL

PREP: 40 MIN. + FREEZING
BAKE: 10 MIN./BATCH
MAKES: ABOUT 1½ DOZEN

- ½ **cup shortening**
- ½ **cup packed brown sugar**
- ½ **cup molasses**
- ¼ **cup water**
- 3 **cups all-purpose flour**
- 1 **teaspoon ground ginger**
- ½ **teaspoon ground nutmeg**
- ⅛ **teaspoon ground allspice**
- ½ **teaspoon baking soda**
- ½ **teaspoon salt**
  Vanilla frosting, optional

1. In a large bowl, cream shortening and brown sugar until light and fluffy. Beat in molasses and water. In another bowl, whisk flour, spices, baking soda and salt; gradually beat into creamed mixture.

2. Divide dough in half. Shape each into a disk; wrap in plastic wrap. Freeze 1 hour or until firm enough to roll.

3. Preheat oven to 375°. On a floured surface, roll each portion of dough to ¼-in. thickness. Cut with a floured 5-in. moose-shaped cookie cutter. Carefully place cookies 1 in. apart on ungreased baking sheets. Bake 7-9 minutes or until set. Cool on pans for 5 minutes. Remove to wire racks to cool. If desired, pipe with vanilla frosting.

FREEZE OPTION *Transfer wrapped disks to a resealable plastic freezer bag; freeze. To use, thaw dough in refrigerator until soft enough to roll. Prepare and bake as directed.*

JoJo's Ginger Cookies

Santa Claus
Sugar Cookies

Frosted Anise Sugar Cookies

Santa Claus Sugar Cookies

My mom taught me how to make Santa cookies and hang them on the tree. Her buttery cookie tradition has lasted 40 years.
—**ANN BUSH** COLORADO CITY, CO

PREP: 45 MIN. + CHILLING
BAKE: 10 MIN./BATCH + COOLING
MAKES: ABOUT 4 DOZEN

- 1 **cup unsalted butter**
- 1½ **cups sugar**
- 2 **large eggs**
- 1 **teaspoon vanilla extract**
- 3½ **cups all-purpose flour**
- 1 **teaspoon baking soda**
- 1 **teaspoon cream of tartar**
- ½ **teaspoon ground nutmeg**
- ¼ **teaspoon salt**

FROSTING

- ¾ **cup unsalted butter, softened**
- 6 **tablespoons 2% milk**
- 2¼ **teaspoons vanilla extract**
- ¼ **teaspoon salt**
- 6¾ **cups confectioners' sugar**
  Optional decorations: red colored sugar and Red Hots

1. In a large bowl, cream butter and sugar until light and fluffy. Beat in eggs and the vanilla. In another bowl, whisk flour, baking soda, cream of tartar, nutmeg and salt; gradually beat into creamed mixture.

2. Divide dough in half. Shape each into a disk; wrap in plastic wrap. Refrigerate 1 hour or until firm enough to roll.

3. Preheat oven to 375°. On a lightly floured surface, roll each portion of dough to ¼-in. thickness. Cut with a floured 3-in. Santa-shaped cookie cutter. Place 2 in. apart on greased baking sheets.

4. Bake 8-10 minutes or until light brown. Remove from pans to wire racks to cool completely.

5. For the frosting, in a large bowl, beat butter until creamy. Beat in milk, vanilla and salt. Gradually beat in confectioners' sugar until smooth. Pipe onto cookies and decorate as desired.

Frosted Anise Sugar Cookies

The anise flavor in these cookies is distinct but not overpowering. I like to add red and green sprinkles for Christmas, but you can decorate them to suit any occasion.
—**JANICE EANNI** WILLOWICK, OH

PREP: 30 MIN. • **BAKE:** 10 MIN./BATCH + COOLING
MAKES: 7 DOZEN

- 1 **cup butter, softened**
- 1½ **cups sugar**
- 6 **large eggs**
- 1 **teaspoon vanilla extract**
- ¾ **teaspoon anise extract**
- 3½ **cups all-purpose flour**
- 4 **teaspoons baking powder**

GLAZE

- 3 **cups confectioners' sugar**
- 4 **teaspoons butter, softened**
- ¾ **teaspoon vanilla extract**
- ¼ to ⅓ **cup whole milk**
  Colored sprinkles, optional

1. Preheat oven to 350°. In a large bowl, cream butter and sugar until light and fluffy. Beat in eggs and extracts. In another bowl, whisk flour and baking powder; gradually beat into creamed mixture.

2. Drop dough by tablespoonfuls 2 in. apart onto greased baking sheets. Bake for 8-10 minutes or until light brown. Remove from pans to wire racks to cool completely.

3. For glaze, in a large bowl, mix confectioners' sugar, butter, vanilla and enough milk to achieve spreading consistency. Dip tops of cookies into glaze. If desired, decorate with colored sprinkles. Let stand until set.

Meringue Santa Hats

Cranberry Pistachio Biscotti

This crunchy Italian cookie is wonderful for dunking, but is just as delicious on its own. It features a classic holiday combo of cranberries and pistachios.

—**RUTH KNOL** ANNVILLE, PA

PREP: 40 MIN. • **BAKE:** 25 MIN. + COOLING
MAKES: 3½ DOZEN

- ½ **cup dried cranberries**
- ½ **cup boiling water**
- ½ **cup butter, softened**
- 1 **cup sugar**
- 3 **large eggs**
- 2 **teaspoons vanilla extract**
- 3 **cups all-purpose flour**
- 2 **teaspoons baking powder**
- ½ **teaspoon salt**
- ½ **cup chopped pistachios**

TOPPING
- 1 **large egg, beaten**
- 3 **tablespoons coarse sugar**

1. Place cranberries in a small bowl. Cover with boiling water; let stand for 5 minutes. Set aside. In a large bowl, cream the butter and sugar until light and fluffy. Add eggs, one at a time, beating well after each addition. Stir in vanilla. Combine the flour, baking powder and salt; gradually add to creamed mixture and mix well. Stir in pistachios and cranberries with liquid.

2. Divide dough into three portions. On a parchment paper-lined baking sheet, shape each dough portion into a 12x1½-in. rectangle. Brush egg over rectangles and sprinkle with coarse sugar. Bake at 375° for 18-22 minutes or until set and lightly browned. Carefully remove to wire racks; cool for 15 minutes.

3. Transfer to a cutting board; cut diagonally with a serrated knife into ¾-in. slices. Place cut side down on ungreased baking sheets. Bake for 6-8 minutes on each side or until edges are browned. Remove to wire racks to cool completely. Store in an airtight container.

---

(5) INGREDIENTS

Meringue Santa Hats

My grandkids love it when I make meringues and call them Santa Hats. I love having the children help by sprinkling on the red sugar.

—**BONNIE HAWKINS** ELKHORN, WI

PREP: 30 MIN. • **BAKE:** 40 MIN. + STANDING
MAKES: 3 DOZEN

- 2 **large egg whites**
- ½ **teaspoon cream of tartar**
- ¼ **teaspoon vanilla extract**
- ½ **cup sugar**
  Red colored sugar

1. Place egg whites in a small bowl; let stand at room temperature 30 minutes.

2. Preheat the oven to 250°. Add cream of tartar and vanilla to egg whites; beat on medium speed until foamy. Gradually add sugar, 1 tablespoon at a time, beating on high after each addition until sugar is dissolved. Continue beating until stiff glossy peaks form.

3. Cut a hole in the tip of a pastry bag or in a corner of a food-safe plastic bag; insert a #8 round tip. Fill bag with one-fourth of the meringue; set aside. Prepare a second piping bag, using a #12 round tip; fill with the remaining meringue.

4. Using bag with the #12 tip, pipe 36 Santa hat triangles (2 in. tall) onto parchment paper-lined baking sheets. Sprinkle with red sugar. Use first bag to pipe white trim and pompoms on hats.

5. Bake 40-45 minutes or until firm to the touch. Turn off oven (do not open oven door); leave meringues in oven for 1 hour.

6. Remove hats from paper. Store in an airtight container at room temperature.

Creme de Menthe
Cheesecake Cookies

BIG BATCH

Creme de Menthe Cheesecake Cookies

Stir cream cheese and creme de menthe baking chips into purchased dough for richness and a refreshing hint of mint. For a festive finish, pipe candy-coating trees on top.

—SHEILA SPORN HOUSTON, TX

PREP: 15 MIN.
BAKE: 15 MIN./BATCH + COOLING
MAKES: 4 DOZEN

- 1 tube (16½ ounces) refrigerated sugar cookie dough
- 6 tablespoons all-purpose flour
- 1 large egg
- 1 package (8 ounces) cream cheese, softened
- 1⅓ cups Andes creme de menthe baking chips
  Green candy coating disks and sprinkles, optional

1. Preheat oven to 350°. In a large bowl, beat cookie dough and flour until blended and dough is softened. Beat in egg. Add cream cheese; beat until smooth. Stir in baking chips. (Dough will be soft.)

2. Drop dough by tablespoonfuls 2 in. apart onto ungreased baking sheets. Bake 11-13 minutes or until bottoms are golden brown. Cool for 2 minutes before removing from pans to wire racks to cool completely.

3. If decorating cookies, melt candy coating in a microwave. Cut a small hole in the tip of a pastry bag or in a corner of a food-safe plastic bag; insert a small round pastry tip. Fill bag with melted coating. Pipe designs onto cookies; decorate with sprinkles.

FREEZE OPTION *Freeze undecorated cookies in freezer containers. To use, thaw and decorate as desired.*

Red Velvet Peppermint Thumbprints

I love red velvet cookies and cakes. In this pretty thumbprint cookie, I added my favorite holiday ingredient: peppermint. It's a fun seasonal twist!
—**PRISCILLA YEE** CONCORD, CA

PREP: 30 MIN. • **BAKE:** 10 MIN./BATCH + COOLING
MAKES: ABOUT 4 DOZEN

- 1 cup butter, softened
- 1 cup sugar
- 1 large egg
- 4 teaspoons red food coloring
- 1 teaspoon peppermint extract
- 2½ cups all-purpose flour
- 3 tablespoons baking cocoa
- 1 teaspoon baking powder
- ¼ teaspoon salt
- 2 cups white baking chips
- 2 teaspoons canola oil
- ¼ cup crushed peppermint candies

1. Preheat oven to 350°. In a large bowl, cream butter and sugar until light and fluffy. Beat in egg, food coloring and extract. In another bowl, whisk flour, cocoa, baking powder and salt; gradually beat into creamed mixture.
2. Shape dough into 1-in. balls. Place 1 in. apart on ungreased baking sheets. Press a deep indentation in center of each with the end of a wooden spoon handle.
3. Bake 9-11 minutes or until set. Remove from pans to wire racks to cool completely.
4. In a microwave, melt baking chips with oil; stir until smooth. Spoon a scant teaspoon into each cookie. Drizzle tops with remaining mixture. Sprinkle with peppermint candies. Let stand until set.

Almond Bonbon Cookies

Almond Bonbon Cookies

These bonbons remind me of England, with a touch of America. Dip cooled cookies into one frosting or dip each side into a different flavor of frosting. Have fun adding any kind of sprinkle toppings you like.
—**TERI RASEY** CADILLAC, MI

PREP: 20 MIN. • **BAKE:** 10 MIN./BATCH
MAKES: 4 DOZEN

- 1 cup butter, softened
- ⅔ cup confectioners' sugar
- ¼ cup 2% milk
- 1 teaspoon vanilla extract
- 3 cups all-purpose flour
- 1 package (7 ounces) almond paste

VANILLA ICING
- 1 cup confectioners' sugar
- 4½ teaspoons 2% milk
- 1 teaspoon vanilla extract

CHOCOLATE ICING
- 1 cup confectioners' sugar
- 1 ounce unsweetened chocolate, melted and cooled
- 3 tablespoons 2% milk
- 1 teaspoon vanilla extract
  Assorted sprinkles

1. Preheat oven to 375°. In a large bowl, cream butter and confectioners' sugar until light and fluffy. Beat in milk and vanilla. Gradually beat in flour.
2. Cut almond paste into 12 slices (about ¼ in. thick); cut each into quarters. Shape into balls. Wrap tablespoons of cookie dough around almond paste to cover completely. Place 2 in. apart on ungreased baking sheets.
3. Bake for 10-12 minutes or until golden brown. Remove to wire racks to cool completely.
4. In a small bowl, mix vanilla icing ingredients until smooth. For chocolate icing, mix confectioners' sugar, cooled chocolate, milk and vanilla until smooth. Dip cookies in icings as desired; allow excess to drip off. Decorate with sprinkles. Place on waxed paper; let stand until set. Store in airtight containers.

FREEZE IT BIG BATCH

Holiday Cutout Cookies

Mom always made these for special occasions including Christmas and Valentine's Day. For crisp cookies, do not frost but sprinkle with colored sugar before baking. Do not over-bake cookies.
—**ANNE GRISHAM** HENDERSON, NV

PREP: 20 MIN. • **BAKE:** 5 MIN./BATCH
MAKES: ABOUT 10 DOZEN

- 1 **cup butter, softened**
- 1 **cup shortening**
- 3 **cups sugar**
- 4 **large eggs**
- 6 **tablespoons evaporated milk**
- 2 **teaspoons vanilla extract**
- 2 **teaspoons almond extract**
- 6 **cups all-purpose flour**
- 1 **teaspoon baking soda**
- ½ **teaspoon salt**

FROSTING

- 3 **cups confectioners' sugar**
- 1 **teaspoon vanilla extract**
- 4 **to 6 tablespoons half-and-half cream**
   Food coloring of your choice, optional
   Assorted sprinkles

1. In a large bowl, cream butter, shortening and sugar until light and fluffy. Beat in eggs, milk and extracts. In another bowl, whisk flour, baking soda and salt; gradually beat into creamed mixture. Divide dough into four portions. Shape each into a disk; wrap in plastic wrap. Refrigerate, covered, overnight or until firm enough to roll.

2. Preheat oven to 400°. On lightly floured surface, roll each portion of dough to ⅛-in. thickness. Cut with floured 3-in. holiday cookie cutters. Place cookies 1 in. apart on ungreased baking sheets.

3. Bake 5-7 minutes or until edges are lightly brown. Remove from pans to wire racks to cool completely.

4. In a large bowl, beat confectioners' sugar, vanilla and enough cream to reach a spreading consistency. If desired, beat in food coloring. Frost and decorate cookies as desired.

FREEZE OPTION *Freeze undecorated cookies in freezer containers. To use, thaw in covered containers and decorate as desired.*

BIG BATCH

Ginger-Macadamia Nut Snowballs

You'll go nuts over these ginger-spiced cookies made with love and coated with sweet confectioners' sugar to look like snow.
—**JENNY HUMPHRIES** OCEAN VIEW, HI

PREP: 25 MIN. • **BAKE:** 15 MIN./BATCH
MAKES: ABOUT 5 DOZEN

- 1 **cup butter, softened**
- ¾ **cup plus 1½ cups confectioners' sugar, divided**
- 2 **teaspoons grated lemon peel**
- 2 **teaspoons lemon extract**
- 2¼ **cups cake flour**
- 1 **cup chopped macadamia nuts**
- 1 **cup chopped crystallized ginger**

1. In a large bowl, cream butter and ¾ cup confectioners' sugar until blended. Beat in lemon peel and lemon extract. Gradually beat flour into creamed mixture. Stir in macadamia nuts and ginger. Refrigerate for 1 hour or until easy to handle.

2. Shape dough into 1-in. balls; place 2 in. apart on parchment paper-lined baking sheets. Bake at 350° for 14-16 minutes or until lightly browned.

3. Roll warm cookies in remaining confectioners' sugar. Cool on wire racks. Roll again in confectioners' sugar.

Holiday Cutout Cookies

Classic Candy Cane Butter Cookies

Classic Candy Cane Butter Cookies

To make cookies that look like candy canes, we color half the dough red and twist away. They're fun to hang on the side of a glass or mug, or devour all on their own.

—**SHANNON ROUM** MILWAUKEE, WI

PREP: 45 MIN. + CHILLING • **BAKE:** 10 MIN./BATCH
MAKES: 3 DOZEN

- 1 cup butter, softened
- ⅔ cup sugar
- ¼ teaspoon salt
- 1 large egg yolk
- 2 teaspoons vanilla extract
- 2¼ cups all-purpose flour
  Red paste food coloring

1. In a large bowl, cream butter, sugar and salt until light and fluffy. Beat in egg yolk and vanilla; gradually beat in flour. Divide dough in half; mix food coloring into one half. Roll each dough into a 6-in. square. Wrap each in plastic wrap; refrigerate at least 1 hour or overnight.

2. Preheat oven to 350°. Cut each dough into 36 squares. Working with a quarter of the dough at a time, keep remaining dough refrigerated. Roll one piece of plain dough into a 6-in. rope; roll one piece of red dough into a 6-in. rope. Place ropes side by side. Lift left rope over the right; repeat to form a twist. Repeat with remaining dough. Place 1 in. apart on parchment paper-lined baking sheets, curving top of each twist to form hook of cane.

3. Bake 7-9 minutes or until set. Cool on pans for 3 minutes. Remove to wire racks to cool.

TOP TIP

Coloring Consistency

Food coloring is available in liquids, gels and pastes. To get the best color, follow the form listed in a recipe.

Snow-Capped Mocha Fudge Drops

Everyone loves seeing chocolate on a cookie tray. My version is fudgy with a hint of mocha. Add red- and green-colored sugar for a festive touch.
—**PATRICIA HARMON** BADEN, PA

PREP: 40 MIN. • **BAKE:** 10 MIN./BATCH + COOLING
MAKES: ABOUT 3½ DOZEN

- 1 cup (6 ounces) semisweet chocolate chips, divided
- ½ cup butter, cubed
- 1 tablespoon instant coffee granules or espresso powder
- ¾ cup sugar
- ¾ cup packed brown sugar
- 2 large eggs
- 2 teaspoons vanilla extract
- 2 cups all-purpose flour
- ¼ cup baking cocoa
- ½ teaspoon baking powder
- ¼ teaspoon salt
- ½ cup chopped pecans or walnuts
- 10 ounces white candy coating, melted
  White edible glitter and/or red and green colored sugar

1. Preheat oven to 350°. In a large microwave-safe bowl, microwave ½ cup chocolate chips and butter until butter is melted; stir until chocolate is melted. Stir in coffee granules; cool slightly.

2. Whisk in sugars. Whisk in eggs, one at a time, and vanilla until blended. In small bowl, whisk flour, cocoa, baking powder and salt; stir into chocolate mixture. Stir in pecans and remaining chocolate chips.

3. Drop dough by tablespoonfuls 1 in. apart onto ungreased baking sheets. Bake 8-10 minutes or until set. Cool on pans for 2 minutes. Remove to wire racks to cool completely.

4. Dip tops of cookies into melted candy coating; sprinkle with glitter and/or colored sugar. Let stand until set.
NOTE *Edible glitter is available from Wilton Industries. Call 800-794-5866 or visit wilton.com.*

Snow Angel Cookies

BIG BATCH

Snow Angel Cookies

Get a little snow at the holidays, no matter where you are. Head to the kitchen and bake a batch of angel cookies dusted with coarse sugar.
—**CAROLYN MOSELEY** DAYTON, OH

PREP: 40 MIN. + CHILLING
BAKE: 15 MIN./BATCH + COOLING
MAKES: ABOUT 5 DOZEN

- 1 cup butter, softened
- 1 cup sugar
- 1½ teaspoons vanilla extract
- 2 large eggs
- 3½ cups all-purpose flour
- 1 teaspoon ground cinnamon
- ½ teaspoon baking powder
- ½ teaspoon salt
- ¼ teaspoon ground nutmeg
- ¼ teaspoon ground cloves

FROSTING
- 9 cups confectioners' sugar
- ¾ cup shortening
- ½ cup lemon juice
- 4 to 6 tablespoons water
  Coarse sugar, optional

1. In a large bowl, beat butter, sugar and vanilla until blended. Beat in eggs, one at a time. In another bowl, whisk flour, cinnamon, baking powder, salt, nutmeg and cloves; gradually beat into creamed mixture.

2. Divide dough in half. Shape each into a disk; wrap in plastic wrap. Refrigerate 1 hour or until firm enough to roll.

3. Preheat oven to 350°. On a lightly floured surface, roll each portion of dough to ⅛-in. thickness. Cut with a floured 4-in. angel-shaped cookie cutter. Place 1 in. apart on ungreased baking sheets.

4. Bake for 12-14 minutes or until edges begin to brown. Remove cookies from pans to wire racks to cool completely.

5. For frosting, in a large bowl, beat confectioners' sugar, shortening, lemon juice and enough water to reach a spreading consistency. Spread or pipe over cookies; sprinkle with coarse sugar if desired.

Lemon-Blueberry
Pound Cake, page 165

Sunny Flower
Cake, page 161

Chocolate Chiffon Cake, page 137

Coconut Cheesecake & Rhubarb Compote, page 212

Cakes

IS IT TIME FOR DESSERT? NO MATTER HOW YOU SLICE IT, EVERYONE LOVES CAKE! BAKE UP A FAVORITE WITH RECIPES THAT FIT ANY OCCASION. FROM SHEET CAKES TO LAYERED TREATS AND FROM CREAMY CHEESECAKES TO CUTE CUPCAKES, THIS CHAPTER OFFERS THE IDEAL FINALE TO BIRTHDAYS, ANNIVERSARIES AND GRADUATIONS AS WELL AS SPECIAL HOLIDAY GET-TOGETHERS.

CHERRY COLA CAKE
PAGE 129

Layered Cakes & Tortes

DO YOU HAVE A SPECIAL OCCASION COMING UP? THESE ARE THE CAKES THAT WILL IMPRESS! MAKE A BIRTHDAY MEMORABLE WITH ANY ONE OF THE RECIPES FOUND HERE. TOWERING LAYER CAKES PROVIDE A GREAT CENTERPIECE, AND FLAVORFUL TORTES WILL HAVE GUESTS ASKING FOR MORE.

MINT CHOCOLATE TORTE
PAGE 120

LEMON-FILLED COCONUT CAKE *PAGE 129*

RICH CHOCOLATE PEANUT BUTTER CAKE *PAGE 126*

**Raspberry Lemon
Layer Cake**

❝I made this cake last year for my husband on Father's Day and he requested it again this year.❞

—**JEDDY123** FROM TASTEOFHOME.COM

Raspberry Lemon Layer Cake

Cooking is my favorite hobby. I love trying recipes with different flavor combinations such as pound cake with lemon curd and fresh raspberries.

—**JANICE BAKER** LONDON, KY

START TO FINISH: 25 MIN.
MAKES: 6 SERVINGS

- 1½ cups heavy whipping cream
- 3 tablespoons confectioners' sugar
- 3 tablespoons orange juice
- 1 loaf (10¾ ounces) frozen pound cake, thawed
- 1 jar (10 ounces) lemon curd
- 2½ cups fresh raspberries

1. In a small bowl, beat cream until it begins to thicken. Add confectioners' sugar and orange juice; beat until stiff peaks form. Using a long serrated knife, cut cake horizontally into three layers.

2. Place bottom cake layer on a serving plate; spread with about ⅓ cup lemon curd. Top with 1 cup raspberries and ⅓ cup cream mixture; repeat layers. Replace cake top; spread with remaining lemon curd.

3. Frost top and sides of cake with remaining cream mixture. Top with remaining raspberries; refrigerate until serving.

TOP TIP

Making Homemade Lemon Curd

In a heavy saucepan, beat 3 eggs and 1 cup sugar. Stir in ½ cup lemon juice (about 2 lemons), ¼ cup melted butter or margarine, and 1 tablespoon grated lemon peel. Cook and stir over medium-low heat for 15 minutes or until mixture is thickened and reaches 160°. Cover and store in the refrigerator for up to 1 week. Yield: 1⅔ cups.

Dr Pepper Cake

Any time I have to take food anywhere, this is my favorite go-to recipe. Everyone loves it. When it is baked in layers rather than in a single layer, it will make people say "wow." It is a crowd-pleaser!
—**SHANNON PARUM** VERNON, TX

PREP: 30 MIN. • **BAKE:** 20 MIN. + COOLING
MAKES: 12 SERVINGS

- 1 package German chocolate cake mix, regular size
- 1 package (3.4 ounces) instant chocolate pudding mix
- 4 large eggs
- 1 can (12 ounces) Dr Pepper
- 1 teaspoon vanilla extract

FROSTING
- 1 container (12 ounces) whipped cream cheese, room temperature
- ⅓ cup butter, softened
- ⅓ cup baking cocoa
- 3½ cups confectioners' sugar
- 1½ teaspoons vanilla extract

1. Preheat oven to 350°. Line bottoms of three greased 9-in. round baking pans with parchment paper; grease paper.
2. In a large bowl, combine the cake and pudding mixes. Add the eggs, one at a time, beating well after each addition. Gradually beat in Dr Pepper and vanilla.
3. Transfer batter to prepared pans. Bake 20-25 minutes or until top springs back when lightly touched. Cool in pans for 10 minutes before removing to wire racks; remove paper. Cool completely.
4. For frosting, in a large bowl, beat cream cheese and butter until smooth. Beat in cocoa. Add confectioners' sugar and vanilla; beat until creamy.
5. Place one cake layer on a serving plate; spread with ½ cup frosting. Repeat layers. Top with remaining cake layer. Frost top and sides of cake with remaining frosting.

Chocolate Lover's Mousse Torte

Chocolate Lover's Mousse Torte

With layer after luscious layer of creamy filling and cake, this delicious chocolate torte proves irresistible every time.
—**BRENDA FISHER** STELLA, MO

PREP: 40 MIN. • **BAKE:** 15 MIN. + COOLING
MAKES: 12 SERVINGS

- 1 cup butter, softened
- 1 cup sugar
- 3 large eggs
- 1½ teaspoons vanilla extract
- 2 cups all-purpose flour
- ⅔ cup baking cocoa
- 1 teaspoon baking powder
- ¼ teaspoon baking soda
- 1⅓ cups whole milk

FILLING
- 1 teaspoon unflavored gelatin
- 3 tablespoons cold water
- ⅓ cup confectioners' sugar
- 3 tablespoons baking cocoa
- 1 cup heavy whipping cream
- 1 teaspoon vanilla extract

1. Preheat oven to 350°. Line a greased 15x10x1-in. baking pan with waxed paper; grease paper.
2. In a large bowl, cream the butter and sugar until light and fluffy. Add eggs, one at a time, beating well after each addition. Beat in vanilla. In another bowl, whisk flour, baking cocoa, baking powder and baking soda; add to creamed mixture alternately with milk, beating just until combined. Transfer to prepared pan.
3. Bake 15-20 minutes or until a toothpick inserted in the center comes out clean. Cool for 10 minutes before inverting onto a wire rack to cool completely. Remove waxed paper.
4. In a small saucepan, sprinkle gelatin over cold water; let stand 1 minute. Heat and stir over low heat until gelatin is completely dissolved. Cool to room temperature.
5. Sift confectioners' sugar and cocoa together. In a large bowl, beat cream until it begins to thicken. Beat in confectioners' sugar mixture and vanilla. While beating, gradually add gelatin until stiff peaks form.
6. Trim cake edges; cut crosswise into fourths. Place one cake layer on a serving plate; spread with ½ cup filling. Repeat layers three times. Refrigerate until serving.

Coconut Italian Cream Cake

Coconut Italian Cream Cake

I'd never tasted an Italian Cream Cake before moving to Colorado. Now I bake for people in the area, and this beauty is one of the most requested cakes.

—**ANN BUSH** COLORADO CITY, CO

PREP: 50 MIN. • **BAKE:** 20 MIN. + COOLING
MAKES: 16 SERVINGS

- 5 large eggs, separated
- 1 cup butter, softened
- 1⅔ cups sugar
- 1½ teaspoons vanilla extract
- 2 cups all-purpose flour
- ¾ teaspoon baking soda
- ½ teaspoon salt
- 1 cup buttermilk
- 1⅓ cups flaked coconut
- 1 cup chopped pecans, toasted

FROSTING
- 12 ounces cream cheese, softened
- 6 tablespoons butter, softened
- 2¼ teaspoons vanilla extract
- 5⅔ cups confectioners' sugar
- 3 to 4 tablespoons heavy whipping cream
- ½ cup chopped pecans, toasted
- ¼ cup toasted flaked coconut, optional

1. Place egg whites in a small bowl; let stand at room temperature 30 minutes.
2. Preheat oven to 350°. Line bottoms of three greased 9-in. round baking pans with parchment paper; grease paper.
3. In a large bowl, cream butter and sugar until light and fluffy. Add egg yolks, one at a time, beating well after each addition. Beat in vanilla. In another bowl, whisk flour, baking soda and salt; add to creamed mixture alternately with buttermilk, beating well after each addition. Fold in coconut and pecans.
4. With clean beaters, beat egg whites on medium speed until stiff peaks form. Gradually fold into batter. Transfer to prepared pans. Bake 20-25 minutes or until a toothpick inserted in the center comes out clean. Cool in pans for 10 minutes before removing to wire racks; remove paper. Cool completely.
5. For frosting, in a large bowl, beat cream cheese and butter until smooth. Beat in the vanilla. Gradually beat in confectioners' sugar and enough cream to reach spreading consistency. Spread frosting between layers and over top and sides of cake. Sprinkle with pecans and, if desired, coconut. Refrigerate leftovers.
NOTE *To toast pecans and coconut, spread each, one at a time, in a 15x10x1-in. baking pan. Bake at 350° for 5-10 minutes or until lightly browned, stirring occasionally.*

Mint Chocolate Torte

I combined two different recipes here: the chocolate cake from my childhood and the filling from a pie I saw in a cookbook. The flavor is reminiscent of an after-dinner chocolate mint.

—**NADINE TAYLOR** DURHAM, NC

PREP: 30 MIN. + CHILLING
BAKE: 15 MIN. + COOLING
MAKES: 14 SERVINGS

- ¾ cup baking cocoa
- ½ cup hot water
- 2 cups sugar
- 1¾ cups all-purpose flour
- 1 teaspoon baking soda
- 1 teaspoon salt
- ¼ teaspoon baking powder
- 1 cup milk
- ½ cup mayonnaise
- 2 large eggs
- 2 teaspoons vanilla extract

FILLING
- 2 cups miniature marshmallows
- ¼ cup milk
- Dash salt
- ⅛ to ¼ teaspoon peppermint extract
- 2 to 3 drops green food coloring, optional
- 1 cup heavy whipping cream, whipped

TOPPING
- 1 cup (6 ounces) semisweet chocolate chips
- ⅓ cup heavy whipping cream

1. In a small bowl, combine cocoa and water until smooth; set aside. In a large bowl, combine the sugar, flour, baking soda, salt and baking powder. Add the milk, mayonnaise, eggs, vanilla and cocoa mixture; beat on medium speed for 2 minutes.
2. Pour into three greased and floured 9-in. round baking pans. Bake at 350° for 15-20 minutes or until a toothpick inserted near the center comes out clean. Cool for 10 minutes before removing from pans to wire racks to cool completely.
3. For the torte filling, combine the marshmallows, milk and salt in a small saucepan; cook and stir over low heat until marshmallows are melted. Remove from the heat; stir in peppermint extract and food coloring if desired. Transfer to a bowl; refrigerate until chilled.
4. Fold in whipped cream. Place bottom cake layer on a serving plate; spread with a third of the filling. Repeat layers twice.
5. For topping, combine chocolate chips and cream in a small saucepan; cook and stir over low heat until chips are melted. Drizzle over top and down sides of cake. Store in the refrigerator.

"I made this torte a few times, and plan on making two for St. Patrick's Day. It's so easy to make."
—**TRODRIGUES**
FROM TASTEOFHOME.COM

Mamaw Emily's Strawberry Cake

My husband loved his Mamaw's strawberry cake. He thought no one could duplicate it. I made it, and it's just as scrumptious as he remembers.
—**JENNIFER BRUCE** MANITOU, KY

PREP: 15 MIN. • **BAKE:** 25 MIN. + COOLING
MAKES: 12 SERVINGS

- 1 **package white cake mix (regular size)**
- 1 **package (3 ounces) strawberry gelatin**
- 3 **tablespoons sugar**
- 3 **tablespoons all-purpose flour**
- 1 **cup water**
- ½ **cup canola oil**
- 2 **large eggs**
- 1 **cup finely chopped strawberries**

FROSTING
- ½ **cup butter, softened**
- ½ **cup crushed strawberries**
- 4½ **to 5 cups confectioners' sugar**

1. Preheat oven to 350°. Line the bottoms of two greased 8-in. round baking pans with parchment paper; grease paper.

2. In a large bowl, combine cake mix, gelatin, sugar and flour. Add water, oil and eggs; beat on low speed for 30 seconds. Beat on medium speed for 2 minutes. Fold in chopped strawberries. Transfer to prepared pans.

3. Bake 25-30 minutes or until a toothpick inserted in the center comes out clean. Cool in pans for 10 minutes before removing to wire racks; remove paper. Cool completely.

4. For frosting, in a small bowl, beat butter until creamy. Beat in crushed strawberries. Gradually beat in enough confectioners' sugar to reach desired consistency. Spread frosting between layers and over top and sides of cake.

Mamaw Emily's Strawberry Cake

Cherry Chocolate Layer Cake

Heads will turn when you bring this divine cake to the table. A luscious almond-cherry filling is sandwiched between four layers of rich, tender chocolate cake. The finishing touch is a creamy chocolate frosting. Your guests will eat every last crumb on their plates!

—**VICTORIA FAULLING** METHUEN, MA

PREP: 35 MIN. • **BAKE:** 25 MIN. + COOLING
MAKES: 12 SERVINGS

- 1 **cup butter, softened**
- 1¼ **cups sugar**
- ¾ **cup packed brown sugar**
- 3 **large eggs**
- 2 **teaspoons vanilla extract**
- 2 **cups all-purpose flour**
- 1 **cup baking cocoa**
- 1½ **teaspoons baking soda**
- ½ **teaspoon baking powder**
- ¼ **teaspoon salt**
- 1½ **cups buttermilk**

FILLING

- 1 **package (8 ounces) cream cheese, softened**
- 6 **tablespoons butter, softened**
- 1 **teaspoon almond extract**
- 3 **cups confectioners' sugar**
- 1 **tablespoon maraschino cherry juice**
- ⅔ **cup finely chopped pecans**
- ⅔ **cup chopped maraschino cherries**

FROSTING

- 3 **cups confectioners' sugar**
- ½ **cup baking cocoa**
- ½ **cup butter, softened**
- ⅓ **cup half-and-half cream**
- 1 **teaspoon vanilla extract**
  Chocolate curls and maraschino cherry, optional

1. Preheat oven to 350°. In a large bowl, cream butter, sugar and brown sugar until light and fluffy. Add eggs, one at a time, beating well after each addition. Beat in vanilla. Combine flour, cocoa, baking soda, baking powder and salt; add to creamed mixture alternately with buttermilk, beating well after each addition.

Cherry Chocolate Layer Cake

2. Transfer batter to two greased and floured 9-in. round baking pans. Bake for 25-30 minutes or until a toothpick inserted in the center comes out clean. Cool for 10 minutes before removing from pans to wire racks to cool completely.

3. In a large bowl, beat the cream cheese, butter and extract until smooth. Add confectioners' sugar and cherry juice; beat until smooth. Stir in pecans and cherries. In another bowl, combine the frosting ingredients; beat until smooth.

4. Cut each cake horizontally into two layers. Place one layer on a serving plate; spread with 1 cup filling. Repeat layers twice. Top with remaining layer. Spread frosting over top and sides of cake. If desired, garnish with chocolate curls and a cherry. Refrigerate until serving.

TOP TIP

Layer Splitting

Using a ruler, mark the center of the side of the cake with a toothpick. Continue inserting toothpicks around the cake. Using toothpicks as a guide, cut the cake horizontally in half with a long serrated knife. Carefully remove the top half. Frost or spread the bottom half with filling as a recipe instructs and then replace the top half, cut side down.

Pink Lemonade Stand Cake

If you love a moist and creamy cake, this is it. Lemon juice and lemonade give the layers a tangy touch, and the subtle pink frosting makes the cake beautiful.

—LAUREN KNOELKE MILWAUKEE, WI

PREP: 50 MIN. • **BAKE:** 20 MIN. + COOLING
MAKES: 12 SERVINGS

- 1 cup buttermilk
- 2 tablespoons lemon juice
- 2 tablespoons seedless strawberry jam, warmed
- 2 tablespoons thawed pink lemonade concentrate
- 2 tablespoons grenadine syrup
- 1 cup unsalted butter, softened
- 1¼ cups sugar
- 3 tablespoons grated lemon peel
- 4 large eggs
- ½ teaspoon vanilla extract
- 2½ cups all-purpose flour
- 1 teaspoon baking powder
- ½ teaspoon baking soda
- ½ teaspoon salt

FROSTING

- 1 cup unsalted butter, softened
- 1 package (8 ounces) cream cheese, softened
- 1 tablespoon grated lemon peel
- 4 cups confectioners' sugar
- ⅓ cup plus 3 tablespoons thawed pink lemonade concentrate, divided
- Pink sprinkles

1. Preheat oven to 350°. Line bottoms of three greased 8-in. round baking pans with parchment paper; grease paper.

2. In a small bowl, whisk the first five ingredients until blended. In a large bowl, cream butter, sugar and lemon peel until light and fluffy. Add eggs, one at a time, beating well after each addition. Beat in vanilla. In another bowl, whisk flour, baking powder, baking soda and salt; add to creamed mixture alternately with buttermilk mixture, beating well after each addition.

3. Transfer batter to prepared pans. Bake 20-24 minutes or until a toothpick inserted in the center comes out clean. Cool in pans for 10 minutes before removing to wire racks; remove paper. Cool completely.

4. For frosting, in a large bowl, beat butter, cream cheese and lemon peel until smooth. Gradually beat in confectioners' sugar and ⅓ cup lemonade concentrate. If necessary, refrigerate until spreadable, up to 1 hour.

5. Place one cake layer on a serving plate. Brush 1 tablespoon lemonade concentrate over cake; spread with ½ cup frosting. Repeat layers. Top with remaining cake layer; brush remaining lemonade concentrate over top.

6. Spread remaining frosting over top and sides of cake. Decorate with sprinkles. Refrigerate until serving.

FOR CUPCAKES *Make batter as directed; fill 24 paper-lined muffin cups three-fourths full. Bake in a preheated 350° oven 16-19 minutes or until a toothpick comes out clean. Cool in pans for 10 minutes before removing to wire racks to cool completely. Prepare the frosting as directed, omitting 3 tablespoons lemonade concentrate for brushing layers; pipe or spread frosting over tops. Yield: 2 dozen cupcakes.*

Pink Lemonade Stand Cake

Mocha
Hazelnut
Torte

BIG BATCH

Mocha Hazelnut Torte

I make this cake on special occasions and birthdays because it's so amazing in appearance and taste. The mild hazelnut and coffee flavor combination is impossible to resist and definitely adds to the overall deliciousness of the cake.
—**CHRISTINA POPE** SPEEDWAY, IN

PREP: 35 MIN. • **BAKE:** 25 MIN. + COOLING
MAKES: 16 SERVINGS

- ¾ cup butter, softened
- 1¼ cups packed brown sugar
- 1 cup sugar
- 3 large eggs
- 3 ounces unsweetened chocolate, melted and cooled slightly
- 2 teaspoons vanilla extract
- 2¼ cups all-purpose flour
- 1 tablespoon instant espresso powder
- 1 teaspoon baking soda
- ½ teaspoon baking powder
- ¼ teaspoon salt
- 1½ cups 2% milk

FROSTING
- 1 cup butter, softened
- 1 cup Nutella
- 4 cups confectioners' sugar
- 1 teaspoon vanilla extract
- 3 to 4 tablespoons 2% milk
- ½ cup chopped hazelnuts, toasted

1. Preheat oven to 350°. Line bottoms of two greased 9-in. round baking pans with parchment paper; grease paper.
2. In a large bowl, cream butter and sugars until light and fluffy. Add eggs, one at a time, beating well after each addition. Beat in melted chocolate and vanilla. In another bowl, whisk flour, espresso powder, baking soda, baking powder and salt; add to creamed mixture alternately with milk, beating well after each addition.
3. Transfer batter to prepared pans. Bake 25-30 minutes or until a toothpick inserted in the center comes out clean. Cool in pans for 10 minutes before removing to wire racks; remove paper. Cool completely.

4. For frosting, in a large bowl, beat butter and Nutella until blended. Gradually beat in confectioners' sugar, vanilla and enough milk to reach desired consistency.
5. Place one cake layer on a serving plate; spread with 1 cup frosting. Sprinkle with ¼ cup hazelnuts. Top with remaining cake layer. Frost top and sides with remaining frosting. Sprinkle with remaining hazelnuts.
NOTE *To toast nuts, bake in a shallow pan in a 350° oven for 5-10 minutes or cook in a skillet over low heat until lightly browned, stirring occasionally.*

Southern Lane Cake

I just love this impressive and festive cake and so do my dinner guests. With the fruit filling and topping, it's reminiscent of a fruit cake but so much more delightful!
—**MABEL PARVI** RIDGEFIELD, WA

PREP: 40 MIN. • **BAKE:** 20 MIN. + CHILLING
MAKES: 12 SERVINGS

- 6 large egg whites
- ¾ cup butter, softened
- 1½ cups sugar
- 1 teaspoon vanilla extract
- 2¼ cups all-purpose flour
- 2½ teaspoons baking powder
- ½ teaspoon salt
- ¾ cup 2% milk

FILLING
- 6 large egg yolks
- 1 cup sugar
- ½ cup butter, cubed
- ¼ cup bourbon
- 1 tablespoon grated orange peel
- ¼ teaspoon salt
- ¾ cup raisins
- ¾ cup flaked coconut
- ¾ cup chopped pecans
- ¾ cup coarsely chopped red candied cherries
- 1 cup heavy whipping cream, whipped and sweetened

1. Line the bottoms of three greased 9-in. round baking pans with parchment paper; grease paper; set aside. Place egg

Southern Lane Cake

whites in a large bowl; let stand at room temperature 30 minutes.
2. In another large bowl, cream butter and sugar until light and fluffy. Beat in vanilla. In another bowl, whisk flour, baking powder and salt; add to creamed mixture alternately with milk, beating well after each addition. Beat egg whites until stiff peaks form; fold into batter. Transfer to prepared pans.
3. Bake at 325° for 20-25 minutes or until a toothpick inserted near the center comes out clean. Cool for 10 minutes before removing from pans to wire racks; remove paper. Cool completely.
4. For filling, combine egg yolks and sugar in a large saucepan. Add butter; cook and stir over medium-low heat until sugar is dissolved and mixture thickens (do not boil). Remove from the heat. Stir in bourbon, orange peel and salt. Fold in the raisins, coconut, pecans and cherries. Cool.
5. Place one cake layer on a serving plate; spread with a third of the filling. Repeat layers twice. Frost sides of cake with whipped cream. Refrigerate until serving.
TO MAKE AHEAD *Cake can be made a day in advance. Cover and refrigerate. Remove from the refrigerator 30 minutes before serving.*

Red Velvet Marble Cake

Red Velvet Marble Cake

I watched my grandma prepare her red velvet showstopper many times for family get-togethers. The fluffy butter frosting perfectly complements the flavor of this gorgeous cake.

—**JODI ANDERSON** OVERBROOK, KS

PREP: 20 MIN. • **BAKE:** 30 MIN. + COOLING
MAKES: 12 SERVINGS

- ¾ cup butter, softened
- 2¼ cups sugar
- 3 large eggs
- 4½ teaspoons white vinegar
- 1½ teaspoons vanilla extract
- 3¾ cups cake flour
- 1½ teaspoons baking soda
- 1½ cups buttermilk
- 3 tablespoons baking cocoa
- 4½ teaspoons red food coloring

FROSTING
- 1 cup butter, softened
- 9 cups confectioners' sugar
- 3 teaspoons vanilla extract
- ⅔ to ¾ cup 2% milk

1. Preheat oven to 350°. Line bottoms of two greased 9-in. round baking pans with parchment paper; grease paper.
2. In a large bowl, cream butter and sugar until light and fluffy. Add eggs, one at a time, beating well after each addition. Beat in vinegar and vanilla. In another bowl, whisk flour and baking soda; add to creamed mixture alternately with buttermilk, beating well after each addition.

3. Transfer half of the batter to another bowl; stir in cocoa and food coloring into one half until blended. Alternately drop plain and chocolate batters by ¼ cupfuls into prepared pans, dividing batter evenly between pans. To make batter level in pans, bang the cake pans several times on the counter.
4. Bake 30-35 minutes or until a toothpick inserted in the center comes out clean. Cool for 10 minutes before removing from pans to wire racks to cool completely.
5. In a large bowl, beat butter, confectioners' sugar, vanilla and enough milk to reach a spreading consistency. Spread frosting between layers and over top and sides of cake.

Rich Chocolate Peanut Butter Cake

For an elegant holiday dessert, try this. The combination of mocha cake and peanut butter filling will satisfy every sweet tooth at your table.

—**TAMMY BOLLMAN** MINATARE, NE

PREP: 35 MIN. + CHILLING
BAKE: 25 MIN. + COOLING
MAKES: 12 SERVINGS

- 2 cups sugar
- 1 cup 2% milk
- 1 cup strong brewed coffee
- 1 cup canola oil
- 2 large eggs
- 1 teaspoon vanilla extract
- 2 cups all-purpose flour
- ¾ cup baking cocoa
- 1 tablespoon instant coffee granules
- 2 teaspoons baking soda
- 1 teaspoon salt

FILLING
- 1 cup butter, softened
- ¾ cup creamy peanut butter
- 1½ cups confectioners' sugar

FROSTING
- ½ cup creamy peanut butter
- 6 ounces bittersweet chocolate, chopped
- 1 cup butter, softened
- 2 cups marshmallow creme

- ⅓ cup confectioners' sugar
- ¾ teaspoon vanilla extract
  Chocolate curls

1. In a large bowl, beat the sugar, milk, coffee, oil, eggs and vanilla until well blended. Combine the flour, cocoa, coffee granules, baking soda and salt; gradually beat into sugar mixture until blended.
2. Transfer batter to two greased and floured 9-in. round baking pans. Bake at 350° for 25-30 minutes or until a toothpick inserted near the center comes out clean.
3. Cool for 10 minutes before removing from pans to wire racks to cool completely.
4. For filling, in a large bowl, beat butter and peanut butter until blended. Add confectioners' sugar; beat until smooth.
5. For frosting, melt peanut butter and chocolate in a microwave; stir until smooth. Cool. In a large bowl, beat butter and chocolate mixture until fluffy. Add the marshmallow creme, confectioners' sugar and vanilla; beat until smooth. If necessary, refrigerate until frosting reaches spreading consistency.
6. Place one cake layer on a serving plate; spread with filling. Top with remaining cake layer. Spread frosting over top and sides of cake. Garnish with chocolate curls. Refrigerate for at least 1 hour before serving.

BIG BATCH
Carrot Cake with Pecan Frosting

My husband constantly requests this homey, old-fashioned version of carrot cake. It's perfect for special holidays like Thanksgiving.

—**ADRIAN BADON** DENHAM SPRINGS, LA

PREP: 35 MIN. • **BAKE:** 40 MIN. + COOLING
MAKES: 16 SERVINGS

- 1 cup shortening
- 2 cups sugar
- 4 large eggs
- 1 can (8 ounces) unsweetened crushed pineapple, undrained

- 2½ **cups all-purpose flour**
- 2 **teaspoons ground cinnamon**
- 1 **teaspoon baking powder**
- 1 **teaspoon baking soda**
- ¾ **teaspoon salt**
- 3 **cups shredded carrots (about 6 medium carrots)**

FROSTING
- 1 **package (8 ounces) reduced-fat cream cheese**
- ½ **cup butter, softened**
- 1 **teaspoon vanilla extract**
- 3¾ **cups confectioners' sugar**
- 1 **cup chopped pecans**

1. Preheat oven to 325°. Line bottoms of two greased 9-in. round baking pans with parchment paper; grease paper.

2. In a large bowl, cream shortening and sugar until fluffy. Add eggs, one at a time, beating well after each addition. Beat in pineapple. In another bowl, whisk flour, cinnamon, baking powder, baking soda and salt; gradually add to creamed mixture. Stir in carrots.

3. Transfer batter to prepared pans. Bake 40-45 minutes or until a toothpick inserted in the center comes out clean. Cool in pans for 10 minutes before removing to wire racks; remove paper. Cool completely.

4. In a large bowl, beat cream cheese, butter and vanilla until blended. Gradually beat in confectioners' sugar until smooth. Stir in pecans.

5. Spread frosting between layers and over top and sides of cake. Refrigerate until serving.

"The best tasting carrot cake I've ever eaten! It is simple yet has an excellent crumb, texture and taste."

—MELEL1717
FROM TASTEOFHOME.COM

Carrot Cake with Pecan Frosting

Ladyfinger Ice
Cream Cake

Ladyfinger Ice Cream Cake

No one will believe you didn't fuss when you bring out this delightfully layered cake. On a hot summer day, it will melt all resistance to dessert—one cool, creamy slice at a time.

—BARBARA MCCALLEY

ALLISON PARK, PA

PREP: 25 MIN. + FREEZING
MAKES: 16 SERVINGS

- 2 **packages (3 ounces each) ladyfingers,** split
- 3 **cups vanilla ice cream,** softened
- 1 **jar (16 ounces) hot fudge ice cream topping**
- 1 **package (8 ounces) toffee bits**
- 3 **cups chocolate ice cream,** softened
- 3 **cups coffee ice cream,** softened

1. Arrange ladyfingers around the edge and on the bottom of a 9-in. springform pan coated with cooking spray.

2. Spoon vanilla ice cream into prepared pan. Top with a third of the ice cream topping and toffee bits. Freeze for 20 minutes. Repeat layers, using chocolate and coffee ice creams (pan will be full). Freeze overnight or until firm.

BIG BATCH

Lemon-Filled Coconut Cake

One of my co-workers brought this cake to a luncheon almost 40 years ago. It was so delicious that I asked for the recipe, and she shared it. I have baked it ever since, and it's always a hit!

—JACKIE BERGENHEIER WICHITA FALLS, TX

PREP: 35 MIN. • **BAKE:** 25 MIN. + COOLING
MAKES: 16 SERVINGS

- 1 cup butter, softened
- 2 cups sugar
- 3 large eggs
- 2 teaspoons vanilla extract
- 3¼ cups all-purpose flour
- 3¼ teaspoons baking powder
- ¾ teaspoon salt
- 1½ cups 2% milk

FILLING

- 1 cup sugar
- ¼ cup cornstarch
- 1 cup water
- 4 large egg yolks, lightly beaten
- ⅓ cup lemon juice
- 2 tablespoons butter

FROSTING

- 1½ cups sugar
- 2 large egg whites
- ⅓ cup water
- ¼ teaspoon cream of tartar
- 1 teaspoon vanilla extract
- 3 cups flaked coconut

1. In a large bowl, cream butter and sugar until light and fluffy. Add eggs, one at a time, beating well after each addition. Beat in vanilla. Combine the flour, baking powder and salt; add to creamed mixture alternately with milk, beating well after each addition.
2. Transfer to three greased and floured 9-in. round baking pans. Bake at 350° for 25-30 minutes or until a toothpick inserted near the center comes out clean. Cool for 10 minutes before removing from pans to wire racks to cool completely.
3. For filling, in a small saucepan, combine the sugar, cornstarch and water until smooth. Bring to a boil; cook and stir 2 minutes longer or until thickened and bubbly. Remove from the heat.
4. Stir a small amount of hot mixture into egg yolks; return all to the pan, stirring constantly. Bring to a gentle boil; cook and stir 2 minutes longer. Remove from the heat; gently stir in lemon juice and butter. Cool to room temperature without stirring.
5. Place one cake on serving plate; spread with half of the filling. Repeat layers. Top with remaining cake.
6. For frosting, in a large heavy saucepan, combine the sugar, egg whites, water and cream of tartar. With a portable mixer, beat on low speed for 1 minute. Continue beating on low over low heat until frosting reaches 160°, about 10 minutes.
7. Transfer to a large bowl; add vanilla. Beat on high until stiff peaks form, about 7 minutes. Frost top and sides of cake. Sprinkle with coconut. Store in the refrigerator.

Cherry Cola Cake

Cherry cola and marshmallows make a zippy chocolate dessert that is even better when topped with vanilla ice cream.

—CHERI MASON HARMONY, NC

PREP: 30 MIN. • **BAKE:** 25 MIN. + COOLING
MAKES: 12 SERVINGS

- 1½ cups miniature marshmallows
- 2 cups all-purpose flour
- 2 cups sugar
- 1 teaspoon baking soda
- 1 cup butter, cubed
- 1 cup cherry-flavored cola
- 3 tablespoons baking cocoa
- 2 large eggs
- ½ cup buttermilk
- 1 teaspoon vanilla extract

FROSTING

- ¾ cup butter, softened
- 1 cup confectioners' sugar
- 1 jar (7 ounces) marshmallow creme
- 2 tablespoons frozen cherry-pomegranate juice concentrate, thawed
  Fresh sweet cherries with stems

Cherry Cola Cake

1. Preheat oven to 350°. Line bottoms of two greased 9-in. round baking pans with parchment paper; grease paper. Divide marshmallows between pans.
2. In a large bowl, whisk flour, sugar and baking soda. In a small saucepan, combine butter, cola and cocoa; bring just to a boil, stirring occasionally. Add to flour mixture, stirring just until moistened.
3. In a small bowl, whisk eggs, buttermilk and vanilla until blended; add to flour mixture, whisking constantly. Pour batter into prepared pans, dividing evenly. (Marshmallows will float to the top.)
4. Bake 25-30 minutes or until a toothpick inserted in the center comes out clean. Cool in pans for 10 minutes before removing to wire racks; remove paper. Cool completely.
5. For frosting, in a small bowl, beat butter and confectioners' sugar until smooth. Beat in marshmallow creme and juice concentrate on low speed just until blended.
6. Place one cake layer on a serving plate; spread top with 1 cup frosting. Top with remaining cake layer; spread with remaining frosting. Decorate with cherries.
NOTE *To frost sides as well as top of cake, double amounts for frosting.*

BIG BATCH
Three-Layered Carrot Cake

My mom loved carrots so much that she put them in various dishes at least five times a week when I was growing up. Her specialty was a homemade carrot cake that was requested for every special occasion. When I made this for her 70th birthday, she cried with each bite.

—PAULA MARCHESI LENHARTSVILLE, PA

PREP: 1 HOUR + COOLING
BAKE: 20 MIN. + COOLING
MAKES: 16 SERVINGS

Three-Layered
Carrot Cake

- 6 **large eggs, separated**
- 2¼ **cups all-purpose flour**
- 1 **teaspoon baking soda**
- ½ **teaspoon salt**
- ⅔ **cup orange juice**
- ⅓ **cup sour cream**
- 1½ **cups butter, softened**
- 1½ **cups sugar**
- ½ **cup packed brown sugar**
- 1 **teaspoon grated orange peel**
- 1½ **teaspoons minced fresh thyme, optional**
- 2 **cups finely shredded carrots (about 4 medium)**
- 1 **cup chopped pecans**

FROSTING
- 2 **packages (8 ounces each) cream cheese, softened**
- 1 **tablespoon grated orange peel**
- 1 **tablespoon orange juice**
- 8 **to 8¼ cups confectioners' sugar**

1. Place egg whites in a small bowl; let stand at room temperature 30 minutes. Preheat oven to 350°. Line bottoms of three greased 8-in.-square baking pans with parchment paper; grease the paper.
2. In another bowl, whisk flour, baking soda and salt. In a small bowl, whisk orange juice and sour cream. In a large bowl, cream butter, sugars and orange peel until light and fluffy. Add egg yolks, one at a time, beating well after each addition. If desired, beat in thyme. Add flour mixture alternately with orange juice mixture, beating well after each addition.

3. With clean beaters, beat egg whites on medium speed until stiff peaks form. Fold into batter. Gently fold in shredded carrots and pecans.
4. Transfer to prepared pans. Bake 20-25 minutes or until a toothpick inserted in the center comes out clean. Cool in pans for 10 minutes before removing to wire racks; remove paper. Cool completely.
5. For frosting, in a large bowl, beat cream cheese, orange peel and juice until blended. Gradually beat in enough confectioners' sugar to reach desired consistency.
6. Spread frosting between layers and over top and sides of cake. Refrigerate until serving.

NOTE *To decorate cake with carrot ribbons, use a vegetable peeler to shave one large carrot into long ribbon-like strips. Reserve four of the longest strips for sides of cake; roll up remaining strips to make curls for the bow. Arrange long and rolled-up strips on a paper towel-lined baking sheet; let dry 30-45 minutes before placing on cake. Decorate frosted cake with carrot ribbons just before serving; if desired, add fresh thyme sprigs.*

BIG BATCH

Marvelous Marble Cake

Pound cake and chocolate make the best marble cake. After putting together these ingredients, I developed this recipe after about five tries. It is now a staple dessert at all my parties and a nice treat with a good cup of coffee.
—**ELLEN RILEY** MURFREESBORO, TN

PREP: 45 MIN. • **BAKE:** 20 MIN. + COOLING
MAKES: 16 SERVINGS

- 4 ounces bittersweet chocolate, chopped
- 3 tablespoons plus 1¼ cups butter, softened, divided
- 2 cups sugar
- 5 large eggs
- 3 teaspoons vanilla extract
- 2¼ cups all-purpose flour
- 2 teaspoons baking powder
- ½ teaspoon salt
- ½ cup sour cream
- ½ cup miniature semisweet chocolate chips, optional

FROSTING
- ¾ cup butter, softened
- 6¾ cups confectioners' sugar
- 2 teaspoons vanilla extract
- ½ to ⅔ cup 2% milk
- 2 tablespoons miniature semisweet chocolate chips

1. In top of a double boiler or a metal bowl over barely simmering water, melt chocolate and 3 tablespoons butter; stir until smooth. Cool to room temperature.
2. Preheat oven to 375°. Line bottoms of three greased 8-in. round baking pans with parchment paper; grease paper.
3. In a large bowl, cream remaining butter and sugar until light and fluffy. Add eggs, one at a time, beating well after each addition. Beat in vanilla. Whisk flour, baking powder and salt; add to creamed mixture alternately with sour cream, beating well after each addition.
4. Remove 2 cups batter to a small bowl; stir in cooled chocolate mixture and, if desired, chocolate chips until blended. Drop plain and chocolate batters by tablespoonfuls into prepared pans, dividing batters evenly among pans. To make batter level in pans, bang the cake pans several times on the counter.
5. Bake 20-25 minutes or until a toothpick inserted in the center comes out clean. Cool in pans for 10 minutes before removing to wire racks; remove paper. Cool completely.
6. For frosting, in a large bowl, beat butter until smooth. Gradually beat in confectioners' sugar, vanilla and enough milk to reach desired consistency.
7. If cake layers have rounded tops, trim with a serrated knife to make level. In a microwave, melt chocolate chips; stir until smooth. Cool slightly.
8. Place one cake layer on a serving plate; spread with ½ cup frosting. Repeat layers. Top with remaining cake layer. Frost the top and sides of cake. Drop cooled chocolate by ½ teaspoonfuls over frosting. Using a large offset spatula, smear chocolate to create a marble design in frosting.

Marvelous Marble Cake

“I love this cake, the presentation is perfect for a marble cake. The taste is 5 plus stars.”
—**JELLYBUG**
FROM TASTEOFHOME.COM

Maple Walnut Cake

BIG BATCH
Maple Walnut Cake

My beloved grandpa made delicious maple syrup when I was a child, and whenever I make this cake, I am reminded of him. The recipe honors his memory and has proved to be a favorite with family and friends.
—**LORI FEE** MIDDLESEX, NY

PREP: 45 MIN. • **BAKE:** 15 MIN. + COOLING
MAKES: 16 SERVINGS

- ½ cup unsalted butter, softened
- 1½ cups packed light brown sugar
- 3 large eggs
- 1 teaspoon maple flavoring or maple syrup
- 2 cups all-purpose flour
- 1 teaspoon baking powder
- 1 teaspoon baking soda
- ¼ teaspoon salt
- 1 cup buttermilk

CANDIED WALNUTS
- 1 tablespoon unsalted butter
- 1½ cups coarsely chopped walnuts
- 1 tablespoon maple syrup
- ¼ teaspoon salt

FROSTING
- 2 cups unsalted butter, softened
- 5 cups confectioners' sugar
- 1 teaspoon maple flavoring or maple syrup
- ¼ teaspoon salt
- ¼ to ½ cup half-and-half cream
- 3 tablespoons maple syrup, divided

1. Preheat oven to 350°. Line bottoms of three greased 9-in. round baking pans with parchment paper; grease paper.
2. In a large bowl, cream butter and brown sugar until blended. Add eggs, one at a time, beating well after each addition. Beat in the maple flavoring. In another bowl, whisk flour, baking powder, baking soda and salt; add to creamed mixture alternately with buttermilk, beating after each addition.
3. Transfer to prepared pans. Bake 11-13 minutes or until a toothpick inserted in the center comes out clean. Cool in pans for 10 minutes before removing to wire racks. Cool completely.
4. For candied walnuts, in a large skillet, melt butter. Add walnuts; cook and stir over medium heat until nuts are toasted, about 5 minutes. Stir in maple syrup and salt; cook and stir 1 minute longer. Spread on foil to cool completely.
5. For the frosting, in a large bowl, beat the butter until creamy. Beat in confectioners' sugar, maple flavoring, salt and enough cream to reach desired consistency.
6. Place one cake layer on a serving plate; spread with 1 cup frosting. Sprinkle with ½ cup candied walnuts and drizzle with 1 tablespoon maple syrup. Repeat layers.
7. Top with remaining cake layer. Frost top and sides of cake. Top with remaining walnuts and syrup.

Strawberries & Cream Torte

Enjoy this festive strawberry summer treat that is one of my mom's favorites. It wows guests every time, yet it is simple to make.
—**CATHY BRANCIAROLI** WILMINGTON, DE

PREP: 25 MIN. • **BAKE:** 15 MIN. + COOLING
MAKES: 12 SERVINGS

- 2 large eggs, separated
- ¼ cup butter, softened
- ½ cup plus ½ teaspoon sugar, divided
- ½ teaspoon vanilla extract
- 1 cup all-purpose flour
- 1½ teaspoons baking powder
- ¼ teaspoon salt
- ½ cup 2% milk

ASSEMBLY
- 2 cups heavy whipping cream
- 1 pint fresh strawberries, hulled and sliced
- ½ teaspoon sugar
  Additional fresh strawberries

1. Place egg whites in a large bowl; let stand at room temperature 30 minutes. Preheat oven to 350°. Line the bottoms of two greased 8-in. round baking pans with parchment paper; grease paper.
2. In a large bowl, cream butter and ½ cup sugar until light and fluffy. Add egg yolks, beating well. Beat in vanilla.
3. In another bowl, whisk flour, baking powder and salt; add to creamed mixture alternately with milk, beating well after each addition. Transfer to prepared pans.
4. With clean beaters, beat egg whites on medium speed until foamy. Add remaining sugar, beating on high until sugar is dissolved. Continue beating until soft peaks form. Spread over batter in pans.
5. Bake 12-15 minutes or until a toothpick inserted in the center comes out clean. Cool completely in pans on wire racks. (Cake layers will be thin.)
6. In a large bowl, beat cream until stiff peaks form. Loosen edges of cakes from pans with a knife. Carefully remove one cake to a serving plate, meringue side up.
7. Arrange sliced strawberries over top; sprinkle with sugar. Gently spread with half of the whipped cream. Top with remaining cake layer, meringue side up; spread with remaining whipped cream. Top with whole strawberries. Refrigerate until serving.

❝I made this torte for Easter dinner. Lovely and tasty! A winner all around.❞
—**GAILARDITH**
FROM TASTEOFHOME.COM

Strawberries &
Cream Torte

CHOCOLATE-FILLED CHERRY ANGEL CAKE *PAGE 140*

Foam Cakes

THE TASTE AND TEXTURE OF THESE CAKES ARE SURE TO PLEASE! BAKE A LIGHT, AIRY DESSERT FOR A CASUAL GET-TOGETHER WITH FRIENDS OR SIMPLY PREPARE ONE AS A SURPRISE FOR YOUR FAMILY. HERE YOU'LL FIND LOVELY ANGEL FOOD, CHIFFON AND SPONGE CAKES WITH SWEET FRUITY FLAVORS, CHOCOLATE FILLINGS AND MORE!

BERRIED TREASURE ANGEL FOOD CAKE *PAGE 139*

HOLIDAY WALNUT TORTE *PAGE 140*

CHOCOLATE-FILLED ANGEL FOOD CAKE *PAGE 147*

"Delicious! The cake doesn't need any topping or sauce. It rose up beautifully, the color was nice with the top slightly carmelized, and the flavor was to die for."

—ALEECE
FROM TASTEOFHOME.COM

Orange Dream
Angel Food Cake

Chocolate Chiffon Cake

BIG BATCH

Orange Dream Angel Food Cake

Angel food cake becomes a heavenly indulgence with a pretty swirl of orange in every bite. Here's the perfect light summertime dessert. Try it with a small scoop of sherbet for a special treat.
—**LAUREN OSBORNE** HOLTWOOD, PA

PREP: 25 MIN. • **BAKE:** 30 MIN. + COOLING
MAKES: 16 SERVINGS

- 12 **large egg whites**
- 1 **cup all-purpose flour**
- 1¾ **cups sugar, divided**
- 1½ **teaspoons cream of tartar**
- ½ **teaspoon salt**
- 1 **teaspoon almond extract**
- 1 **teaspoon vanilla extract**
- 1 **teaspoon grated orange peel**
- 1 **teaspoon orange extract**
- 6 **drops red food coloring, optional**
- 6 **drops yellow food coloring, optional**

1. Place egg whites in a large bowl; let stand at room temperature for 30 minutes. Sift flour and ¾ cup sugar together twice; set aside.
2. Add cream of tartar, salt and almond and vanilla extracts to egg whites; beat on medium speed until soft peaks form. Gradually add remaining sugar, about 2 tablespoons at a time, beating on high until stiff glossy peaks form and sugar is dissolved. Gradually fold in flour mixture, about ½ cup at a time.
3. Gently spoon half of batter into an ungreased 10-in. tube pan. To the remaining batter, stir in the orange peel, orange extract and, if desired, food colorings. Gently spoon orange batter over white batter. Cut through both layers with a knife to swirl the orange and remove air pockets.
4. Bake on the lowest oven rack at 375° for 30-35 minutes or until lightly browned and entire top appears dry. Immediately invert pan; cool completely, about 1 hour.
5. Run a knife around side and center tube of pan. Remove to a serving plate.

BIG BATCH

Chocolate Chiffon Cake

If you want to offer family and friends a dessert that really stands out from the rest, this is the cake to make. The beautiful rich sponge cake is drizzled with a succulent chocolate glaze.
—**ERMA FOX** MEMPHIS, MO

PREP: 25 MIN. + COOLING
BAKE: 1 HOUR + COOLING
MAKES: 16-20 SERVINGS

- 7 **large eggs, separated**
- ½ **cup baking cocoa**
- ¾ **cup boiling water**
- 1¾ **cups cake flour**
- 1¾ **cups sugar**
- 1½ **teaspoons baking soda**
- 1 **teaspoon salt**
- ½ **cup canola oil**
- 2 **teaspoons vanilla extract**
- ¼ **teaspoon cream of tartar**

ICING

- ⅓ **cup butter**
- 2 **cups confectioners' sugar**
- 2 **ounces unsweetened chocolate, melted and cooled**
- 1½ **teaspoons vanilla extract**
- 3 **to 4 tablespoons hot water**
  Chopped nuts, optional

1. Let eggs stand at room temperature for 30 minutes. In a bowl, combine the cocoa and water until smooth; cool for 20 minutes. In a large bowl, combine flour, sugar, baking soda and salt. In a bowl, whisk the egg yolks, oil and the vanilla; add to dry ingredients along with the cocoa mixture. Beat until well blended. In another large bowl and with clean beaters, beat egg whites and cream of tartar on high speed until stiff peaks form. Gradually fold into egg yolk mixture.
2. Gently spoon batter into an ungreased 10-in. tube pan. Cut through the batter with a knife to remove air pockets. Bake on lowest rack at 325° for 60-65 minutes or until top springs back when lightly touched. Immediately invert pan; cool completely. Run a knife around sides and center tube of pan. Invert cake onto a serving plate.
3. For icing, melt butter in a saucepan. Remove from heat; stir in confectioners' sugar, chocolate, vanilla and water. Drizzle over cake. Sprinkle with nuts if desired.

Layered Orange Sponge Cake

rack 45-55 minutes or until top springs back when lightly touched. Immediately invert pan; cool the cake in the pan, about 1½ hours.

5. Meanwhile, in a large heavy saucepan, mix the sugar and flour for the frosting. Whisk in orange juice and orange peel. Cook and stir over medium heat until thickened and bubbly. Reduce heat to low; cook and stir 2 minutes longer. Remove from heat.

6. In a small bowl, whisk a small amount of hot mixture into eggs; return to pan, whisking constantly. Bring to a gentle boil; cook and stir 2 minutes. Immediately transfer to a clean bowl. Cool for 30 minutes. Press plastic wrap onto surface of orange mixture; refrigerate until cold.

7. In a large bowl, beat cream until soft peaks form; fold into orange mixture. Run a knife around sides and center tube of pan. Remove cake to a serving plate. Using a long serrated knife, cut cake horizontally into three layers. Spread frosting between layers and over top and sides of cake. Sprinkle with pecans. Refrigerate until serving.

Layered Orange Sponge Cake

The recipe for this cake has been handed down in my family for 40 years. It's from a relative who was a French baker. It's light and delicate, just like a great cake should be.
—**JOYCE SPEERBRECHER** GRAFTON, WI

PREP: 30 MIN. • **BAKE:** 45 MIN. + COOLING
MAKES: 12 SERVINGS

- 8 **large eggs, separated**
- 1 **cup plus 2 tablespoons all-purpose flour**
- ⅔ **cup plus ⅔ cup sugar, divided**
- ½ **cup orange juice**
- 3 **tablespoons grated orange peel**
- ½ **teaspoon salt**
- ¼ **teaspoon cream of tartar**

FROSTING
- 1½ **cups sugar**
- 6 **tablespoons all-purpose flour**
- ⅔ **cup orange juice**
- 3 **tablespoons grated orange peel**
- 2 **large eggs**

- 2 **cups heavy whipping cream**
- 1 **cup chopped pecans**

1. Place egg whites in a large bowl; let stand at room temperature 30 minutes. Meanwhile, preheat oven to 325°. Sift flour twice.

2. In another large bowl, beat egg yolks until slightly thickened. Gradually add ⅔ cup sugar, beating on high speed until thick and lemon-colored. Beat in orange juice and orange peel. Fold in flour.

3. Add salt and cream of tartar to the egg whites; with clean beaters, beat on medium until soft peaks form. Gradually add remaining sugar, 1 tablespoon at a time; beat on high after each addition until sugar is dissolved. Continue beating until soft glossy peaks form. Fold a fourth of the egg whites into batter, then fold in remaining whites.

4. Gently transfer to an ungreased 10-in. tube pan. Bake on lowest oven

---

5 INGREDIENTS

Cake with Pineapple Pudding

I serve this light and refreshing recipe often. It was given to me by a dear friend. I frequently take it to church luncheons.
—**JUDY SELLGREN** GRAND RAPIDS, MI

START TO FINISH: 10 MIN.
MAKES: 6 SERVINGS

- 2 **cups cold 2% milk**
- 1 **package (3.4 ounces) instant French vanilla pudding mix**
- 1 **can (8 ounces) unsweetened crushed pineapple, drained**
- 1 **cup whipped topping**
- 6 **slices angel food cake**

In a large bowl, whisk the milk and pudding mix for 2 minutes. Let stand for 2 minutes or until soft-set. Fold in pineapple and whipped topping. Chill until serving. Serve with cake.

Berried Treasure Angel Food Cake

My husband grills anything and everything—even dessert! With his encouragement, I came up with this easy recipe that takes just a few minutes to prepare, yet impresses dinner guests.

—ANITA ARCHIBALD AURORA, ON

START TO FINISH: 25 MIN.
MAKES: 4 SERVINGS

- 8 **slices angel food cake (1½ inches thick)**
- ¼ **cup butter, softened**
- ½ **cup heavy whipping cream**
- ¼ **teaspoon almond extract**
- ¼ **cup almond cake and pastry filling**
- ½ **cup fresh blueberries**
- ½ **cup fresh raspberries**
- ½ **cup sliced fresh strawberries**
- ¼ **cup mixed nuts, coarsely chopped**
  Confectioners' sugar

1. Using a 1½-in. round cookie cutter, cut out the centers of half of the cake slices (discard removed cake or save for another use). Spread butter over both sides of cake slices. Grill, covered, over medium heat or broil 4 in. from heat 1-2 minutes on each side or until toasted.
2. In a small bowl, beat cream until it begins to thicken. Add extract; beat until soft peaks form.
3. To serve, stack one solid and one cutout slice of cake on each dessert plate, placing the outer edges on opposite sides for a more even thickness. Spoon almond filling into holes; top with whipped cream, berries and nuts. Dust with confectioners' sugar.

Berried Treasure
Angel Food Cake

BIG BATCH
Chocolate-Filled Cherry Angel Cake

Here's a cake that will catch the eye of all your guests. It's beautiful and it's ideal for parties or holidays. If you love chocolate and cherries together, you'll love this cake!
—**BARBARA WHEELER** ROYAL OAK, MI

PREP: 20 MIN. • **BAKE:** 45 MIN. + COOLING
MAKES: 16 SERVINGS

- 1 **package (16 ounces) angel food cake mix**
- ½ **cup finely chopped maraschino cherries**
- 1 **cup semisweet chocolate chips**
- 1 **tablespoon maraschino cherry juice**
- 2 **teaspoons strong brewed coffee**
- ½ **teaspoon vanilla extract**
- 1 **container (8 ounces) sour cream**
- 1 **container (8 ounces) frozen whipped topping, thawed**
  Chopped walnuts, grated chocolate and additional maraschino cherries

1. Prepare cake mix batter according to package directions; fold in chopped cherries. Gently spoon into an ungreased 10-in. tube pan. Cut through batter with a knife to remove air pockets.
2. Bake on lowest oven rack at 350° for 45-55 minutes or until lightly browned and entire top appears dry. Immediately invert pan; cool completely, about 1 hour. Run a knife around side and center tube of pan. Cut the cake horizontally into three layers.
3. For the filling, in a small heavy saucepan, cook and stir the chocolate chips, cherry juice, coffee and vanilla over medium-low heat until melted. Remove from the heat; stir in the sour cream.
4. To assemble, place one cake layer on a serving plate; spread with one half of the filling. Repeat layers. Top with remaining cake layer. Spread whipped topping over top and sides of cake. Garnish with walnuts, chocolate and cherries. Refrigerate until serving.

Holiday Walnut Torte

Holiday Walnut Torte

One of my grandma's best-loved recipes, this torte has tender layers of nut-filled cake put together with apricot glaze and cream cheese frosting. It is just divine!
—**EILEEN KORECKO** HOT SPRINGS VILLAGE, AR

PREP: 40 MIN. • **BAKE:** 25 MIN. + COOLING
MAKES: 10-12 SERVINGS

- 3 **large eggs**
- 1½ **cups sugar**
- 3 **teaspoons vanilla extract**
- 1¾ **cups all-purpose flour**
- 1 **cup ground walnuts**
- 2 **teaspoons baking powder**
- ½ **teaspoon salt**
- 1½ **cups heavy whipping cream**

GLAZE
- ⅔ **cup apricot preserves**
- 1 **tablespoon sugar**

FROSTING
- ½ **cup butter, softened**
- 1 **package (3 ounces) cream cheese, softened**
- 2 **cups confectioners' sugar**
- 1 **teaspoon vanilla extract**
- ¾ **cup ground walnuts, divided**

1. In a large bowl, beat eggs, sugar and vanilla on high speed for 5 minutes or until thick and lemon-colored. Combine the flour, walnuts, baking powder and salt; beat into egg mixture. Beat cream until stiff peaks form; fold into batter.
2. Pour into two greased and floured 9-in. round baking pans. Bake at 350° for 25-30 minutes or until a toothpick inserted near the center comes out clean. Cool for 10 minutes before removing from the pans to wire racks to cool completely.
3. In a small saucepan over medium heat, cook and stir preserves and sugar until sugar is dissolved. Set aside ½ cup. Brush remaining glaze over cake tops.
4. In a large bowl, beat butter and cream cheese until fluffy. Add confectioners' sugar and vanilla; beat until smooth. Spread ½ cup frosting over one cake; top with second cake and ¾ cup frosting. Sprinkle ½ cup walnuts over the top.
5. Brush reserved glaze over sides of cake; press remaining walnuts onto sides. Pipe remaining frosting around top edge of cake. Store in the refrigerator.

(5) INGREDIENTS

Rainbow Sherbet Angel Food Cake

Talk about a dessert that pops off the plate. I sometimes make this cake even more eye-catching by coloring the whipped cream, too. Use whatever sherbet flavor combination you like.

—BONNIE HAWKINS ELKHORN, WI

PREP: 25 MIN. + FREEZING
MAKES: 12 SERVINGS

- 1 prepared angel food cake (8 to 10 ounces)
- 3 cups rainbow sherbet, softened if necessary

WHIPPED CREAM

- 2 cups heavy whipping cream
- ⅓ cup confectioners' sugar
- 1 teaspoon vanilla extract

1. Using a long serrated knife, cut cake horizontally into four layers. Place bottom layer on a freezer-safe serving plate; spread with 1 cup sherbet. Repeat twice. Top with remaining cake layer. Freeze, covered, until the sherbet is firm, about 1 hour.

2. In a large bowl, beat the cream until it begins to thicken. Add confectioners' sugar and vanilla; beat until soft peaks form. Frost top and sides of the cake. Freeze until firm.

3. Thaw cake in refrigerator for 30 minutes before serving. Cut with a serrated knife.

Caramelized Angel Food Cake Sundaes

Angel food gets a sinful makeover with this easy recipe. If you have them on hand, fresh sliced strawberries make a wonderful addition. Yum!

—JESSICA RING CHICAGO, IL

START TO FINISH: 20 MIN.
MAKES: 6 SERVINGS

- 1 package (3 ounces) cream cheese, softened
- ¼ cup sour cream
- 2 tablespoons confectioners' sugar
- ¼ cup butter, softened
- ¼ cup packed brown sugar
- ⅛ teaspoon ground cinnamon
- 6 slices angel food cake
- 6 scoops fudge ripple ice cream

1. In a small bowl, beat the cream cheese, sour cream and confectioner's sugar until smooth. In another bowl, cream the butter, brown sugar and cinnamon until light and fluffy.

2. Spread butter mixture over the top and sides of each cake slice. Place on an ungreased baking sheet. Broil 4-6 in. from the heat for 1-2 minutes or until bubbly. Cool slightly. Serve with ice cream and sour cream mixture.

Rainbow Sherbet Angel Food Cake

TOP TIP

Accurate Measurements

The moisture in brown sugar tends to trap air between the crystals, so it should be firmly packed when measuring. *Taste of Home* recipes specify packed brown sugar in the ingredients.

Mini Rum Cakes

Mini Rum Cakes

Mom often kept sponge cakes in her freezer and pudding in the pantry. We tried many rum cakes to get the best recipe. We think this has the most flavor.

—**DONA HOFFMAN** ADDISON, IL

START TO FINISH: 10 MIN.
MAKES: 6 SERVINGS

- 2 **cups cold 2% milk**
- 1 **package (3.4 ounces) instant vanilla pudding mix**
- 1 **teaspoon rum extract**
- 6 **individual round sponge cakes**
- 1½ **cups whipped topping**
  Fresh or frozen raspberries

1. In a small bowl, whisk milk and pudding mix for 2 minutes; stir in extract. Let stand for 2 minutes or until soft-set.

2. Place the individual sponge cakes on dessert plates; top with pudding. Garnish with whipped topping and raspberries.

BIG BATCH
Snowballs Cake

I couldn't pry this secret family recipe from my sister-in-law, but her mother did, and I was thrilled! The old-fashioned flavor never goes out of style.
—NORMA WEHRUNG GETZVILLE, NY

PREP: 25 MIN. • **BAKE:** 40 MIN. + CHILLING
MAKES: 20 SERVINGS

- 1 package (16 ounces) angel food cake mix
- 2 envelopes unflavored gelatin
- ¼ cup cold water
- 1 cup boiling water
- 1 can (20 ounces) crushed pineapple, undrained
- 1 cup sugar
- 3 tablespoons lemon juice
- ¼ teaspoon salt
- 4 envelopes whipped topping mix (Dream Whip)
- 2 cups milk
  Toasted flaked coconut and maraschino cherries

1. Prepare and bake cake according to package directions, using an ungreased 10-in. tube pan. Immediately invert cake onto a wire rack; cool completely, about 1 hour.
2. Meanwhile, in a large bowl, sprinkle gelatin over cold water; let stand for 1 minute. Stir in boiling water until gelatin is dissolved. Add pineapple, sugar, lemon juice and salt. Refrigerate until partially thickened, about 40 minutes.
3. In a large bowl, beat whipped topping mixes and milk until stiff. Fold into pineapple mixture.
4. Run a knife around sides and center tube of cake pan; remove cake from pan and cut into 1-in. cubes. Place half of the cake cubes in a 13x9-in. dish; top with half of the filling. Repeat layers. Refrigerate for at least 1 hour.
5. Sprinkle with coconut. Cut into squares; top each with a cherry.

Lime Angel Food Cake

Lime Angel Food Cake

For my husband's family reunion, I took a store-bought angel food cake and turned it into this special dessert with a lovely lime cream frosting topped with toasted coconut. It went over big!
—NANCY FOUST STONEBORO, PA

PREP: 20 MIN. + CHILLING
COOK: 15 MIN. + CHILLING
MAKES: 12 SERVINGS

- 2 large eggs
- 2 large egg yolks
- ½ cup plus 3 tablespoons sugar, divided
- 6 tablespoons lime juice
- 2 teaspoons grated lime peel
- ½ cup cold butter, cubed
- 1 cup heavy whipping cream
- ½ teaspoon vanilla extract
- 1 prepared angel food cake (8 to 10 ounces)
- 1 cup flaked coconut, toasted

1. In the top of a double boiler, beat eggs and yolks. Stir in ½ cup sugar, lime juice and peel. Cook over simmering water while gradually whisking in butter. Cook and stir until mixture is thickened and reaches 160°. Strain; refrigerate until completely cool.
2. In a small bowl, beat the cream and vanilla until stiff peaks form; gradually beat in remaining sugar. Gently fold into lime mixture.
3. Split cake horizontally into three layers. Place bottom layer on a serving plate. Spread with ⅔ cup lime mixture. Repeat. Place top layer on cake. Frost top and sides with remaining lime mixture. Sprinkle with the coconut. Refrigerate for at least 30 minutes before slicing.

Lemon Curd-Filled Angel Food Cake

Lemon Curd-Filled Angel Food Cake

For a sunny angel food cake, I make a filling of mascarpone, cream cheese and lemon curd, and then drizzle the cake with a lemony sweet glaze.
—**LEAH REKAU** MILWAUKEE, WI

PREP: 55 MIN. + CHILLING
BAKE: 45 MIN. + COOLING
MAKES: 16 SERVINGS

- 12 **large egg whites (about 1⅔ cups)**
- 1 **cup cake flour**
- 1½ **cups sugar, divided**
- 1 **vanilla bean or 1 teaspoon vanilla extract**
- ½ **teaspoon cream of tartar**
- ¼ **teaspoon salt**

FILLING
- ½ **cup heavy whipping cream**
- ½ **cup mascarpone cheese**
- 2 **tablespoons confectioners' sugar**
- 1 **jar (10 ounces) lemon curd, divided**
- 1 **cup sliced fresh strawberries, patted dry**

GLAZE
- 2 **cups confectioners' sugar**
- 1 **teaspoon grated lemon peel**
- 3 **to 4 tablespoons lemon juice**

1. Place egg whites in a large bowl; let stand at room temperature 30 minutes.
2. Preheat oven to 325°. In a small bowl, mix flour and ¾ cup sugar until blended.
3. Add seeds from the vanilla bean (or extract if using), cream of tartar and salt to egg whites. Beat on medium speed until soft peaks form. Gradually add remaining ¾ cup sugar, 1 tablespoon at a time, beating on high after each addition until sugar is dissolved. Continue beating until soft glossy peaks form. Gradually fold in flour mixture, about ½ cup at a time.
4. Gently transfer batter to an ungreased 10-in. tube pan. Cut through batter with a knife to remove air pockets. Bake on lowest oven rack 45-55 minutes or until top springs back when lightly touched. Immediately invert the pan; cool completely in pan, about 1½ hours.
5. Run a knife around sides and center tube of pan. Remove cake to a serving plate. Using a serrated knife, cut a 1-in. slice off top of cake. Hollow out remaining cake, leaving a 1-in.-thick shell (save removed cake for another use).
6. For the filling, in a small bowl, beat cream until it begins to thicken. Add mascarpone cheese and confectioners' sugar; beat until soft peaks form. Fold in ¼ cup of the lemon curd.
7. Line bottom of tunnel with strawberries. Spoon mascarpone mixture over berries; top with remaining lemon curd. Replace cake top; refrigerate, covered, at least 4 hours or overnight.
8. For glaze, in a small bowl, mix confectioners' sugar, lemon peel and enough juice to reach desired consistency. Unwrap cake; spread glaze over top, allowing some to drip down sides. Refrigerate until serving.
NOTE *To remove the seeds from a vanilla bean, cut bean lengthwise in half with a sharp knife; scrape out the dark, pulpy seeds.*

⑤ INGREDIENTS *BIG BATCH*
Apple-Spice Angel Food Cake

Angel food cake mix is lower in fat and calories than regular cake mix. Apple pie spice and toasted nuts add a festive fall flavor.
—**JOAN BUEHNERKEMPER** TEUTOPOLIS, IL

PREP: 10 MIN. • **BAKE:** 35 MIN. + COOLING
MAKES: 16 SERVINGS

- 1 **package (16 ounces) angel food cake mix**
- 1 **cup water**
- ⅔ **cup unsweetened applesauce**
- ½ **cup finely chopped pecans, toasted**
- 1 **teaspoon apple pie spice**
  Reduced-fat whipped topping and/or apple slices, optional

1. In a large bowl, combine cake mix and water. Beat on low speed for 30 seconds. Beat on medium speed for 1 minute. Fold in the applesauce, pecans and pie spice.
2. Gently spoon into an ungreased 10-in. tube pan. Cut through the batter with a knife to remove air pockets. Bake on lowest oven rack at 350° for 35-45 minutes or until lightly browned and entire top appears dry. Immediately invert pan; cool completely, about 1 hour.
3. Run a knife around side and center tube of pan. Remove cake to a serving plate. Garnish with whipped topping and/or apple slices if desired.

> ❝My husband and I ate up this apple-spice cake all by ourselves... it was absolutely delicious!❞
> —**ACARBAUGH**
> FROM TASTEOFHOME.COM

Apple-Spice
Angel Food Cake

(5)INGREDIENTS
Pineapple-Caramel Sponge Cakes

Want the flavor of pineapple upside-down cake without the heat and hassle of turning on the oven? Then try my tasty no-bake riff.
—**LYNN MAHLE** QUINCY, FL

START TO FINISH: 10 MIN.
MAKES: 4 SERVINGS

- 1 **can (8 ounces) unsweetened crushed pineapple, drained**
- ½ **cup caramel ice cream topping**
- 4 **individual round sponge cakes**
- 1 **pint vanilla ice cream, softened**

1. In a small saucepan, combine drained pineapple and caramel topping. Cook over medium heat for 2-3 minutes or until heated through, stirring occasionally.
2. Place sponge cakes on dessert plates. Top each with a scoop of ice cream and ¼ cup pineapple sauce. Serve immediately.

BIG BATCH
Vanilla Bean Angel Food Cake

Angel food cake is my favorite blank slate for making awesome desserts. Serve it with a simple glaze, or pile on fresh fruit, chocolate sauce or nutty sprinkles.
—**ELLEN RILEY** MURFREESBORO, TN

PREP: 30 MIN. • **BAKE:** 45 MIN. + COOLING
MAKES: 16 SERVINGS

- 12 **large egg whites (about 1⅔ cups)**
- 1 **cup cake flour**
- 1½ **cups sugar, divided**
- 1 **vanilla bean or 1 teaspoon vanilla extract**
- ½ **teaspoon cream of tartar**
- ¼ **teaspoon salt**
- GLAZE
- 2 **cups confectioners' sugar**
- 1 **vanilla bean or 1 teaspoon vanilla extract**
- 3 **to 4 tablespoons 2% milk**

1. Place egg whites in a large bowl; let stand at room temperature 30 minutes.

2. Preheat oven to 325°. In a small bowl, mix flour and ¾ cup sugar until blended.
3. Add seeds from vanilla bean (or extract if using), cream of tartar and salt to egg whites. Beat on medium speed until soft peaks form. Gradually add remaining ¾ cup sugar, 1 tablespoon at a time, beating on high after each addition until sugar is dissolved. Continue beating until soft glossy peaks form. Gradually fold in flour mixture, about ½ cup at a time.
4. Gently transfer the batter to an ungreased 10-in. tube pan. Cut through batter with a knife to remove air pockets. Bake on lowest oven rack 45-55 minutes or until top springs back when lightly touched. Immediately invert pan; cool completely in pan, about 1½ hours.
5. Run a knife around sides and center tube of pan. Remove cake to a serving plate.
6. For glaze, in a small bowl, mix confectioners' sugar, seeds from vanilla bean (or extract if using) and enough milk to reach desired consistency. Spread glaze over cake, allowing some to drip down sides.
NOTE *To remove the seeds from a vanilla bean, cut bean lengthwise in half with a sharp knife; scrape out the dark, pulpy seeds.*

Vanilla Bean Angel Food Cake

BIG BATCH

Chocolate-Filled Angel Food Cake

If you are looking to impress, try this decadent cake with a chocolate glaze and a secret tunnel of Amaretto-and-chocolate-flavored whipped cream.

—LEAH REKAU MILWAUKEE, WI

PREP: 1 HOUR 5 MIN. + CHILLING
BAKE: 45 MIN. + COOLING
MAKES: 16 SERVINGS

- 12 **large egg whites (about 1⅔ cups)**
- 1 **cup cake flour**
- 1½ **cups sugar, divided**
- 1 **vanilla bean or 1 teaspoon vanilla extract**
- ½ **teaspoon cream of tartar**
- ¼ **teaspoon salt**

FILLING

- 1 **cup (6 ounces) 60% cacao bittersweet chocolate baking chips**
- 1 **cup heavy whipping cream, divided**
- 1 **tablespoon amaretto**
- 1 **tablespoon sugar**

GLAZE

- 1 **cup (6 ounces) 60% cacao bittersweet chocolate baking chips**
- ½ **cup heavy whipping cream**
- 1 **tablespoon sugar**
- 2 **tablespoons amaretto**
- ¼ **cup sliced almonds, toasted**

1. Place egg whites in a large bowl; let stand at room temperature 30 minutes.

2. Preheat oven to 325°. In a small bowl, mix flour and ¾ cup sugar until blended.

3. Add the seeds from the vanilla bean (or extract if using), cream of tartar and salt to egg whites. Beat on medium speed until soft peaks form. Gradually add remaining ¾ cup sugar, 1 tablespoon at a time, beating on high after each addition until the sugar is dissolved. Continue beating until soft glossy peaks form. Gradually fold in flour mixture, about ½ cup at a time.

4. Gently transfer the batter to an ungreased 10-in. tube pan. Cut through batter with a knife to remove air pockets. Bake on lowest oven rack 45-55 minutes or until top springs back when lightly touched. Immediately invert pan; cool completely in pan, about 1½ hours.

5. For filling, in a large microwave-safe bowl, combine the baking chips, ¼ cup cream and amaretto; microwave on high for 60-90 seconds or until chocolate is melted, stirring every 30 seconds. Continue stirring until mixture is smooth and glossy; cool to lukewarm (90°), about 25-30 minutes.

6. Meanwhile, run a knife around sides and center tube of pan. Remove cake to a serving plate. Using a serrated knife, cut a 1-in. slice off top of cake. Hollow out remaining cake, leaving a 1-in.-thick shell (save removed cake for another use). In a small bowl, beat remaining ¾ cup cream until it begins to thicken. Add sugar; beat until soft peaks form.

7. Fold whipped cream into lukewarm chocolate; spoon into tunnel. Replace cake top. Refrigerate, covered, at least 4 hours or overnight.

8. For glaze, place baking chips in a small bowl. In a small saucepan, combine cream and sugar; bring just to a boil, stirring to dissolve sugar. Pour over baking chips; stir with a whisk until smooth. Stir in amaretto. Cool slightly, about 15 minutes.

9. Unwrap cake; pour glaze over top, allowing some to drip down sides. Sprinkle with almonds.

NOTE *To remove the seeds from a vanilla bean, cut bean lengthwise in half with a sharp knife; scrape out the dark, pulpy seeds.*

Chocolate-Filled Angel Food Cake

Cherrimisu

Grilled Cake and Fruit

Bring the convenience of outdoor cooking to dessert with toasted angel food cake "sandwiches" that hold melted chocolate and are served with grilled fruit.

—**TERRI TRUDEAU** SAN GABRIEL, CA

START TO FINISH: 30 MIN.
MAKES: 4 SERVINGS

- 4 slices angel food cake (1 inch thick)
- 1 ounce bittersweet chocolate
- 1 medium firm banana, cut into fourths
- 8 pineapple chunks
- 1 tablespoon lemon juice
- ¼ cup sugar
- ¼ teaspoon ground cinnamon
- 2 medium kiwifruit, peeled and diced
- 8 fresh strawberries, sliced

1. Cut a pocket in each slice of cake by cutting from one long side to within ½ in. of the opposite side. Insert a chocolate piece into each opening; set aside.
2. In a small bowl, toss the banana, pineapple chunks and lemon juice; drain. In a large resealable plastic bag, combine sugar and cinnamon. Add banana and pineapple; toss to coat. Thread onto four 4-in. metal or soaked wooden skewers.
3. Using long-handled tongs, moisten a paper towel with cooking oil and lightly coat the grill rack. Prepare the grill for indirect heat using a drip pan. Place fruit over drip pan and grill over indirect medium heat for 4-6 minutes or until heated through, turning frequently.
4. Grill cake for 30-60 seconds on each side or until chocolate is melted. Remove fruit from skewers. Combine the kiwi, strawberries and grilled fruit; serve with cake slices.

Cherrimisu

Inspired by traditional Italian tiramisu, this easy dessert dresses up a prepared angel food cake with a cherry cream filling and frosting. Dust the top with baking cocoa for a decadent finishing touch.

—**KELLY BYLER** GOSHEN, IN

START TO FINISH: 25 MIN.
MAKES: 12 SERVINGS

- 1 jar (10 ounces) maraschino cherries
- ½ cup ricotta cheese
- 4 ounces cream cheese, softened
- 2 tablespoons confectioners' sugar
- ¼ teaspoon cherry extract
- 1½ cups heavy whipping cream
- 1 prepared angel food cake (8 to 10 ounces)
- 1 tablespoon baking cocoa

1. Drain the cherries; reserving ¼ cup juice. In a large bowl, beat ricotta cheese, cream cheese, confectioners' sugar and extract until blended. Gradually beat in cream and reserved cherry juice until stiff peaks form.
2. Using a long serrated knife, cut cake horizontally in half. Place one cake layer on a serving plate; spread with 1 cup whipped cream mixture. Arrange cherries over cream layer. Top with remaining cake layer. Frost top and sides of cake with remaining cream mixture. Dust with cocoa.

TOP TIP

Ripening Trick

To ripen kiwifruit, place it in a brown paper bag with a banana or an apple and leave at room temperature. When they are ready to eat, kiwis should yield to slight pressure. Store ripe fruits in the refrigerator for up to 1 week.

Moist Lemon
Chiffon Cake

Moist Lemon Chiffon Cake

I think this cake is a real treat with its attractive drizzle of sweet-tart lemon glaze. For brunch, a coffee break or dessert, it's the kind of treat that's great for guests.

—REBECCA BAIRD SALT LAKE CITY, UT

PREP: 15 MIN. • **BAKE:** 45 MIN. + COOLING
MAKES: 16 SERVINGS

- ½ cup fat-free evaporated milk
- ½ cup reduced-fat sour cream
- ¼ cup lemon juice
- 2 tablespoons canola oil
- 2 teaspoons vanilla extract
- 1 teaspoon grated lemon peel
- 1 teaspoon lemon extract
- 2 cups cake flour
- 1½ cups sugar
- 1 tablespoon baking powder
- ½ teaspoon salt
- 1 cup egg whites (about 7)
- ½ teaspoon cream of tartar

LEMON GLAZE
- 1¾ cups confectioners' sugar
- 3 tablespoons lemon juice

1. In a large bowl, combine the first seven ingredients. Sift together the flour, sugar, baking powder and salt; gradually beat into lemon mixture until smooth. In a small bowl, beat egg whites until foamy. Add cream of tartar; beat until stiff peaks form. Gently fold into the lemon mixture.
2. Pour into an ungreased 10-in. tube pan. Bake at 325° for 45-55 minutes or until cake springs back when lightly touched. Immediately invert pan; cool completely. Remove cake to a serving platter. Combine glaze ingredients; drizzle over cake.

AUTUMN TREE CAKE
PAGE 153

Party & Theme Cakes

IF YOU'RE LOOKING FOR SOME SWEETS TO TOP OFF A HOLIDAY PARTY, A FEW CUTE CLASSROOM TREATS OR EVEN A MEMORABLE CONTRIBUTION TO A BAKE SALE, TURN TO THE EYE-APPEALING BITES FOUND HERE. BAKE UP A SNOW GLOBE CAKE, RED VELVET CREPES OR MINIATURE CASTLES THAT'LL HAVE EVERYONE'S SWEET TOOTH SINGING!

SHERBET CREAM CAKE
PAGE 156

CHIRPY CHICK CUPCAKES
PAGE 154

OCEAN CAKE
PAGE 160

**Summer Celebration
Ice Cream Cake**

Summer Celebration Ice Cream Cake

I wanted to make my youngest son an ice cream cake one year for his summer birthday because he prefers ice cream to traditional cake. He picked the flavors, and I decided to try my favorite brownie recipe as a crust. It worked!

—**KRISTA FRANK** RHODODENDRON, OR

PREP: 15 MIN. • **BAKE:** 20 MIN. + FREEZING
MAKES: 9 SERVINGS

- 1 cup sugar
- 3 tablespoons butter, melted
- 3 tablespoons orange yogurt
- 1 large egg
- 1 teaspoon grated orange peel
- 1 teaspoon vanilla extract
- ¾ cup all-purpose flour
- ⅓ cup baking cocoa
- 1 cup (6 ounces) semisweet chocolate chips
- 1¾ quarts vanilla ice cream, softened
- 4 to 6 ounces semisweet chocolate, chopped
- 1 tablespoon shortening
  Mixed fresh berries

1. Line an 8-in. square baking dish with foil and grease the foil; set aside. In a large bowl, combine the sugar, butter, yogurt, egg, orange peel and vanilla until blended. Combine flour and cocoa; stir into sugar mixture. Add chocolate chips.

2. Spread into prepared dish. Bake at 325° for 20-25 minutes or until a toothpick inserted near the center comes out with moist crumbs. Cool on a wire rack.

3. Spread ice cream over the cake. Cover and freeze for 3 hours or until firm.

4. Remove from the freezer 10 minutes before serving. In a microwave-safe bowl, melt chocolate and shortening; stir until smooth. Using foil, lift dessert out of dish; gently peel off the foil. Cut into squares. Garnish with mixed fresh berries and drizzle with chocolate.

Holiday Snow Globe Cake

Autumn Tree Cake

I love the changing colors that come with fall. I make this pretty cake using orange and yellow candy to celebrate.
—**MARIE PARKER** MILWAUKEE, WI

PREP: 40 MIN. • **BAKE:** 20 MIN. + COOLING
MAKES: 12 SERVINGS

- 1 package butter recipe golden cake mix (regular size)
- 1 cup orange juice
- ⅓ cup butter, softened
- 3 large eggs

FROSTING
- 6 cups confectioners' sugar
- ⅔ cup butter, softened
- Orange food coloring, optional
- 5 to 6 tablespoons orange juice
- ½ cup crushed chocolate wafers (about 8 wafers)
- 1 cup (6 ounces) semisweet chocolate chips
- 1 tablespoon shortening
- Assorted candy and chocolate leaves

1. Preheat oven to 350°. Line bottoms of two greased 9-in. round baking pans with parchment paper; grease paper. In a large bowl, combine the cake mix, orange juice, butter and eggs; beat on low speed 30 seconds. Beat on medium 2 minutes. Transfer to prepared pans. Bake 20-25 minutes or until a toothpick inserted in the center comes out clean. Cool in pans 10 minutes before removing to wire racks; remove paper. Cool completely.
2. For frosting, in a large bowl, beat confectioners' sugar, butter, if desired, food coloring and enough orange juice to achieve desired consistency. Spread frosting between layers and over top and sides of cake. Lightly press wafer crumbs onto sides of cake.
3. In a microwave-safe bowl, melt chocolate and shortening; stir until smooth. Transfer to a pastry bag or a food-safe plastic bag; cut a small hole in the tip of the bag. Pipe a tree on top of the cake. Decorate as desired with candy and chocolate leaves.

Holiday Snow Globe Cake

I can change up the decorations on this cake depending on the holiday—or birthday. My daughter loves this Christmas version.
—**MARIE LOUISE LUDWIG** PHOENIXVILLE, PA

PREP: 65 MIN. • **BAKE:** 25 MIN. + COOLING
MAKES: 12 SERVINGS

- 4 large eggs, separated
- ⅔ cup butter, softened
- 1 cup sugar, divided
- 2 tablespoons dark rum
- 2 cups cake flour
- 3 teaspoons baking powder
- ½ teaspoon salt
- ⅔ cup coconut milk

FROSTING/FILLING
- 1¼ cups heavy whipping cream
- 2 tablespoons confectioners' sugar
- ¾ teaspoon vanilla extract
- ¾ cup seedless raspberry jam
- 2 cups flaked coconut

DECORATIONS
- Frosted Christmas Tree (see below)
- Porcelain snowman ornament
- 8-inch glass bubble bowl (about 6-inch opening)

1. Preheat oven to 350°. Place egg whites in a large bowl; let stand at room temperature for 30 minutes. Line bottoms of two greased 8-in. round baking pans with parchment paper; grease paper.
2. In a large bowl, cream butter and ½ cup sugar until light and fluffy. Add egg yolks, one at a time, beating well after each addition. Beat in rum. In another bowl, whisk flour, baking powder and salt; add to creamed mixture alternately with coconut milk, beating well after each addition.
3. With clean beaters, beat egg whites on medium speed until soft peaks form. Gradually add remaining sugar, 1 tablespoon at a time, beating on high after each addition until the sugar is dissolved. Continue beating until stiff glossy peaks form. Fold into batter. Transfer batter to prepared pans.
4. Bake 20-25 minutes or until

a toothpick inserted in the center comes out clean. Cool in pans 10 minutes before removing to wire racks; remove paper. Cool completely.
5. Using a long serrated knife, trim tops of cakes if domed. In a large bowl, beat cream until it begins to thicken. Add confectioners' sugar and vanilla; beat until stiff peaks form.
6. Place one cake layer on a serving plate, bottom side down. Spread jam over top to within ¾ in. of edge; top with ½ cup whipped cream. Place second cake layer over whipped cream, bottom side up.
7. Spread remaining whipped cream over top and sides of cake; sprinkle with coconut. Refrigerate at least 15 minutes. Just before serving, place Frosted Christmas Tree and snowman on center of cake. Carefully invert bowl over decorations.

FROSTED CHRISTMAS TREE
Lightly brush a small star-shaped sugar cookie with corn syrup; sprinkle with silver edible glitter. For tree, tint canned vanilla frosting with green paste food coloring. Stack two ice cream sugar cones. Using a #32 open star tip, pipe tree branches onto top cone to resemble a pine tree. Decorate with candy-coated sunflower kernels or colored sprinkles; sprinkle with coarse sugar. Place star cookie at top.

⑤INGREDIENTS

Chirpy Chick Cupcakes

These adorable cupcakes are so much fun to make and share. They're perfect for an Easter dessert.

—**SARA MARTIN** BROOKFIELD, WI

START TO FINISH: 30 MIN.
MAKES: VARIES

- 1 to 2 cans vanilla frosting
(16 ounces each)
Yellow paste food coloring
Cupcakes of your choice
Miniature semisweet chocolate chips
Orange spice drop or candy corn

1. Set aside ¼ cup frosting for eyes. Tint remaining frosting yellow; transfer to a pastry bag. Insert #17 star tip; pipe stars to cover top of cupcake. Pipe a large ball for head. Place tip on each side of the head and pull out for each wing.

2. Place white icing in a pastry bag; insert #2 round tip. Pipe eyes and decorate with mini chocolate chips. For the beak, flatten an orange gum drop and cut into 2 triangles or add candy corn.

⑤INGREDIENTS *BIG BATCH*

Rainbow Cake with Clouds

Some cakes stand on their own without icing. For this Rainbow Cake, use a little whipped cream to make fluffy clouds.

—**JANET TIGCHELAAR** JERSEYVILLE, ON

PREP: 30 MIN. • **BAKE:** 40 MIN. + COOLING
MAKES: 16 SERVINGS

- 1 package white cake mix (regular size)
Purple, blue, green, yellow, orange and red paste food coloring
- 1 cup heavy whipping cream
- 3 tablespoons confectioners' sugar
- ½ teaspoon vanilla extract

1. Preheat oven to 325°. Grease and flour a 10-in. fluted tube pan. Prepare the cake mix according to package directions. Transfer 1⅓ cups batter to prepared pan; spread evenly. Reserve an additional 2 tablespoons batter in a small bowl.

2. Divide remaining batter into six separate bowls, tinting each with the food coloring to make the following: 2 tablespoons purple batter, ¼ cup blue batter, ⅓ cup green batter, ½ cup yellow batter, ⅔ cup orange batter, and the remaining batter red.

3. Fill six small food-safe plastic bags with a different color batter. Cut a hole in a corner of the red batter bag; pipe a wide ring onto white batter to within ½ in. of pan edges. Pipe a ring of orange in the middle of the red ring, leaving some red visible on each side. Repeat by piping remaining colors in the middle of the previous layer, in rainbow color

order. (Each ring will be narrower than the previous layer.) Fill a bag with reserved white batter; pipe over purple ring only.

4. Bake 40-45 minutes or until a toothpick inserted in the center comes out clean. Cool completely in pan on a wire rack.

5. Remove cake from pan; place on a serving plate. In a bowl, beat cream until it begins to thicken. Add confectioners' sugar and vanilla; beat until soft peaks form. Serve with whipped cream clouds.

NOTE *To remove cakes easily, use solid shortening to grease plain and fluted tube pans.*

Rainbow Cake with Clouds

BIG BATCH
Easter Basket Cupcakes

My mother and I would make these when I was growing up, and I had just as much fun sharing the same experience with my own children when they were young.
—**KATHY KITTELL** LENEXA, KS

PREP: 35 MIN. • **BAKE:** 20 MIN. + COOLING
MAKES: 2½ DOZEN

- 4 large eggs
- 1 cup sugar
- 1 cup packed brown sugar
- 1 cup canola oil
- 3 teaspoons vanilla extract
- 3 cups all-purpose flour
- 2 teaspoons baking powder
- 2 teaspoons ground cinnamon
- 1 teaspoon salt
- 1 teaspoon baking soda
- ½ teaspoon ground ginger
- ¼ teaspoon ground nutmeg
- ¾ cup buttermilk
- 1 pound carrots, grated
- 2 cups chopped walnuts, toasted
- 1 can (8 ounces) crushed pineapple, drained
- 1 cup flaked coconut

FROSTING/DECORATIONS
- 1 package (8 ounces) cream cheese, softened
- ½ cup butter, softened
- 1 teaspoon grated orange peel
- 1 teaspoon vanilla extract
- 4 cups confectioners' sugar
- 1 teaspoon water
- 6 drops green food coloring
- 3 cups flaked coconut
  Optional candies: jelly beans, bunny Peeps candy and Sour Punch straws

1. Preheat oven to 350°. Line 30 muffin cups with paper liners. In a large bowl, beat eggs, sugars, oil and vanilla until well blended. In another bowl, whisk flour, baking powder, cinnamon, salt, baking soda, ginger and nutmeg; add to egg mixture alternately with buttermilk, beating well after each addition. Stir in carrots, walnuts, pineapple and coconut.
2. Fill prepared cups three-fourths full. Bake 20-25 minutes or until a toothpick inserted in the center comes out clean. Cool in pans for 10 minutes before removing to wire racks to cool completely.
3. In a large bowl, beat cream cheese and butter until blended. Beat in the orange peel and vanilla. Gradually beat in confectioners' sugar until smooth. Frost cupcakes.
4. In a large resealable plastic bag, mix water and food coloring; add coconut. Seal bag and shake until coconut is evenly tinted. Sprinkle over cupcakes. Decorate with candies, as desired. Refrigerate until serving.
NOTE *To toast nuts, bake in a shallow pan in a 350° oven for 5-10 minutes or cook in a skillet over low heat until lightly browned, stirring occasionally.*

Easter Basket Cupcakes

❝The recipe for the carrot cake itself was very tasty and moist. Everyone thought these were good and very cute. The frosting was also very good.❞
—**MILLSAPM**
FROM TASTEOFHOME.COM

Chocolate Peppermint Log

FREEZE IT

Chocolate Peppermint Log

What a great make-ahead dessert! It's perfect for the holidays because you can make it when you have time, store it in the freezer and scratch dessert off of your to-do list.

—BRENDA SINCLAIR PRINCETON, MO

PREP: 35 MIN. + CHILLING
BAKE: 15 MIN. + COOLING
MAKES: 12 SERVINGS

- 3 **large eggs, separated**
- ½ **cup all-purpose flour**
- ⅓ **cup baking cocoa**
- ½ **teaspoon baking powder**
- ¼ **teaspoon baking soda**
- ⅛ **teaspoon salt**
- ⅓ **cup plus ½ cup sugar, divided**
- ⅓ **cup water**
- 1 **teaspoon vanilla extract**

FILLING
- 1 **package (8 ounces) reduced-fat cream cheese**
- ½ **cup sugar**
- 1 **carton (8 ounces) frozen reduced-fat whipped topping, thawed**
- ¼ **cup crushed peppermint candies**

GLAZE
- 5 **teaspoons butter**
- 2 **tablespoons baking cocoa**
- 2 **tablespoons water**
- 1 **cup confectioners' sugar**
- ½ **teaspoon vanilla extract**
- 2 **tablespoons crushed peppermint candies**

1. Place egg whites in a small bowl; let stand at room temperature 30 minutes.
2. Meanwhile, preheat oven to 375°. Line the bottom of a 15x10x1-in. baking pan with parchment paper. Sift flour, cocoa, baking powder, baking soda and salt twice.
3. In a large bowl, beat egg yolks until slightly thickened. Gradually add ⅓ cup sugar, beating on high speed until thick and lemon-colored. Beat in water and vanilla. Fold in flour mixture (batter will be very thick).
4. With clean beaters, beat egg whites on medium until soft peaks form. Gradually add the remaining sugar, 1 tablespoon at a time, beating on high after each addition until sugar is dissolved. Continue beating until soft glossy peaks form. Fold a fourth of the whites into batter, then fold in the remaining whites. Transfer to prepared pan, spreading evenly.
5. Bake 12-15 minutes or until top springs back when lightly touched. Cool 5 minutes. Invert onto a kitchen towel dusted with cocoa. Gently peel off paper. Roll up cake in the towel jelly-roll style, starting with a short side. Cool completely on a wire rack.
6. For filling, in a large bowl, beat cream cheese and sugar until smooth. Fold in whipped topping and crushed peppermint candies.
7. Unroll cake; spread filling over cake to within ½ in. of edges. Roll up again, without the towel. Place on a platter, seam side down. Refrigerate, covered, until cold.
8. For glaze, in a small saucepan, melt butter. Whisk in cocoa and water until blended. Bring to a boil. Remove from heat. Whisk in confectioners' sugar and vanilla until smooth. Cool slightly.
9. Spread glaze over cake. Sprinkle with peppermint candies. Refrigerate until set, about 10 minutes.
FREEZE OPTION *Securely wrap and freeze cake before glazing. To use, thaw wrapped cake in refrigerator overnight. Unwrap cake and glaze as directed.*

BIG BATCH

Sherbet Cream Cake

For an Easter ice cream social, it doesn't get any more showstopping than this. In my family, this is how we celebrate special occasions and birthdays. It takes a little time to prepare, but it's easy and turns out beautiful and delicious!

—PAULA WIPF ARLINGTON, VA

PREP: 30 MIN. + FREEZING
MAKES: 14-16 SERVINGS

- 3 **cups each raspberry, orange and lime sherbet**
- 3 **quarts vanilla ice cream, softened, divided**
- 2 **cups chopped pecans, divided**
- 2 **cups miniature semisweet chocolate chips, divided**
- 3 **cups heavy whipping cream, whipped Raspberries and orange and lime slices, optional**

1. Using a ¼-cup ice cream scoop, shape sherbet into balls. Place on a waxed paper-lined baking sheet. Freeze for 1 hour or until firm.
2. In a large bowl, combine 1 qt. vanilla ice cream, 1 cup pecans and 1 cup chocolate chips. Spread into a 10-in. tube pan.
3. Alternately arrange 12 sherbet balls, four of each color, against the center tube and outer edge of pan. Freeze for 30 minutes.
4. Spread with 1 qt. ice cream; freeze for 30 minutes. Top with remaining sherbet balls. Combine remaining ice cream, pecans and chips; spread over sherbet balls. Cover and freeze overnight.
5. Run a knife around edge of pan; dip pan in lukewarm water until loosened. Invert cake onto a serving plate. Frost with whipped cream. Return to freezer. Remove from freezer 10 minutes before serving. Garnish with raspberries and orange and lime slices if desired.

Miniature Castle Cakes

You can easily make several of these pretty palaces with a boxed cake mix, canned frosting and a few common confections. Grab a goblet of milk and enjoy one with your prince or princess.

—*TASTE OF HOME* **TEST KITCHEN**

PREP: 45 MIN. • **BAKE:** 20 MIN. + COOLING
MAKES: 6 CAKES

- 1 **package white cake mix (regular size)**
- 2½ **cups vanilla frosting**
- 2 **milk chocolate candy bars (1.55 ounces each)**
- 27 **nonpareil candies**
- 12 **pretzel sticks**
- ½ **cup flaked coconut**
- 1 **drop blue food coloring**
- 3 **sticks Fruit Stripe gum**
- 6 **small ice cream sugar cones**
- 36 **star sprinkles**

1. Prepare cake mix according to package directions. Pour batter into a greased 11x7-in. baking pan and six greased muffin cups. Bake at 350° for 20-30 minutes for cake and 15-18 minutes for cupcakes or until a toothpick comes out clean. Cool cupcakes for 5 minutes and cake for 10 minutes before removing from pans to wire racks.

2. Cut the cake into six square pieces; place on serving plates. Frost tops and sides of cakes. Position a cupcake on top of each; frost cupcakes.

3. For the drawbridges, divide each candy bar into four three-piece sections. Center one section on one side of each cake; gently press into the cake. Divide the two remaining chocolate sections into three pieces; place one piece above each drawbridge for a door. Cut three nonpareil candies in half; arrange a half circle above each door. Press pretzels into cake on each side of bridge.

4. In a resealable plastic bag, shake coconut and food coloring until coconut is evenly colored. Sprinkle around bases of castles to represent water in the moat. Cut each stick of gum in half widthwise; cut one end to form a flag. Trim sugar cone tips; dot with frosting, and attach flags to frosted cone tips.

5. Place three nonpareil candies on each cupcake for windows. Frost backs of remaining candies; place one on the front of each cone. Attach star sprinkles to cones. Position cones on cupcakes.

Miniature Castle Cakes

Sunshine Cake

BIG BATCH
Sunshine Cake

I brought this cake to the county fair for 4-H and easily took home a purple ribbon. For a quicker lemon filling, use a cup of lemon curd from a jar.
—**LEAH WILL** BEL AIRE, KS

PREP: 1 HOUR + CHILLING
BAKE: 25 MIN. + COOLING
MAKES: 16 SERVINGS

- 1 cup butter, softened
- 1⅔ cups sugar
- 4 large eggs
- 1½ teaspoons vanilla extract
- 1½ teaspoons each grated lemon, orange and lime peel
- 2¾ cups all-purpose flour
- 3 teaspoons baking powder
- ¾ teaspoon salt
- 1 cup 2% milk

FILLING
- ½ cup sugar
- ¼ cup cornstarch
- ¼ teaspoon salt
- ¾ cup water
- 2 large egg yolks
- 2 tablespoons butter
- ⅓ cup lemon juice

FROSTING
- ½ cup butter, softened
- 3¾ cups confectioners' sugar
- ¼ cup light corn syrup
- 3 tablespoons orange juice
- 1 teaspoon vanilla extract
- ½ teaspoon grated orange peel
  Dash salt
- 3 drops yellow food coloring
- 1 drop red food coloring
  Assorted lollipops, unwrapped

1. Preheat oven to 350°. Line bottom of a greased 15x10x1-in. jelly-roll pan with parchment paper; grease paper.
2. In a large bowl, cream butter and sugar until light and fluffy. Add eggs, one at a time, beating well after each addition. Beat in vanilla and citrus peels. In another bowl, whisk flour, baking powder and salt; add to creamed mixture alternately with milk, beating well after each addition.
3. Transfer to prepared pan. Bake 25-30 minutes or until a toothpick inserted in the center comes out clean. Cool in pan for 5 minutes before removing to a wire rack; remove paper. Cool completely.
4. For the filling, in a small saucepan, combine sugar, cornstarch and salt. Whisk in water. Cook and stir over medium heat until thickened and bubbly. Remove from heat.
5. In a small bowl, whisk a small amount of hot mixture into egg yolks; return all to pan, whisking constantly. Bring to a gentle boil; cook and stir 2 minutes. Remove from heat. Stir in butter. Gently stir in lemon juice. Press plastic wrap onto surface of filling; cool slightly. Refrigerate until cold.
6. For frosting, in a large bowl, cream butter until fluffy. Beat in confectioners' sugar, corn syrup, orange juice, vanilla, orange peel and salt until smooth. Tint orange with yellow and red food coloring.
7. Trim edges of cake; cut crosswise into thirds. Place one cake layer on a serving plate; spread with half of the filling. Repeat layers. Top with remaining cake layer. Frost the top and sides of cake with frosting. Insert lollipops in top for flowers. Refrigerate leftovers.

TO MAKE A WINDOW BOX CAKE
For window box, press 28 cream-filled wafer cookies against sides of cake. Tie two shoestring licorice together to make longer strands. Wrap and tie strands around window box. For flowers, cut Fruit Roll-Ups with flower-shaped cutters. Sandwich two cutouts around each unwrapped small lollipop, moistening edges with water. For stems and leaves, insert drinking straws in cake. Top with lollipop flowers. Cut leaves from green licorice twists and insert in cake.

Giant Cupcake Pumpkin

BIG BATCH
Giant Cupcake Pumpkin

Make a smiley statement by decorating a whole tray of chocolate-spice cupcakes. Once everyone's seen the big picture, they can each take a treat.
—**GENA LOTT** OGDEN, UT

PREP: 35 MIN. • **BAKE:** 20 MIN. + COOLING
MAKES: 26 CUPCAKES

- 1 package spice cake mix (regular size)
- 1 cup solid-pack pumpkin
- 1 cup water
- 2 large eggs
- 1 cup (6 ounces) miniature semisweet chocolate chips
- 2 cans (16 ounces each) vanilla frosting
- 1 teaspoon maple flavoring
  Orange food coloring
  Reese's pieces

1. Preheat oven to 350°. Line 26 muffin cups with paper liners.
2. In a large bowl, combine cake mix, pumpkin, water and eggs; beat on low speed 30 seconds. Beat on medium 2 minutes. Stir in chocolate chips. Fill prepared cups two-thirds full.
3. Bake 16-20 minutes or until a toothpick inserted in the center comes out clean. Cool in pans for 10 minutes before removing to wire racks to cool completely.
4. In a large bowl, beat the frosting and flavoring; tint frosting orange. Arrange cupcakes on a large platter, forming a pumpkin. Spread frosting over the cupcakes. Decorate with Reese's pieces.

Ocean Cake

Whether it's for a pool or birthday party, this fish-themed cake will snag smiles from kids of all ages!

—**TASTE OF HOME** TEST KITCHEN

PREP: 30 MIN. • **BAKE:** 25 MIN. + COOLING
MAKES: 12 SERVINGS

- **1   package white cake mix (regular size)**
- **2⅔ cups canned vanilla frosting**
  Blue and green Fruit Roll-Ups
  Fish candies
  Black shoestring licorice
  Candy stick

1. Prepare and bake cake according to package directions, using two greased 9-in. round baking pans. Cool for 10 minutes before removing from pans to wire racks to cool completely.
2. Spread 1⅔ cups frosting between layers and over top and sides of cake. Using the back of a spoon, make waves on top of the cake with remaining frosting.
3. Cut wave shapes out of Fruit Roll-Ups; gently press along bottom of cake. Arrange additional wave shapes and fish candies on top of cake as desired. Tie licorice on one end of candy stick to create a fishing pole.

HOW-TO *To create ocean waves, smooth frosting first. Then use the back of a spoon to make a small twisting motion in one direction. Next, move spoon over slightly and make another twist the opposite way. Repeat. Cut the Fruit Roll-Ups in half vertically. Then fold in half, keeping the plastic sides together. Cut into wave shapes.*

❝I made a variation of this for my son's 6th birthday. Instead of gummy fish, I used sharks.❞

—PIERSTAR
FROM TASTEOFHOME.COM

Red Velvet Crepe Cakes

It's well worth the time to make this absolutely stunning cake. Each thin layer is separated by a rich and creamy filling. Treat your family on special occasions with this cake.

—**CRYSTAL HEATON** ALTON, UT

PREP: 1¼ HOURS • **COOK:** 25 MIN.
MAKES: 2 CREPE CAKES (8 SERVINGS EACH)

- **1   package red velvet cake mix (regular size)**
- **2¾ cups whole milk**
- **1   cup all-purpose flour**
- **3   large eggs**
- **3   large egg yolks**
- **¼   cup butter, melted**
- **3   teaspoons vanilla extract**

FROSTING
- **2   packages (8 ounces each) cream cheese, softened**
- **1¼ cups butter, softened**
- **½   teaspoon salt**
- **12 cups confectioners' sugar**
- **5   teaspoons vanilla extract**
  Fresh blueberries

1. In a large bowl, combine the cake mix, milk, flour, eggs, egg yolks, butter and vanilla; beat on low speed for 30 seconds. Beat on medium for 2 minutes.
2. Heat a lightly greased 8-in. nonstick skillet over medium heat; pour ¼ cup batter into center of skillet. Lift and tilt pan to coat bottom evenly. Cook until top appears dry; turn and cook for 15-20 seconds longer. Remove to a wire rack. Repeat with remaining batter, greasing skillet as needed. When cool, stack crepes with waxed paper or paper towels in between.
3. For frosting, in a large bowl, beat the cream cheese, butter and salt until fluffy. Add confectioners' sugar and vanilla; beat until smooth.
4. To assemble two crepe cakes, place one crepe on each of two cake plates. Spread each with one rounded tablespoon frosting to within ½ in. of edges. Repeat layers until all crepes are used. Spread remaining frosting over tops and sides of crepe cakes. Garnish with blueberries.

Red Velvet Crepe Cakes

Sunny Flower Cake

(5) INGREDIENTS *BIG BATCH*

Sunny Flower Cake

I made this cake for my niece's 4th birthday party and again for a baby shower. Both times, it was the hit of the party!

—**DEBRA HARASZKIEWICZ** CEMENT CITY, MI

PREP: 1 HOUR
MAKES: 1 CAKE (19 SERVINGS)

  19 cupcakes of your choice
     Frosting of your choice
     Food coloring
     Assorted cake decorations

1. Place one cupcake in the center of a large platter; arrange six cupcakes around the center cupcake. Add an outer ring of remaining cupcakes, forming a flower shape.

2. Tint frosting as desired; generously spread over tops of cupcakes. Pipe on additional frosting to define the flower petals and the center. Decorate as desired.

TOP TIP

Evenly Divided

To easily fill cupcake liners or muffin cups, our Test Kitchen prefers to use a dry measuring cup if the batter is thin and a spring-loaded ice cream scoop for thicker batters. This assures that the batter is divided evenly.

Creative Cake

If you have patience and strong hands ready for kneading, I suggest making the fondant yourself. Whether you use store-bought or homemade, this artistic cake will get rave reviews.

—**KATIE MOLITOR** CEDAR, MN

PREP: 2 HOURS
MAKES: 12 SERVINGS

     Two-layer cake of your choice
       (9 inches)
     Frosting of your choice
       (in a pale color)
     White and dark brown ready-to-use
       rolled fondant
     New paintbrush
  1 tablespoon clear vanilla extract
     or water
     White pearl dragees
     Fresh strawberries

1. Place cake on a serving platter; spread frosting between layers and over top and sides of cake (save 2 teaspoons frosting for decorating the cake).

2. Roll out white fondant into a 16-in. circle; place over cake. Smooth top and sides of cake; trim excess. (Keep unused fondant wrapped in plastic wrap to prevent it from drying out.)

3. Roll brown fondant into a 16x4-in. rectangle; cut with a 3x2-in. diamond-shaped cookie cutter. Dip paintbrush in vanilla; lightly brush over a diamond. Secure diamond to side of cake. Repeat. Decorate with dragees, securing with reserved frosting. Top with strawberries.

COCONUT FRUITCAKE
PAGE 173

Tube & Pound Cakes

THESE BEAUTIFULLY SHAPED CAKES ARE MOIST AND FLAVORFUL. IF YOU ARE LOOKING FOR SOMETHING TO HAVE WITH YOUR COFFEE OR SHARE AT A BREAKFAST OR BRUNCH, YOU'LL FIND A TERRIFIC RECIPE WITHIN THESE PAGES. EVERYONE WILL BE ASKING FOR SECONDS!

SOUR CREAM BUNDT COFFEE CAKE
PAGE 165

ALMOND FUDGE CAKES
PAGE 171

BLUEBERRY BOUNTY CAKE
PAGE 169

Sparkling Cider
Pound Cake

Sparkling Cider Pound Cake

I love everything about this pound cake!
It's incredible and completely reminds me
of fall with every bite. Using sparkling apple
cider in the batter and in the glaze gives it
a delicious and unique flavor.

—**NIKKI BARTON** PROVIDENCE, UT

PREP: 20 MIN. • **BAKE:** 40 MIN. + COOLING
MAKES: 12 SERVINGS

¾ **cup butter, softened**
1½ **cups sugar**
3 **large eggs**
1½ **cups all-purpose flour**
¼ **teaspoon baking powder**
¼ **teaspoon salt**
½ **cup sparkling apple cider**
GLAZE
¾ **cup confectioners' sugar**
3 **to 4 teaspoons sparkling apple cider**

1. Preheat oven to 350°. Line the
bottom of a greased 9x5-in. loaf pan
with parchment paper; grease paper.
2. In a large bowl, cream butter and
sugar until light and fluffy. Add eggs,
one at a time, beating well after each
addition. In another bowl, whisk flour,
baking powder and salt; add to creamed
mixture alternately with cider, beating
well after each addition.
3. Transfer to pan. Bake 40-50 minutes
or until a toothpick inserted in the center
comes out clean. Cool in the pan for
10 minutes before removing to a wire
rack to cool completely.
4. In a small bowl, mix glaze ingredients
until smooth; spoon over top of cake,
allowing it to flow over the sides.

**❝The cake is easy
to make, and it didn't
survive the night
I made it!❞**

—**CINDYCAR**
FROM TASTEOFHOME.COM

BIG BATCH

Sour Cream Bundt Coffee Cake

You won't even need the cup of coffee with this yummy and moist cake! Make it for your next get-together—your guests will thank you.

—**KATHLEEN LARIMER** DAYTON, OH

PREP: 40 MIN. • **BAKE:** 45 MIN. + COOLING
MAKES: 16 SERVINGS

- ⅔ **cup chopped pecans**
- 2 **tablespoons brown sugar**
- 1½ **teaspoons ground cinnamon**

BATTER
- 1 **cup butter, softened**
- 2 **cups sugar**
- 2 **large eggs**
- ½ **teaspoon vanilla extract**
- 2 **cups all-purpose flour**
- 1 **teaspoon baking powder**
- ¼ **teaspoon baking soda**
- ¼ **teaspoon salt**
- 1 **cup (8 ounces) sour cream**
  Confectioners' sugar

1. Preheat oven to 350°. In a small bowl, combine pecans, brown sugar and cinnamon; set aside. In a large bowl, cream butter and sugar until light and fluffy. Add eggs, one at a time, beating well after each addition. Beat in vanilla. Combine flour, baking powder, baking soda and salt; add to creamed mixture alternately with sour cream, beating well after each addition.

2. Pour half of the batter into a greased and floured 10-in. fluted tube pan; sprinkle with half of the pecan mixture. Gently top with the remaining batter and pecan mixture.

3. Bake 45-50 minutes or until a toothpick inserted in the center comes out clean. Cool for 10 minutes before removing from pan to a wire rack to cool completely. Sprinkle with confectioners' sugar.

Lemon-Blueberry Pound Cake

Lemon-Blueberry Pound Cake

Pair a slice of this soft cake with a scoop of vanilla ice cream and you won't be disappointed. Mmmm!

—**REBECCA LITTLE** PARK RIDGE, IL

PREP: 25 MIN. • **BAKE:** 55 MIN. + COOLING
MAKES: 12 SERVINGS

- ⅓ **cup butter, softened**
- 4 **ounces cream cheese, softened**
- 2 **cups sugar**
- 3 **large eggs**
- 1 **large egg white**
- 1 **tablespoon grated lemon peel**
- 2 **teaspoons vanilla extract**
- 2 **cups fresh or frozen unsweetened blueberries**
- 3 **cups all-purpose flour, divided**
- 1 **teaspoon baking powder**
- ½ **teaspoon baking soda**
- ½ **teaspoon salt**
- 1 **cup (8 ounces) lemon yogurt**

GLAZE
- 1¼ **cups confectioners' sugar**
- 2 **tablespoons lemon juice**

1. Preheat oven to 350°. Grease and flour a 10-in. fluted tube pan. In a large bowl, cream the butter, cream cheese and sugar until blended. Add eggs and egg white, one at a time, beating well after each addition. Beat in lemon peel and vanilla.

2. Toss blueberries with 2 tablespoons of flour. In another bowl, mix the remaining flour with baking powder, baking soda and salt; add to creamed mixture alternately with the yogurt, beating after each addition just until combined. Fold in blueberry mixture.

3. Transfer batter to prepared pan. Bake 55-60 minutes or until a toothpick inserted in the center comes out clean. Cool in the pan for 10 minutes before removing to wire rack; cool completely.

4. In a small bowl, mix confectioners' sugar and lemon juice until smooth. Drizzle over cake.

NOTE *For easier removal of cake, use solid shortening when greasing a fluted or plain tube pan.*

Molly's Sweet and Spicy Tzimmes Cake

Fluted Lemon Cake with Fresh Fruit

Bake this citrusy, golden-brown cake in a fancy fluted tube pan, and it will look especially beautiful. Serve each slice with a dollop of whipped cream and fresh fruit.

—**DONNA POCHODAY-STELMACH**
MORRISTOWN, NJ

PREP: 20 MIN. • **BAKE:** 1 HOUR + COOLING
MAKES: 12 SERVINGS

- 1 cup butter, softened
- 2 cups sugar
- 4 large eggs
- 2 tablespoons grated lemon peel
- 1 teaspoon lemon extract
- 2½ cups all-purpose flour
- 2 teaspoons baking powder
- ½ teaspoon salt
- 1 cup (8 ounces) fat-free strawberry Greek yogurt
  Confectioners' sugar, optional
  Assorted fresh fruit
  Whipped cream

1. Preheat oven to 325°. Grease and flour a 10-in. fluted tube pan. In a large bowl, cream butter and sugar until light and fluffy. Add eggs, one at a time, beating well after each addition. Beat in lemon peel and extract.
2. In another bowl, whisk flour, baking powder and salt; add to creamed mixture alternately with yogurt, beating well after each addition.
3. Transfer to prepared pan. Bake 60-70 minutes or until a toothpick inserted in the center comes out clean. Cool in pan for 10 minutes before removing to a wire rack to cool completely. If desired, dust with confectioners' sugar. Serve with fresh fruit and whipped cream.
NOTE *For easier removal of cake, use solid shortening when greasing a fluted or plain tube pan.*

Molly's Sweet and Spicy Tzimmes Cake

My husband and I are always looking for new ways to incorporate Jewish traditions into our interfaith home. Rich with apples, carrots and sweet potato, this sweet and spicy cake is perfect for Rosh Hashanah or any fall holiday.

—**MOLLY HAENDLER** PHILADELPHIA, PA

PREP: 35 MIN. • **BAKE:** 45 MIN. + COOLING
MAKES: 12 SERVINGS

- 1 cup sugar
- ½ cup canola oil
- 2 large eggs
- 1 cup mashed sweet potatoes
- ¼ cup white wine or orange juice
- 1 tablespoon lemon juice
- 1 teaspoon vanilla extract
- 1⅔ cups all-purpose flour
- 3 teaspoons grated orange peel
- 1 teaspoon baking soda
- ½ teaspoon baking powder
- ½ teaspoon salt
- ½ teaspoon ground ginger
- ½ teaspoon ground cinnamon
- ¼ teaspoon ground cloves
- 1 large tart apple, peeled and chopped
- 1 cup dried cranberries
- 1 cup shredded carrots
- ½ cup golden raisins

1. Preheat oven to 350°. Grease and flour a 10-in. fluted tube pan.
2. In a large bowl, beat sugar and oil until blended. Add eggs, one at a time, beating well after each addition. Beat in sweet potatoes, wine, lemon juice and vanilla.
3. In another bowl, whisk flour, orange peel, baking soda, baking powder, salt and spices; gradually beat into sweet potato mixture. Gently fold in apple, cranberries, carrots and raisins.
4. Transfer the batter to prepared pan. Bake 45-55 minutes or until a toothpick inserted in the center comes out clean. Cool in the pan for 10 minutes before removing to a wire rack to cool.
NOTE *For easier removal of cake, use solid shortening when greasing a fluted or plain tube pan.*

Fluted Lemon Cake with Fresh Fruit

Aunt Lou's Fresh Apple Cake

My great aunt Lou made a luscious apple cake that became a family tradition. My mom makes it for our annual beach trip to the Outer Banks.

—**CRISTY KING** SCOTT DEPOT, WV

PREP: 15 MIN. • **BAKE:** 50 MIN. + COOLING
MAKES: 12 SERVINGS

- 2 **cups sugar**
- 1 **cup canola oil**
- 3 **large eggs**
- 2 **teaspoons vanilla extract**
- 3 **cups all-purpose flour**
- 1 **teaspoon salt**
- 1 **teaspoon baking powder**
- 3 **cups chopped peeled apples (about 3 medium)**

1. Preheat oven to 350°. Grease and flour a 10-in. fluted tube pan.
2. In a large bowl, beat sugar, oil, eggs and vanilla until well blended. In another bowl, whisk flour, salt and baking powder; gradually beat into oil mixture. Stir in apples. Transfer batter to prepared pan.
3. Bake 50-60 minutes or until a toothpick inserted in the center comes out clean. Cool in pan for 10 minutes. Run a knife around sides and center tube of the pan. Remove cake to a wire rack to cool.
NOTE *For easier removal of cake, use solid shortening when greasing a fluted or plain tube pan.*

Aunt Lou's Fresh Apple Cake

Blueberry Bounty Cake

You'll have a hard time deciding whether to serve this blueberry beauty for dessert, breakfast or brunch. Don't worry if the berries sink to the bottom; it makes a lovely presentation when the cake is inverted.

—ALICE TESCH WATERTOWN, WI

PREP: 20 MIN. • **BAKE:** 45 MIN. + COOLING
MAKES: 12 SERVINGS (1 CUP SAUCE)

- 1½ cups butter, softened
- 1¾ cups sugar
- 4 large eggs
- 1 tablespoon grated lemon peel
- 2 teaspoons vanilla extract
- 3 cups cake flour
- 2½ teaspoons baking powder
- ¼ teaspoon salt
- 1 cup lemonade
- 1½ cups fresh or frozen blueberries

BLUEBERRY SAUCE

- 2 teaspoons cornstarch
- ¼ cup sugar
- ¼ cup water
- 1 cup fresh or frozen blueberries, thawed

1. In a large bowl, cream butter and sugar until light and fluffy. Add eggs, one at a time, beating well after each addition. Beat in lemon peel and vanilla.
2. Combine flour, baking powder and salt; add to creamed mixture alternately with lemonade, beating well after each addition. Fold in blueberries.
3. Pour into a greased and floured 10-in. fluted tube pan. Bake at 350° for 45-50 minutes or until a toothpick inserted near the center comes out clean. Cool for 20 minutes before removing from pan to a wire rack to cool completely.
4. In a small saucepan, combine the cornstarch and sugar. Stir in water until smooth. Add blueberries; bring to a boil over medium heat, stirring constantly. Cook and stir 1 minute longer or until thickened. Serve warm with cake.
NOTE *If using frozen blueberries, use without thawing to avoid discoloring the batter.*

Coconut Pound Cake
with Lime Glaze

BIG BATCH

Coconut Pound Cake with Lime Glaze

I have made several versions of this recipe, and this one is my favorite. The lime glaze adds an additional layer of flavor to an already terrific cake. Oven temps will vary, so if the cake is not done after 1 hour and 20 minutes, place back in oven for another 5 minutes and continue cooking in 5-minute intervals until it's done. Do not use bottled lime juice for the glaze. Only pure lime juice works.

—JO MCFARLAND STERLING, VA

PREP: 30 MIN. • **BAKE:** 1¼ HOURS MIN. + COOLING
MAKES: 16 SERVINGS

- 1½ cups butter, softened
- 1 package (8 ounces) cream cheese, softened
- 3 cups sugar
- 6 large eggs, room temperature
- 2 teaspoons coconut extract
- 1 teaspoon vanilla extract
- ⅛ teaspoon almond extract
- 3 cups all-purpose flour
- ½ teaspoon baking powder
- ½ teaspoon salt
- 2 cups flaked coconut

GLAZE

- ½ cup sugar
- ¼ cup lime juice
- 1 teaspoon grated lime peel
- 1 teaspoon coconut extract
  Toasted flaked coconut, optional

1. Preheat oven to 350°. Grease and flour a 10-in. fluted tube pan.
2. In a large bowl, cream butter, cream cheese and sugar until light and fluffy. Add eggs, one at a time, beating well after each addition. Beat in extracts. In another bowl, whisk flour, baking powder and salt; gradually beat into creamed mixture just until combined. Fold in coconut.
3. Transfer batter to prepared pan. Bake for 75-85 minutes or until a toothpick inserted in the center comes out clean. Cool in pan for 20 minutes before removing to a wire rack to cool completely.
4. In a small saucepan, combine glaze ingredients. Cook and stir over medium heat 2-3 minutes or until sugar is dissolved. Brush over cake. If desired, sprinkle with coconut.

Holiday Cranberry Eggnog Cake

Got eggnog and cranberries? I use both in this tasty cake for the holidays. It's delicious with a sweet topping of whipped cream and mascarpone.

—ROXANNE PEELEN FRANKLIN, WI

PREP: 15 MIN. • **BAKE:** 40 MIN. + COOLING
MAKES: 12 SERVINGS

- 1 package yellow cake mix (regular size)
- 1½ cups eggnog
- 3 large eggs
- ¼ cup butter, softened
- 2 teaspoons ground nutmeg
- 1 teaspoon vanilla extract
- 1 cup dried cranberries

MASCARPONE TOPPING

- ½ cup heavy whipping cream
- 1 carton (8 ounces) mascarpone cheese
- 2 tablespoons confectioners' sugar
- ½ teaspoon vanilla extract
  Additional ground nutmeg

1. Preheat oven to 350°. Grease and flour a 10-in. fluted tube pan. In a large bowl, combine cake mix, eggnog, eggs, butter, nutmeg and vanilla; beat on low speed 30 seconds. Beat on medium speed 2 minutes. Fold in cranberries.
2. Transfer to prepared pan. Bake 40-45 minutes or until a toothpick inserted in the center comes out clean. Cool in pan for 10 minutes before removing from pan to a wire rack to cool completely.
3. For topping, in a small bowl, beat cream until stiff peaks form. In another small bowl, mix mascarpone cheese, confectioners' sugar and vanilla just until combined. Fold in whipped cream. Serve with cake; sprinkle with additional nutmeg.
NOTE *This recipe was tested with commercially prepared eggnog.*

Pistachio Cake with Walnuts

Pistachio Cake with Walnuts

It didn't take long for this dessert to become my husband's favorite birthday cake. The frosting gives it an extra appetizing look.

—PATTY LANOUE STEARNS
TRAVERSE CITY, MI

PREP: 20 MIN. • **BAKE:** 40 MIN. + COOLING
MAKES: 12 SERVINGS

- 1 package white cake mix (regular size)
- 1 package (3.4 ounces) instant pistachio pudding mix
- 3 large eggs
- 1 cup club soda
- ¾ cup canola oil
- 1 cup chopped walnuts

FROSTING

- 1 package (3.4 ounces) instant pistachio pudding mix
- 1 cup 2% milk
- 1 carton (8 ounces) frozen whipped topping, thawed

1. Preheat oven to 350°. Grease and flour a 10-in. fluted tube pan.
2. In a large bowl, combine the first five ingredients; beat on low speed 30 seconds. Beat on medium speed 2 minutes. Fold in walnuts. Transfer to prepared pan. Bake 40-45 minutes or until a toothpick inserted in the center comes out clean. Cool in pan for 10 minutes before removing to a wire rack to cool completely.
3. For frosting, in a large bowl, combine pudding mix and milk; beat on low speed 1 minute. Fold in the whipped topping. Spread over cake. Refrigerate leftovers.
NOTE *For easier removal of cake, use solid shortening when greasing a fluted or plain tube pan.*

Almond Fudge Cakes

I teach in a school where there are three or four teachers per grade. I bake these little cakes in small pans so that each group can grab a cake before school and divide it among themselves later. Sometimes I slice the cakes into three or four layers and fill the additional layers with strawberry preserves or cherry pie filling.

—CARLEEN JOHNS BROWNWOOD, MO

PREP: 1 HOUR **BAKE:** 20 MIN. + COOLING
MAKES: 10 SERVINGS

- 1 package chocolate cake mix (regular size)
- 1 cup (8 ounces) sour cream
- ¾ cup water
- ½ cup butter, softened
- 3 large eggs

FILLING

- 1 package (8 ounces) cream cheese, softened
- 1 cup confectioners' sugar
- ½ cup heavy whipping cream, whipped
- 1 teaspoon almond extract

GLAZE

- 1½ cups confectioners' sugar
- 1 cup milk chocolate chips
- ½ cup butter, cubed
- ¼ cup sweetened condensed milk
- 5 teaspoons heavy whipping cream
- 1 teaspoon vanilla extract
- 1 cup chopped almonds, toasted

1. In a large bowl, combine the cake mix, sour cream, water, butter and eggs; beat on low speed for 30 seconds. Beat on medium speed for 2 minutes.

2. Spoon ½ cupfuls into 10 greased 4-in. fluted tube pans. Bake at 350° for 20-25 minutes. Cool for 10 minutes before removing from pans to wire racks to cool completely.

3. In a small bowl, combine cream cheese and confectioners' sugar until creamy. Fold in whipped cream and almond extract; set aside.

4. For glaze, in a large saucepan, combine the confectioners' sugar, chocolate chips, butter and milk. Cook and stir over medium heat until smooth. Remove from the heat. Stir in cream and vanilla.

5. Cut each cake horizontally into two layers. Place each bottom layer on a serving plate; top with 3 tablespoons filling. Replace tops. Spoon glaze over cakes; sprinkle with almonds.

NOTE *To bake in 6-oz. ramekins, divide among eight greased ramekins. Bake at 350° for 25-30 minutes or until a toothpick comes out clean.*

BIG BATCH

Orange Chocolate Cake

I received this recipe from one of the best cooks in my ladies' Bible class at church. The orange and chocolate combination is fantastic. One of my hobbies is collecting recipes, especially those for desserts, which suits my chocolate-loving husband just fine!

—LINDA HARRIS WICHITA, KS

PREP: 20 MIN. • **BAKE:** 1 HOUR + COOLING
MAKES: 16-20 SERVINGS

- 1 package orange cake mix (regular size)
- 5 large eggs
- 1 cup orange juice or water
- 1 package (3.4 ounces) instant vanilla pudding mix
- 1 teaspoon orange extract, optional
- ½ cup semisweet chocolate chips
- ½ cup chopped walnuts or pecans
- ¾ cup chocolate syrup

1. In a large bowl, beat cake mix, eggs, juice, pudding mix and extract, if desired, until well-blended and smooth. Sprinkle the chocolate chips and nuts into greased and floured 10-in. fluted tube pan. Pour two-thirds of batter into pan. Combine chocolate syrup with the remaining batter; pour into pan.

2. Bake at 350° for 1 hour or until a toothpick inserted near the center comes out clean. Cool for 10 minutes before inverting onto a wire rack.

Almond Fudge Cakes

Coconut
Fruitcake

BIG BATCH
Coconut Fruitcake

A neighbor gave me this recipe when we first moved to the small town of Ferryville, Wisconsin, saying it dated back to the 1800s and everybody in the area made it. I soon discovered why when I took a taste...and I'm not a fruitcake fan!

—LORRAINE GROH FERRYVILLE, WI

PREP: 20 MIN. • **BAKE:** 80 MIN. + COOLING
MAKES: 16 SERVINGS

- ½ cup butter, softened
- 1 cup sugar
- 3 large eggs
- 1 teaspoon lemon extract
- 2 cups all-purpose flour
- 1 teaspoon baking powder
- 1 teaspoon salt
- ½ cup orange juice
- 1 pound chopped mixed candied fruit
- 1½ cups flaked coconut
- 1 cup golden raisins
- 1 cup chopped nuts
- Additional confectioners' sugar and candied fruit or nuts, optional

1. In a large bowl, cream butter and sugar until light and fluffy. Add eggs, one at a time, beating well after each addition. Beat in extract. Combine the flour, baking powder and salt; gradually add to creamed mixture alternately with orange juice. Stir in the candied fruit, coconut, raisins and nuts.

2. Press into a greased and waxed paper-lined 10-in. tube pan. Bake at 300° for 80-90 minutes or until a toothpick comes out clean. Cool for 10 minutes before removing from pan to a wire rack to cool completely. If desired, dust with confectioners' sugar and sprinkle with candied fruit or nuts.

Pina Colada Bundt Cake

Pina Colada Bundt Cake

I named this cake a "pina colada" because it has coconut, pineapple and rum. It's a soothing finish at the end of a big spread.

—DEBRA KEIL OWASSO, OK

PREP: 15 MIN. • **BAKE:** 45 MIN. + COOLING
MAKES: 12 SERVINGS

- 1 package white cake mix (regular size)
- 1 package (3.4 ounces) instant coconut cream pudding mix
- 1 cup canola oil
- ¾ cup water
- 2 large eggs
- ¼ cup rum
- 1 cup crushed pineapple, drained

GLAZE
- 2 cups confectioners' sugar, divided
- 2 tablespoons unsweetened pineapple juice
- ¼ cup cream of coconut
- 1 tablespoon rum
- ¼ cup flaked coconut

1. Preheat oven to 350°. Grease and flour a 10-in. fluted tube pan.

2. In a large bowl, combine cake mix, pudding mix, oil, water, eggs and rum; beat on low speed 30 seconds. Beat on medium speed 2 minutes. Stir in the pineapple. Transfer batter to prepared pan. Bake for 45-50 minutes or until a toothpick inserted in the center comes out clean. Cool in the pan for 15 minutes before removing to wire rack.

3. Meanwhile, in a small bowl, mix 1 cup confectioners' sugar and pineapple juice; brush over warm cake. Cool cake completely.

4. In another bowl, mix the cream of coconut, rum and remaining confectioners' sugar; drizzle over cake. Sprinkle with coconut.

NOTE *This recipe was tested with Coco Lopez cream of coconut. Look for it in the liquor section. For easier removal of cake, use solid shortening when greasing a fluted or plain tube pan.*

Triple-Chocolate Cake
with Raspberry Sauce

Taste-of-Summer Light Pound Cake

Bring the bright look and taste of summer to your table year-round with this delicious, reduced-calorie pound cake.

—JILL BELLROSE PORTLAND, OR

PREP: 20 MIN. • **BAKE:** 35 MIN. + COOLING
MAKES: 12 SERVINGS

- ½ cup butter, softened
- 1 cup sugar
- 2 large egg whites
- 1 large egg
- 1 tablespoon lemon juice
- 1 teaspoon lemon extract
- 1 teaspoon vanilla extract
- 1½ cups all-purpose flour
- 1 cup whole wheat pastry flour
- 2 teaspoons baking powder
- ½ teaspoon salt
- ¼ teaspoon baking soda
- ¾ cup (6 ounces) fat-free lemon yogurt

GLAZE
- ¾ cup confectioners' sugar
- 4 teaspoons lemon juice
- 1 teaspoon grated lemon peel
- ⅓ cup dried apricots, finely chopped

1. In a large bowl, cream butter and sugar until light and fluffy. Add egg whites, then egg, beating well after each addition. Beat in lemon juice and extracts. Combine the flours, baking powder, salt and baking soda; add to the creamed mixture alternately with yogurt.

2. Transfer to a 10-in. fluted tube pan coated with cooking spray. Bake at 350° for 35-40 minutes or until a toothpick inserted near the center comes out clean. Cool for 10 minutes before removing from pan to a wire rack to cool completely.

3. For glaze, in a small bowl, whisk the confectioners' sugar, lemon juice and lemon peel until blended. Stir in apricots. Drizzle over cake.

Triple-Chocolate Cake with Raspberry Sauce

Chocolate lovers, brace yourselves. This cocoa creation and its saucy accompaniment make an absolutely heavenly combination.

—JENNY STANIEC OAK GROVE, MN

PREP: 20 MIN. • **BAKE:** 1 HOUR + COOLING
MAKES: 12 SERVINGS (2⅔ CUPS SAUCE)

- 1 package chocolate cake mix (regular size)
- 1 package (3.4 ounces) instant vanilla pudding mix
- 1 package (3.4 ounces) instant chocolate pudding mix
- 4 large eggs
- 1½ cups water
- ½ cup canola oil
- 1 cup (6 ounces) semisweet chocolate chips

RASPBERRY SAUCE
- 1 cup water
- 2 packages (10 ounces each) frozen sweetened raspberries, thawed
- 1 tablespoon sugar
- 3 tablespoons cornstarch
- 2 tablespoons lemon juice
  Confectioners' sugar

1. Preheat the oven to 325°. In a large bowl, combine the cake mix, pudding mixes, eggs, water and oil; beat on low speed 30 seconds. Beat on medium speed 2 minutes. Fold in chocolate chips.

2. Pour into a well-greased 10-in. fluted tube pan. Bake 60-65 minutes or until a toothpick inserted near the center comes out clean. Cool for 10 minutes before removing from pan to a wire rack to cool completely.

3. Meanwhile, place water, raspberries and sugar in a blender; cover and process until well blended. In a small saucepan, combine cornstarch and lemon juice; stir in raspberry puree. Bring to a boil. Cook and stir 2 minutes or until thickened. Refrigerate until serving.

4. Dust cake with confectioners' sugar. Serve with sauce.

BIG BATCH

Banana Chip Cake

One of my favorite treats is Ben & Jerry's Chunky Monkey ice cream, so I decided to create a cake with the same flavors. The hardest part is waiting for it to cool.

—**BARBARA PRYOR** MILFORD, MA

PREP: 25 MIN. • **BAKE:** 40 MIN. + COOLING
MAKES: 16 SERVINGS

- 1 **package yellow cake mix (regular size)**
- 1¼ **cups water**
- 3 **large eggs**
- ½ **cup unsweetened applesauce**
- 2 **medium bananas, mashed**
- 1 **cup miniature semisweet chocolate chips**
- ½ **cup chopped walnuts**

1. In a large bowl, combine the cake mix, water, eggs and applesauce; beat on low speed for 30 seconds. Beat on medium speed for 2 minutes. Stir in the bananas, chips and walnuts.

2. Transfer to a 10-in. fluted tube pan coated with cooking spray and sprinkled with flour. Bake at 350° for 40-50 minutes or until a toothpick inserted near the center comes out clean. Cool for 10 minutes before removing from pan to a wire rack to cool completely.

TOP TIP

Try Baking with Applesauce

For every ½ cup of oil replaced with applesauce, you will save 900 calories and 110 grams of fat. Replacing the same amount of butter with applesauce reduces the calories by 850 and the fat by 91 grams, of which a whopping 56 grams is saturated fat (the "bad" fat). Sodium also is reduced by 925 mg.

Banana Chip Cake

BOSTON CREAM CUPCAKES
PAGE 186

Delightful Cupcakes

INDULGE IN THE CUTE CUPCAKES FOUND HERE! THERE ARE SO MANY VARIETIES, AND THE CHOICES FOR HOW YOU DECORATE THE TREATS ARE ENDLESS. CHECK OUT THE CUPCAKE CONES—KIDS WILL LOVE THEM! BAKE UP A FEW AND MAKE SOMEONE FEEL SPECIAL TODAY!

SPICE CUPCAKES WITH MOCHA FROSTING *PAGE 187*

ZUCCHINI CUPCAKES *PAGE 183*

PUMPKIN PECAN BITES *PAGE 184*

Cupcake Cones

Cupcake Cones

Serve up your cake in a cute ice cream cone. These are really fun treats and popular with little kids. My mom would make them all the time when I was young.

—MINA DYCK BOISSEVAIN, MB

PREP: 25 MIN. • **BAKE:** 25 MIN. + COOLING
MAKES: ABOUT 2 DOZEN

- ⅓ **cup butter, softened**
- ½ **cup creamy peanut butter**
- 1½ **cups packed brown sugar**
- 2 **large eggs**
- 1 **teaspoon vanilla extract**
- 2 **cups all-purpose flour**
- 2½ **teaspoons baking powder**
- ½ **teaspoon salt**
- ¾ **cup 2% milk**
- 24 **ice cream cake cones**
  (about 3 inches tall)
  Frosting of your choice
  Sprinkles or chopped
     peanuts, optional

1. In a large bowl, cream butter, peanut butter and brown sugar until light and fluffy. Beat in eggs and vanilla. Combine dry ingredients; add to creamed mixture alternately with milk, beating well after each addition.
2. Place ice cream cones in muffin cups. Spoon about 3 tablespoons batter into each cone, filling to ¾ in. from the top.
3. Bake at 350° for 25-30 minutes or until a toothpick inserted near the center of cake comes out clean. Cool completely on wire racks. Frost and decorate as desired.
NOTE *Reduced-fat peanut butter is not recommended for this recipe.*

❝Very easy to make. Put icing in a freezer bag then cut the edge for easier frosting.❞

—BROOKRACH
FROM TASTEOFHOME.COM

Carrot Cupcakes

Carrot Cupcakes

To get my family to eat more vegetables, I often hide nutritional foods inside sweet treats. Now we can have our cake and eat our vegetables, too!

—DOREEN KELLY ROSYLN, PA

PREP: 15 MIN. • **BAKE:** 20 MIN.
MAKES: 2 DOZEN

- 4 **large eggs**
- 2 **cups sugar**
- 1 **cup canola oil**
- 2 **cups all-purpose flour**
- 2 **teaspoons ground cinnamon**
- 1 **teaspoon baking soda**
- 1 **teaspoon baking powder**
- 1 **teaspoon ground allspice**
- ½ **teaspoon salt**
- 3 **cups grated carrots**
- **CHUNKY FROSTING**
- 1 **package (8 ounces) cream**
  cheese, softened
- ¼ **cup butter, softened**
- 2 **cups confectioners' sugar**
- ½ **cup flaked coconut**
- ½ **cup chopped pecans**
- ½ **cup chopped raisins**

1. In a large bowl, beat the eggs, sugar and oil. Combine the flour, cinnamon, baking soda, baking powder, allspice and salt; gradually add to egg mixture. Stir in carrots.
2. Fill greased or paper-lined muffin cups two-thirds full. Bake at 325° for 20-25 minutes or until a toothpick inserted near the center comes out clean. Cool for 5 minutes before removing from pans to wire racks.
3. For frosting, in a large bowl, beat cream cheese and butter until fluffy. Gradually beat in confectioners' sugar until smooth. Stir in coconut, pecans and raisins. Frost cupcakes. Store in the refrigerator.

Key Lime Pie Cupcakes

Key Lime Pie Cupcakes

I bake more than 200 of these cupcakes for our church suppers, and we always run out. If you can't find Key lime juice, use lime juice instead, just make sure to add a tad more sugar.

—**JULIE HERRERA-LEMLER** ROCHESTER, MN

PREP: 45 MIN. • **BAKE:** 20 MIN. + COOLING
MAKES: 32 CUPCAKES

- 2 packages (14.1 ounces each) refrigerated pie pastry
- 1 cup butter, softened
- 2½ cups sugar
- 4 large eggs
- ½ cup Key lime juice
- 2 cups all-purpose flour
- 1½ cups self-rising flour
- 1½ cups buttermilk

FROSTING

- 12 ounces cream cheese, softened
- 1½ cups butter, softened
- 1½ teaspoons vanilla extract
- 2¾ to 3 cups confectioners' sugar
- 6 tablespoons Key lime juice
  Fresh raspberries

1. Preheat oven to 350°. Line 32 muffin cups with foil liners. On a lightly floured work surface, unroll pastry sheets. Cut 32 circles with a floured 2¼-in. round cookie cutter (discard remaining pastry or save for another use). Press one pastry circle into each liner. Bake for 10-12 minutes or until lightly browned. Cool on wire racks.
2. In a large bowl, beat butter and sugar until crumbly. Add eggs, one at a time, beating well after each addition. Beat in lime juice. In another bowl, whisk flours; add to butter mixture alternately with buttermilk, beating well after each addition.
3. Pour batter into prepared cups. Bake for 20-22 minutes or until a toothpick inserted in the center comes out clean. Cool in pans for 10 minutes before removing to wire racks to cool completely.
4. In a large bowl, beat cream cheese, butter and vanilla until blended. Beat in enough of the confectioners' sugar, alternately with lime juice, to reach desired consistency. Frost cupcakes; top with fresh raspberries. Refrigerate leftovers.
NOTE *As a substitute for 1½ cups self-rising flour, place 2¼ teaspoons baking powder and ¾ teaspoon salt in a measuring cup. Add all-purpose flour to measure 1 cup. Combine with an additional ½ cup all-purpose flour.*

Rosy Rhubarb Cupcakes

If you're in a big hurry, skip the frosting—the cupcakes are just as good without it. But don't skip the nutmeg because it provides the flavor spark.

—**SHARON NICHOLS** BROOKINGS, SD

PREP: 15 MIN. • **BAKE:** 30 MIN.
MAKES: 1½ DOZEN

- ½ cup shortening
- 1 cup packed brown sugar
- ¼ cup sugar
- 1 large egg
- 2 cups all-purpose flour
- ½ teaspoon baking soda
- ¼ teaspoon baking powder
- ¼ teaspoon ground nutmeg
- 1 cup buttermilk
- 1½ cups finely chopped fresh or frozen rhubarb, thawed
  Cream cheese frosting, optional

1. In a large bowl, cream shortening and sugars until light and fluffy. Beat in the egg. Combine the flour, baking soda, baking powder and nutmeg; add to creamed mixture alternately with buttermilk, beating well after each addition. Fold in rhubarb.
2. Fill paper-lined muffin cups two-thirds full. Bake at 350° for 30-35 minutes or until a toothpick inserted near the center comes out clean. Frost if desired.
NOTE *If using frozen rhubarb, measure rhubarb while still frozen, then thaw completely. Drain in a colander, but do not press liquid out.*

Creamy Center
Cupcakes

BIG BATCH

Creamy Center Cupcakes

My mother made these cupcakes from scratch when I was growing up. I simplified it with a cake mix. Sometimes Mom would replace the smooth filling with homemade whipped cream. They are really good with either filling.

—CAROLINE ANDERSON WAUPACA, WI

PREP: 45 MIN. + COOLING
MAKES: 2 DOZEN

- 1 **package devil's food cake mix (regular size)**
- ¾ **cup shortening**
- ⅔ **cup confectioners' sugar**
- 1 **cup marshmallow creme**
- 1 **teaspoon vanilla extract**
- 2 **cans (16 ounces each) chocolate frosting**

1. Prepare and bake cake according to package directions for cupcakes, using paper-lined muffin cups. Cool for 10 minutes before removing from pans to wire racks to cool completely.
2. Meanwhile in a large bowl, cream shortening and confectioners' sugar until light and fluffy. Beat in the marshmallow creme and vanilla.
3. Cut a small hole in the corner of a pastry or plastic bag; insert a very small tip. Fill with cream filling. Push the tip through the bottom of paper liner to fill each cupcake. Frost with chocolate frosting.

TOP TIP

No-Stick Muffin Liners

When baking muffins or cupcakes in paper liners, I spray them with nonstick cooking spray. The liner peels off very nicely, leaving no crumbs behind!
—PAMELA K. MARTINSBURG, WV

Peanut Butter-Filled Brownie Cupcakes

Folks love brownies and cupcakes, so why not combine them? You'll watch these snacks disappear before your very eyes.

—CAROL GILLESPIE
CHAMBERSBURG, PA

PREP: 15 MIN. • **BAKE:** 15 MIN. + COOLING
MAKES: 1 DOZEN

- 1 package fudge brownie mix (8-inch square pan size)
- ½ cup miniature semisweet chocolate chips
- ⅓ cup creamy peanut butter
- 3 tablespoons cream cheese, softened
- 1 large egg
- ¼ cup sugar
  Confectioners' sugar

1. Preheat oven to 350°. Prepare brownie batter according to the package directions; stir in the chocolate chips. For filling, in a small bowl, beat peanut butter, cream cheese, egg and the sugar until smooth.

2. Fill paper-lined muffin cups one-third full with batter. Drop filling by teaspoonfuls into the center of each cupcake. Cover with remaining batter.

3. Bake 15-20 minutes or until a toothpick inserted in brownie portion comes out clean. Cool 10 minutes before removing from pan to a wire rack to cool completely. Dust tops with confectioners' sugar. Store in the refrigerator.

Peanut Butter-Filled Brownie Cupcakes

BIG BATCH
Zucchini Cupcakes

I asked my grandmother for this recipe after trying these irresistible spice cupcakes at her home. I love their creamy caramel frosting. They are such a scrumptious dessert you actually forget you're eating your vegetables, too!

—VIRGINIA LAPIERRE
GREENSBORO BEND, VERMONT

PREP: 20 MIN. • **BAKE:** 20 MIN. + COOLING
MAKES: 1½-2 DOZEN

- 3 **large eggs**
- 1⅓ **cups sugar**
- ½ **cup canola oil**
- ½ **cup orange juice**
- 1 **teaspoon almond extract**
- 2½ **cups all-purpose flour**
- 2 **teaspoons ground cinnamon**
- 2 **teaspoons baking powder**
- 1 **teaspoon baking soda**
- 1 **teaspoon salt**
- ½ **teaspoon ground cloves**
- 1½ **cups shredded zucchini**

FROSTING

- 1 **cup packed brown sugar**
- ½ **cup butter, cubed**
- ¼ **cup 2% milk**
- 1 **teaspoon vanilla extract**
- 1½ **to 2 cups confectioners' sugar**

1. Preheat oven to 350°. Beat the first five ingredients together. Combine dry ingredients; gradually add to egg mixture and blend well. Stir in zucchini.
2. Fill paper-lined muffin cups two-thirds full. Bake until a toothpick inserted in the center comes out clean, 20-25 minutes. Cool for 10 minutes before removing to a wire rack.
3. For frosting, combine brown sugar, butter and milk in a large saucepan. Bring to a boil over medium heat; cook and stir until thickened, 1-2 minutes. Remove from heat; stir in vanilla. Cool to lukewarm.
4. Gradually beat in confectioners' sugar until frosting reaches spreading consistency. Frost cupcakes.

Orange Dream
Mini Cupcakes

BIG BATCH
Orange Dream Mini Cupcakes

The sweet taste of these cute cupcakes reminds me and my friends of orange-and-vanilla frozen treats.

—JEN SHEPHERD ST. PETERS, MO

PREP: 1 HOUR • **BAKE:** 15 MIN. + COOLING
MAKES: 4 DOZEN

- ½ **cup butter, softened**
- 1 **cup sugar**
- 2 **large eggs**
- 1 **tablespoon grated orange peel**
- 1 **tablespoon orange juice**
- ½ **teaspoon vanilla extract**
- 1½ **cups all-purpose flour**
- 1½ **teaspoons baking powder**
- ¼ **teaspoon salt**
- ½ **cup buttermilk**

BUTTERCREAM

- ½ **cup butter, softened**
- ¼ **teaspoon salt**
- 2 **cups confectioners' sugar**
- 2 **tablespoons 2% milk**
- 1½ **teaspoons vanilla extract**
- ½ **cup orange marmalade**

1. Preheat oven to 325°. Line 48 mini-muffin cups with paper liners. In a large bowl, cream butter and sugar until light and fluffy. Add eggs, one at a time, beating well after each addition. Beat in orange peel, orange juice and vanilla. In another bowl, whisk flour, baking powder and salt; add to creamed mixture alternately with buttermilk, beating well after each addition.
2. Fill prepared cups two-thirds full. Bake for 11-13 minutes or until a toothpick inserted in the center comes out clean. Cool in pans for 5 minutes before removing to wire racks to cool completely.
3. For buttercream, in a large bowl, beat butter and salt until creamy. Gradually beat in confectioners' sugar, milk and vanilla until smooth.
4. Using a paring knife, cut a 1-in.-wide cone-shaped piece from the top of each cupcake; discard removed portion. Fill cavity with marmalade. Pipe or spread buttercream over tops.

BIG BATCH
Pumpkin Pecan Bites

Because this recipe makes a lot, these bite-size treats are ideal for potlucks. Easily frost by putting the frosting in a pastry bag and piping it on top of the cupcakes.
—**CAROL BEYERL** EAST WENATCHEE, WA

PREP: 20 MIN. • **BAKE:** 20 MIN. + COOLING
MAKES: ABOUT 6 DOZEN

- 1 package spice cake mix (regular size)
- 1 can (15 ounces) solid-pack pumpkin
- 3 large eggs
- ½ cup canola oil
- 1 tablespoon ground cinnamon
- 1 teaspoon baking soda
- ¼ teaspoon ground cloves
- 36 pecan halves, cut in half

CREAM CHEESE FROSTING
- ½ cup butter, softened
- 4 ounces cream cheese, softened
- 1 teaspoon vanilla extract
- 3¾ cups confectioners' sugar
- 2 to 3 tablespoons milk
   Ground cinnamon

1. In a large bowl, combine the cake mix, pumpkin, eggs, oil, cinnamon, baking soda and cloves; beat on low speed for 30 seconds. Beat on medium speed for 2 minutes.
2. Fill paper-lined miniature muffin cups two-thirds full. Press a pecan piece into each. Bake at 350° for 17-20 minutes or until a toothpick inserted near the center comes out clean. Cool for 5 minutes before removing from pans to wire racks to cool completely.
3. In a small bowl, cream the butter, cream cheese and vanilla until light and fluffy. Gradually add confectioners' sugar and mix well. Add enough milk to achieve spreading consistency. Frost cupcakes. Sprinkle with cinnamon.
NOTE *This recipe can be prepared in 2 dozen regular-size muffin cups. Bake for 22-26 minutes.*

Dark Chocolate Bacon Cupcakes

Dark Chocolate Bacon Cupcakes

These adventurous cupcakes were a challenge by my friends that turned into a great success. Use extra-smoky bacon to really get the salty, rich flavor.
—**SANDY PLOY** WHITEFISH BAY, WI

PREP: 25 MIN. • **BAKE:** 20 MIN. + COOLING
MAKES: 22 CUPCAKES

- 2 cups sugar
- 1 cup buttermilk
- 2 large eggs
- ½ cup canola oil
- ½ cup strong brewed coffee
- 2 cups all-purpose flour
- ¾ cup plus 1 tablespoon baking cocoa, divided
- 1¼ teaspoons baking powder
- ½ teaspoon sea salt
- ¼ teaspoon baking soda
- ¾ pound bacon strips, cooked and crumbled, divided
- 1 can (16 ounces) chocolate frosting

1. In a large bowl, beat the sugar, buttermilk, eggs, oil and coffee until well blended. In a small bowl, combine the flour, ¾ cup cocoa, baking powder, salt and baking soda; gradually beat into sugar mixture until blended. Stir in two-thirds of the bacon.
2. Fill paper-lined muffin cups two-thirds full. Bake at 375° for 18-22 minutes or until a toothpick inserted near the center comes out clean. Cool for 10 minutes before removing from pans to wire racks to cool completely.
3. Frost cupcakes. Sprinkle with the remaining bacon; dust with remaining cocoa. Refrigerate leftovers.

Coconut Tres Leches Cupcakes

Three types of milk provide rich flavor for these little cakes, and the toasted coconut is an elegant touch.

—TASTE OF HOME TEST KITCHEN

PREP: 30 MIN. • **BAKE:** 20 MIN. + CHILLING
MAKES: ABOUT 1½ DOZEN

- ½ cup butter, softened
- 1½ cups sugar
- 4 large egg whites
- 1½ teaspoons vanilla extract
- 2 cups all-purpose flour
- 1 teaspoon baking powder
- ½ teaspoon baking soda
- ¼ teaspoon salt
- 1⅓ cups buttermilk
- 1 can (14 ounces) sweetened condensed milk
- ⅔ cup evaporated milk
- ½ cup coconut milk
- 1 cup heavy whipping cream
- 3 tablespoons confectioners' sugar
  Toasted flaked coconut

1. In a large bowl, cream butter and sugar until light and fluffy. Add egg whites, one at a time, beating well after each addition. Beat in vanilla. Combine the flour, baking powder, baking soda and salt; add to the creamed mixture alternately with buttermilk, beating well after each addition.

2. Fill paper-lined muffin cups two-thirds full. Bake at 350° for 18-22 minutes or until a toothpick inserted near the center comes out clean. Place pan on a wire rack; cool for 10 minutes. Remove the paper liners from cupcakes; return to pan.

3. Poke holes in cupcakes with a skewer, about ½ in. apart. Combine the sweetened condensed milk, evaporated milk and coconut milk; slowly pour over cupcakes, allowing mixture to absorb into cake. Cover and refrigerate for 2 hours.

4. In a large bowl, beat cream until it begins to thicken. Add confectioners' sugar; beat until soft peaks form. Frost cupcakes. Sprinkle with coconut. Store in the refrigerator.

BIG BATCH
Chocolate Chip Cupcakes

These crowd-pleasing cupcakes are quick, moist and yummy. You just can't go wrong with chocolate chips.

—PAULA ZSIRAY LOGAN, UT

PREP: 15 MIN. • **BAKE:** 20 MIN. + COOLING
MAKES: 2½ DOZEN

- 1 package yellow cake mix (regular size)
- 1 package (3.4 ounces) instant vanilla pudding mix
- 1 cup water
- ½ cup canola oil
- 4 large eggs
- 1 cup (6 ounces) miniature semisweet chocolate chips
- 1 can (16 ounces) chocolate or vanilla frosting
  Additional miniature semisweet chocolate chips, optional

1. In a large bowl, combine the cake and pudding mixes, water, oil and eggs; beat on low speed for 30 seconds. Beat on medium speed for 2 minutes. Stir in chocolate chips.

2. Fill paper-lined muffin cups two-thirds full. Bake at 375° for 18-22 minutes or until a toothpick inserted near the center comes out clean. Cool for 10 minutes before removing to wire racks to cool completely. Frost cupcakes. Sprinkle with additional chips if desired.

Coconut Tres Leches Cupcakes

Boston Cream Cupcakes

Boston Cream Cupcakes

Boston cream bismarcks have been my favorite bakery treat since I was a child, so I put together this easy-to-make cupcake version.

—JEANNE HOLT MENDOTA HEIGHTS, MN

PREP: 25 MIN. • **BAKE:** 15 MIN. + COOLING
MAKES: ½ DOZEN

- 3 **tablespoons shortening**
- ⅓ **cup sugar**
- 1 **large egg**
- ½ **teaspoon vanilla extract**
- ½ **cup all-purpose flour**
- ½ **teaspoon baking powder**
- ¼ **teaspoon salt**
- 3 **tablespoons 2% milk**
- ⅔ **cup prepared vanilla pudding**
- ½ **cup semisweet chocolate chips**
- ¼ **cup heavy whipping cream**

1. In a small bowl, cream shortening and sugar until light and fluffy. Beat in egg. Beat in vanilla. Combine the flour, baking powder and salt; add to the creamed mixture alternately with milk, beating well after each addition.

2. Filled paper-lined muffin cups half full. Bake at 350° for 15-20 minutes or until a toothpick inserted near the center comes out clean. Cool for 10 minutes before removing from pan to a wire rack to cool completely.

3. Cut a small hole in the corner of a pastry or plastic bag; insert a small tip. Fill with pudding. Push the tip through the top to fill each cupcake.

4. Place chocolate chips in a small bowl. In a small saucepan, bring cream just to a boil. Pour over chocolate; whisk until smooth. Cool, stirring occasionally, to room temperature or until ganache thickens slightly, about 10 minutes. Spoon over cupcakes. Let stand until set. Store in an airtight container in the refrigerator.

Spice Cupcakes with Mocha Frosting

Old-fashioned flavor comes through with the molasses, cinnamon, cloves and nutmeg in these light, fluffy cupcakes. The mocha frosting is a fresh touch that makes them extra special.

—**SARAH VAUGHAN** WATERVILLE, ME

PREP: 30 MIN. • **BAKE:** 20 MIN. + COOLING
MAKES: 15 CUPCAKES

- ½ cup butter, softened
- ½ cup sugar
- 1 large egg
- ½ cup molasses
- 1½ cups all-purpose flour
- ½ teaspoon baking soda
- ¼ teaspoon salt
- ¼ teaspoon each ground cinnamon, cloves and nutmeg
- ½ cup buttermilk

FROSTING
- 1¾ cups confectioners' sugar
- 1 tablespoon baking cocoa
- 2 tablespoons strong brewed coffee
- 1 tablespoon butter, softened
- ¼ teaspoon vanilla extract
  Chocolate-covered coffee beans and assorted candies, optional

1. In a large bowl, cream butter and sugar until light and fluffy. Beat in egg and molasses. Combine the flour, baking soda, salt, cinnamon, cloves and nutmeg; add to creamed mixture alternately with buttermilk.
2. Fill paper-lined muffin cups two-thirds full. Bake at 350° for 20-25 minutes or until a toothpick inserted near the center comes out clean. Cool for 10 minutes before removing from pans to wire racks to cool completely.
3. In a small bowl, combine confectioners' sugar and cocoa. Stir in the coffee, butter and vanilla until smooth. Frost cupcakes. Garnish with coffee beans and candies if desired.
NOTE *Warmed buttermilk will appear curdled.*

Marshmallow-Filled Banana Cupcakes

Marshmallow-Filled Banana Cupcakes

A friend gave me this recipe when I first moved into my neighborhood 40 years ago. It might seem more time consuming than it is, but it's easy and the results are incredible.

—**MONIQUE CARON** BUXTON, ME

PREP: 40 MIN. • **BAKE:** 20 MIN. + COOLING
MAKES: 1½ DOZEN

- ¾ cup shortening
- 1½ cups sugar
- 2 large eggs
- 1 cup mashed ripe bananas (about 2 medium)
- 1 teaspoon vanilla extract
- 2 cups all-purpose flour
- 1 teaspoon baking soda
- ¼ teaspoon salt
- ¼ cup buttermilk

FILLING
- 1 cup butter, softened
- 2 cups marshmallow creme
- 1½ cups confectioners' sugar
  Additional confectioners' sugar

1. Preheat oven to 375°. Line 18 muffin cups with paper or foil liners.
2. In a large bowl, cream shortening and sugar until light and fluffy. Add eggs, one at a time, beating well after each addition. Beat in bananas and vanilla. In another bowl, whisk flour, baking soda and salt; add to creamed mixture alternately with buttermilk, beating well after each addition.
3. Fill prepared cups two-thirds full. Bake 18-22 minutes or until a toothpick inserted in the center comes out clean. Cool in pans for 10 minutes before removing to wire racks to cool completely.
4. For filling, in a large bowl, beat butter, marshmallow creme and confectioners' sugar until smooth. Using a sharp knife, cut a 1-in. circle, 1 in. deep, in the top of each cupcake. Carefully remove cut portion and set aside. Fill cavity with about 1 teaspoon filling. Replace tops, pressing down lightly. Dollop or pipe remaining filling over tops. Dust with confectioners' sugar.

Chocolate Raspberry Cupcakes

teaspoonfuls into the center of each cupcake. Bake at 350° for 18-23 minutes or until a toothpick inserted in the cake portion comes out clean.

4. Cool cupcakes for 10 minutes before removing from pans to wire racks to cool completely. Spread ½ teaspoon jam over each cupcake.

5. For frosting, spoon 1 cup cream from top of coconut milk and place in a small saucepan. Bring just to a boil; remove from the heat. Add chocolate chips; whisk until smooth. Stir in the butter, confectioners' sugar and coffee liqueur. Refrigerate for 1½ hours or until chilled.

6. In a small bowl, beat chocolate mixture until soft peaks form, about 15 seconds. Frost cupcakes. Garnish with coconut.

BIG BATCH
German Chocolate Cupcakes

These cupcakes disappear in a flash when I take them to the school where I teach. The coconut-pecan topping dresses them up nicely, so no one misses the icing.
—**LETTICE CHARMASSON** SAN DIEGO, CA

PREP: 20 MIN. • **BAKE:** 15 MIN. + COOLING
MAKES: ABOUT 2 DOZEN

- 1 **package German chocolate cake mix (regular size)**
- 1 **cup water**
- 3 **large eggs**
- ½ **cup canola oil**
- 3 **tablespoons chopped pecans**
- 3 **tablespoons flaked coconut**
- 3 **tablespoons brown sugar**

1. In a large bowl, combine the cake mix, water, eggs and oil. Beat on low speed for 30 seconds. Beat on medium speed for 2 minutes.

2. Fill the paper-lined muffin cups three-fourths full. Combine the pecans, coconut and brown sugar; sprinkle over batter. Bake at 400° for 15-20 minutes or until a toothpick inserted near the center comes out clean. Cool for 10 minutes before removing from pans to wire racks to cool completely.

BIG BATCH
Chocolate Raspberry Cupcakes

These cupcake are so amazing that people have been know to inhale them in two bites. But most prefer to savor each decadent morsel. They can be kept in the fridge for about a week.
—**KIM BEJOT** AINSWORTH, NE

PREP: 30 MIN. + CHILLING
BAKE: 20 MIN. + COOLING
MAKES: 2½ DOZEN

- 1 **cup baking cocoa**
- 2 **cups boiling water**
- 1 **cup butter, softened**
- 2½ **cups sugar**
- 4 **large eggs**
- 2 **tablespoons cold strong brewed coffee**
- 2 **teaspoons vanilla extract**
- 2¾ **cups all-purpose flour**
- 2 **teaspoons baking soda**
- ½ **teaspoon baking powder**
- ½ **teaspoon salt**
- 1 **cup seedless raspberry jam**

FROSTING
- 1 **can (13.66 ounces) coconut milk**
- 1 **package (12 ounces) dark chocolate chips**
- ½ **cup butter, cubed**
- ⅓ **cup confectioners' sugar**
- 2 **tablespoons coffee liqueur**
  Toasted coconut

1. In a small bowl, combine cocoa and water; set aside to cool.

2. In a large bowl, cream butter and sugar until light and fluffy. Add eggs, one at a time, beating well after each addition. Beat in coffee and vanilla. Combine the flour, baking soda, baking powder and salt; add to the creamed mixture alternately with cocoa mixture, beating well after each addition.

3. Fill paper-lined muffin cups two-thirds full. Drop jam by

⑤INGREDIENTS *BIG BATCH*

Cowabunga Root Beer Cupcakes

I created these small delights especially for my daughter's first birthday party. They're the perfect summertime treat.

—MINDY CARSWELL WALKER, MI

PREP: 10 MIN. • **BAKE:** 15 MIN. + COOLING
MAKES: 24 SERVINGS

- **1 package butter recipe golden cake mix (regular size)**
- **4 teaspoons root beer concentrate, divided**
- **1 carton (12 ounces) frozen whipped topping, thawed Vanilla ice cream**

1. Prepare and bake cupcakes according to package directions, adding 2 teaspoons root beer concentrate when mixing the batter. Remove to wire racks to cool completely.

2. In a small bowl, mix whipped topping and remaining root beer concentrate until blended; spread over cupcakes. Serve with ice cream.

NOTE *This recipe was tested with McCormick root beer concentrate.*

Cowabunga Root
Beer Cupcakes

CHOCOLATE-PEANUT BUTTER SHEET CAKE *PAGE 198*

Snack & Single Layer Cakes

THE SNACK CAKES FOUND HERE ARE TERRIFIC FOR JUST THAT—SNACKING! THE SHEET CAKES ARE THE PERFECT ADDITION TO POTLUCKS, CHURCH SUPPERS, SHOWERS AND PARTIES. THE SINGLE-LAYER SWEETS ALSO MAKE IDEAL ENDINGS TO SMALLER GET-TOGETHERS SUCH AS LUNCHEONS, TEAS AND MORE. MAKE THESE SIMPLE SENSATIONS THE HIT OF YOUR NEXT EVENT.

CHERRY PECAN UPSIDE-DOWN CAKE *PAGE 197*

MOCHA FROSTED SNACK CAKE *PAGE 194*

RHUBARB BERRY UPSIDE-DOWN CAKE *PAGE 199*

Banana-Pecan Sheet Cake

FREEZE IT *BIG BATCH*

Banana-Pecan Sheet Cake

A dear friend of mine gave me this recipe, and I make it often, especially for potlucks. Sometimes I make it ahead and freeze it, then I frost the cake before a party.
—**MERRILL POWERS** SPEARVILLE, KS

PREP: 35 MIN. • **BAKE:** 20 MIN. + COOLING
MAKES: 24 SERVINGS

- ½ cup butter, softened
- 1⅔ cups sugar
- 2 large eggs
- 1½ cups mashed ripe bananas
- 2½ cups all-purpose flour
- 3 teaspoons baking powder
- 1 teaspoon salt
- ¼ teaspoon baking soda
- ⅔ cup buttermilk
- ½ cup chopped pecans

FROSTING
- ⅓ cup butter, softened
- 3 cups confectioners' sugar
- 1½ teaspoons vanilla extract
- 3 to 4 tablespoons fat-free milk
- ⅓ cup finely chopped pecans, toasted

1. Preheat the oven to 350°. Coat a 15x10x1-in. baking pan with cooking spray.
2. In a large bowl, beat butter and sugar until blended. Add eggs, one at a time, beating well after each addition. Add bananas, mixing well (mixture will appear curdled).
3. In another bowl, whisk flour, baking powder, salt and baking soda; add to the butter mixture alternately with buttermilk, beating well after each addition. Fold in pecans.
4. Transfer to prepared pan. Bake for 20-25 minutes or until a toothpick inserted in the center comes out clean. Cool completely in pan on a wire rack.
5. For frosting, in a large bowl, combine butter, confectioners' sugar and vanilla. Add enough milk to achieve the desired consistency. Frost cake. Sprinkle with toasted pecans.

Kahlua Fudge Sheet Cake

BIG BATCH
Mini Pineapple Upside-Down Cakes

These individual pineapple upside-down cakes are an eye-catching addition to a dessert table. A cake mix makes them easy to bake anytime.
—**CINDY COLLEY** OTHELLO, WA

PREP: 30 MIN. • **BAKE:** 20 MIN. + COOLING
MAKES: 2 DOZEN

- ⅔ cup packed brown sugar
- ⅓ cup butter, melted
- 1 can (20 ounces) pineapple tidbits
- 12 maraschino cherries, halved
- 1 package yellow cake mix (regular size)
- 3 large eggs
- ⅓ cup canola oil

1. In a small bowl, combine brown sugar and butter until blended. Spoon into 24 greased muffin cups. Drain pineapple, reserving the juice; spoon pineapple into prepared cups. Place a cherry half with the cut side down in the center of each.
2. In a large bowl, combine the cake mix, eggs, oil and reserved pineapple juice. Beat on low speed for 30 seconds. Beat on medium speed for 2 minutes. Spoon over pineapple, filling each cup three-fourths full.
3. Bake at 350° for 18-22 minutes or until a toothpick inserted near the center comes out clean. Immediately invert onto wire racks to cool.

TOP TIP

Precut a Sheet Cake

Preparing a decorated sheet cake to serve to a large group? Before frosting and decorating, cut the cooled cake into serving-size pieces in the pan. Then frost and decorate as usual. To serve, remove one piece at a time. The rest of the cake stays pretty without cuts going through the frosting.
—**MARY S.** MILTON, WI

BIG BATCH
Kahlua Fudge Sheet Cake

I make this cake for my grandsons. It's a quick and easy recipe that's perfect for chocolate and marshmallow creme lovers.
—**NANCY HEISHMAN** LAS VEGAS, NV

PREP: 35 MIN. • **BAKE:** 20 MIN. + COOLING
MAKES: 24 SERVINGS

- 2 cups all-purpose flour
- 1¾ cups sugar
- 2 teaspoons ground cinnamon
- 1 teaspoon baking soda
- 1 cup Kahlua (coffee liqueur) or strong brewed coffee
- ½ cup butter, cubed
- ½ cup marshmallow creme
- ⅓ cup baking cocoa
- 2 large eggs
- ½ cup buttermilk
- ½ cup chopped pecans

FROSTING
- ½ cup butter, cubed
- ⅓ cup baking cocoa
- ¼ cup marshmallow creme
- 3¾ cups confectioners' sugar
- ½ to ⅔ cup Kahlua (coffee liqueur) or strong brewed coffee
- ¼ cup chopped pecans

1. Preheat oven to 350°. Grease a 15x10x1-in. baking pan. In a large bowl, whisk flour, sugar, cinnamon and baking soda. In a small saucepan, combine Kahlua, butter, marshmallow creme and cocoa; bring just to a boil, stirring occasionally. Add to flour mixture, stirring just until moistened.
2. In a small bowl, whisk eggs and buttermilk until blended; add to the Kahlua mixture, whisking constantly. Fold in pecans. Transfer to prepared pan, spreading evenly. Bake for 18-22 minutes or until a toothpick inserted in the center comes out clean.
3. Meanwhile, for frosting, combine butter, cocoa and marshmallow creme in a small saucepan; stir over medium heat until smooth. Transfer to a bowl. Beat in confectioners' sugar and enough Kahlua to reach a spreading consistency.
4. Remove the cake from oven; place on a wire rack. Spread frosting evenly over warm cake; sprinkle with pecans. Cool completely.

Mocha Frosted Snack Cake

Mocha Frosted Snack Cake

Here's a lighter version of a chocolate mocha cake I've been baking for my family for more than 30 years. I replaced part of the sugar with a lower-calorie sugar blend and some of the oil with applesauce. It turned out just as delicious.
—**DONNA ROBERTS** MANHATTAN, KS

PREP: 20 MIN. • **BAKE:** 35 MIN. + COOLING
MAKES: 9 SERVINGS

- 1 teaspoon instant coffee granules
- 1 cup boiling water
- 1¼ cups all-purpose flour
- ½ cup packed brown sugar
- ¼ cup cornstarch
- ¼ cup sugar blend
- 3 tablespoons baking cocoa
- 1 teaspoon baking soda
- ½ teaspoon salt
- ¼ cup unsweetened applesauce
- 2 tablespoons canola oil
- 1 tablespoon white vinegar
- ½ teaspoon vanilla extract

FROSTING
- ½ teaspoon instant coffee granules
- 1 tablespoon fat-free milk
- 1½ cups confectioners' sugar
- 2 tablespoons baking cocoa
- 3 tablespoons reduced-fat butter, softened
- ½ teaspoon vanilla extract

1. Preheat oven to 350°. In a small bowl, dissolve coffee granules in boiling water; cool slightly. Coat an 8-in.-square baking dish with cooking spray.

2. In a large bowl, whisk flour, brown sugar, cornstarch, sugar blend, cocoa, baking soda and salt. Whisk applesauce, oil, vinegar and vanilla into the coffee mixture. Add to flour mixture; stir just until moistened.

3. Transfer to prepared dish. Bake 35-40 minutes or until a toothpick inserted in the center comes out clean. Cool completely on a wire rack.

4. For frosting, in a small bowl, dissolve coffee granules in milk. In a large bowl, mix confectioners' sugar and cocoa until blended; beat in butter, vanilla and enough coffee mixture to reach a spreading consistency. Spread over the cake.

NOTE *This recipe was tested with Splenda Sugar Blend for Baking and Land O'Lakes light stick butter.*

Golden Apple Snack Cake

It is hard to beat this moist, old-fashioned cake, especially warmed up and finished off with a dollop of whipped topping.
—**CARRIE GRAVOT** BELLEVILLE, IL

PREP: 15 MIN. • **BAKE:** 35 MIN. + COOLING
MAKES: 9 SERVINGS

- ½ cup butter, softened
- 1 cup sugar
- 1 large egg
- 1 cup all-purpose flour
- ½ teaspoon baking soda
- ½ teaspoon ground cinnamon
- 2½ cups chopped peeled tart apples
- ½ cup chopped pecans

1. In a large bowl, cream butter and sugar until light and fluffy. Add egg. Combine the flour, baking soda and cinnamon; gradually beat into the creamed mixture. Fold in apples and pecans.

2. Transfer batter to a greased 9-in.-square baking pan. Bake at 350° for 32-38 minutes or until a toothpick inserted near the center comes out clean. Cool on a wire rack.

Gingered Apple Upside-Down Cake

I like that this gingerbread delight is so deeply flavored and delicious. A nice scoop of vanilla bean ice cream is definitely the icing on this cake, which can be served warm from the oven.

—**RAYMONDE BOURGEOIS** SWASTIKA, ON

PREP: 30 MIN. • **BAKE:** 30 MIN.+ COOLING
MAKES: 8 SERVINGS

- ¼ cup butter, cubed
- ¼ cup packed brown sugar
- 1 tablespoon finely chopped crystallized ginger
- 2 large apples, peeled and cut into ⅛-in. slices

BATTER

- ¼ cup butter, softened
- ⅔ cup packed brown sugar
- 2 large eggs
- 1 teaspoon vanilla extract
- 1½ cups all-purpose flour
- 2 teaspoons baking powder
- 1 teaspoon ground ginger
- ¼ teaspoon salt
- ½ cup 2% milk

1. Preheat oven to 375°. Place butter in a 9-in. round baking pan; heat in oven until melted. Tilt pan to coat bottom and sides. Sprinkle brown sugar and ginger onto bottom of pan. Arrange the apple slices in circles over brown sugar mixture.

2. For batter, in a large bowl, beat butter and brown sugar until blended. Add eggs, one at a time, beating well after each addition. Beat in vanilla. In another bowl, whisk flour, baking powder, ginger and salt; add to creamed mixture alternately with milk. Spoon over apples.

3. Bake 30-35 minutes or until a toothpick inserted in the center comes out clean. Cool for 10 minutes before inverting onto a serving plate. Serve warm.

**Gingered Apple
Upside-Down Cake**

Spiced Pear Upside-Down Cake

BIG BATCH
Yummy S'more Snack Cake

Try this cake that is a close second to s'mores by the campfire. You can adjust the amount of marshmallows and chocolate chips to your liking.
—**DEBORAH WILLIAMS** PEORIA, AZ

PREP: 20 MIN. • **BAKE:** 20 MIN. + COOLING
MAKES: 20 SERVINGS

- 2½ cups reduced-fat graham cracker crumbs (about 15 whole crackers)
- ½ cup sugar
- ⅓ cup cake flour
- ⅓ cup whole wheat flour
- 2 teaspoons baking powder
- ¼ teaspoon salt
- 3 large egg whites
- 1 cup light soy milk
- ¼ cup unsweetened applesauce
- ¼ cup canola oil
- 2 cups miniature marshmallows
- 1 cup (6 ounces) semisweet chocolate chips

1. In a large bowl, combine the first six ingredients. In a small bowl, whisk the egg whites, soy milk, applesauce and oil. Stir into the dry ingredients just until moistened. Transfer to a 13x9-in. baking pan coated with cooking spray.
2. Bake at 350° for 12-15 minutes or until a toothpick inserted near the center comes out clean. Sprinkle with marshmallows. Bake 4-6 minutes longer or until marshmallows are softened. Cool on a wire rack for 10 minutes.
3. In a microwave, melt chocolate chips; stir until smooth. Drizzle over cake. Cool completely on a wire rack.

> "It's super yummy! It's best warm, and reheats very well in the microwave."
> —**KIMBERLYJDUNCAN**
> FROM TASTEOFHOME.COM

Spiced Pear Upside-Down Cake

The flavors of fresh, sweet pears and gingerbread blend beautifully in this intriguing variation on pineapple upside-down cake. Leftovers—if there are any—taste great with coffee or tea the next day.
—**LISA VARNER** EL PASO, TX

PREP: 25 MIN. • **BAKE:** 35 MIN. + COOLING
MAKES: 9 SERVINGS

- ½ cup butter, melted
- ½ cup coarsely chopped walnuts
- ¼ cup packed brown sugar
- 2 large pears, peeled and sliced
- ½ cup butter, softened
- ⅓ cup sugar
- 1 large egg
- ⅓ cup molasses
- 1½ cups all-purpose flour
- ¾ teaspoon ground ginger
- ¾ teaspoon ground cinnamon
- ½ teaspoon salt
- ½ teaspoon baking powder
- ¼ teaspoon baking soda
- ½ cup warm water
  Ice cream, optional

1. Pour melted butter into a 9-in. square baking pan; sprinkle with the nuts and brown sugar. Arrange pears over nuts.
2. In a large bowl, cream softened butter and sugar until light and fluffy. Beat in egg and molasses. Combine the flour, ginger, cinnamon, salt, baking powder and baking soda; add to creamed mixture alternately with water, beating well after each addition.
3. Spread batter over pears. Bake at 350° for 35-40 minutes or until a toothpick inserted near the center comes out clean. Cool for 10 minutes before inverting onto a serving plate. Serve warm with ice cream if desired.

BIG BATCH

Holiday White Fruitcake

Years ago, when I attended Koloa Missionary Church in Hawaii, a friend gave me this recipe. Now I whip up at least 60 loaves for the holidays.

—EILEEN ORTH-SOKOLOWSKI
CHANDLER, AZ

PREP: 20 MIN. • **BAKE:** 50 MIN. + COOLING
MAKES: 4 LOAVES (16 SLICES EACH)

- 1 package (8 ounces) chopped mixed candied fruit
- 1¼ cups golden raisins
- 1 cup chopped walnuts, toasted
- 3 cups all-purpose flour, divided
- 2 cups butter, softened
- 2 cups sugar
- 6 large eggs

1. Preheat oven to 275°. Line bottoms of four greased 9x5-in. loaf pans with parchment paper; grease paper.
2. In a small bowl, toss the candied fruit, raisins and walnuts with ½ cup flour. In a large bowl, cream butter and sugar until light and fluffy. Add eggs, one at a time, beating well after each addition. Gradually beat in remaining flour. Fold in fruit mixture.
3. Transfer to prepared pans. Bake 50-60 minutes or until a toothpick inserted in the center comes out clean. Cool in pans for 10 minutes before removing to wire racks to cool.
NOTE *To toast nuts, bake in a shallow pan in a 350° oven for 5-10 minutes or cook in a skillet over low heat until lightly browned, stirring occasionally.*

Holiday White Fruitcake

Cherry Pecan Upside-Down Cake

Use cherries to make a terrific take on traditional pineapple upside-down cake. The crowning touch: the cheesy topping.

—ELEANOR FROEHLICH ROCHESTER, MI

PREP: 25 MIN. • **BAKE:** 40 MIN. + COOLING
MAKES: 8 SERVINGS

- ¼ cup butter, melted
- ¾ cup packed brown sugar
- 2 cans (15 ounces each) pitted dark sweet cherries, drained
- ½ cup chopped pecans

CAKE
- ½ cup butter, softened
- 1 cup plus 2 tablespoons sugar
- 3 large eggs
- ½ teaspoon vanilla extract
- 1½ cups cake flour
- 1 teaspoon baking powder
- ¼ teaspoon salt
- ½ cup buttermilk

TOPPING
- ½ cup heavy whipping cream
- ½ cup mascarpone cheese
- 2 tablespoons confectioners' sugar
- ⅛ teaspoon almond extract
- ⅛ teaspoon vanilla extract

1. Pour the butter into an ungreased 9-in. round baking pan; sprinkle with brown sugar. Arrange cherries in a single layer over brown sugar; top with pecans.
2. In a large bowl, cream butter and sugar until light and fluffy. Add eggs, one at a time, beating well after each addition. Beat in vanilla. Combine the flour, baking powder and salt; add to the creamed mixture alternately with buttermilk, beating well after each addition.
3. Spoon over pecan layer. Bake at 350° for 40-45 minutes or until a toothpick inserted near the center comes out clean. Cool for 10 minutes before inverting.
4. In a large bowl, beat cream and cheese until it begins to thicken. Gradually add confectioners' sugar and extracts; beat until stiff peaks form. Serve with cake.

Chocolate-Peanut Butter Sheet Cake

FREEZE IT

Tiny Texas Sheet Cakes

These tiny sheet cakes boast a homemade chocolate flavor as big as Texas itself. The cakes are moist, freeze well unfrosted and always bring compliments.

—**HOPE MEECE** AMBIA, IN

PREP: 25 MIN. • **BAKE:** 20 MIN. + COOLING
MAKES: 4 SERVINGS

- ¼ cup butter, cubed
- ¼ cup water
- 1 tablespoon baking cocoa
- ½ cup all-purpose flour
- ½ cup sugar
- ½ teaspoon baking powder
- ¼ teaspoon ground cinnamon
  Dash salt
- 2 tablespoons beaten large egg
- 2 tablespoons 2% milk

FROSTING

- 2 tablespoons butter
- 4½ teaspoons 2% milk
- 1 tablespoon baking cocoa
- ¾ cup confectioners' sugar
- ¼ teaspoon vanilla extract
- 2 tablespoons chopped pecans, toasted, optional

1. In a large saucepan, bring the butter, water and the cocoa just to a boil. Immediately remove from the heat. Combine the flour, sugar, baking powder, cinnamon and salt; stir into butter mixture. Add egg and milk; mix well.
2. Pour into two 5¾x3x2-in. loaf pans coated with cooking spray. Bake at 350° for 20-25 minutes or until a toothpick inserted near the center comes out clean. Cool for 10 minutes before removing from pans to a wire rack to cool completely.
3. In a small microwave-safe bowl, melt butter; add milk and cocoa. Microwave on high for 30 seconds. Whisk in confectioners' sugar and vanilla until smooth. Spread over cakes. Sprinkle with pecans if desired.
NOTE *This recipe was tested in a 1,100-watt microwave.*

BIG BATCH

Chocolate-Peanut Butter Sheet Cake

I love peanut butter and chocolate, so I combined recipes to blend the two. This cake is heavenly served plain or topped with ice cream.

—**LISA VARNER** EL PASO, TX

PREP: 25 MIN. • **BAKE:** 25 MIN. + COOLING
MAKES: 15 SERVINGS

- 2 cups all-purpose flour
- 2 cups sugar
- 1 teaspoon baking soda
- ½ teaspoon salt
- 1 cup water
- ½ cup butter, cubed
- ½ cup creamy peanut butter
- ¼ cup baking cocoa
- 3 large eggs
- ½ cup sour cream
- 2 teaspoons vanilla extract

FROSTING

- 3 cups confectioners' sugar
- ½ cup creamy peanut butter
- ½ cup 2% milk
- ½ teaspoon vanilla extract
- ½ cup chopped salted or unsalted peanuts

1. Preheat oven to 350°. Grease a 13x9-in. baking pan.
2. In a large bowl, whisk flour, sugar, baking soda and salt. In a small saucepan, combine water, butter, peanut butter and cocoa; bring just to a boil, stirring occasionally. Add to flour mixture, stirring just until moistened.
3. In a small bowl, whisk eggs, sour cream and vanilla until blended; add to flour mixture, whisking constantly. Transfer to prepared pan. Bake for 25-30 minutes or until a toothpick inserted in the center comes out clean.
4. Prepare the frosting while cake is baking. In a large bowl, beat the confectioners' sugar, peanut butter, milk and vanilla until smooth.
5. Remove cake from oven; place on a wire rack. Immediately spread with frosting; sprinkle with peanuts. Cool completely.

Rhubarb Berry Upside-Down Cake

I had leftover rhubarb and wanted to create something fresh. With dried cranberries, blueberries and strawberries on hand, I had discovered I had a berry upside-down cake.
—**JUNE PAUL** PORTAGE, WI

PREP: 30 MIN. • **BAKE:** 35 MIN. + COOLING
MAKES: 8 SERVINGS

- 2 **tablespoons butter**
- 1¾ **cups chopped fresh rhubarb**
- ½ **cup fresh blueberries**
- 2 **tablespoons dried cranberries**
- 2 **tablespoons brown sugar**

CAKE
- 6 **tablespoons butter, softened**
- 1 **cup sugar**
- 1 **tablespoon brown sugar**
- 2 **large eggs**
- 1 **tablespoon seedless strawberry jam**
- 1 **teaspoon vanilla extract**
- 1¼ **cups all-purpose flour**
- 1½ **teaspoons baking powder**
- ½ **teaspoon salt**
- ½ **cup 2% milk**
- ¼ **cup orange juice**

1. Preheat oven to 350°. Place butter in an 11x7-in. baking dish. Place in oven for 5-6 minutes or until the butter is melted; carefully swirl to coat evenly.
2. Place rhubarb, blueberries and cranberries in a bowl; sprinkle with sugar and toss to combine. Transfer to baking dish.
3. In a large bowl, beat butter and sugars until blended. Add eggs, one at a time, beating well after each addition. Beat in jam and vanilla. In a small bowl, whisk flour, baking powder and salt. Add to creamed mixture alternately with milk and orange juice, beating well after each addition. Pour over fruit.
4. Bake 35-45 minutes or until top is golden brown and a toothpick inserted in the center comes out clean. Cool for 10 minutes.
5. Loosen cake edges from pan with a knife; invert onto a serving plate. Serve warm or at room temperature.

Rhubarb Berry Upside-Down Cake

BIG BATCH

Pineapple Sheet Cake

Serve a crowd perfectly with this cake. It keeps so well that you can easily prepare it a day ahead and it will stay moist. I often take it to potluck meals at our church, and I have yet to take much of it home.

—KIM MILLER SPIEK SARASOTA, FL

PREP: 15 MIN. • **BAKE:** 35 MIN. + COOLING
MAKES: ABOUT 24 SERVINGS

CAKE
- 2 cups all-purpose flour
- 2 cups sugar
- 2 large eggs
- 1 cup chopped nuts
- 2 teaspoons baking soda
- ½ teaspoon salt
- 1 teaspoon vanilla extract
- 1 can (20 ounces) crushed pineapple, undrained

CREAM CHEESE ICING
- 1 package (8 ounces) cream cheese, softened
- ½ cup butter, softened
- 3¾ cups confectioners' sugar
- 1 teaspoon vanilla extract
- ½ cup chopped nuts

1. In a large bowl, combine the cake ingredients; beat until smooth. Pour into a greased 15x10x1-in. baking pan. Bake at 350° for 35 minutes. Cool.
2. For icing, in a small bowl, combine the cream cheese, butter, confectioners' sugar and vanilla until smooth. Spread over cake and sprinkle with nuts.

Pineapple Sheet Cake

Apple Raisin Spice Cake

Grandma wrote down the recipe for this inviting cake on a piece of a brown paper bag. It's loaded with popular spices, so the aroma while baking is out of this world! The warm sauce makes it moist—and special. Add a dollop of whipped topping for a real treat.

—SHIRLEY JOAN HELFENBEIN LAPEER, MI

PREP: 25 MIN. • **BAKE:** 40 MIN. + COOLING
MAKES: 8 SERVINGS

- 1 cup raisins
- 1 cup boiling water
- ½ cup butter, softened
- ¼ cup shortening
- 1¼ cups sugar
- 2 large eggs
- 1 cup chunky applesauce
- 1 teaspoon vanilla extract
- 2½ cups all-purpose flour
- 2 teaspoons ground cinnamon
- 1 teaspoon baking powder
- ½ teaspoon salt
- ½ teaspoon ground nutmeg
- ¼ teaspoon baking soda
- ¼ teaspoon ground ginger
- ½ cup chopped walnuts

1. Place raisins in a small bowl; cover with boiling water. Let stand for 5 minutes; drain and set aside.
2. In a large bowl, cream the butter, shortening and sugar. Add eggs, one at a time, beating well after each addition. Beat in applesauce and vanilla. Combine the flour, cinnamon, baking powder, salt, nutmeg, baking soda and ginger; add to creamed mixture just until blended. Stir in walnuts and raisins.
3. Pour into a greased 11x7-in. baking dish. Bake at 350° for 40-45 minutes or until a toothpick inserted near the center comes out clean. Cool on a wire rack.

Blueberry
Upside-Down
Skillet Cake

Blueberry Upside-Down Skillet Cake

Living in Maine, I am lucky to have an endless amount of wild blueberries. This recipe is easy, light and also works with cranberries.

—NETTIE MOORE BELFAST, ME

PREP: 25 MIN. • **BAKE:** 20 MIN.
MAKES: 8 SERVINGS

- ¼ cup butter, cubed
- 1 cup packed brown sugar
- ¼ cup orange juice
- 1 cup fresh or frozen blueberries
- 1½ cups all-purpose flour
- ½ cup sugar
- 2 teaspoons baking powder
- ½ teaspoon salt
- 1 large egg
- ½ cup 2% milk
- ½ cup butter, melted
- ½ teaspoon almond extract
  Optional toppings: vanilla ice cream, whipped cream and toasted almonds

1. Preheat the oven to 400°. In a 10-in. ovenproof skillet, melt cubed butter over medium-low heat; stir in brown sugar until dissolved. Remove from heat. Stir in orange juice; sprinkle with blueberries.
2. In a large bowl, whisk flour, sugar, baking powder and salt. In another bowl, whisk egg, milk, melted butter and extract until blended. Add to flour mixture; stir just until moistened. Pour over blueberries.
3. Bake 18-22 minutes or until a toothpick inserted in the center comes out clean. Cool for 10 minutes; invert. Top as desired.
NOTE *To toast nuts, bake in a shallow pan in a 350° oven for 5-10 minutes or cook in a skillet over low heat until lightly browned, stirring occasionally.*

APPLE COBBLER
CHEESECAKE *PAGE 212*

Cheesecakes

FOR SOME, A SOFT, CREAMY CHEESECAKE JUST CAN'T BE BEAT. ENJOY THE MANY VARIATIONS ON THIS TIMELESS DESSERT WITH THIS TOOTH-TINGLING CHAPTER. FROM LEMONY FAVORITES TO CHOCOLATY DELIGHTS, THESE CROWD-PLEASING DINNER FINALES ARE PERFECT FOR ANY HOLIDAY, MENU OR GET-TOGETHER.

GRASSHOPPER CHEESECAKE
PAGE 208

DULCE DE LECHE CHEESECAKE
PAGE 209

CAPPUCCINO CHEESECAKE
PAGE 204

Very Vanilla Slow Cooker Cheesecake

Very Vanilla Slow Cooker Cheesecake

Cinnamon and vanilla give this cheesecake so much flavor, and making it in the slow cooker creates a silky, smooth texture that's hard to resist.

—**KRISTA LANPHIER** MILWAUKEE, WI

PREP: 40 MIN. • **COOK:** 2 HOURS + CHILLING
MAKES: 6 SERVINGS

- ¾ cup graham cracker crumbs
- 1 tablespoon sugar plus ⅔ cup sugar, divided
- ¼ teaspoon ground cinnamon
- 2½ tablespoons butter, melted
- 2 packages (8 ounces each) cream cheese, softened
- ½ cup sour cream
- 2 to 3 teaspoons vanilla extract
- 2 large eggs, lightly beaten

TOPPING
- 2 ounces semisweet chocolate, chopped
- 1 teaspoon shortening
  Toasted sliced almonds

1. Grease a 6-in. springform pan; place on a double thickness of heavy-duty foil (about 12 in. square). Wrap foil securely around pan.
2. Pour 1 in. water into a 6-qt. slow cooker. Layer two 24-in. pieces of aluminum foil. Starting with a long side, roll up foil to make a 1-in.-wide strip; shape into a circle. Place in bottom of slow cooker to make a rack.

3. In a small bowl, mix cracker crumbs, 1 tablespoon sugar and cinnamon; stir in butter. Press onto bottom and about 1 in. up sides of prepared pan.
4. In a large bowl, beat cream cheese and remaining sugar until smooth. Beat in sour cream and vanilla. Add eggs; beat on low speed just until combined. Pour into crust.
5. Place springform pan on foil circle without touching slow cooker sides. Cover slow cooker with a double layer of white paper towels; place lid securely over towels. Cook, covered, on high for 2 hours.
6. Do not remove the lid; turn off slow cooker and let cheesecake stand, covered, in slow cooker for 1 hour.
7. Remove springform pan from slow cooker; remove foil around pan. Cool cheesecake on a wire rack 1 hour longer. Loosen sides from pan with a knife. Refrigerate overnight, covering when completely cooled.
8. For topping, in a microwave, melt chocolate and shortening; stir until smooth. Cool slightly. Remove rim from springform pan. Pour chocolate mixture over cheesecake; sprinkle with almonds.
NOTE *Wilton Industries sells 6-inch springform pans. Call 800-794-5866 or visit wilton.com.*

BIG BATCH
Cappuccino Cheesecake

Instead of pouring the decadent ganache over the top of this coffee-flavored cheesecake, I use most of it to cover the chocolate crust. It's the perfect dessert for a holiday spread.

—**LINDA STEMEN** MONROEVILLE, IN

PREP: 40 MIN. • **BAKE:** 65 MIN. + CHILLING
MAKES: 16 SERVINGS

- 24 Oreo cookies
- ⅓ cup butter, melted

GANACHE
- 1 package (10 ounces) 60% cacao bittersweet chocolate baking chips
- 1 cup heavy whipping cream
- ⅓ cup coffee liqueur

FILLING
- 1 tablespoon instant coffee granules
- 2 tablespoons dark rum
- 4 packages (8 ounces each) cream cheese, softened
- 1⅓ cups sugar
- 2 tablespoons all-purpose flour
- 2 tablespoons ground coffee
- 3 teaspoons vanilla extract
- 2 teaspoons molasses
- 4 large eggs, lightly beaten

TOPPING
- 1½ cups (12 ounces) sour cream
- ⅓ cup sugar
- 2 teaspoons vanilla extract

1. Place cookies in a food processor. Cover and pulse until fine crumbs form. Transfer to a bowl and stir in butter. Press onto the bottom of a greased 10-in. springform pan; set aside.
2. Place chocolate in a small bowl. In a small saucepan, bring cream just to a boil. Pour over chocolate; whisk until smooth. Stir in liqueur. Pour 1¾ cups over the crust. Freeze for 30 minutes or until firm. For the garnishes, drop remaining ganache by teaspoonfuls onto waxed paper-lined sheets; cover and refrigerate.
3. Dissolve coffee granules in rum. In a large bowl, beat cream cheese and sugar until smooth. Beat in the flour, ground coffee, vanilla, molasses and rum mixture. Add eggs; beat on low speed just until combined. Pour over ganache in pan. Place pan on a baking sheet.
4. Bake at 350° for 1-1¼ hours or until center is almost set. Let stand for 5 minutes. Combine the sour cream, sugar and vanilla; spread over top of cheesecake. Bake for 5 minutes longer. Cool on a wire rack for 10 minutes. Carefully run a knife around edge of pan to loosen; cool 1 hour longer. Refrigerate overnight.
5. Remove sides of pan. Just before serving, arrange the garnishes over the top.

BIG BATCH

Butter Pecan Cheesecake

Fall always makes me yearn for this pecan cheesecake, but it's delicious any time of the year. You'll want to put it on your list of favorite desserts.

—LAURA SYLVESTER MECHANICSVILLE, VA

PREP: 30 MIN. • **BAKE:** 70 MIN. + CHILLING
MAKES: 16 SERVINGS

1½ cups graham cracker crumbs
½ cup finely chopped pecans
⅓ cup sugar
⅓ cup butter, melted

FILLING
3 packages (8 ounces each) cream cheese, softened
1½ cups sugar
2 cups (16 ounces) sour cream
1 teaspoon vanilla extract
½ teaspoon butter flavoring
3 large eggs, lightly beaten
1 cup finely chopped pecans

1. In a large bowl, combine the cracker crumbs, pecans, sugar and butter; set aside ⅓ cup for topping. Press remaining crumb mixture onto the bottom and 1 in. up the sides of a greased 9-in. springform pan.
2. Place springform pan on a double thickness of heavy-duty foil (about 18 in. square). Securely wrap foil around pan.
3. In a large bowl, beat the cream cheese and sugar until smooth. Beat in the sour cream, vanilla and butter flavoring. Add eggs; beat on low speed just until combined. Fold in pecans. Pour into crust; sprinkle with reserved crumb mixture. Place springform pan in a large baking pan; add 1 in. of hot water to larger pan.
4. Bake at 325° for 70-80 minutes or until center is almost set. Remove springform pan from water bath. Cool on a wire rack for 10 minutes. Carefully run a knife around edge of pan to loosen; cool 1 hour longer. Refrigerate overnight. Remove sides of pan.

Butter Pecan Cheesecake

"Definitely a 5-star recipe. I shared it with my neighbors and they all called to rave about it."
—LAZYDAYSL
FROM TASTEOFHOME.COM

Lovely Lemon
Cheesecake

Lovely Lemon Cheesecake

Listen for the oohs and ahhs when you present this luxurious cheesecake. The lemon flavor gives it a bright and tangy flair.

—MARGARET ALLEN ABINGDON, VA

PREP: 25 MIN. • **BAKE:** 70 MIN. + CHILLING
MAKES: 14 SERVINGS

- ¾ cup graham cracker crumbs
- 2 tablespoons sugar
- 3 teaspoons ground cinnamon
- 2 tablespoons butter, melted

FILLING

- 5 packages (8 ounces each) cream cheese, softened
- 1⅔ cups sugar
- ⅛ teaspoon salt
- ¼ cup lemon juice
- 1½ teaspoons vanilla extract
- 5 large eggs, lightly beaten
  Thin lemon slices, optional

1. Preheat oven to 325°. Place a greased 10-in. springform pan on a double thickness of heavy-duty foil (about 18 in. square). Wrap foil securely around pan.

2. In a small bowl, mix cracker crumbs, sugar and cinnamon; stir in butter. Press onto bottom of prepared pan; refrigerate while preparing filling.

3. In a large bowl, beat cream cheese, sugar and salt until smooth. Beat in lemon juice and vanilla. Add eggs; beat on low speed just until blended. Pour over crust. Place springform pan in a larger baking pan; add 1 in. of hot water to larger pan.

4. Bake 70-80 minutes or until center is just set and top appears dull. Remove springform pan from water bath. Cool cheesecake on a wire rack for 10 minutes. Loosen sides of pan with a knife; remove foil. Cool 1 hour longer. Refrigerate overnight, covering when completely cooled.

5. Remove rim from pan. If desired, top cheesecake with lemon slices.

Maple-Chestnut Cheesecake

There are so many delightful flavors that perfectly complement each other in this rich, impressive cheesecake. The hint of cinnamon in the crust goes wonderfully well with the maple-brown sugar filling. The homemade maple-glazed chestnuts just take it over the top.

—TASTE OF HOME TEST KITCHEN

PREP: 30 MIN. • **BAKE:** 1¾ HOURS
MAKES: 12 SERVINGS

- 2 **cups graham cracker crumbs**
- 3 **tablespoons sugar**
- ½ **teaspoon ground cinnamon**
- ⅓ **cup butter, melted**

FILLING
- 1½ **cups pure maple syrup**
- 3 **packages (8 ounces each) cream cheese, softened**
- ½ **cup packed brown sugar**
- ⅔ **cup sour cream**
- 3 **tablespoons all-purpose flour**
- 2 **teaspoons vanilla extract**
- ¼ **teaspoon salt**
- 4 **large eggs, lightly beaten**

CANDIED CHESTNUTS
- ½ **cup confectioners' sugar**
- ¼ **teaspoon salt**
- 1 **package (7 ounces) whole cooked and peeled chestnuts, quartered**
- ¾ **cup pure maple syrup**

1. Place a greased 9-in. springform pan on a double thickness of heavy-duty foil (about 18 in. square). Securely wrap foil around pan.
2. In a small bowl, combine the cracker crumbs, sugar and cinnamon; stir in butter. Press onto the bottom and 1½ in. up the sides of prepared pan. Place pan on a baking sheet. Bake at 375° for 8-10 minutes or until set. Cool on a wire rack. Reduce heat to 325°.
3. For filling, in a small saucepan, bring 1½ cups maple syrup to a low boil; cook until reduced to about 1 cup. Cool to room temperature.
4. In a large bowl, beat cream cheese and brown sugar until smooth. Beat in the sour cream, flour, vanilla, salt and cooled syrup. Add eggs; beat on low speed just until combined. Pour into crust. Place springform pan in a large baking pan; add 1 in. of hot water to larger pan.
5. Bake at 325° for 1¼-1½ hours or until center is just set and top appears dull. Remove springform pan from water bath; remove foil. Cool cheesecake on a wire rack for 10 minutes; loosen edges from pan with a knife. Cool 1 hour longer. Refrigerate overnight.
6. For candied chestnuts, in a small bowl, combine sugar and salt. Add chestnuts; toss to coat. Spread evenly onto a greased 15x10x1-in. baking pan. Bake at 350° for 15-19 minutes or until golden brown, stirring once after 10 minutes. Immediately transfer to a waxed paper-lined baking sheet; cool completely.
7. Remove rim from pan. Serve cheesecake with chestnuts and maple syrup.

BIG BATCH
Raspberry & White Chocolate Cheesecake

My mom makes this cheesecake a lot because it's so good and really pretty. She calls it a "go-to recipe." Someday I'll try to make it myself.

—PEGGY ROOS MINNEAPOLIS, MN

PREP: 40 MIN. • **BAKE:** 1¾ HOURS + CHILLING
MAKES: 16 SERVINGS

- 1 **package (10 ounces) frozen sweetened raspberries, thawed**
- 1 **tablespoon cornstarch**

CRUST
- 1 **cup all-purpose flour**
- 2 **tablespoons sugar**
- ½ **cup cold butter**

FILLING
- 4 **packages (8 ounces each) cream cheese, softened**
- 1½ **cups sugar**
- 1¼ **cups heavy whipping cream**
- 2 **teaspoons vanilla extract**
- 2 **large eggs, lightly beaten**
- 12 **ounces white baking chocolate, melted and cooled**

Raspberry & White Chocolate Cheesecake

1. In a small saucepan, mix raspberries and cornstarch until blended. Bring to a boil; cook and stir 1-2 minutes or until thickened. Press through a fine-mesh strainer into a bowl; discard seeds. Cool completely.
2. Preheat oven to 350°. Place a greased 9x3-in. deep springform pan on a double thickness of heavy-duty foil (about 18 in. square). Wrap foil securely around pan.
3. For crust, in a small bowl, mix flour and sugar. Cut in butter until crumbly. Press onto bottom of prepared pan. Place pan on a baking sheet. Bake for 20-25 minutes or until golden brown. Cool on a wire rack. Reduce oven setting to 325°.
4. In a large bowl, beat cream cheese and sugar until smooth. Beat in cream and vanilla. Add the eggs; beat on low speed just until blended. Stir in cooled chocolate. Pour half of the mixture over crust. Spread with half of the raspberry puree. Top with remaining batter. Drop remaining puree by tablespoonfuls over top. Cut batter with a knife to swirl.
5. Place springform pan in a larger baking pan; add 1 in. of hot water to larger pan. Bake 1¾-2 hours or until edge of cheesecake is set and golden. (Center will jiggle when moved.) Remove springform pan from water bath. Cool cheesecake on a wire rack for 10 minutes. Loosen from pan with a knife; remove the foil. Cool 1 hour longer. Refrigerate overnight. Remove rim from pan.

Grasshopper Cheesecake

What do you get when you combine a popular mint-chocolate drink with a cheesecake? Pure delight! Garnish the top with piped whipped cream and cookie crumbs.

—**MARIE RIZZIO** INTERLOCHEN, MI

PREP: 25 MIN. + CHILLING
MAKES: 12 SERVINGS

Toffee Truffle Cheesecake

- 35 **chocolate wafers, finely crushed (about 1²/₃ cups)**
- ¼ **cup butter, melted**
- 1 **tablespoon plus ¾ cup sugar, divided**
- 1 **envelope unflavored gelatin**
- ½ **cup cold water**
- 1 **package (8 ounces) cream cheese, softened**
- ⅓ **cup green creme de menthe**
- 2 **cups heavy whipping cream, whipped**

1. In a small bowl, combine the cookie crumbs, butter and 1 tablespoon sugar. Press half of mixture onto the bottom of a greased 9-in. springform pan. Refrigerate until chilled.
2. In a small saucepan, sprinkle gelatin over cold water; let stand for 1 minute. Heat over low heat, stirring until gelatin is completely dissolved. Cool.
3. In a large bowl, beat cream cheese and the remaining sugar until fluffy. Gradually beat in gelatin mixture. Stir in creme de menthe. Set aside ½ cup whipped cream for garnish. Fold remaining whipped cream into cream cheese mixture.
4. Pour half of the filling over crust. Top with remaining crumb mixture, reserving 2 tablespoons for garnish. Pour remaining filling into pan; garnish with reserved whipped cream. Sprinkle with reserved crumbs. Chill until set. Remove sides of pan before slicing.
TO MAKE AHEAD *Cheesecake can be made a few days in advance. Cover and refrigerate.*

Toffee Truffle Cheesecake

I put together two of my absolute favorite cheesecake recipes and added the delicious homemade caramel sauce for a cheesecake that's now my favorite!

—**HANNAH HALSTEAD** BLAIR, NE

PREP: 40 MIN. • **BAKE:** 45 MIN. + CHILLING
MAKES: 12 SERVINGS (¾ CUP SAUCE)

- 1½ **cups graham cracker crumbs**
- 3 **tablespoons sugar**
- 1 **tablespoon baking cocoa**
- ⅓ **cup butter, melted**

FILLING
- 2 **packages (8 ounces each) cream cheese, softened**
- ⅔ **cup sugar**
- 8 **ounces bittersweet chocolate, melted and cooled**
- 1 **tablespoon all-purpose flour**
- 1 **teaspoon vanilla extract**
- 3 **large eggs, lightly beaten**
- 1 **cup milk chocolate English toffee bits**

SAUCE
- ¼ **cup butter, cubed**
- ⅔ **cup packed brown sugar**
- 1 **tablespoon corn syrup**
- ¼ **cup heavy whipping cream**
- 2 **tablespoons plus ½ cup milk chocolate English toffee bits, divided**

1. Preheat oven to 325°. In a small bowl, mix cracker crumbs, sugar and cocoa; stir in butter. Press onto bottom of a greased 9-in. springform pan.
2. In a large bowl, beat cream cheese and sugar until smooth. Beat in cooled chocolate, flour and vanilla. Add eggs; beat on low speed just until blended. Fold in toffee bits. Pour over crust. Place pan on a baking sheet.
3. Bake 45-50 minutes or until center is almost set. Cool on a wire rack for 10 minutes. Loosen sides from pan with a knife. Cool 1 hour longer. Refrigerate overnight, covering when completely cooled.
4. For sauce, melt butter in a small saucepan. Stir in brown sugar and corn syrup; bring to a boil. Reduce heat to medium; cook and stir until sugar is completely dissolved, about 2 minutes. Stir in cream; return to a boil. Remove from heat; stir in 2 tablespoons toffee bits.
5. Remove rim from springform pan. Sprinkle remaining toffee bits over top of cheesecake. Warm the sauce if necessary; serve with cheesecake.

BIG BATCH
Dulce de Leche Cheesecake

I'm originally from Paraguay, and dulce de leche reminds me of where I came from. If you can't find it at your grocery store, try caramel ice cream topping instead. It tastes different, but this decadent dessert will still be amazing.
—**SONIA LIPHAM** RANBURNE, AL

PREP: 40 MIN. • **BAKE:** 1 HOUR + CHILLING
MAKES: 16 SERVINGS

- 1¾ cups crushed gingersnap cookies (about 35 cookies)
- ¼ cup finely chopped walnuts
- 1 tablespoon sugar
- ½ teaspoon ground cinnamon
- 6 tablespoons butter, melted

FILLING

- 3 packages (8 ounces each) cream cheese, softened
- 1 cup plus 2 tablespoons sugar
- ¼ cup 2% milk
- 2 tablespoons all-purpose flour
- 1 teaspoon vanilla extract
- 3 large eggs, lightly beaten
- 1 can (13.4 ounces) dulce de leche

TOPPINGS

- 1 cup (6 ounces) semisweet chocolate chips
- 1½ teaspoons chili powder
- ½ cup dulce de leche
- 3 tablespoons hot water

1. Preheat oven to 350°. Place a greased 9-in. springform pan on a double thickness of heavy-duty foil (about 18 in. square). Securely wrap foil around pan. In a large bowl, combine cookie crumbs, walnuts, sugar, cinnamon and butter. Press onto bottom and 2 in. up sides of prepared pan.

2. In a large bowl, beat cream cheese and sugar until smooth. Beat in milk, flour and vanilla. Add eggs; beat on low speed just until combined. Pour into crust.

3. Pour dulce de leche into a microwave-safe bowl; microwave at 50% power until softened. Drop dulce de leche by tablespoonfuls over batter; cut through batter with a knife to swirl.

4. Place the springform pan in a large baking pan; add 1 in. of hot water to larger pan. Bake 60-70 minutes or until center is just set and top appears dull.

5. Remove springform pan from water bath. Cool on a wire rack for 10 minutes. Carefully run a knife around edge of pan to loosen; cool 1 hour.

6. In a microwave-safe bowl, melt chips; stir until smooth. Stir in chili powder. Spread over cheesecake. Refrigerate overnight. Remove sides of pan.

7. In a small bowl, whisk dulce de leche and hot water until smooth; drizzle over cheesecake.

NOTE *This recipe was tested with Nestle La Lechera dulce de leche; look for it in the international foods section. If using Eagle Brand dulce de leche (caramel flavored sauce), thicken according to package directions before using.*

Dulce de Leche Cheesecake

TOP TIP
Quick Crust

Use a flat-bottomed measuring cup or glass to firmly press the prepared crumb mixture onto the bottom (and up the sides if recipe directs) of a springform pan.

Pumpkin Cranberry Cheesecake

Pumpkin Cranberry Cheesecake

One Thanksgiving, I was eating pumpkin pie and decided to have some cranberry sauce with it. I loved it so much that I came up with a cheesecake that combines both flavors.
—**JOHN ABRAHAM** BOCA RATON, FL

PREP: 45 MIN. • **BAKE:** 70 MIN. + CHILLING
MAKES: 12 SERVINGS

- 1½ cups graham cracker crumbs
- ¾ cup ground pecans
- 2 tablespoons sugar
- ¼ cup butter, melted

CRANBERRY LAYER
- 1 package (12 ounces) fresh or frozen cranberries
- 1 cup sugar
- 2 tablespoons cornstarch
- 2 tablespoons water
- 4 teaspoons grated orange peel

FILLING
- 3 packages (8 ounces each) cream cheese, softened
- ¾ cup sugar
- ¾ cup packed brown sugar
- 1 can (15 ounces) solid-pack pumpkin
- 3 teaspoons vanilla extract
- 1 teaspoon ground cinnamon
- 4 large eggs, lightly beaten

1. Preheat the oven to 350°. Place a greased 9-in. springform pan on a double thickness of heavy-duty foil (about 18 in. square). Wrap foil securely around pan. Place pan on a baking sheet.
2. In a small bowl, mix cracker crumbs, pecans and sugar; stir in butter. Press onto bottom and 2 in. up sides of the prepared pan. Bake 15 minutes. Cool on a wire rack. Reduce oven setting to 325°.
3. In a large saucepan, combine the cranberry layer ingredients. Bring to a boil, stirring to dissolve sugar. Reduce heat to medium; cook, uncovered, 8-10 minutes or until berries pop and mixture is slightly thickened, stirring occasionally. Remove from heat. Cool slightly. Gently spread into crust.
4. In a large bowl, beat cream cheese and sugars until smooth. Beat in the pumpkin, vanilla and cinnamon. Add eggs; beat on low speed just until blended. Pour over cranberry layer. Place springform pan in a larger baking pan; add 1 in. of hot water to larger pan.
5. Bake 70-80 minutes or until the center is just set and top appears dull. Remove springform pan from water bath. Cool cheesecake on a wire rack for 10 minutes. Loosen sides from pan with a knife; remove foil. Cool 1 hour longer. Refrigerate overnight, covering when completely cooled. Remove rim from pan.

Raspberry Almond Cheesecake

My son requests this cheesecake for his birthday every year, and our school auction committee asks me to make it for the annual auction. It's definitely one of my best recipes.
—**DIANE SCHUMANN** FREDONIA, WI

PREP: 45 MIN. • **BAKE:** 65 MIN. + CHILLING
MAKES: 14 SERVINGS

- 2 cups vanilla wafers (about 60 wafers)
- ½ cup butter, melted
- ¼ cup sugar

FILLING
- 4 packages (8 ounces each) cream cheese, softened
- 1¼ cups sugar
- 1 tablespoon Triple Sec
- 1 teaspoon almond extract
- ⅛ teaspoon salt
- 4 large eggs, lightly beaten
- ⅓ cup seedless raspberry spreadable fruit
- ½ teaspoon raspberry extract

TOPPING
- 2 cups (16 ounces) sour cream
- ¼ cup sugar
- ½ teaspoon almond extract

1. Place a greased 10-in. springform pan on a double thickness of heavy-duty foil (about 18 in. square). Securely wrap foil around pan. In a small bowl, combine the wafer crumbs, butter and sugar. Press onto the bottom and 1 in. up the sides of prepared pan.
2. In a large bowl, beat cream cheese and sugar until smooth. Beat in the Triple Sec, extract and salt. Add eggs; beat on low speed just until combined.

3. Remove 1 cup batter to a small bowl; stir in the spreadable fruit and extract until well-blended. Pour plain batter over crust. Drop raspberry batter by tablespoons over plain batter; spread evenly. Place springform pan in a large baking pan; add 1 in. of hot water to larger pan.

4. Bake at 325° for 50-60 minutes or until almost set and top appears dull. Remove springform pan from water bath. Let stand for 5 minutes.

5. Combine all the topping ingredients; spread over top of the cheesecake. Bake for 5 minutes longer. Cool on a wire rack for 10 minutes. Carefully run a knife around edge of pan to loosen; cool 1 hour longer. Refrigerate overnight. Remove sides of pan.

Marbled Cappuccino Fudge Cheesecake

I came up with this recipe because I love the frozen cappuccino drinks at coffee shops and wanted a cheesecake with the same goodness. If you try it, don't hold back on the topping. It's the best part!
—**BECKY MCCLAFLIN** BLANCHARD, OK

PREP: 45 MIN. • **BAKE:** 70 MIN. + CHILLING
MAKES: 12 SERVINGS

- 1½ cups chocolate graham cracker crumbs (about 8 whole crackers)
- 3 tablespoons sugar
- ¼ cup butter, melted

FILLING
- 4 packages (8 ounces each) cream cheese, softened
- 1¼ cups sugar
- ¼ cup heavy whipping cream
- 3 tablespoons double mocha cappuccino mix
- 2 tablespoons all-purpose flour
- 1½ teaspoons vanilla extract
- 3 large eggs, lightly beaten
- ⅔ cup hot fudge ice cream topping, warmed

CAPPUCCINO CREAM TOPPING
- 1 cup heavy whipping cream
- 2 tablespoons double mocha cappuccino mix

- 1 tablespoon confectioners' sugar
  Chocolate curls, optional

1. Place a greased 9-in. springform pan on a double thickness of heavy-duty foil (about 18 in. square). Securely wrap foil around pan.

2. In a small bowl, combine the cracker crumbs, sugar and butter. Press onto the bottom and 2 in. up the sides of prepared pan. Place pan on a baking sheet. Bake at 325° for 7-9 minutes. Cool on a wire rack.

3. In a large bowl, beat cream cheese and sugar until smooth. Beat in the cream, cappuccino mix, flour and vanilla. Add eggs; beat on low speed just until combined. Pour half of batter into crust. Drizzle with ⅓ cup fudge topping. Repeat layers. Cut through batter with a knife to swirl fudge topping. Place springform pan in a large baking pan; add 1 in. of hot water to larger pan.

4. Bake at 325° for 70-80 minutes or until center is just set and top appears dull. Remove springform pan from water bath. Cool on a wire rack for 10 minutes. Carefully run a knife around edge of pan to loosen; cool for 1 hour longer. Refrigerate overnight. Remove sides of pan.

5. For topping, in a small bowl, beat cream until it begins to thicken. Add cappuccino mix and confectioners' sugar; beat until soft peaks form. Spread over cheesecake. Garnish with chocolate curls if desired.

Marbled Cappuccino Fudge Cheesecake

Coconut Cheesecake
& Rhubarb Compote

BIG BATCH

Coconut Cheesecake & Rhubarb Compote

I took my daughter's love of cheesecake plus my mom's love of coconut and rhubarb and ran with it. Try it with a smidge of chocolate sauce, too.
—**WENDY RUSCH** TREGO, WI

PREP: 55 MIN. • **BAKE:** 1 HOUR 20 MIN. + CHILLING
MAKES: 16 SERVINGS (3½ CUPS COMPOTE)

- 14 **whole graham crackers**
- 1 **cup flaked coconut, toasted**
- ¼ **cup sugar**
- ⅓ **cup butter, melted**

FILLING
- 5 **packages (8 ounces each) cream cheese, softened**
- 1¼ **cups sugar**
- 1¼ **cups sour cream**
- 1 **tablespoon vanilla extract**
- 1 **tablespoon lemon or lime juice**
- 5 **large eggs, lightly beaten**
- 1 **cup flaked coconut**

COMPOTE
- 6 **cups chopped fresh rhubarb (about 1½ pounds)**
- 1 **cup sugar**
- ½ **cup orange juice or water**
  Additional toasted flaked coconut, optional

1. Preheat oven to 325°. Place a greased 9-in. (3-in.-deep) springform pan on a double thickness of heavy-duty foil (about 18 in. square). Wrap foil securely around pan.

2. Break graham crackers into quarters; place in a food processor. Add coconut and sugar; pulse until fine crumbs form. While pulsing, add melted butter just until blended. Press onto bottom and 1½ in. up sides of prepared pan.

3. In a large bowl, beat cream cheese and sugar until smooth. Beat in sour cream, vanilla and lemon juice. Add eggs; beat on low speed just until blended. Fold in coconut. Pour into crust. Place springform pan in a larger baking pan; add 1 in. of hot water to larger pan.

4. Bake 80-90 minutes or until center is just set and top appears dull. Remove springform pan from water bath. Cool cheesecake on a wire rack for 10 minutes. Loosen sides from pan with a knife; remove foil. Cool 1 hour longer.

5. In a large saucepan, combine rhubarb, sugar and orange juice; bring to a boil. Reduce heat; simmer, uncovered, 7-9 minutes or until thickened. Cool slightly; transfer to a covered container. Refrigerate cheesecake and compote overnight, covering cheesecake when cooled completely.

6. Remove rim from springform pan. If desired, press additional coconut onto sides of cheesecake. Serve with compote, warmed if desired.

NOTE *To toast coconut, bake in a shallow pan in a 350° oven for 5-10 minutes or cook in a skillet over low heat until golden brown, stirring occasionally.*

BIG BATCH

Apple Cobbler Cheesecake

I call this mixture of two classic desserts my "lucky" recipe. It won top honors when I entered the baking contest in my hometown's annual apple festival.
—**JAY HOOVER** THE VILLAGES, FL

PREP: 50 MIN. • **BAKE:** 1¼ HOURS + COOLING
MAKES: 16 SERVINGS

- 2 **cups graham cracker crumbs**
- ¼ **cup sugar**
- ½ **cup butter, melted**

COBBLER LAYER
- 1 **cup butter, softened**
- 1 **cup sugar**
- 2 **large eggs**
- 2 **cups all-purpose flour**
- 2 **tablespoons baking powder**
- 2 **medium tart apples, peeled and thinly sliced**
- 1 **jar (12 ounces) hot caramel ice cream topping, divided**

CHEESECAKE LAYER
- 3 **packages (8 ounces each) cream cheese, softened**
- 1 **cup sugar**
- ¼ **cup all-purpose flour**
- ¼ **cup water**
- 3 **large eggs, lightly beaten**
  Whipped cream

1. Preheat oven to 325°. In a small bowl, mix cracker crumbs and sugar; stir in butter. Press onto bottom and 1 in. up sides of a greased 10-in. springform pan. Place pan on a 15x10x1-in. baking pan.

2. For cobbler layer, in a large bowl, cream butter and sugar until light and fluffy. Add eggs, one at a time, beating well after each addition. In a small bowl, whisk flour and baking powder; add to creamed mixture. Drop half of the dough by tablespoonfuls into crust. Top with half of the apple slices; drizzle with ⅓ cup caramel topping.

3. For cheesecake layer, in a large bowl, beat cream cheese and sugar until smooth. Beat in flour and water. Add eggs; beat on low speed just until combined. Pour over caramel. Repeat cobbler layer with remaining dough, apple and an additional ⅓ cup caramel topping.

4. Bake for 1¼-1½ hours or until the cheesecake layer no longer jiggles when moved. Cool on a wire rack 30 minutes.

5. Serve warm or refrigerate overnight, covering when completely cooled, and serve cold. Loosen sides of cheesecake with a knife. Remove rim from pan. Warm remaining caramel topping. Serve with cheesecake; top with whipped cream.

Maple-Nut Cheesecake

To vary this delicious cheesecake, add cherries to the top, or swirl raspberry jam throughout before it's baked.

—WENDY PAFFENROTH PINE ISLAND, NY

PREP: 45 MIN. • **BAKE:** 45 MIN. + CHILLING
MAKES: 12 SERVINGS

- ¾ **cup graham cracker crumbs**
- ½ **cup finely chopped walnuts**
- 3 **tablespoons sugar**
- ¼ **cup butter, melted**

FILLING

- 4 **packages (8 ounces each) cream cheese, softened**
- ¾ **cup sugar**
- 2 **teaspoons maple flavoring**
- ½ **teaspoon almond extract**
- ⅛ **teaspoon grated lemon peel**
- 3 **large eggs, lightly beaten**
   Melted chocolate, optional

1. Place a greased 9-in. springform pan on a double thickness of heavy-duty foil (about 18 in. square). Wrap foil securely around pan.

2. In a small bowl, mix the cracker crumbs, walnuts and sugar; stir in butter. Press onto bottom and 1 in. up sides of prepared pan. Place pan on a baking sheet. Bake at 325° for 10 minutes. Cool on a wire rack.

3. For filling, in a large bowl, beat cream cheese and sugar until smooth. Beat in the maple flavoring, extract and lemon peel. Add eggs; beat on low speed just until blended. Pour into crust. Place springform pan in a larger baking pan; add 1 in. of hot water to larger pan.

4. Bake for 45-55 minutes or until center is just set and top appears dull. Remove springform pan from water bath. Cool cheesecake on a wire rack for 10 minutes. Loosen sides from pan with a knife; remove foil. Cool 1 hour longer. Refrigerate overnight.

5. Remove rim from the pan. If desired, drizzle the cheesecake with melted chocolate.

Maple-Nut Cheesecake

Tart Cherry Lattice Pie, page 231

Personal Pear Pot Pies, page 303

Cookie Ice Cream Pie, page 275

Old-Fashioned Banana Cream Pie, page 236

Pies

MMM, PIE! WHETHER YOU PREFER FRUITY SWEETNESS, CREAMY GOODNESS, COZY COMFORT OR FUN AND FROSTY THIS IS THE SECTION FOR YOU! YOU'LL EVEN FIND CLASSIC TARTS, CRISPS AND COBBLERS. THESE SENSATIONAL MOST-REQUESTED PIE RECIPES PROMISE TO HAVE YOUR TASTE TESTERS GRINNING FROM EAR TO EAR WITH DELIGHT!

BERRY CREAM PIE *PAGE 220*

Fruit Pies

A FRESHLY BAKED PIE FROM THE OVEN WILL ENTICE ANYONE WITH ITS AROMA. BRING ONE OF THESE WHIMSICAL PIES TO A LUNCH OR PICNIC AND EVERYONE WILL WANT TO SKIP RIGHT TO DESSERT! TRY RECIPES FOR APPLE, BLUEBERRY, CHERRY, MANGO, PEAR, RASPBERRY AND OTHERS.

STONE FRUIT PIE
PAGE 223

BLUEBERRY DREAM PIE
PAGE 226

PERFECT RHUBARB PIE
PAGE 229

"I made this pie for my sister and her daughter, and not a single slice was left after 24 hours!"

—JEANJEANNE56
FROM TASTEOFHOME.COM

Berry Patch Pie

Berry Patch Pie

Enjoy a gorgeous, made-for-summer pie with this mouthwatering recipe. Each bite bursts with sweet, juicy berries.
—TASTE OF HOME TEST KITCHEN

PREP: 30 MIN. + CHILLING
MAKES: 8 SERVINGS

Pastry for single-crust pie (9 inches)
¾ cup sugar
¼ cup cornstarch
2 cups halved fresh strawberries
1½ cups fresh raspberries
1 cup fresh blackberries
1 cup fresh blueberries
1 tablespoon lemon juice

1. On a lightly floured surface, unroll pastry. Transfer to a 9-in. pie plate.
2. Trim pastry to ½ in. beyond edge of plate; flute edges. Line unpricked pastry with a double thickness of heavy-duty foil. Bake at 450° for 8 minutes. Remove foil; bake for 5-7 minutes longer or until golden brown. Cool on a wire rack.
3. Meanwhile, in a large saucepan, combine sugar and cornstarch. Stir in berries and lemon juice. Cook, stirring occasionally, over medium heat until mixture just comes to a boil; pour into prepared crust. Cool completely on a wire rack.

> **TOP TIP**
>
> ## Fruit Filling Done Right
>
> • Blackberries, raspberries and strawberries stay fresh for up to two days. Blueberries should be used within five days.
> • To wash delicate berries, soak them in cold water, drain, then dry them in a single layer on a paper towel.
> • To add some spice, simmer the fruit filling with a few slices of fresh ginger or a cinnamon stick.

Cran-Raspberry Pie

Jewel-toned fruits team up to pack this lattice-topped pie. It's a lovely addition to the end of any meal.

—VERONA KOEHLMOOS PILGER, NE

PREP: 15 MIN. • **BAKE:** 40 MIN. + COOLING
MAKES: 6-8 SERVINGS

- 2 cups chopped fresh or frozen cranberries
- 5 cups fresh or frozen unsweetened raspberries, thawed
- ½ teaspoon almond extract
- 1 to 1¼ cups sugar
- ¼ cup quick-cooking tapioca
- ¼ teaspoon salt
  Pastry for double-crust pie (9 inches)

1. In a large bowl, combine cranberries, raspberries and extract. Combine the sugar, tapioca and salt in another bowl. Add to fruit mixture; toss gently to coat. Let stand for 15-20 minutes.

2. Line pie plate with bottom pastry; trim to 1 in. beyond edge of plate. Add filling. Roll out remaining pastry; make a lattice crust. Trim, seal and flute edges. Cover edges loosely with foil.

3. Bake at 375° for 40-45 minutes or until crust is golden brown and filling is bubbly. Cool on a wire rack.

Apple-Cherry Cream Cheese Pie

Apple-Cherry Cream Cheese Pie

A layer of sweetened cream cheese topped with a tart fruit filling makes this pie popular with family, friends and co-workers. It won the blue ribbon at a local fair.

—DONNA RETTEW JONESTOWN, PA

PREP: 45 MIN. + CHILLING
BAKE: 45 MIN. + COOLING
MAKES: 8 SERVINGS

- 2¼ cups all-purpose flour
- 2 teaspoons sugar
- ¾ teaspoon salt
- 1 cup cold unsalted butter, cubed
- 6 to 8 tablespoons ice water

FILLING

- 1 package (8 ounces) cream cheese, softened
- 1¼ cups sugar, divided
- 1 teaspoon vanilla extract
- 9 cups thinly sliced peeled McIntosh apples (about 11 medium)
- ½ cup all-purpose flour
- 1 teaspoon apple pie spice
- ¼ teaspoon salt
- 1 can (14½ ounces) pitted tart cherries, drained
- 2 tablespoons butter

1. In a large bowl, mix flour, sugar and salt; cut in butter until crumbly. Gradually add ice water, tossing with a fork until dough holds together when pressed. Divide dough in half. Shape each into a disk; wrap in plastic wrap. Refrigerate 1 hour or overnight.

2. Preheat oven to 425°. For filling, in a small bowl, beat cream cheese, ¼ cup sugar and vanilla until blended. In a large bowl, toss apples with flour, pie spice, salt and remaining sugar. Stir in cherries.

3. On a lightly floured surface, roll one half of dough to a ⅛-in.-thick circle; transfer to a 9-in. pie plate. Trim pastry even with rim.

4. Spread cream cheese mixture onto bottom of pastry. Add apple mixture; dot with butter. Roll remaining dough to a ⅛-in.-thick circle. Place over filling. Trim, seal and flute edge. Cut slits in top.

5. Bake 45-50 minutes or until crust is golden brown and filling is bubbly. Cover top loosely with foil during the last 10-15 minutes if needed to prevent overbrowning. Cool on a wire rack. Refrigerate leftovers.

Berry Cream Pie

Berry Cream Pie

I found this recipe in a very old cookbook and made it for a family gathering. The pie was gone in no time. It's a perfect summertime treat.

—SUE YAEGER BOONE, IA

PREP: 15 MIN. • **COOK:** 15 MIN. + CHILLING
MAKES: 6-8 SERVINGS

FILLING
- ½ **cup sugar**
- 3 **tablespoons cornstarch**
- 3 **tablespoons all-purpose flour**
- ½ **teaspoon salt**
- 2 **cups 2% milk**
- 1 **large egg, lightly beaten**
- ½ **teaspoon vanilla extract**
- ½ **teaspoon almond extract, optional**
- ½ **cup heavy whipping cream**
- 1 **pastry shell (9 inches), baked**

GLAZE
- ½ **cup crushed strawberries**
- ½ **cup water**
- ¼ **cup sugar**
- 2 **teaspoons cornstarch**
- 1½ **cups quartered strawberries**
- 1½ **cups fresh raspberries**

1. In a large saucepan, combine the sugar, cornstarch, flour and the salt; gradually stir in milk until smooth. Cook and stir over medium-high heat until thickened and bubbly. Reduce heat; cook and stir 2 minutes more.
2. Remove from heat and stir a small amount of hot filling into egg; return all to the saucepan, stirring constantly. Bring to a gentle boil; cook and stir for 2 minutes. Remove from the heat; gently stir in vanilla and almond extract, if desired. Cool to room temperature.
3. In a small bowl, beat cream until stiff peaks form; fold into filling. Pour into pastry shell. Chill for at least 2 hours.
4. About 2 hours before serving, prepare glaze. In a large saucepan, combine crushed strawberries and water; cook for 2 minutes. Combine sugar and cornstarch; gradually add to the pan. Cook and stir until thickened and clear; strain. Cool for 20 minutes.
5. Meanwhile, arrange quartered strawberries and raspberries over filling; pour glaze evenly over the berries. Refrigerate for 1 hour.

BIG BATCH
Lattice-Topped Pear Slab Pie

When I make a lattice top for pears and candied fruit, it's a charming frame for this dessert. Dollop with whipped cream.

—JOHNNA JOHNSON SCOTTSDALE, AZ

PREP: 30 MIN. + CHILLING
BAKE: 40 MIN. + COOLING
MAKES: 24 SERVINGS

- 1 **cup butter, softened**
- 1 **package (8 ounces) cream cheese, softened**
- 2 **tablespoons sugar**
- ½ **teaspoon salt**
- 2¼ **cups all-purpose flour**

FILLING
- ¾ **cup sugar**
- 3 **tablespoons all-purpose flour**
- 2 **teaspoons grated lemon peel**
- 8 **cups thinly sliced peeled fresh pears (about 7 medium)**
- 1 **cup chopped mixed candied fruit**
- 1 **tablespoon 2% milk**
- 3 **tablespoons coarse sugar**

1. In a small bowl, beat butter, cream cheese, sugar and salt until blended. Gradually beat in flour. Divide dough in two portions so that one portion is slightly larger than the other. Shape each into a rectangle; wrap in plastic wrap. Refrigerate 1 hour or overnight.
2. Preheat oven to 350°. For filling, in a large bowl, combine sugar, flour and lemon peel. Add the pears and candied fruit; toss to coat.
3. On a lightly floured surface, roll out larger portion of dough into an 18x13-in. rectangle. Transfer to a greased 15x10x1-in. baking pan. Press onto the bottom and up the sides of pan; add filling.
4. Roll remaining dough to a ⅛-in.-thick rectangle; cut into ½-in.-wide strips. Arrange over filling in a lattice pattern. Trim and seal strips to edges. Brush pastry with milk; sprinkle with sugar.
5. Bake 40-45 minutes or until crust is golden brown and filling is bubbly. Cool on a wire rack.

Lattice-Topped
Pear Slab Pie

Rhu-berry Pie

Rhu-berry Pie

I cook in a coffee shop, so I am always looking for new and unique pies to serve my customers. The combination of blueberries and rhubarb in this recipe caught my eye and it was an instant best seller.

—KAREN DOUGHERTY FREEPORT, IL

PREP: 20 MIN. • **BAKE:** 45 MIN.
MAKES: 8 SERVINGS

Pastry for single-crust pie (9 inches)

½ cup sugar
¼ cup cornstarch
1 cup unsweetened apple juice
3½ cups diced fresh rhubarb
2½ cups fresh blueberries

1. Roll out pastry to fit a 9-in. pie plate. Transfer pastry to pie plate. Trim pastry to ½ in. beyond edge of plate; flute edges.

2. In a large heavy saucepan, combine sugar and cornstarch. Stir in apple juice until smooth. Cook and stir over medium heat until thickened. Add rhubarb; cook and stir gently 2-3 minutes or just until heated through. Stir in the blueberries. Spoon mixture into pie shell.

3. Place a foil-lined baking sheet on a rack below the pie to catch any spills. Bake at 375° for 45-50 minutes or until bubbly. Cool completely on a wire rack.

Stone Fruit Pie

You can use any type of stone fruit in this pie. I love combining white peaches with sour cherries as a variation. The flavor is complex, and the filling is so pretty.

—**CRYSTAL JO BRUNS** ILIFF, CO

PREP: 30 MIN. • **BAKE:** 45 MIN.
MAKES: 8 SERVINGS

- 2 **cups fresh or frozen pitted tart cherries, thawed**
- 3 **medium nectarines, chopped**
- 3 **apricots, sliced**
- ⅔ **cup sugar**
- 1 **tablespoon cornstarch**
- 2 **tablespoons plus 2 cups all-purpose flour, divided**
- ⅛ **teaspoon ground cinnamon**
- 1 **teaspoon salt**
- ¾ **cup plus 2 tablespoons cold butter, divided**
- 6 **to 7 tablespoons ice water**
- 1 **large egg yolk**
- 1 **teaspoon water**

1. Preheat the oven to 400°. In a small bowl, combine the cherries, nectarines, apricots, sugar, cornstarch, 2 tablespoons flour and cinnamon; set aside.

2. In another bowl, combine salt and remaining flour; cut in ¾ cup butter until crumbly. Gradually add ice water, tossing with a fork until dough forms a ball. Divide dough into two portions so that one is slightly larger than the other. Roll out larger portion to fit a 9-in. pie plate; transfer pastry to pie plate. Add filling; dot with remaining butter.

3. Roll out remaining pastry; make a lattice crust. Trim, seal and flute edges. In a small bowl, whisk egg yolk and water; brush over lattice top.

4. Bake 45-50 minutes or until filling is bubbly and crust is golden brown. Cover edges with foil during the last 15 minutes to prevent overbrowning if necessary. Cool on a wire rack.

Fresh Strawberries & Amaretto Cream Pie

Strawberry pie is even more luscious when covered with a generous layer of amaretto cream. Keep this recipe in mind whenever you have a bounty of fresh berries.

—**CHARIS O'CONNELL** MOHNTON, PA

PREP: 40 MIN.+ COOLING
BAKE: 15 MIN. + CHILLING
MAKES: 8 SERVINGS

- ¾ **cup sliced almonds, toasted**
- 1 **cup all-purpose flour**
- ¼ **cup confectioners' sugar**
- ⅛ **teaspoon salt**
- ¼ **cup cold butter, cubed**
- 2 **tablespoons shortening**
- 3 **to 4 tablespoons ice water**

FILLING
- 4 **cups sliced fresh strawberries, divided**
- 1 **tablespoon lemon juice**
- ½ **cup water**
- ½ **cup sugar**
- ¼ **cup cornstarch**
- 4 **to 6 drops red food coloring, optional**

AMARETTO CREAM
- 1 **cup heavy whipping cream**
- 2 **tablespoons sour cream**
- 1 **tablespoon confectioners' sugar**
- 2 **tablespoons amaretto or ½ teaspoon almond extract**
  Optional toppings: additional fresh strawberries and toasted almonds

1. Place almonds in a food processor; cover and pulse until almonds are finely ground. Add flour, confectioners' sugar and salt; pulse until blended. Add butter and shortening; pulse until butter and shortening are the size of peas. While pulsing, add just enough ice water to form moist crumbs. Shape dough into a disk; wrap in plastic wrap. Refrigerate for 30 minutes or until easy to handle.

2. On a lightly floured surface, roll dough to a ⅛-in. thick circle; transfer to a 9-in. deep-dish plate. Trim pastry to ½ in. beyond edge of plate; flute edges. Line unpricked pastry shell with a double thickness of heavy-duty

Fresh Strawberries & Amaretto Cream Pie

foil. Fill with dried beans, uncooked rice or pie weights.

3. Bake at 425° for 8 minutes. Remove the foil and weights; bake 5-7 minutes longer or until golden brown. Cool on a wire rack.

4. In a large bowl, mash 1 cup of the strawberries with the lemon juice. Add water. In a large saucepan, combine sugar and cornstarch; stir in mashed berry mixture. Bring to a boil over medium heat, stirring constantly. Cook and stir for 2 minutes or until thickened. Transfer to a large bowl; stir in the food coloring if desired. Refrigerate for 20 minutes or until cooled slightly, stirring occasionally.

5. Fold in the remaining sliced berries; transfer to crust. Refrigerate for at least 3 hours or until set.

6. In a small bowl, beat the whipping cream until it begins to thicken. Add sour cream, confectioners' sugar and amaretto; beat until stiff peaks form. Spread over filling. Top with additional strawberries and almonds if desired.

NOTE *To toast nuts, spread in a 15x10x1-in. baking pan. Bake at 350° for 5-10 minutes or until lightly browned, stirring occasionally. Or, spread in a dry nonstick skillet and heat over low heat until lightly browned, stirring occasionally. When using pie weights, cool before storing. Beans and rice may be reused for pie weights, but not for cooking.*

Browned Butter Apple Pie with Cheddar Crust

Browned Butter Apple Pie with Cheddar Crust

How do you make good old-fashioned apple pie even better? Enhance the crust with shredded cheddar cheese and stir browned butter into the filling. Wonderful!

—**KATHRYN CONRAD** MILWAUKEE, WI

PREP: 40 MIN. + CHILLING
BAKE: 45 MIN. + COOLING
MAKES: 8 SERVINGS

- 2½ cups all-purpose flour
- 3 tablespoons semolina flour
- ¾ teaspoon salt
- 14 tablespoons cold butter, cubed
- ½ cup shredded aged sharp cheddar cheese
- 10 to 12 tablespoons ice water

FILLING

- ¼ cup butter, cubed
- 8 large Honeycrisp apples, peeled and cut into ¾-inch pieces (about 12 cups)
- ⅓ cup sugar
- 3 tablespoons brown sugar
- 3 tablespoons all-purpose flour
- 1 large egg
- 1 tablespoon water

1. Place the flours and salt in a food processor; pulse until blended. Add butter; pulse until butter is the size of peas. Add cheese; pulse 1-2 times. Transfer flour mixture to a large bowl. Gradually add ice water to flour mixture tossing with a fork until dough holds together when pressed. Divide dough in half. Shape each into a disk; wrap in plastic wrap. Refrigerate 30 minutes or overnight.

2. Preheat oven to 400°. For filling, in a Dutch oven, melt butter over medium heat. Heat 5-7 minutes or until golden brown, stirring constantly.

3. Stir in apples and sugars; bring to a boil. Reduce heat; simmer, covered, 6-8 minutes or until apples are almost tender. Uncover; cook 4-6 minutes longer or until slightly thickened, stirring occasionally. Stir in flour. Transfer apple mixture to a large bowl; refrigerate until cool.

4. On a lightly floured surface, roll out half of the dough to fit a 9-in. deep-dish pie plate. Transfer pastry to pie plate; trim pastry to ½ in. beyond edge of plate. Refrigerate 30 minutes.

5. Add filling to pastry. Roll remaining dough to a 12-in. circle; cut into eight wedges. Place wedges over filling. Trim, seal and flute edges. In a small bowl, whisk egg with water; brush over pastry.

6. Bake 45-55 minutes or until crust is golden brown and filling is bubbly. Cover edge loosely with foil during the last 15 minutes if needed to prevent overbrowning. Remove foil. Cool on a wire rack.

Lemon Pear Pie

My husband loves all kinds of fruit, so he's a big fan of this fast-to-fix pie. The lemon and pear flavors taste fantastic paired together.

—**CAROLINA HOFELDT** LLOYD, MT

PREP: 20 MIN. • **BAKE:** 50 MIN. + COOLING
MAKES: 6-8 SERVINGS

- 2 large eggs, lightly beaten
- 1 cup sugar
- ¼ cup lemon juice
- 1 tablespoon butter
- 1 teaspoon grated lemon peel
- 3 cans (15 ounces each) pear halves, drained and cubed
- 1 unbaked pastry shell (9 inches)

1. In a saucepan, combine the first five ingredients. Cook and stir over low heat for 10 minutes or until thickened and bubbly. Remove from heat; fold in pears. Pour into pastry shell.

2. Bake at 350° for 50-55 minutes

or until crust is golden brown and filling is bubbly. Cool on a wire rack for 1 hour. Store pie in the refrigerator.

Rhubarb Cheese Pie

Savor this tangy rhubarb pie topped with a luscious cream cheese layer. The rich cheese tempers the tart rhubarb to create a balanced dessert.
—STACEY MEYER PLYMOUTH, WI

PREP: 35 MIN. • **BAKE:** 25 MIN. + CHILLING
MAKES: 8 SERVINGS

Pastry for single-crust pie (9 inches)
- 4½ teaspoons all-purpose flour
- 1 tablespoon cornstarch
- 1 cup sugar, divided
- ½ cup water
- 3 cups sliced fresh or frozen rhubarb
- 1 teaspoon vanilla extract, divided
- 12 ounces cream cheese, softened
- 2 large eggs, lightly beaten
- 1 large egg yolk

1. Line a 9-in. pie plate with pastry; flute edges. Line unpricked pastry shell with a double thickness of heavy-duty foil. Bake at 450° for 8 minutes. Remove foil; bake 5 minutes longer. Cool on a wire rack.
2. In a small saucepan, combine the flour, cornstarch and ½ cup sugar. Add water and rhubarb; stir until blended. Bring to a boil; cook and stir for 2 minutes or until thickened. Remove from heat; stir in ½ teaspoon vanilla. Transfer to prepared pastry.
3. In a small bowl, beat the cream cheese with remaining sugar and vanilla until smooth. Add eggs and egg yolk; beat on low speed just until combined. Spread over top of pie.
4. Cover edges with foil. Bake at 325° for 25-30 minutes or until set. Cool on a wire rack for 1 hour. Refrigerate for at least 4 hours before serving.
NOTE *If using frozen rhubarb, measure rhubarb while still frozen, then thaw completely. Drain in a colander, but do not press liquid out.*

"This pie is a new family favorite! The perfect blend of sweet and tart, so yummy!"
—WADDINGTON6
FROM TASTEOFHOME.COM

Rhubarb
Cheese Pie

Tropical Coconut Pie

A breeze to prepare, this tropical-tasting pie is tops with whoever tries it, especially those who like pineapple and coconut.
—**NANCY MENDOZA** YAKIMA, WA

PREP: 20 MIN. + COOLING
BAKE: 10 MIN. + CHILLING
MAKES: 8 SERVINGS

- 2¼ **cups flaked coconut, divided**
- 2 **tablespoons butter, melted**
- 1 **can (20 ounces) crushed pineapple, undrained**
- 32 **large marshmallows**
- 2 **teaspoons rum or vanilla extract**
- ¼ **teaspoon salt**
- 1 **cup heavy whipping cream, whipped**

1. In a bowl, combine 2 cups coconut and the butter. Press onto the bottom and up the sides of a greased 9-in. pie plate. Bake at 325° for 8-10 minutes or until golden brown. Cool on a wire rack. Toast the remaining coconut; set aside.
2. Drain pineapple, reserving ½ cup juice (discard the remaining juice or refrigerate for another use); set the pineapple aside. In a saucepan, combine the marshmallows and reserved juice. Cook and stir over medium heat until marshmallows are melted. Remove from the heat. Add pineapple, extract and salt; mix well. Refrigerate for 2 hours or until cool.
3. Fold in the whipped cream; spoon into prepared crust. Sprinkle with toasted coconut. Refrigerate for 2 hours or until set. Refrigerate leftovers.

Blueberry Dream Pie

Decorate this showstopping pie to fit any season. I like to make stars for Independence Day, leaves for fall, hearts for Valentine's Day and flowers for spring.
—**KERRY NAKAYAMA** NEW YORK, NY

PREP: 40 MIN. • **BAKE:** 35 MIN. + COOLING
MAKES: 8 SERVINGS

- **Pastry for double-crust pie (9 inches)**
- **CHEESE FILLING**
- 4 **ounces reduced-fat cream cheese**

Blueberry Dream Pie

- ½ **cup confectioners' sugar**
- 1 **tablespoon lemon juice**
- 1 **large egg yolk**
- **BLUEBERRY FILLING**
- ½ **cup plus 1 tablespoon sugar, divided**
- 2 **tablespoons all-purpose flour**
- 1 **tablespoon cornstarch**
- ¼ **cup cold water**
- 6 **cups fresh or frozen blueberries, divided**
- 2 **tablespoons lemon juice**
- 1 **tablespoon minced fresh mint or 1 teaspoon dried mint**
- 1 **large egg white, beaten**

1. Line a 9-in. deep-dish pie plate with bottom crust. Trim pastry to ½ in. beyond edge of plate; flute edges. Line unpricked pastry shell with a double thickness of heavy-duty foil. Bake at 450° for 8 minutes. Remove foil; bake 5 minutes longer. Cool on a wire rack. Reduce the heat to 375°.
2. In a small bowl, beat the cream cheese, confectioners' sugar and lemon juice until light and fluffy. Beat in egg yolk until blended. Spread into crust.
3. In a large saucepan, combine ½ cup sugar, flour and cornstarch; stir in water until smooth. Stir in 2 cups berries. Bring to a boil; cook and stir for 1-2 minutes or until thickened. Cool slightly. Gently stir in the lemon juice, mint and remaining berries. Pour over cheese filling.
4. Cut decorative cutouts in remaining pastry; arrange over the filling, leaving center uncovered. Brush the pastry with egg white; sprinkle with remaining sugar.
5. Bake at 375° for 35-40 minutes or until crust is golden brown and filling is bubbly. Cover edges with foil during the last 15 minutes to prevent overbrowning if necessary. Cool on a wire rack. Refrigerate leftovers.

BIG BATCH
Apple Cranberry Slab Pie

My husband loves pie, so I created this recipe. It's so good, I bend the rules and let the grandkids have it for breakfast.
—BRENDA SMITH CURRAN, MI

PREP: 45 MIN. • **BAKE:** 40 MIN. + COOLING
MAKES: 15 SERVINGS

- Pastry for two double-crust pies (9 inches)
- 1½ cups sugar
- ¼ cup all-purpose flour
- 4 medium tart apples, peeled and sliced (about 4½ cups)
- 4 cups frozen or fresh raspberries
- 2 cups fresh or frozen cranberries
- 2 teaspoons grated orange peel
- ½ cup orange juice
- 1 teaspoon ground nutmeg
- 1 teaspoon ground cinnamon
- Additional orange juice and sugar, optional

1. Divide pastry dough into two portions so that one is slightly larger than the other; wrap each in plastic wrap. Refrigerate 1 hour or overnight.
2. In a Dutch oven, mix sugar and flour; stir in fruit, orange peel, orange juice and spices. Bring to a boil. Reduce heat; simmer, uncovered, 10-12 minutes or until apples are tender and juices are thickened, stirring occasionally. Cool slightly.
3. Preheat the oven to 375°. Roll out the larger portion of pastry dough between two pieces of waxed paper into a 16x12-in. rectangle. Remove top sheet of waxed paper; place a 13x9-in. baking pan upside down over pastry. Lifting with waxed paper, carefully invert pastry into pan. Remove waxed paper; press pastry onto bottom and up sides of pan. Add filling.
4. On a well-floured surface, roll the remaining dough into a 14x10-in. rectangle; cut into ¾-in.-wide strips. Arrange strips over filling, sealing ends to edges of bottom pastry. If desired, brush pastry with additional orange juice; sprinkle with additional sugar.
5. Bake 40-50 minutes or until crust is golden brown and filling is bubbly. Cool on a wire rack.

PASTRY FOR TWO DOUBLE-CRUST PIES (9 INCHES) *In a large bowl, combine 4½ cups all-purpose flour, 1 Tbsp. sugar and 2 tsp. salt; cut in 1¾ cups shortening until crumbly. Whisk 1 large egg, 1 Tbsp. white vinegar and ½ cup ice water; gradually add to flour mixture, tossing with a fork until dough holds together when pressed. Proceed as directed.*

Apple-Berry Crumb Pie

Enjoy this delectable pie that saves time and effort because you don't have to roll out a crust or cut up any apples!
—LAURIE JONAS PORTAGE, WI

PREP: 20 MIN. • **BAKE:** 25 MIN. + COOLING
MAKES: 8 SERVINGS

- 1½ cups quick-cooking oats
- 1 cup all-purpose flour
- ½ cup packed brown sugar
- 10 tablespoons butter, melted
- 1 can (21 ounces) apple pie filling
- ¾ cup dried cranberries
- 1½ teaspoons lemon juice
- ½ teaspoon ground cinnamon
- Vanilla ice cream, optional

1. Preheat oven to 375°. In a large bowl, combine oats, flour, brown sugar and butter; set aside ¾ cup for topping. Press remaining mixture onto the bottom and up the sides of a greased 9-in. pie plate. Bake for 13-17 minutes or until lightly browned.
2. In another bowl, combine apple pie filling, cranberries, lemon juice and cinnamon. Spoon into crust. Sprinkle with reserved oat mixture.
3. Bake 25-30 minutes or until topping is lightly browned. Cool on a wire rack. Serve with ice cream if desired.

Apple Cranberry Slab Pie

Perfect
Rhubarb Pie

Perfect Rhubarb Pie

Nothing hides the tangy rhubarb in this lovely pie, which has just the right balance of sweet and tart tastiness.
—**ELLEN BENNINGER** GREENVILLE, PA

PREP: 20 MIN. + STANDING • **BAKE:** 55 MIN.
MAKES: 8 SERVINGS

- 4 **cups sliced fresh or frozen rhubarb, thawed**
- 4 **cups boiling water**
- 1½ **cups sugar**
- 3 **tablespoons all-purpose flour**
- 1 **teaspoon quick-cooking tapioca**
- 1 **large egg**
- 2 **teaspoons cold water**
  Pastry for double-crust pie (9 inches)
- 1 **tablespoon butter**

1. Place rhubarb in a colander; pour boiling water over rhubarb and allow to drain. In a large bowl, mix sugar, flour and tapioca. Add drained rhubarb; toss to coat. Let stand 15 minutes. In a small bowl, whisk egg and cold water; stir into rhubarb mixture.

2. Preheat oven to 400°. On a lightly floured surface, roll one half of the pastry dough to a ⅛-in.-thick circle; transfer to a 9-in. pie plate. Trim the pastry even with rim. Add filling; dot with butter. Roll remaining dough to a ⅛-in.-thick circle. Place over filling. Trim, seal and flute edge. Cut slits in top. Bake for 15 minutes.

3. Reduce oven setting to 350°. Bake 40-50 minutes longer or until crust is golden brown and filling is bubbly. Cool on a wire rack.

NOTE *If using frozen rhubarb, measure rhubarb while still frozen, then thaw completely. Drain in a colander, but do not press liquid out.*

PASTRY FOR DOUBLE-CRUST PIE (9 INCHES): *Combine 2½ cups all-purpose flour and ½ tsp. salt; cut in 1 cup cold butter until crumbly. Gradually add ⅓ to ⅔ cup ice water, tossing with a fork until dough holds together when pressed. Wrap in plastic wrap and refrigerate for 1 hour.*

Sour Cream Peach Pecan Pie

Sour Cream Peach Pecan Pie

Fresh peaches, good Southern pecans and real vanilla make this pie impossible to resist. Make sure to have a big slice!
—**SHERRELL DIKES** HOLIDAY ISLE, AR

PREP: 30 MIN. • **BAKE:** 45 MIN. + COOLING
MAKES: 8 SERVINGS

- **Pastry for single-crust pie (9 inches)**
- 4 **cups sliced peeled peaches**
- 2 **tablespoons peach preserves**
- 1 **cup sugar**
- 1 **cup (8 ounces) sour cream**
- 3 **large egg yolks**
- ¼ **cup all-purpose flour**
- 1 **teaspoon vanilla extract**

TOPPING
- ½ **cup all-purpose flour**
- ½ **cup packed brown sugar**
- ¼ **cup sugar**
- 3 **tablespoons chopped pecans**
- 1 **teaspoon ground cinnamon**
- ¼ **cup cold butter, cubed**

1. Line a 9-in. pie plate with pastry; trim and flute edge. In a large bowl, combine peaches and preserves. Transfer to pastry shell. In a small bowl, whisk the sugar, sour cream, egg yolks, flour and vanilla. Pour over peaches.

2. Bake at 425° for 30 minutes. Meanwhile, in a small bowl, combine flour, sugars, pecans and cinnamon. Cut in butter until crumbly; sprinkle over pie.

3. Bake for 15-20 minutes or until a knife inserted in the center comes out clean and topping is golden brown. Cover edge with foil during the last 15 minutes to prevent overbrowning if necessary. Cool completely on a wire rack for 3 hours before serving. Store in the refrigerator.

Mango Pie with Coconut Crust

Mango Pie with Coconut Crust

Mangoes are one of my favorite fruits. They deserve to be represented in a pie. And, of course, everything is better with coconut. This is the first pie I created myself.
—**JENNIFER WORRELL** NILES, IL

PREP: 50 MIN. + CHILLING
BAKE: 45 MIN. + COOLING
MAKES: 8 SERVINGS

- 2½ cups all-purpose flour
- ½ teaspoon salt
- ⅔ cup cold butter, cubed
- ⅔ to ¾ cup ice water
- 5 cups sliced peeled mangoes (about 4 large)
- 2 tablespoons dark rum or orange juice
- ⅓ cup sugar
- 2 tablespoons quick-cooking tapioca
- ¾ teaspoon ground ginger
- ¼ teaspoon ground cardamom
  Dash white pepper
- ⅛ teaspoon salt
- ⅓ cup flaked coconut, toasted

1. In a large bowl, mix flour and salt; cut in butter until crumbly. Gradually add ice water, tossing with a fork until dough holds together when pressed. Divide dough in half. Shape each into a disk; wrap in plastic wrap. Refrigerate 30 minutes or overnight.
2. Preheat oven to 400°. In a large bowl, toss mangoes with rum. In a small bowl, mix sugar, tapioca, spices and salt. Gently stir into fruit mixture; let stand 15 minutes.
3. Sprinkle the coconut on a lightly floured surface. Place one half of dough on coconut; roll dough to a ⅛-in.-thick circle. Transfer to a 9-in. pie plate, coconut side down. Trim pastry even with rim. Add filling.
4. Roll the remaining dough to a ⅛-in.-thick circle; cut into ½-in.-wide strips. Arrange over filling in a lattice pattern. Trim and seal strips to edge of bottom pastry; flute edge.
5. Bake 45-50 minutes or until crust is golden brown and filling is bubbly. Cover edge loosely with foil during the last 15 minutes if needed to prevent overbrowning. Remove foil. Cool on a wire rack.
NOTE *To toast coconut, bake in a shallow pan in a 350° oven for 5-10 minutes or cook in a skillet over low heat until golden brown, stirring occasionally.*

Very Raspberry Pie

We live along an old railroad track (our house once was a train station), and wild raspberries pop up for a few weeks every year. I harvest the berries for this incredibly delicious pie.
—**KATHY JONES** WEST WINFIELD, NY

PREP: 30 MIN. + CHILLING
MAKES: 8 SERVINGS

RASPBERRY TOPPING
- 6 cups fresh raspberries, divided
- 1 cup sugar
- 3 tablespoons cornstarch
- ½ cup water

CREAM FILLING
- 1 package (8 ounces) cream cheese, softened
- 1 cup whipped topping
- 1 cup confectioners' sugar
- 1 graham cracker crust (9 inches)
  Fresh mint, optional

1. Mash about 2 cups raspberries to measure 1 cup; place in a small saucepan. Add the sugar, cornstarch and water.
2. Bring to a boil, stirring constantly; cook and stir 2 minutes longer. Strain to remove berry seeds if desired. Cool to room temperature, about 20 minutes.
3. Meanwhile, for filling, beat the cream cheese, whipped topping and confectioners' sugar in a small bowl. Spread in bottom of crust.
4. Top with remaining raspberries. Pour cooled raspberry sauce over top. Refrigerate until set, about 3 hours.
5. Store in the refrigerator. Garnish with mint if desired.

Tart Cherry Lattice Pie

Tart Cherry Lattice Pie

Whenever my mom is invited to a party or potluck, everyone requests her homemade double-crust fruit pies. In the summer, she uses fresh, tart cherries for this recipe. I love a slice topped with vanilla ice cream.
—**PAMELA EATON** MONCLOVA, OH

PREP: 20 MIN. • **BAKE:** 40 MIN. + COOLING
MAKES: 8 SERVINGS

1⅓ cups sugar
⅓ cup all-purpose flour
4 cups fresh or frozen pitted tart cherries, thawed and drained
¼ teaspoon almond extract

Pastry for double-crust pie (9 inches)
2 tablespoons butter, cut into small pieces

1. Preheat oven to 400°. In a large bowl, combine sugar and flour; stir in cherries and extract.
2. On a lightly floured surface, roll one half of the pastry dough to a ⅛-in.-thick circle; transfer to a 9-in. pie plate. Trim pastry to ½ in. beyond rim of plate. Add filling; dot with butter.
3. Roll remaining dough to a ⅛-in.-thick circle; cut into 1½-in.-wide strips. Arrange over filling in a lattice pattern. Trim and seal strips to edge of bottom pastry; flute edge. Cover edge loosely with foil.
4. Bake 40-50 minutes or until crust is golden brown and filling is bubbly. Remove foil. Cool on a wire rack.

PASTRY FOR DOUBLE-CRUST PIE (9 INCHES) *Combine 2½ cups all-purpose flour and ½ tsp. salt; cut in 1 cup cold butter until crumbly. Gradually add ⅓ to ⅔ cup ice water, tossing with a fork until dough holds together when pressed. Wrap in plastic wrap and refrigerate for 1 hour.*

DAR'S COCONUT CREAM PIE
PAGE 241

Cream & Custard Pies

WITH SILKY SMOOTH CONSISTENCIES AND CLOUD-LIKE TEXTURES, THESE DESSERTS ARE A BAKER'S DREAM COME TRUE! WHETHER YOU LIKE MERINGUE, CUSTARD OR CREAM, THE PIES HERE WILL SATISFY ANY CRAVING. KEEP FORKS HANDY, BECAUSE THESE TIMELESS TREATS WILL GO FAST.

CHOCOLATE-HAZELNUT CREAM PIE
PAGE 239

CONTEST-WINNING GERMAN CHOCOLATE CREAM PIE *PAGE 240*

MARSHMALLOW-ALMOND KEY LIME PIE *PAGE 247*

**Chocolate Cream
Cheese Pie**

Chocolate Cream Cheese Pie

Nothing could be better than a cool and creamy finish to a meal. Since the pudding needs time to set, I usually make this first before starting the rest of a dinner.

—**RHONDA HOGAN** EUGENE, OR

PREP: 25 MIN. + CHILLING
MAKES: 6 SERVINGS

- 1 package (3 ounces) cream cheese, softened
- 2 tablespoons sugar
- 1¾ cups milk, divided
- 2 cups whipped topping, divided
- 1 graham cracker crust (9 inches)
- 1 package (3.9 ounces) instant chocolate pudding mix
      Miniature semisweet chocolate chips, optional

1. In a small bowl, beat the cream cheese, sugar and 1 tablespoon milk until smooth. Fold in 1 cup whipped topping. Spread evenly into crust.
2. In a small bowl, whisk pudding mix and remaining milk for 2 minutes. Let stand for 2 minutes or until soft-set. Pour over cream cheese mixture. Chill until set.
3. Just before serving, garnish with remaining whipped topping and chocolate chips if desired.

❝We bring this pie to every family gathering and it's always well received. Everyone loves it!❞
—**MADAMBABETTE**
FROM TASTEOFHOME.COM

Pina Colada Macadamia Pies

I first made this dessert for my husband, who enjoys all things Hawaiian—especially pina coladas and macadamia nuts. Refreshing, light and different, these personalized tarts are a taste of the tropics.

—JONI HILTON ROCKLIN, CA

PREP: 25 MIN. • **BAKE:** 10 MIN. + CHILLING
MAKES: 5 MINI PIES

- 35 **vanilla wafers**
- ½ **cup macadamia nuts, toasted**
- ½ **cup flaked coconut**
- ¼ **cup butter, melted**

FILLING

- 2 **teaspoons unflavored gelatin**
- 2 **tablespoons cold water**
- ½ **cup unsweetened pineapple juice**
- 1 **can (15 ounces) cream of coconut**
- ¾ **cup (6 ounces) pina colada yogurt**

TOPPING

- ¾ **cup heavy whipping cream**
- 2 **tablespoons confectioners' sugar**
- ⅓ **cup macadamia nuts, toasted**
  Fresh pineapple wedges

1. Place wafers and macadamia nuts in a food processor. Cover and pulse until fine crumbs form. Add coconut and butter; cover and pulse until blended. Press onto the bottom and up the sides of five greased 5-in. pie pans. Refrigerate for 30 minutes.

2. Transfer pie pans to a baking sheet. Bake at 350° for 10-12 minutes or until lightly browned. Cool on a wire rack.

3. In a small saucepan, sprinkle gelatin over cold water; let stand for 1 minute. Add pineapple juice. Heat over low heat, stirring until gelatin is completely dissolved. Remove from the heat.

4. In a large bowl, stir the cream of coconut until blended. Stir in yogurt. Add the gelatin mixture and pour into crusts. Refrigerate for 8 hours or overnight.

5. In a small bowl, beat cream until it begins to thicken. Add confectioners' sugar; beat until soft peaks form. Spread over filling. Sprinkle with nuts and garnish with pineapple.

Banana
Chocolate
Cream Pie

Banana Chocolate Cream Pie

English toffee bits add a buttery crunch to this cool and creamy layered pie. The little monkeys in your family will love it!

—PAT YAEGER NAPLES, FL

PREP: 15 MIN. • **BAKE:** 15 MIN. + CHILLING
MAKES: 4 SERVINGS

- 1 **sheet refrigerated pie pastry**
- ¾ **cup plus 2 tablespoons 2% milk**
- ⅓ **cup instant chocolate pudding mix**
- ¼ **cup English toffee bits or almond brickle chips**
- 1 **small ripe banana, sliced**
- ¾ **cup whipped topping**

1. Cut pastry sheet in half. Repackage and refrigerate one half for another use. On a lightly floured surface, roll out remaining half into an 8-in. circle. Transfer to a 7-in. pie plate; flute edges.

2. Line unpricked pastry shell with a double thickness of heavy-duty foil. Bake at 450° for 8 minutes. Remove foil; bake 5 minutes longer. Cool on a wire rack.

3. In a small bowl, whisk milk and pudding mix for 2 minutes. Let stand for 2 minutes or until soft-set. Sprinkle the toffee bits over crust; layer with banana and pudding. Spread with the whipped topping. Refrigerate for at least 1 hour before serving. Store leftovers in the refrigerator.

NOTE *We do not recommend substituting sugar-free pudding mix in this recipe.*

Contest-Winning Raspberry Cream Pie

Old-Fashioned Banana Cream Pie

I love this fluffy no-bake pie. It's full of old-fashioned flavor, with only a fraction of the work. Because it uses instant pudding, it's ready in just minutes.

—**PERLENE HOEKEMA** LYNDEN, WA

START TO FINISH: 10 MIN.
MAKES: 8 SERVINGS

- 1 **cup cold 2% milk**
- ½ **teaspoon vanilla extract**
- 1 **package (3.4 ounces) instant vanilla pudding mix**
- 1 **carton (12 ounces) frozen whipped topping, thawed, divided**
- 1 **graham cracker crust (9 inches)**
- 2 **medium firm bananas, sliced**
  Additional banana slices, optional

1. In a large bowl, whisk the milk, vanilla and pudding mix for 2 minutes (mixture will be thick). Fold in 3 cups whipped topping.
2. Pour 1⅓ cups of pudding mixture into the pie crust. Layer with banana slices and remaining pudding mixture. Top with remaining whipped topping. Garnish with additional banana slices if desired. Refrigerate until serving.

Contest-Winning Raspberry Cream Pie

Either fresh-picked or frozen raspberries are perfect for this recipe, which means you can make it year-round. But no matter when you eat it, this chilled fruit pie is a tribute to summer.

—**JULIE PRICE** NASHVILLE, TN

PREP: 30 MIN. + CHILLING
MAKES: 8 SERVINGS

- 1½ **cups crushed vanilla wafers (about 45 wafers)**
- ⅓ **cup chopped pecans**
- ¼ **cup butter, melted**

FILLING
- 1 **package (8 ounces) cream cheese, softened**
- ⅔ **cup confectioners' sugar**
- 2 **tablespoons orange liqueur**
- 1 **teaspoon vanilla extract**
- 1 **cup heavy whipping cream, whipped**

TOPPING
- 1 **cup sugar**
- 3 **tablespoons cornstarch**
- 3 **tablespoons water**
- 2½ **cups fresh or frozen raspberries, divided**

1. Combine the wafer crumbs, pecans and butter. Press onto the bottom and up the sides of a greased 9-in. pie plate.
2. In a large bowl, beat the cream cheese, confectioners' sugar, liqueur and vanilla until light and fluffy. Fold in whipped cream. Spread into crust. Chill until serving.
3. In a small saucepan, combine sugar and cornstarch; stir in water and 1½ cups raspberries. Bring to a boil; cook and stir for 2 minutes or until thickened. Transfer to a bowl; refrigerate until chilled.
4. Spread topping over filling. Garnish with remaining berries.

TOP TIP

The Skinny on Skinning a Pie

To prevent a "skin" from forming on cream pies and puddings, place a piece of plastic wrap on the surface immediately after pouring the mixture into dishes or a pie shell.

Old-Fashioned
Banana Cream Pie

(5) INGREDIENTS
Root Beer Float Pie

Give this fun and easy dessert a try. It's the kind of recipe your kids will look back on and always remember. It's so smooth and yummy, and the only appliance you need to make it is the refrigerator.

—CINDY REAMS PHILIPSBURG, PA

PREP: 15 MIN. + CHILLING
MAKES: 8 SERVINGS

1 carton (8 ounces) frozen reduced-fat whipped topping, thawed, divided
¾ cup cold diet root beer
½ cup fat-free milk
1 package (1 ounce) sugar-free instant vanilla pudding mix
1 graham cracker crust (9 inches)
  Maraschino cherries, optional

1. Set aside and refrigerate ½ cup whipped topping for garnish. In a large bowl, whisk the root beer, milk and pudding mix for 2 minutes. Fold in half of the remaining whipped topping. Spread into graham cracker crust.
2. Spread remaining whipped topping over pie. Refrigerate for at least 8 hours or overnight.
3. Dollop the reserved whipped topping over each serving; top with a maraschino cherry if desired.

Sour Cream-Lemon Pie

I first tasted this pie at a local restaurant and hunted around until I found a similar recipe. Now it's my husband's favorite.
—MARTHA SORENSEN FALLON, NV

PREP: 20 MIN. + CHILLING
MAKES: 8 SERVINGS

   Pastry for single-crust pie (9 inches)
1 **cup sugar**
3 **tablespoons plus 1½ teaspoons cornstarch**
1 **cup milk**
½ **cup lemon juice**
3 **large egg yolks, lightly beaten**
¼ **cup butter, cubed**
1 **tablespoon grated lemon peel**
1 **cup (8 ounces) sour cream**
1 **cup heavy whipping cream, whipped**

1. Preheat the oven to 450°. On a lightly floured surface, roll the dough to a ⅛-in.-thick circle; transfer to a 9-in. pie plate. Trim pastry to ½ in. beyond rim of plate; flute edge.
2. Line unpricked pastry with a double thickness of foil. Fill with pie weights, dried beans or uncooked rice. Bake for 8 minutes or until bottom is lightly browned. Remove the foil and weights; bake 5-7 minutes longer or until golden brown. Cool on a wire rack.
3. In a large heavy saucepan, mix sugar and cornstarch. Whisk in milk and lemon juice until smooth. Cook and stir over medium-high heat until thickened and bubbly. Reduce heat to low; cook and stir 2 minutes longer. Remove from heat.
4. In a small bowl, whisk a small amount of hot mixture into egg yolks; return all to the pan, whisking constantly. Bring to a gentle boil; cook and stir 2 minutes. Remove from heat. Stir in butter and lemon peel. Cool without stirring.
5. Stir in sour cream. Add the filling to crust. Top with whipped cream. Store in the refrigerator.
NOTE *Let pie weights cool before storing. Beans and rice may be reused for pie weights, but not for cooking.*

Chocolate-Hazelnut Cream Pie

Chocolate-Hazelnut Cream Pie

We've all seen peanut butter pies, so why not try a Nutella pie? This luscious dessert is just fabulous. I sometimes add sliced bananas on top of the crust and then spoon the Nutella mixture over them for a Banana-Hazelnut Cream Pie.
—ANNA SMITH NORTH SALT LAKE, UT

PREP: 20 MIN. • **BAKE:** 15 MIN. + CHILLING
MAKES: 8 SERVINGS

16 **Oreo cookies**
¼ **cup butter, melted**
1 **package (8 ounces) cream cheese, softened**
¾ **cup Nutella**
½ **cup confectioners' sugar**
1 **teaspoon vanilla extract**
1 **cup heavy whipping cream**
TOPPING
¼ **cup heavy whipping cream**
1 **tablespoon light corn syrup**
2 **teaspoons butter**
⅛ **teaspoon salt**
2 **ounces semisweet chocolate, finely chopped**
2 **tablespoons chopped hazelnuts, toasted**

1. Preheat oven to 350°. Pulse cookies in a food processor until ground. Add butter; pulse until blended. Press the mixture onto bottom and up the sides of a greased 9-in. pie plate. Bake for 15 minutes. Cool completely on a wire rack.
2. Beat the cream cheese, Nutella, confectioners' sugar and vanilla until smooth. In another bowl, beat cream until stiff peaks form; fold into cream cheese mixture. Add to crust; refrigerate for 30 minutes.
3. For the topping, in a small saucepan, bring the cream, corn syrup, butter and salt to a boil over medium heat. Remove from heat; add chocolate. Let stand for 5 minutes. Stir until smooth; cool to spreading consistency. Spread over pie; sprinkle with hazelnuts. Refrigerate for 1 hour.

Texas Lemon Chess Pie

Slice into Southern comfort and go back to a simpler time with this classic, feel-good pie. We consider it a must-have menu item for our family gatherings all year long.
—**CHRISTIAN_ROSE**
TASTE OF HOME ONLINE COMMUNITY

PREP: 30 MIN. • **BAKE:** 35 MIN. + CHILLING
MAKES: 8 SERVINGS

- 1 **sheet refrigerated pie pastry**
- 3 **large eggs, separated**
- ½ **cup butter, softened**
- 1½ **cups sugar**
- 3 **tablespoons grated lemon peel**
- 1 **tablespoon cornmeal**
- 1 **teaspoon vanilla extract**
- ¼ **cup evaporated milk**
- ¼ **cup lemon juice**
   Whipped cream, optional

1. Unroll pastry into a 9-in. pie plate; flute edges. Line unpricked pastry with a double thickness of foil. Fill with dried beans, uncooked rice or pie weights.
2. Bake at 400° on a lower oven rack for 8 minutes. Remove foil and weights; bake 6-9 minutes longer or until bottom of crust is light brown. Cool on a wire rack. Reduce heat to 325°.
3. In a small bowl, beat the egg whites until soft peaks form. Set aside.
4. In a large bowl, cream butter and sugar until light and fluffy; beat in the egg yolks, lemon peel, cornmeal and vanilla. Stir in the milk and lemon juice. Fold in beaten egg whites. Pour into crust. Cover edges with foil to prevent overbrowning.
5. Bake at 325° for 35-40 minutes or until a knife inserted near the center comes out clean. Remove foil. Cool on a wire rack. Refrigerate, covered, for 3 hours or until chilled. Serve with whipped cream if desired.
NOTE *Let pie weights cool before storing. Beans and rice may be reused for pie weights, but not for cooking.*

Contest-Winning
German Chocolate
Cream Pie

Contest-Winning German Chocolate Cream Pie

I've won quite a few awards in recipe contests over the years, and I was truly delighted when this luscious pie sent me to the Great American Pie Show finals in Branson, Missouri.
—**MARIE RIZZIO** INTERLOCHEN, MI

PREP: 20 MIN. • **BAKE:** 45 MIN. + COOLING
MAKES: 8 SERVINGS

   Pastry for single-crust pie (9 inches)
- 4 **ounces German sweet chocolate, chopped**
- ¼ **cup butter, cubed**
- 1 **can (12 ounces) evaporated milk**
- 1½ **cups sugar**
- 3 **tablespoons cornstarch**
   Dash salt
- 2 **large eggs**
- 1 **teaspoon vanilla extract**
- 1⅓ **cups flaked coconut**
- ½ **cup chopped pecans**
TOPPING
- 2 **cups heavy whipping cream**
- 2 **tablespoons confectioners' sugar**
- 1 **teaspoon vanilla extract**
   Additional flaked coconut and chopped pecans

1. Line a 9-in. pie plate with pastry; trim and flute edges.
2. Place the chocolate and butter in a small saucepan. Cook and stir over low heat until smooth. Remove from the heat; stir in milk. In a large bowl, combine the sugar, cornstarch and salt. Add the eggs, vanilla and chocolate mixture; mix well. Pour into crust. Sprinkle with coconut and pecans.
3. Bake at 375° for 45-50 minutes or until a knife inserted near the center comes out clean. Cool completely on a wire rack.
4. For the topping, in a large bowl, beat cream until it begins to thicken. Add confectioners' sugar and vanilla; beat until stiff peaks form. Spread over pie; sprinkle with additional coconut and pecans. Refrigerate until serving.

Dar's Coconut Cream Pie

When I make this pie, my family goes wild! We never have any leftovers. Make your own pie crust to add a little extra homemade touch.

—DARLENE BARTOS SHOREVIEW, MN

PREP: 1 HOUR + CHILLING
BAKE: 20 MIN. + COOLING
MAKES: 10 SERVINGS

	Pastry for single-crust pie (9 inches)
4	large egg yolks
2	cups coconut milk
1½	cups half-and-half cream
1	cup sugar
⅓	cup cornstarch
¼	teaspoon salt
2	teaspoons vanilla extract
1½	cups flaked coconut, toasted, divided
2	cups heavy whipping cream
¼	cup confectioners' sugar
½	teaspoon vanilla extract

1. On a lightly floured surface, roll pastry dough to a ⅛-in.-thick circle; transfer to a 9-in. pie plate. Trim the pastry to ½ in. beyond rim of plate; flute edge. Refrigerate for 30 minutes. Preheat oven to 425°.

2. Line pastry with a double thickness of foil. Fill with pie weights, dried beans or uncooked rice. Bake on a lower oven rack for 20-25 minutes or until edges are golden brown. Remove foil and weights; bake 3-6 minutes longer or until bottom is golden brown. Cool completely on a wire rack.

3. In a large heavy saucepan, whisk egg yolks, coconut milk, cream, sugar, cornstarch and salt until blended. Bring to a gentle boil over medium heat, whisking constantly. Reduce heat to medium-low; cook for 2 minutes longer, whisking vigorously. Remove from heat; stir in vanilla and 1 cup coconut. Immediately transfer to crust.

4. Press plastic wrap onto surface of filling. Refrigerate 2 hours or until cold.

5. In a large bowl, beat the whipping cream until it begins to thicken. Add confectioners' sugar and vanilla; beat until soft peaks form. Spread over pie. Sprinkle with remaining coconut.

PASTRY FOR SINGLE-CRUST PIE (9 INCHES) *Combine 1¼ cups all-purpose flour and ¼ tsp. salt; cut in ½ cup cold butter until crumbly. Gradually add 3-5 Tbsp. ice water, tossing with a fork until dough holds together when pressed. Wrap in plastic wrap and refrigerate 1 hour.*

NOTE *Let pie weights cool before storing. Beans and rice may be reused for pie weights, but not for cooking.*

---

⑤INGREDIENTS

Fluffy Lemon-Lime Pie

You just can't go wrong with this refreshing treat. Simply mix together three ingredients, put the combination into a prepared crust and pop it into the refrigerator.

—MRS. C.G. ROWLAND CHATTANOOGA, TN

PREP: 15 MIN. + CHILLING
MAKES: 6-8 SERVINGS

1	envelope (.13 ounce) unsweetened lemon-lime soft drink mix
1	can (14 ounces) sweetened condensed milk
1	carton (8 ounces) frozen whipped topping, thawed
1	graham cracker crust (9 inches)

In a large bowl, dissolve soft drink mix in milk; fold in whipped topping. Spoon into crust. Cover and refrigerate for 3 hours or until set.

Dar's Coconut Cream Pie

Fluffy Strawberry Meringue Pie

Fluffy Strawberry Meringue Pie

The combination of cool, creamy berry filling and a delightfully different meringue crust guarantees you'll hear "pass the pie, please" all around the table.

—**ROXANNA SHOFFSTALL** LAKEVIEW, OH

PREP: 25 MIN. • **BAKE:** 25 MIN. + CHILLING
MAKES: 8-10 SERVINGS

- 3 **large egg whites**
- ¼ **teaspoon cream of tartar**
- 1 **cup sugar**
- ½ **cup crushed saltines (about 12 crackers)**
- ½ **cup chopped pecans**
- 1 **teaspoon vanilla extract**
- 2 **pints fresh strawberries, divided**
- 4 **cups miniature marshmallows**
- 1 **carton (8 ounces) frozen whipped topping, thawed Red food coloring, optional**

1. In a bowl, beat egg whites and cream of tartar on medium speed until soft peaks form. Gradually beat in sugar, 1 tablespoon at a time, on high speed until stiff glossy peaks form and sugar is dissolved. Fold in the crackers, pecans and vanilla.

2. Spread onto the bottom and up the sides of a greased 10-in. deep-dish pie plate. Bake at 350° for 25-30 minutes or until meringue is lightly browned. Cool on a wire rack.

3. Set aside one strawberry for garnish. Slice half of the strawberries; set aside. In a bowl, mash remaining strawberries; drain the juice, reserving ½ cup. In a saucepan, combine the marshmallows and reserved juice. Cook and stir over low heat until marshmallows are melted. Refrigerate until partially set.

4. Fold the sliced and mashed strawberries and whipped topping into the marshmallow mixture. Add food coloring if desired. Spoon into meringue shell. Garnish with the reserved strawberry. Refrigerate for 3 hours or until set. Refrigerate leftovers.

French Silk Pie

I first prepared French Silk Pie when I was in high school. Years later, I experimented with the recipe until I was happy with it. Now it's one of my husband's favorites.

—**LISA FRANCIS** ELBA, AL

PREP: 40 MIN. • **COOK:** 10 MIN. + CHILLING
MAKES: 6 SERVINGS

- 1 **sheet refrigerated pie pastry**
- ⅔ **cup sugar**
- 2 **large eggs**
- 2 **ounces unsweetened chocolate, melted**
- 1 **teaspoon vanilla extract**
- ⅓ **cup butter, softened**
- ⅔ **cup heavy whipping cream**
- 2 **teaspoons confectioners' sugar Whipped cream and chocolate curls, optional**

1. Cut pastry sheet in half. Repackage and refrigerate one half for another use. On a lightly floured surface, roll out remaining half into an 8-in. circle. Transfer to a 7-in. pie plate; flute edges.

2. Line shell with a double thickness of heavy-duty foil. Bake at 450° for 4 minutes. Remove foil; bake 2 minutes longer or until crust is golden brown. Cool on a wire rack.

3. In a small saucepan, combine sugar and eggs until well blended. Cook over low heat, stirring constantly, until the mixture reaches 160° and coats the back of a metal spoon. Remove from the heat. Stir in chocolate and vanilla until smooth. Cool to lukewarm (90°), stirring occasionally.

4. In a small bowl, cream butter until light and fluffy. Add cooled chocolate mixture; beat on high speed for 5 minutes or until light and fluffy.

5. In another large bowl, beat the cream until it begins to thicken. Add confectioners' sugar; beat until stiff peaks form. Fold into chocolate mixture.

6. Pour into crust. Chill for at least 6 hours before serving. Garnish with whipped cream and chocolate curls if desired. Refrigerate leftovers.

Chocolate Peanut Pie

Who can resist a tempting chocolate crumb crust and a creamy filling with big peanut butter taste? Be prepared to take an empty plate home when you serve this pie at your next potluck.

—DORIS DOHERTY ALBANY, OR

PREP: 20 MIN. + COOLING
MAKES: 8-10 SERVINGS

1¼ cups chocolate cookie crumbs (20 cookies)
¼ cup sugar
¼ cup butter, melted

FILLING

1 package (8 ounces) cream cheese, softened
1 cup creamy peanut butter
1 cup sugar
1 tablespoon butter, softened
1 teaspoon vanilla extract
1 cup heavy whipping cream, whipped
   Grated chocolate or chocolate cookie crumbs, optional

1. In a small bowl, combine cookie crumbs and sugar; stir in butter. Press onto the bottom and up the sides of a 9-in. pie plate. Bake at 375° for 10 minutes. Cool on a wire rack.

2. For filling, beat the cream cheese, peanut butter, sugar, butter and vanilla in a large bowl until smooth. Fold in whipped cream. Gently spoon into crust. Garnish with chocolate or cookie crumbs if desired. Store in the refrigerator.

> ❝If you have the time, make it the day before. The pie sets up very nicely overnight in the refrigerator.❞
>
> **—CONTRARYWIFE**
> FROM TASTEOFHOME.COM

Chocolate Peanut Pie

Cherry Cream Pie

Cherry Cream Pie

A favorite vacation spot in Wisconsin— Door County (in the "thumb" of the state)—is known for its abundance of cherry orchards, and that's where this cream pie recipe originated. I think it's a delectable dessert, with a nutty crumb crust, real whipped cream and, of course, cherry pie filling.

—CAROL WENCKA GREENFIELD, WI

PREP: 40 MIN. + CHILLING
MAKES: 6-8 SERVINGS

CRUST
- 1 **cup all-purpose flour**
- 1 **cup finely chopped walnuts**
- ½ **cup butter, softened**
- ¼ **cup packed brown sugar**

FILLING
- 1 **package (8 ounces) cream cheese, softened**
- 1 **cup confectioners' sugar**
- ¼ **teaspoon almond extract**
- ½ **cup heavy whipping cream, whipped**
- 1 **can (21 ounces) cherry pie filling**

1. In a small bowl, combine the flour, walnuts, butter and brown sugar. Transfer to a 13x9-in. baking pan. Bake at 375° for 15 minutes, stirring once. Set aside 1 cup of crumbs. While warm, press the remaining crumbs into a greased 9-in. pie plate, firmly pressing onto the bottom and up the sides. Chill for 30 minutes.
2. In a small bowl, beat the cream cheese, confectioners' sugar and almond extract until smooth. Spread over the bottom of the crust. Gently fold whipped cream into the cherry pie filling; spread over cream cheese layer. Sprinkle with reserved crumbs. Chill for at least 4 hours before serving.

Lemonade Meringue Pie

Lemonade Meringue Pie

Lemonade concentrate and lemon juice give this special pie an excellent citrus flavor. I also like to add some lemon zest on top of the meringue.

—KAY SEILER GREENVILLE, OH

PREP: 30 MIN. • **BAKE:** 15 MIN. + CHILLING
MAKES: 8 SERVINGS

- **Pastry for single-crust pie (9 inches)**
- 3 **large eggs, separated**
- 1¼ **cups 2% milk**
- 1 **cup (8 ounces) sour cream**
- 1 **package (4.6 ounces) cook-and-serve vanilla pudding mix**
- ⅓ **cup thawed lemonade concentrate**
- 1 **teaspoon lemon juice**
- ¼ **teaspoon cream of tartar**
- 6 **tablespoons sugar**

1. Line a 9-in. pie plate with pastry; trim and flute edges. Line unpricked pastry with a double thickness of heavy-duty foil. Bake at 450° for 8 minutes. Remove foil; bake 5-7 minutes longer or until lightly browned. Cool on a wire rack.
2. Place egg whites in a large bowl; let stand at room temperature for 30 minutes. Meanwhile, in a large saucepan, combine the milk, sour cream and pudding mix until smooth. Cook and stir over medium heat until thickened and bubbly. Reduce heat; cook and stir 2 minutes longer.
3. Remove from the heat. Stir a small amount of hot mixture into egg yolks; return all to the pan, stirring constantly. Bring to a gentle boil; cook and stir for 2 minutes longer. Remove from the heat. Gently stir in lemonade concentrate; keep warm.
4. Add lemon juice and cream of tartar to egg whites; beat on medium speed until soft peaks form. Gradually beat in sugar, 1 tablespoon at a time, on high until stiff glossy peaks form and sugar is dissolved.
5. Pour warm filling into pastry shell. Spread meringue evenly over filling, sealing edges to crust.
6. Bake at 350° for 15-20 minutes or until the meringue is golden brown. Cool on a wire rack for 1 hour. Refrigerate pie for at least 3 hours before serving. Store leftovers in the refrigerator.

Lemon Curd Chiffon Pie

350° for 10-12 minutes or until light golden brown. Cool completely on a wire rack.

3. In a small bowl, combine the cream, sugar and vanilla. Beat until stiff peaks form; set aside. In a large bowl, beat the lemon curd, cream cheese and lemon peel until blended; set aside.

4. Sprinkle gelatin over lemon juice; let stand for 1 minute. Microwave on high for 20 seconds. Stir and let stand for 1 minute or until gelatin is completely dissolved. Stir in limoncello. Gradually beat into lemon curd mixture until well blended. Fold in whipped cream; pour into the crust. Refrigerate for 3 hours or until set.

5. In a small saucepan over medium heat, combine the berries, sugar and jam. Cook and stir for 3-5 minutes or until fruit is softened. In a blender, cover and process berry mixture for 1-2 minutes or until blended. Strain, reserving juice. Discard seeds.

6. Return juice to the saucepan; cook for 15-18 minutes or until reduced to desired consistency, stirring occasionally. Stir in lemon juice and raspberry liqueur. Chill for 1 hour. Garnish servings of pie with sauce.

Lemon Curd Chiffon Pie

Normally I am a chocolate lover, but this showstopping pie makes me forget about chocolate with its refreshing and tart flavor. I get frequent requests from my gang to make it.

—CALLIE PALEN-LOWRIE LOUISVILLE, CO

PREP: 30 MIN. • **BAKE:** 10 MIN. + CHILLING
MAKES: 8 SERVINGS

- **9** whole graham crackers, broken into large pieces
- **½** cup chopped pecans
- **3** tablespoons sugar
- **¼** teaspoon vanilla extract
- **⅛** teaspoon salt
- **5** tablespoons butter, melted

FILLING
- **1½** cups heavy whipping cream
- **3** tablespoons sugar
- **3** teaspoons vanilla extract
- **1** jar (11 ounces) lemon curd
- **1** package (8 ounces) cream cheese, softened
- **1** tablespoon grated lemon peel
- **1½** teaspoons unflavored gelatin
- **⅓** cup lemon juice
- **1** tablespoon limoncello

BERRY SAUCE
- **½** pint fresh raspberries
- **½** pint fresh blueberries
- **½** pint fresh strawberries
- **¼** cup sugar
- **1** tablespoon seedless raspberry jam
- **1** tablespoon lemon juice
- **1** tablespoon raspberry liqueur

1. Place the graham crackers, pecans, sugar, vanilla and salt in a food processor; cover and pulse until mixture resembles fine crumbs. Add the butter; process until blended.

2. Press the crumb mixture onto the bottom and up the sides of a greased 9-in. deep-dish pie plate. Bake at

Marshmallow-Almond Key Lime Pie

It's great to see that many grocers now carry Key limes, which give this pie its distinctive sweet-tart flavor. But unlike other Key lime pies, this one has a smooth marshmallow top layer that makes it stand out as a crowd favorite.

—JUDY CASTRANOVA NEW BERN, NC

PREP: 40 MIN. • **BAKE:** 15 MIN. + CHILLING
MAKES: 8 SERVINGS

- 1 cup all-purpose flour
- 3 tablespoons brown sugar
- 1 cup slivered almonds, toasted, divided
- ¼ cup butter, melted
- 1 tablespoon honey
- 1 package (8 ounces) cream cheese, softened, divided
- 1 can (14 ounces) sweetened condensed milk
- 1 tablespoon grated Key lime peel
- ½ cup Key lime juice
  Dash salt
- 1 large egg yolk
- 1¾ cups miniature marshmallows
- 4½ teaspoons butter
- ½ cup heavy whipping cream

1. Preheat oven to 350°. Place flour, brown sugar and ½ cup almonds in a food processor; process until the almonds are finely chopped. Add melted butter and honey; process until crumbly. Press onto the bottom and up sides of a greased 9-in. pie plate. Bake 8-10 minutes or until lightly browned. Cool on a wire rack.

2. In a large bowl, beat 5 ounces of cream cheese, milk, lime peel, lime juice and salt until blended. Add the egg yolk; beat on low speed just until combined. Pour into crust. Bake 15-20 minutes or until the center is almost set. Cool on a wire rack.

3. Meanwhile, place marshmallows and butter in a small heavy saucepan; cook and stir over medium-low heat until melted. Transfer to a large bowl; beat in remaining cream cheese until blended. Beat in cream. Refrigerate, covered, until cold.

4. Beat the chilled marshmallow mixture until light and fluffy. Spread over pie; sprinkle with the remaining almonds. Refrigerate until serving.

NOTE *To toast nuts, bake in a shallow pan in a 350° oven for 5-10 minutes or cook in a skillet over low heat until lightly browned, stirring occasionally.*

Marshmallow-Almond Key Lime Pie

**BUTTERSCOTCH PIE WITH
WALNUT-BACON TOFFEE** *PAGE 257*

Cozy Pies

WHEN THE SMELL OF AUTUMN LEAVES IS IN THE AIR AND THE TEMPERATURE STARTS TO FALL, IT'S TIME TO INDULGE IN ONE OF THESE HEARTWARMING NUT, PUMPKIN, SQUASH AND SWEET POTATO PIES. COZY UP WITH A SLICE BY YOURSELF OR SHARE A PIE WITH FAMILY AND FRIENDS OVER THE HOLIDAY SEASON.

CARAMEL-PECAN CHEESECAKE PIE *PAGE 252*

SWEET POTATO COCONUT PIE WITH MARSHMALLOW MERINGUE *PAGE 254*

PUMPKIN MOUSSE PIE WITH GINGERSNAP CRUST *PAGE 261*

Fluffy Pumpkin Pie

Cranberry & Walnut Pie

For a showstopping pie, I mix cranberries, chocolate and walnuts. It's a dessert similar to a pecan pie—with a little touch of rum.
—**LORRIE MELERINE** HOUSTON, TX

PREP: 30 MIN. + CHILLING
BAKE: 30 MIN. + COOLING
MAKES: 8 SERVINGS

> **Pastry for single-crust pie (9 inches)**
> 3 **large eggs**
> ¾ **cup sugar**
> ½ **cup butter, melted**
> 3 **tablespoons all-purpose flour**
> 1 **cup chopped walnuts**
> 1 **cup fresh or frozen cranberries**
> 1 **cup (6 ounces) semisweet chocolate chips**
> 2 **tablespoons dark rum**

1. On a lightly floured surface, roll pastry dough to a ⅛-in.-thick circle; transfer to a 9-in. pie plate. Trim pastry to ½ in. beyond rim of plate; flute edge. Refrigerate 30 minutes. Preheat oven to 450°.
2. Line unpricked pastry with a double thickness of foil. Fill with pie weights, dried beans or uncooked rice. Bake on a lower oven rack 15-20 minutes or until edges are light golden brown. Remove foil and weights; bake 3-6 minutes longer or until bottom is golden brown. Cool on a wire rack. Reduce oven setting to 350°.
3. In a large bowl, beat the eggs, sugar and melted butter until well-blended. Gradually add flour until blended. Stir in remaining ingredients; pour into crust.
4. Bake 30-35 minutes or until top is bubbly and crust is golden brown. Cool on a wire rack. Refrigerate leftovers.
PASTRY FOR SINGLE-CRUST PIE (9 INCHES) *Combine 1¼ cups all-purpose flour and ¼ tsp. salt; cut in ½ cup cold butter until crumbly. Gradually add 3-5 Tbsp. ice water, tossing with a fork until dough holds together when pressed. Wrap in plastic wrap, refrigerate for 1 hour.* **NOTE** *Let pie weights cool before storing. Beans and rice may be reused for pie weights, but not for cooking.*

Fluffy Pumpkin Pie

Children love this pie—marshmallows and whipped topping make the filling light. It's an easy recipe that I've shared many times.
—**PHYLLIS RENFRO** WHITE BEAR LAKE, MN

PREP: 1 HOUR + CHILLING
COOK: 10 MIN. + CHILLING
MAKES: 8 SERVINGS

> **Pastry for single-crust pie (9 inches)**
> 24 **large marshmallows**
> 1 **can (15 ounces) solid-pack pumpkin**
> ½ **teaspoon ground cinnamon**
> ½ **teaspoon ground allspice**
> ¼ **teaspoon salt**
> 1 **carton (8 ounces) frozen whipped topping, thawed**
> **Additional whipped topping and ground cinnamon, optional**

1. On a lightly floured surface, roll pastry dough to a ⅛-in.-thick circle; transfer to a 9-in. pie plate. Trim pastry to ½ in. beyond rim of plate; flute edge. Refrigerate 30 minutes. Preheat oven to 425°.
2. Line pastry with a double thickness of foil. Fill with pie weights, dried beans or uncooked rice. Bake on a lower oven rack 20-25 minutes or until edges are golden brown. Remove foil and weights; bake 3-6 minutes longer or until bottom is golden brown. Cool completely on a wire rack.
3. In a small heavy saucepan, melt marshmallows over low heat. Remove from the heat. Stir in the pumpkin, cinnamon, allspice and salt; cool to room temperature.
4. Fold in whipped topping. Spoon into pastry shell. Refrigerate for at least 4 hours before serving. Garnish with additional whipped topping and cinnamon if desired.
PASTRY FOR SINGLE-CRUST PIE (9 INCHES) *Combine 1¼ cups all-purpose flour and ¼ tsp. salt; cut in ½ cup cold butter until crumbly. Gradually add 3-5 Tbsp. ice water, tossing with a fork until dough holds together when pressed. Wrap in plastic wrap, refrigerate for 1 hour.* **NOTE** *Let pie weights cool before storing. Beans and rice may be reused for pie weights, but not for cooking.*

Cranberry &
Walnut Pie

Caramel-Pecan Cheesecake Pie

"This is absolutely delicious! I made it last year for Thanksgiving, then again for Christmas! Looks like a new tradition is born."

—LILRIKI FROM TASTEOFHOME.COM

Caramel-Pecan Cheesecake Pie

Cheesecake meets pecan pie. Every slice reveals its two-toned layers of rich cream cheese and caramel-nut topping.

—BECKY RUFF MCGREGOR, IA

PREP: 15 MIN. • **BAKE:** 35 MIN. + CHILLING
MAKES: 6-8 SERVINGS

- 1 sheet refrigerated pie pastry
- 1 package (8 ounces) cream cheese, softened
- ½ cup sugar
- 4 large eggs
- 1 teaspoon vanilla extract
- 1¼ cups chopped pecans
- 1 jar (12¼ ounces) fat-free caramel ice cream topping
  Additional fat-free caramel ice cream topping, optional

1. Preheat oven to 375°. Line a 9-in. deep-dish pie plate with pastry. Trim and flute edges. In a small bowl, beat cream cheese, sugar, 1 egg and vanilla until smooth. Spread into pastry shell; sprinkle with pecans.

2. In a small bowl, whisk remaining eggs; gradually whisk in caramel topping until blended. Pour slowly over pecans.

3. Bake 35-40 minutes or until lightly browned (loosely cover edges with foil after 20 minutes if the pie browns too quickly). Cool on a wire rack 1 hour. Refrigerate for 4 hours or overnight before slicing. If desired, garnish with additional caramel ice cream topping.

NOTE *This recipe was tested with Smucker's ice cream topping.*

TOP TIP

A Familiar Ring

Save yourself trouble by fitting an aluminum foil ring around a pie while it's cold, before baking. Once the ring is formed, remove it and put the pie in the oven. When edges begin to brown, set ring in place and continue baking.

—FAYE HOGENSON GRESHAM, OR

Eggnog Sweet Potato Pie

Pies are therapy to me. This is one I like to make for special events and holiday celebrations. The eggnog and sweet potato make a soft filling that goes nicely with the crunchy topping.

—**SARAH SPAUGH** WINSTON-SALEM, NC

PREP: 25 MIN. • **BAKE:** 55 MIN. + COOLING
MAKES: 8 SERVINGS

- ¼ cup caramel ice cream topping
- 1 unbaked pastry shell (9 inches)
- 2 cups mashed sweet potatoes
- ¾ cup eggnog
- 1 large egg, lightly beaten
- 2 tablespoons butter, melted
- ½ teaspoon vanilla extract
- ½ cup sugar
- ½ cup packed brown sugar
- ¾ teaspoon ground cinnamon

TOPPING

- ½ cup flaked coconut
- ⅓ cup all-purpose flour
- ¼ cup packed brown sugar
- ⅓ cup cold butter, cubed
- ¼ cup chopped pecans

1. Carefully spread caramel topping over bottom of pastry shell; set aside. In a small bowl, combine the sweet potatoes, eggnog, egg, butter and vanilla. Stir in sugars and cinnamon. Carefully spoon over caramel layer.

2. Bake at 400° for 15 minutes. Reduce heat to 350°; bake 30 minutes longer.

3. Meanwhile, in a small bowl, combine the coconut, flour and brown sugar. Cut in butter until crumbly; stir in pecans. Sprinkle over pie.

4. Bake 10-15 minutes or until a knife inserted near the center comes out clean and the topping is golden brown (cover edges with foil if necessary to prevent overbrowning). Cool on a wire rack. Store the pie in the refrigerator.

NOTE *This recipe was tested with commercially prepared eggnog.*

Maple-Caramel Walnut Pie

Maple-Caramel Walnut Pie

Here's a wonderful variation on the nut pies traditionally made during the holiday season. The homemade caramel flavored with maple syrup really complements the walnuts.

—**RUTH EALY** PLAIN CITY, OH

PREP: 40 MIN. + CHILLING
BAKE: 25 MIN. + COOLING
MAKES: 10 SERVINGS

- 1¼ cups all-purpose flour
- ⅛ teaspoon salt
- ¼ cup cold butter, cubed
- ¼ cup shortening
- 3 to 4 tablespoons cold water

FILLING

- 1 cup packed brown sugar
- ⅔ cup maple syrup
- 5 tablespoons butter, cubed
- ¼ cup heavy whipping cream
- ¼ teaspoon salt
- 3 large eggs
- 2 teaspoons vanilla extract
- 2 cups chopped walnuts
- 1 cup walnut halves

1. In a small bowl, combine flour and salt; cut in the butter and shortening until crumbly. Gradually add water, tossing with a fork until dough forms a ball. Wrap in plastic wrap. Refrigerate for 2 hours or until easy to handle.

2. Roll out pastry to fit a 9-in. pie plate. Transfer pastry to pie plate. Trim pastry to ½ in. beyond edge of plate; flute edges. Line unpricked pastry with a double thickness of heavy-duty foil. Fill with dried beans, uncooked rice or pie weights.

3. Bake at 450° for 8 minutes. Remove foil and weights; bake 5 minutes longer. Cool on a wire rack.

4. Meanwhile, in a large saucepan, combine brown sugar, syrup, butter, cream and salt; bring to a boil over medium heat, stirring constantly. Remove from the heat; let stand for 10 minutes.

5. In a large bowl, beat eggs and vanilla. Gradually add the syrup mixture. Stir in chopped walnuts. Pour into crust. Arrange walnut halves over top.

6. Bake at 350° for 25-30 minutes or until set. Cool on a wire rack. Refrigerate leftovers.

NOTE *Let pie weights cool before storing. Beans and rice may be reused for pie weights, but not for cooking.*

Sweet Potato Coconut Pie with Marshmallow Meringue

Sweet Potato Coconut Pie with Marshmallow Meringue

My grandmother's sweet potato casserole contains coconut and marshmallows. I thought it would be even better as a pie.
—**SIMONE BAZOS** BALTIMORE, MD

PREP: 1 HOUR • **BAKE:** 65 MIN. + CHILLING
MAKES: 8 SERVINGS

- 1½ **cups all-purpose flour**
- ¼ **teaspoon salt**
- ¼ **teaspoon ground ginger**
- 6 **tablespoons cold butter**
- 2 **tablespoons shortening**
- 3 **to 4 tablespoons cold water**

FILLING

- 1 **cup coconut milk**
- ¾ **cup packed brown sugar**
- ¼ **cup cream cheese, softened**
- 2 **cups mashed sweet potatoes**
- 3 **large eggs, lightly beaten**
- 2 **teaspoons lemon juice**
- 1½ **teaspoons vanilla extract**
- ¼ **teaspoon salt**
- ¼ **teaspoon ground cinnamon**

MERINGUE

- 4 **large egg whites**
- ¼ **teaspoon cream of tartar**
- ½ **cup sugar**
- 1 **jar (7 ounces) marshmallow creme**
- ½ **cup miniature marshmallows**
- ¼ **cup flaked coconut**

1. In a food processor, combine the flour, salt and ginger; cover and pulse to blend. Add butter and shortening; cover and pulse until mixture resembles coarse crumbs.

2. While processing, gradually add water just until moist crumbs form. Shape into a disk; wrap in plastic wrap and refrigerate for 30 minutes or until easy to handle.

3. Preheat the oven to 425°. Roll out pastry to fit a 9-in. deep-dish pie plate. Transfer pastry to pie plate. Trim pastry to ½ in. beyond edge of plate; flute edges or decorate with pastry cutouts as desired. Line unpricked pastry with a double thickness of heavy-duty foil. Fill with dried beans, uncooked rice or pie weights.

4. Bake 8 minutes. Remove foil and weights; bake 5 minutes longer. Cool on a wire rack. Reduce oven setting to 325°.

5. For filling, in a small saucepan, combine coconut milk, brown sugar and cream cheese. Cook and stir until smooth. Transfer to a large bowl; cool 5 minutes. Whisk in sweet potatoes, eggs, lemon juice, vanilla, salt and cinnamon. Pour into crust.

6. Bake for 50-60 minutes or until a knife inserted near the center comes out clean. Cover edges with foil during the last 15 minutes to prevent overbrowning if necessary.

7. For meringue, in a large bowl, beat the egg whites and cream of tartar on medium speed until soft peaks form. Gradually beat in sugar, 1 tablespoon at a time, on high speed until stiff glossy peaks form and sugar is dissolved.

8. Place the marshmallow creme in a separate large bowl; fold in a third of the egg white mixture, then fold in the remaining mixture. Spread evenly over hot filling, sealing edges to crust. Sprinkle the pie with marshmallows and coconut.

9. Bake for 12-15 minutes longer or until top is golden brown. Cool on a wire rack for 1 hour. Refrigerate for at least 3 hours before serving. Store leftovers in the refrigerator.
NOTE *Let pie weights cool before storing. Beans and rice may be reused for pie weights, but not for cooking.*

Macadamia Nut Pie

When I was young, friends of our family traveled to Hawaii and brought back macadamia nuts. My mom used them in this recipe. It's a tasty twist on traditional pecan pie.
—**BRENDA HILDEBRANDT** MOOSOMIN, SK

PREP: 25 MIN. • **BAKE:** 50 MIN. + COOLING
MAKES: 8-10 SERVINGS

- 1 **sheet refrigerated pie pastry**
- 3 **large eggs**
- 1 **cup dark corn syrup**
- ⅔ **cup sugar**
- 2 **tablespoons butter, melted**
- 2 **teaspoons vanilla extract**
- 2 **cups chopped macadamia nuts**

1. Unroll pastry and place in a 9-in. pie plate; flute edges and set aside. In a small bowl, beat the eggs, corn syrup, sugar, butter and vanilla until combined. Stir in the nuts. Pour into pastry shell.

2. Bake at 325° for 50-55 minutes or until the center is set and the top is golden brown. Cool on a wire rack. Refrigerate leftovers.

Cinnamon Pumpkin Pie

My daughter Jessica claims this is the best pumpkin pie she's ever eaten. The recipe is a breeze to make.

—JACKIE DEIBERT KLINGERSTOWN, PA

PREP: 10 MIN. • **BAKE:** 55 MIN. + COOLING
MAKES: 6 SERVINGS

- 1 cup sugar
- 4 teaspoons cornstarch
- ½ teaspoon salt
- ½ teaspoon ground cinnamon
- 2 large eggs, lightly beaten
- 1 can (15 ounces) solid-pack pumpkin
- 1 cup milk
- 1 unbaked pastry shell (9 inches)
  Whipped cream in a can, optional

1. In a small bowl, combine the sugar, cornstarch, salt and cinnamon. In a large bowl, combine the eggs, pumpkin and sugar mixture. Gradually stir in the milk. Pour into the pastry shell.

2. Bake at 400° for 10 minutes. Reduce heat to 350°; bake for 45-50 minutes longer or until a knife inserted near the center comes out clean. Cool on a wire rack. Top with whipped cream if desired. Refrigerate leftovers.

Cinnamon Pumpkin Pie

Butternut Squash Pie

I have been making this pie for more than 25 years for special occasions. It is so simple to put together, and the taste is wonderful.
—MARY ELLEN SOLESBEE GREER, SC

PREP: 10 MIN. • **BAKE:** 50 MIN. + CHILLING
MAKES: 6-8 SERVINGS

Pastry for single-crust pie (9 inches)
1¼ cups sugar
4½ teaspoons cornstarch
1 tablespoon ground cinnamon
3 cups mashed cooked butternut squash
½ cup butter, softened
2 large eggs
¼ cup water
3 teaspoons vanilla extract
Whipped cream, optional

1. Line a 9-in. pie plate with pastry; trim and flute edges. Use a leaf-shaped cookie cutter on the scraps to cut out garnish if desired; place on a baking sheet and set aside.
2. In a large bowl, combine the sugar, cornstarch and cinnamon. Beat in the squash, butter, eggs, water and vanilla until smooth. Pour into crust.
3. Cover edges loosely with foil. Bake at 350° for 15 minutes. Remove foil. Bake 35-40 minutes longer or until a knife inserted near the center comes out clean. Bake leaf cutouts for 5-7 minutes or until golden brown.
4. Cool pie and cutouts on a wire rack for 1 hour. Refrigerate pie until chilled. Garnish with pastry leaves and whipped cream if desired.

TOP TIP

Shaping a Fluted Edge

Position your index finger on the edge of the crust, pointing out. Place the thumb and index finger of your other hand on the outside edge and pinch dough around the index finger to form a V shape. Continue around the edge.

Contest-Winning Eggnog Pumpkin Pie

Contest-Winning Eggnog Pumpkin Pie

Try a combination of my family's favorite holiday flavors: eggnog and pumpkin. The creamy and crunchy texture of the pie is the perfect finale to a special meal.
—LYN DILWORTH RANCHO CORDOVA, CA

PREP: 40 MIN. + CHILLING
BAKE: 50 MIN. + COOLING
MAKES: 8 SERVINGS

1¼ cups all-purpose flour
¼ teaspoon salt
3 tablespoons shortening, cubed
3 tablespoons cold butter, cubed
3 to 4 tablespoons cold water
FILLING
2 large eggs
1 can (15 ounces) solid-pack pumpkin
1 cup eggnog
½ cup sugar
1 teaspoon ground cinnamon
½ teaspoon salt
½ teaspoon ground ginger
½ teaspoon ground nutmeg
¼ teaspoon ground cloves
TOPPING
½ cup packed brown sugar
2 tablespoons butter, softened
½ cup chopped pecans

1. In a food processor, combine flour and salt; cover and pulse to blend. Add shortening and butter; cover and pulse until mixture resembles coarse crumbs. While processing, gradually add water until dough forms a ball. Wrap in plastic wrap. Refrigerate for 1 to 1½ hours or until easy to handle.
2. Roll out pastry to fit a 9-in. pie plate. Transfer pastry to pie plate. Trim pastry to ½ in. beyond edge of plate; flute edges.
3. In a large bowl, whisk the eggs, pumpkin, eggnog, sugar, cinnamon, salt, ginger, nutmeg and cloves until blended. Pour into crust.
4. In a small bowl, beat the brown sugar and butter until crumbly, about 2 minutes. Stir in pecans; sprinkle over filling.
5. Bake at 350° for 50-60 minutes or until a knife inserted near the center comes out clean. Cool on a wire rack. Refrigerate leftovers.
NOTE *This recipe was tested with commercially prepared eggnog.*

Butterscotch Pie with Walnut-Bacon Toffee

I started to make bacon toffee, but once I got going, I ended up with a sweet and savory pie that's just right for holiday dining.
—**JULIANN STODDART** CHICAGO, IL

PREP: 1¾ HOURS + CHILLING
MAKES: 12 SERVINGS PLUS 1 POUND TOFFEE

- 1½ cups all-purpose flour
- 1¾ teaspoons sugar
- ¼ teaspoon salt
- ⅔ cup cold unsalted butter, cubed
- 5 to 6 tablespoons ice water

BACON TOFFEE
- ½ teaspoon unsalted butter
- 2 cups sugar
  Dash salt
- 2 cups unsalted butter, cubed
- 2 cups chopped walnuts, toasted
- ½ pound bacon strips, cooked and crumbled
- ¼ teaspoon vanilla extract

FILLING
- 3 large egg yolks
- 1½ cups packed brown sugar
- ⅓ cup all-purpose flour
  Dash salt
- 1 cup 2% milk
- ⅓ cup unsalted butter, cubed
- 1 teaspoon vanilla extract
  Sweetened whipped cream

1. For crust, in a large bowl, mix flour, sugar and salt; cut in butter until crumbly. Gradually add the ice water, tossing with a fork until dough holds together when pressed. Shape into a disk; wrap in plastic wrap. Refrigerate 1 hour or overnight.

2. For the toffee, grease a 15x10x1-in. pan with ½ teaspoon butter. In a large heavy saucepan, combine sugar, salt and remaining butter. Cook over medium heat until a candy thermometer reads 300° (hard-crack stage), stirring constantly. Remove from heat. Stir in walnuts, cooked bacon and vanilla. Immediately pour into prepared pan. Let stand until set, about 45 minutes. Coarsely chop enough toffee to measure 4 cups; set aside. Break the remaining toffee into pieces; refrigerate to serve with pie or save for another use.

3. On a lightly floured surface, roll the pastry dough to a ⅛-in.-thick circle; transfer to a 9-in. deep-dish pie plate. Trim pastry to ½ in. beyond rim of plate; flute edge. Refrigerate for 30 minutes. Preheat oven to 425°.

4. Line pastry with a double thickness of foil. Fill with pie weights, dried beans or uncooked rice. Bake on a lower oven rack 20-25 minutes or until edges are golden brown. Remove foil and weights; bake 3-6 minutes longer or until bottom is golden brown. Cool on a wire rack.

5. For filling, place egg yolks in a small bowl; let stand at room temperature 30 minutes. In a large heavy saucepan, mix brown sugar, flour and salt. Whisk in milk. Cook and stir over medium heat until thickened and bubbly. Reduce heat to low; cook and stir 4 minutes longer. Remove from heat.

6. Gradually whisk a small amount of hot mixture into egg yolks; return all to pan, whisking constantly. Bring to a gentle boil; cook and stir 2 minutes. Immediately transfer to a clean bowl; stir in butter and vanilla until smooth.

7. Place 3 cups of the chopped toffee into crust; pour filling over toffee. Top with remaining 1 cup chopped toffee. Refrigerate, covered, at least 2 hours before serving. Serve with whipped cream and remaining toffee pieces.
NOTE *To toast nuts, bake in a shallow pan in a 350° oven for 5-10 minutes or cook in a skillet over low heat until lightly browned, stirring occasionally.*

Butterscotch Pie with Walnut-Bacon Toffee

Coconut
Pecan Pie

Coconut Pecan Pie

I top this sweet and delicious pie with sliced bananas, whipped cream and more sliced bananas. It's based on a recipe that my mom got from a pot holder she bought at the Patti's 1880s Settlement in Grand Rivers, Kentucky.
—**JENNIFER CHOISSER** PADUCAH, KY

PREP: 15 MIN. • **BAKE:** 25 MIN. + COOLING
MAKES: 8 SERVINGS

- **Pastry for single-crust pie (9 inches)**
- 7 **large egg whites**
- 1½ **cups sugar**
- 1½ **cups flaked coconut**
- 1½ **cups graham cracker crumbs**
- 1½ **cups chopped pecans**
- **Whipped cream**

1. Preheat the oven to 325°. On a lightly floured surface, roll the dough to a ⅛-in.-thick circle; transfer to a 9-in. pie plate. Trim pastry to ½ in. beyond rim of plate; flute edge.
2. In a large bowl, combine egg whites, sugar, coconut, cracker crumbs and pecans. Pour into pastry shell. Bake 25-30 minutes or until set. Cool on a wire rack. Serve with whipped cream.
PASTRY FOR SINGLE-CRUST PIE (9 INCHES) *Combine 1¼ cups all-purpose flour and ¼ tsp. salt; cut in ½ cup cold butter until crumbly. Gradually add 3-5 Tbsp. ice water, tossing with a fork until dough holds together when pressed. Wrap in plastic wrap, refrigerate for 1 hour.*

Crumb-Topped Apple & Pumpkin Pie

Make a truly unique presentation with this special pie that combines cozy flavors of the season. At our house, it gets rave reviews each year and has become a holiday tradition.
—**TRISHA FOX** PLAINFIELD, IL

PREP: 35 MIN. • **BAKE:** 50 MIN. + COOLING
MAKES: 10 SERVINGS

- 1 **sheet refrigerated pie pastry**
- 2 **cups thinly sliced peeled tart apples**
- ¼ **cup sugar**

Crumb-Topped Apple & Pumpkin Pie

- 2 **teaspoons all-purpose flour**
- 1 **teaspoon lemon juice**
- ¼ **teaspoon ground cinnamon**

PUMPKIN FILLING
- 1½ **cups canned pumpkin**
- 1 **cup fat-free evaporated milk**
- ½ **cup egg substitute**
- ½ **cup sugar**
- ¾ **teaspoon ground cinnamon**
- ¼ **teaspoon salt**
- ⅛ **teaspoon ground nutmeg**

TOPPING
- ½ **cup all-purpose flour**
- 3 **tablespoons sugar**
- 4½ **teaspoons cold butter**
- 3 **tablespoons chopped walnuts**

1. On a lightly floured surface, unroll pie pastry. Transfer pastry to a 9-in. deep-dish pie plate. Trim pastry to ½ in. beyond edge of plate; flute edges. In a large bowl, combine apples, sugar, flour, lemon juice and cinnamon. Spoon into crust.
2. In another large bowl, whisk the pumpkin filling ingredients. Pour over apple mixture. Bake at 375° for 30 minutes.
3. For topping, combine flour and sugar. Cut in butter until crumbly; stir in walnuts. Sprinkle over pie.
4. Bake 20-25 minutes longer or until a knife inserted into pumpkin layer comes out clean (cover edge with foil during the last 15 minutes to prevent overbrowning if necessary).
5. Cool pie on a wire rack. Refrigerate any leftovers.

Praline Sweet Potato Pie

4. Bake at 450° for 15 minutes. Reduce heat to 350°. Bake 30-35 minutes longer or until center is almost set. Cover edges with foil during the last 15 minutes to prevent overbrowning if necessary.
5. Cool on a wire rack. Garnish with whipped cream and the remaining praline crumbles.

TO MAKE AHEAD *Praline crumbles can be made up to 2 weeks in advance. Store in an airtight container.*

Kentucky Chocolate Pecan Pie

Crunchy pecans fill a rich bourbon and chocolate crust. This is our version of a Southern classic. You can use walnuts in place of the pecans if you prefer.

—*TASTE OF HOME* TEST KITCHEN

PREP: 15 MIN. • **BAKE:** 40 MIN. + COOLING
MAKES: 6-8 SERVINGS

- 3 **large eggs**
- 2 **large egg yolks**
- ¾ **cup packed brown sugar**
- ⅔ **cup light corn syrup**
- ⅓ **cup butter, melted**
- 2 **tablespoons Kentucky bourbon, optional**
- 1 **teaspoon vanilla extract**
  Dash salt
- 1 **cup coarsely chopped pecans or chopped walnuts**
- 1 **unbaked pastry shell (9 inches)**
- 1 **large egg white, lightly beaten**
- ¾ **cup semisweet chocolate chips**
- 1 **cup heavy whipping cream**
- 2 **tablespoons confectioners' sugar**

1. In a large bowl, whisk the eggs, yolks, brown sugar, corn syrup, butter, bourbon if desired, vanilla and salt. Stir in nuts.
2. Brush pastry shell with egg white. Sprinkle with chocolate chips. Pour filling over the chips. Bake at 350° for 40-45 minutes or until set. Cool on a wire rack.
3. In a small bowl, beat cream until it begins to thicken. Add confectioners' sugar; beat until stiff peaks form. Dollop on pie just before serving. Refrigerate leftovers.

Praline Sweet Potato Pie

Adding a pleasant crunch, praline crumbles contrast perfectly with the smooth sweet potato filling in this recipe. It's a fun, festive update on a classic Southern dessert.

—CAROL GILLESPIE CHAMBERSBURG, PA

PREP: 30 MIN. • **BAKE:** 45 MIN.
MAKES: 8 SERVINGS

- ¾ **cup sugar**
- ¾ **cup packed brown sugar**
- ¾ **cup half-and-half cream**
- 3 **tablespoons butter**
- 1¼ **cups chopped pecans**
- ½ **teaspoon vanilla extract**
- 1 **sheet refrigerated pie pastry**

FILLING

- 1¾ **cups mashed sweet potatoes**
- 3 **large egg yolks**
- 1 **cup sugar**
- ½ **cup whole milk**
- ½ **cup half-and-half cream**
- 6 **tablespoons butter, softened**
- 2 **teaspoons lemon extract**
- ½ **teaspoon ground cinnamon**
- ½ **teaspoon ground nutmeg**
  Whipped cream

1. Line a 15x10x1-in. pan with waxed paper; set aside. For praline crumbles, in a large saucepan over medium heat, combine the sugar, brown sugar, cream and butter. Cook and stir until sugar is dissolved. Stir in pecans.
2. Bring to a boil; cook and stir until a candy thermometer reads 238° (soft-ball stage), about 10 minutes. Remove from the heat. Add vanilla; stir for 2-3 minutes or until the mixture thickens slightly and begins to lose its gloss. Quickly drop by heaping tablespoonfuls onto the prepared pan. Let stand at room temperature until set. Coarsely chop.
3. Unroll pastry into a 9-in. pie plate; flute edges. Sprinkle 1 cup praline crumbles into pastry. Place sweet potatoes, egg yolks, sugar, milk, cream, butter, extract and spices in a food processor. Cover and process just until blended. Pour into crust.

Pumpkin Mousse Pie with Gingersnap Crust

Gingersnap cookies and pumpkin taste so good together in this pie. It's a must-have treat at our family get-togethers.

—BERNICE JANOWSKI STEVENS POINT, WI

PREP: 45 MIN. + CHILLING
MAKES: 8 SERVINGS

- 1½ cups finely crushed gingersnap cookies (about 30 cookies)
- 1 cup finely chopped pecans, toasted
- ⅓ cup butter, melted
- 1 envelope unflavored gelatin
- ¼ cup cold water
- ½ cup packed brown sugar
- ½ cup half-and-half cream
- 3 large egg yolks
- 1 can (15 ounces) solid-pack pumpkin
- 2 teaspoons pumpkin pie spice
- 2 cups whipped topping
- ¼ cup butterscotch-caramel ice cream topping
- ½ cup chopped pecans, toasted

1. Preheat oven to 350°. In a small bowl, mix the crushed cookies and chopped pecans; stir in butter. Press onto bottom and up the sides of an ungreased 9-in. deep-dish pie plate. Bake 10-12 minutes or until lightly browned. Cool on a wire rack.

2. In a microwave-safe bowl, sprinkle gelatin over cold water; let stand for 1 minute. Microwave on high for 30-40 seconds. Stir and let stand 1 minute or until gelatin is dissolved.

3. In a large saucepan, whisk brown sugar, cream and egg yolks until blended. Cook over low heat until a thermometer reads at least 160°, stirring constantly. (Do not allow to boil.) Remove from heat; stir in pumpkin, pie spice and gelatin mixture. Cool completely.

4. Fold in whipped topping. Pour into crust; refrigerate until set. Drizzle with ice cream topping; sprinkle with pecans.

NOTE *To toast nuts, bake in a shallow pan in a 350° oven for 5-10 minutes or cook in a skillet over low heat until lightly browned, stirring occasionally.*

Pumpkin Mousse Pie with Gingersnap Crust

Buttermilk Pecan Pie

Whenever we visited my grandmother, she would make this "golden oldie." Grandma grew her own pecans, and we never tired of cracking them and picking out the meat when we knew we'd be treated to her special pie!

—MILDRED SHERRER

FORT WORTH, TX

PREP: 15 MIN. • **BAKE:** 55 MIN.
MAKES: 8 SERVINGS

- ½ **cup butter, softened**
- 2 **cups sugar**
- 5 **large eggs**
- 2 **tablespoons all-purpose flour**
- 2 **tablespoons lemon juice**
- 1 **teaspoon vanilla extract**
- 1 **cup buttermilk**
- 1 **cup chopped pecans**
- 1 **unbaked pastry shell (10 inches)**

In a bowl, cream butter and sugar. Add eggs, one at a time, beating well after each addition. Blend in flour, lemon juice and vanilla. Stir in buttermilk and pecans. Pour into the pie shell. Bake at 325° for 55 minutes or until set. Cool on a wire rack. Store in the refrigerator.

Buttermilk Pecan Pie

Fruits of the Forest Pie

Five kinds of nuts are squirreled away in this deliciously sweet pie. You'll find that there's crunch in every bite!

—MARY LOU TIMPSON COLORADO CITY, AZ

PREP: 30 MIN. • **BAKE:** 45 MIN. + COOLING
MAKES: 8 SERVINGS

Pastry for single-crust pie (9 inches)
- ⅓ cup coarsely chopped macadamia nuts
- ⅓ cup chopped hazelnuts
- ½ cup salted cashew halves
- ½ cup pecan halves
- ⅓ cup slivered almonds
- 4 large eggs
- 1 cup light corn syrup
- ½ cup sugar
- ¼ cup packed brown sugar
- 2 tablespoons butter, melted
- 1 teaspoon vanilla extract
- ¼ teaspoon salt

1. Line a 9-in. pie plate with pastry; trim pastry to ½ in. beyond edge of plate and flute the edges. Sprinkle macadamia nuts and hazelnuts into pastry shell. Arrange cashews, pecans and almonds over the chopped nuts.
2. In a small bowl, beat the eggs, corn syrup, sugars, butter, vanilla and salt until well blended. Pour over nuts.
3. Bake at 350° for 45-50 minutes or until a knife inserted near the center comes out clean. (Cover edges with foil during the last 10 minutes to prevent overbrowning if necessary.) Cool on a wire rack. Store in the refrigerator.

"It was great! Made it twice! It was delicious!"

—DILLBERT
FROM TASTEOFHOME.COM

Gingery Pumpkin Pie

Gingery Pumpkin Pie

My birthday is in late November, so my mom often morphed the Thanksgiving pumpkin pie into my birthday "cake" and had all the family sing for me. This is an update on her recipe, adding lots more of our mutual favorite ingredient: ginger. The pie's best after it's nice and chilled. Birthday candles optional.

—EMILY TYRA MILWAUKEE, WI

PREP: 30 MIN. + CHILLING • **BAKE:** 50 MIN.
MAKES: 8 SERVINGS (1½ CUPS WHIPPED CREAM)

- 1¼ cups all-purpose flour
- 1 tablespoon minced fresh gingerroot
- ¼ teaspoon ground allspice
- ¼ teaspoon salt
- ½ cup butter, cubed
- 3 to 5 tablespoons ice water

FILLING
- 2 large eggs
- 1 large egg yolk
- 1 can (15 ounces) solid-pack pumpkin
- 1¼ cups heavy whipping cream
- ⅔ cup packed brown sugar
- 1 teaspoon ground cinnamon
- 1 teaspoon minced fresh gingerroot
- 1 teaspoon molasses
- ¼ teaspoon ground ginger
- ¼ teaspoon ground allspice
- ⅛ teaspoon ground cardamom
- ⅛ teaspoon ground cloves

WHIPPED CREAM
- ¾ cup heavy whipping cream
- 1 tablespoon maple syrup
- ¼ teaspoon ground cinnamon

1. In a small bowl, mix flour, ginger, allspice and salt; cut in butter until crumbly. Gradually add ice water, tossing with a fork until dough holds together when pressed. Shape into a disk; wrap in plastic wrap. Refrigerate for 1 hour or overnight.
2. Preheat the oven to 375°. On a lightly floured surface, roll the dough to a ⅛-in.-thick circle; transfer to a 9-in. pie plate. Trim pastry to ½ in. beyond rim of plate; flute edge. In a large bowl, whisk filling ingredients until blended; pour into crust.
3. Bake on a lower oven rack for 50-60 minutes or until a knife inserted near the center comes out clean. Cool on a wire rack; serve or refrigerate within 2 hours.
4. For whipped cream, in a small bowl, beat cream until it begins to thicken. Add maple syrup and cinnamon; beat until soft peaks form. Serve with pie.

LEMON-BERRY ICE CREAM PIE
PAGE 270

Frosty Favorites

HOORAY FOR FROSTY TREATS SERVED UP DURING THE DOG DAYS OF SUMMER! YOU'LL ENJOY THE VARIETY OF FROZEN RECIPE OPTIONS HERE, AND SO WILL THE LITTLE ONES. WHIP TOGETHER ANY OF THESE SIMPLE PIES FOR YOUR NEXT POOL PARTY, FAMILY PICNIC OR AFTER-DINNER SURPRISE.

MINTY ICE CREAM PIE
PAGE 268

GRASSHOPPER PIE
PAGE 274

**CARAMEL BANANA
ICE CREAM PIE** *PAGE 277*

Frozen Grasshopper Pie

When I first started experimenting with cream pies, this seemed like the right recipe to create for a house of chocolate lovers. I guessed right. This is more of an adult New Year's Eve pie, but some have made it for Christmas dessert—served after the kids have gone to bed!

—LORRAINE CALAND SHUNIAH, ON

PREP: 20 MIN. + CHILLING
COOK: 15 MIN. + FREEZING
MAKES: 8 SERVINGS

1¼ cups chocolate wafer crumbs
    (about 22 wafers)
¼ cup sugar
¼ cup butter, melted
FILLING
1 package (10 ounces)
    miniature marshmallows
⅓ cup 2% milk
¼ cup creme de menthe
2 tablespoons creme de cacao
¼ teaspoon peppermint
    extract, optional
2 cups heavy whipping cream
    Maraschino cherries and
        additional whipped
        cream, optional

1. In a small bowl, mix wafer crumbs and sugar; stir in butter. Press onto bottom and up the sides of a greased 9-in. pie plate. Refrigerate for 30 minutes.

2. Meanwhile, in a large saucepan, combine marshmallows and milk; cook and stir over medium-low heat for 12-14 minutes or until smooth. Remove from heat. Cool to room temperature, stirring occasionally. Stir in liqueurs and, if desired, extract.

3. In a large bowl, beat cream until soft peaks form; fold in marshmallow mixture. Transfer to crust. Freeze 6 hours or until firm. If desired, top with cherries and additional whipped cream just before serving.

Frozen
Grasshopper
Pie

Raspberry Truffle Pie

A dessert like this is perfect for any occasion and special enough to conclude a holiday meal. The raspberry sauce pairs well with the chocolate pie.

—SUZY HORVATH MILWAUKIE, OR

PREP: 40 MIN. + CHILLING
MAKES: 8 SERVINGS (1¾ CUPS SAUCE)

- 1¼ cups graham cracker crumbs
- ¼ cup sugar
- 1 tablespoon baking cocoa
- ¼ cup butter, melted

FILLING
- 4 ounces semisweet chocolate, chopped
- 2 tablespoons milk
- 1 package (8 ounces) cream cheese, softened
- 3 tablespoons sugar
- ⅓ cup raspberry liqueur
- 1¾ cups heavy whipping cream

RASPBERRY SAUCE
- 2 cups fresh raspberries
- ½ cup sugar
- ¼ cup raspberry liqueur

1. In a bowl, combine the graham cracker crumbs, sugar, cocoa and butter; press onto the bottom and up the sides of a greased 9-in. pie plate. Bake at 375° for 8-10 minutes or until lightly browned. Cool on a wire rack.

2. For filling, in a small saucepan, melt chocolate with milk; stir until smooth. Remove from the heat; set aside to cool.

3. In a large bowl, beat cream cheese and sugar until smooth. Gradually beat in liqueur and cooled chocolate mixture just until combined. In a small bowl, beat cream until stiff peaks form; fold into chocolate mixture. Pour into crust. Cover and refrigerate for at least 4 hours.

4. For sauce, place raspberries and sugar in a blender; cover and process until blended. Press mixture through a fine meshed sieve; discard seeds. Stir in liqueur. Serve with pie.

Cool and Creamy
Watermelon Pie

⑤ INGREDIENTS

Cool and Creamy Watermelon Pie

I like this pie because it's so refreshing. It never lasts long on warm summer days. Watermelon and a few convenience items make it a delightful dessert that's easy to whip up.

—VELMA BECK CARLINVILLE, IL

PREP: 15 MIN. + CHILLING
MAKES: 6-8 SERVINGS

- 1 package (3 ounces) watermelon gelatin
- ¼ cup boiling water
- 1 carton (12 ounces) frozen whipped topping, thawed
- 2 cups cubed seeded watermelon
- 1 graham cracker crust (9 inches)

In a large bowl, dissolve gelatin in boiling water. Cool to room temperature. Whisk in whipped topping; fold in watermelon. Spoon into crust. Refrigerate for 2 hours or until pie is set.

FREEZE IT ⑤ INGREDIENTS

Frosty Key Lime Pie

Give credit to the whipped cream for the fluffy-smooth texture and luscious flavor of this frozen refresher.

—LISA FELD GRAFTON, WI

PREP: 20 MIN. + FREEZING
MAKES: 6-8 SERVINGS

- 1 can (14 ounces) sweetened condensed milk
- 6 tablespoons key lime juice
- 2 cups heavy whipping cream, whipped, divided
- 1 graham cracker crust (9 inches)

1. In a large bowl, combine milk and lime juice. Refrigerate ¼ cup whipped cream for garnish. Fold a fourth of the remaining whipped cream into lime mixture; fold in remaining whipped cream. Spoon into crust. Cover and freeze overnight.

2. Remove from the freezer about 10-15 minutes before serving. Garnish with reserved whipped cream.

Bananas Foster Pie

FREEZE IT

Minty Ice Cream Pie

I love ice cream desserts because they can be fixed in advance and kept on hand for unexpected company. Plus, they never fail to please! This minty pie always makes a refreshing finale.

—LORRAINE DAROCHA MOUNTAIN CITY, TN

PREP: 25 MIN. + FREEZING
MAKES: 6-8 SERVINGS

- 1 package (3 ounces) cream cheese, softened
- 2 tablespoons sugar
- 2 cups heavy whipping cream, divided
- ¼ cup chopped walnuts
- 1 chocolate crumb crust (9 inches)
- 2 packages (4¾ ounces each) chocolate-covered peppermint candies, divided
- 1 pint chocolate ice cream or fudge ripple ice cream
- ¼ cup hot fudge ice cream topping, warmed
- 2 tablespoons confectioners' sugar
- 1 teaspoon peppermint extract
- 2 to 3 drops green food coloring, optional

1. In a small bowl, beat cream cheese and sugar until smooth. Beat in 1 cup cream until soft peaks form. Fold in walnuts. Spread into crust. Coarsely chop 1 package peppermint candies; fold into ice cream. Spread over cream cheese mixture. Drizzle with fudge topping. Freeze for 1 hour.

2. In a small bowl, beat remaining cream until it begins to thicken. Add the confectioners' sugar, extract and food coloring if desired; beat until stiff peaks form. Garnish pie with whipped cream mixture and remaining candies. Freeze. Remove from the freezer 15 minutes before serving.

Bananas Foster Pie

I love peanut butter with banana, so it only made sense to me to create a pie with that tasty combination. I also used the flavors of banana's foster to create this delectable pie.

—EMILY HOBBS OZARK, MO

PREP: 45 MIN. + CHILLING
MAKES: 8 SERVINGS

- 1½ cups crushed vanilla wafers (about 45 wafers)
- ¼ cup butter, melted

FILLING

- 2 tablespoons butter
- ⅓ cup all-purpose flour
- ⅔ cup packed brown sugar
- ¾ teaspoon ground cinnamon
- ¼ teaspoon salt
- ¼ teaspoon ground nutmeg
- 2 cups 2% milk
- 4 large egg yolks
- ⅓ cup creamy peanut butter
- 1 tablespoon dark rum
- 1 teaspoon vanilla extract
- 3 medium bananas

Whipped cream, caramel sundae syrup and chopped salted peanuts

1. Combine wafer crumbs and butter; press onto the bottom and up the sides of a greased 9-in. pie plate. Bake at 350° for 8-10 minutes or until crust is lightly browned. Cool on a wire rack. In a large saucepan, melt 2 tablespoons butter. Stir in the flour, brown sugar, cinnamon, salt and nutmeg until smooth. Gradually add the milk. Bring to a boil; cook and stir for 2 minutes or until thickened. Remove from the heat.

2. Stir a small amount of hot filling into egg yolks; return all to the pan, stirring constantly. Bring to a gentle boil; cook and stir 2 minutes longer. Remove from the heat. Stir in the peanut butter, rum and vanilla. Slice bananas into the crust; pour filling over the top. Refrigerate for 3 hours or until set. Garnish as desired with whipped cream, caramel syrup and peanuts. Store leftovers in the refrigerator.

FREEZE IT

Frosty Toffee Bits Pie

On a hot summer day, or to finish off a wonderful meal any time, this dessert tastes oh-so-good!

—LADONNA REED PONCA CITY, OK

PREP: 10 MIN. + FREEZING
MAKES: 6-8 SERVINGS

- 1 **package (3 ounces) cream cheese, softened**
- 2 **tablespoons sugar**
- ½ **cup half-and-half cream**
- 1 **carton (8 ounces) frozen whipped topping, thawed**
- 1 **package (8 ounces) milk chocolate English toffee bits, divided**
- 1 **graham cracker crust (9 inches)**

1. In a large bowl, beat cream cheese and sugar until smooth. Beat in cream until blended. Fold in whipped topping and 1 cup toffee bits.

2. Spoon into crust; sprinkle with remaining toffee bits. Cover and freeze overnight. Remove from the freezer 10 minutes before serving.

TOP TIP

Homemade Crust

If you decide to make a homemade graham cracker crust, keep the bottom from getting soggy by using only butter or regular margarine, not low fat spreads, which add water. Bake your crust to make it crisp, but make sure it is cooled before adding your filling so moisture will not form between the crust and the filling.

Frosty
Toffee Bits
Pie

Frozen Cranberry Pie with Candied Almonds

It's so convenient to prepare part of a holiday feast in advance. This frosty, ginger-spiced delight goes in the freezer overnight and is ready to enjoy the next day.

—**ROSEMARY JOHNSON** IRONDALE, AL

PREP: 30 MIN. + FREEZING
MAKES: 8 SERVINGS

- 24 **gingersnap cookies**
- ¾ **cup milk**
- 2 **packages (3.4 ounces each) instant French vanilla pudding mix**
- 1 **can (14 ounces) whole-berry cranberry sauce**
- 1 **carton (8 ounces) frozen French vanilla whipped topping, thawed, divided**
- ½ **cup slivered almonds, divided**
- 1 **teaspoon chopped crystallized ginger**
- 1 **teaspoon almond extract**
- 2 **teaspoons butter**
- 2 **tablespoons brown sugar**

1. Arrange cookies around the bottom and up the sides of an ungreased 9-in. pie plate, cutting cookies if necessary to fit.
2. In a small bowl, combine milk and pudding mixes. Stir in the cranberry sauce, ½ cup whipped topping, ⅓ cup almonds, ginger and almond extract. Pour into prepared pie plate; chill for 1 hour.
3. Meanwhile, in a small heavy skillet, melt butter. Add remaining almonds; cook over medium heat until nuts are toasted, about 4 minutes. Sprinkle with brown sugar. Cook and stir for 2-4 minutes or until sugar is melted. Spread on foil to cool.
4. Spread remaining whipped topping over filling; sprinkle with almonds. Cover and freeze overnight.

Lemon-Berry
Ice Cream Pie

Lemon-Berry Ice Cream Pie

I love the combination of fresh strawberries and lemon curd. It's so refreshing, especially in a super easy dessert like this.

—**ROXANNE CHAN** ALBANY, CA

PREP: 15 MIN. + FREEZING
MAKES: 8 SERVINGS

- 1 **pint strawberry ice cream, softened**
- 1 **graham cracker crust (9 inches)**
- 1 **cup lemon curd**
- 2 **cups frozen whipped topping, thawed**
- 1 **pint fresh strawberries, halved**

1. Spoon ice cream into pie crust; freeze 2 hours or until firm.
2. Spread lemon curd over ice cream; top with whipped topping. Freeze, covered, 4 hours or until firm.
3. Remove from freezer 10 minutes before serving. Serve with strawberries.

TOP TIP

We Like Fresh Strawberries

Strawberries will stay fresher for longer if they are stored unwashed, with the stems on, in a sealed glass jar in the refrigerator.

—**MARY M.** WILLIAMSPORT, PA

Chocolate-Caramel Dream Pie

Chocolate, caramel and cream cheese come together to produce a pleasing pie. Adding the chocolate stars on top makes it perfect for a Fourth of July or Memorial Day gathering. Tell guests to save room for dessert!

—ANNA ROBB HARRISON, AR

PREP: 25 MIN. + CHILLING
MAKES: 8 SERVINGS

- 1½ cups crushed crisp ladyfinger cookies
- ⅓ cup butter, melted
- ½ cup Nutella
- ⅔ cup caramel ice cream topping
- 2 tablespoons plus 2 cups heavy whipping cream, divided
- 1½ cups slivered almonds
- 1 package (8 ounces) cream cheese, softened
- ⅓ cup plus 1 tablespoon confectioners' sugar, divided
- 1½ cups semisweet chocolate chips, melted
- 2 teaspoons vanilla extract
  Additional heavy whipping cream, whipped
  Chocolate stars for garnish if desired, optional

1. Combine crushed cookies and butter; press onto the bottom and up the sides of a greased 9-in. pie plate. Refrigerate for 30 minutes.

2. Spread Nutella over crust. In a large bowl, combine caramel topping and 2 tablespoons cream; stir in almonds. Spoon over Nutella layer.

3. In a small bowl, beat cream cheese and ⅓ cup confectioners' sugar; stir in melted chocolate and vanilla until smooth. In a large bowl, beat remaining cream until stiff peaks form; fold into cream cheese mixture. Spread over the caramel-almond layer.

4. Sprinkle with the remaining confectioners' sugar. Garnish with more whipped cream and chocolate stars if desired. Refrigerate for at least 1 hour before serving.

NOTE *This recipe was tested with Alessi crisp ladyfinger cookies. Kept refrigerated, this can be made the day before serving.*

Raspberry Ribbon Pie

While he was growing up, this was my husband's favorite Christmas dessert. When we married, his mother passed it on to me. I take it to family gatherings during the holidays and have yet to bring any home! It's a cool recipe for summer as well.

—VICTORIA NEWMAN ANTELOPE, CA

PREP: 20 MIN. + CHILLING
MAKES: 6-8 SERVINGS

- 2 packages (3 ounces each) cream cheese, softened
- ½ cup confectioners' sugar
  Dash salt
- 1 cup heavy whipping cream, whipped
  Pastry for deep-dish single-crust pie (9 inches), baked
- 1 package (3 ounces) raspberry gelatin
- 1¼ cups boiling water
- 1 tablespoon lemon juice
- 1 package (10 ounces) frozen raspberries in syrup, thawed

1. In a large bowl, beat the cream cheese, confectioners' sugar and salt until smooth. Fold in cream. Spread half into pie shell. Chill 30 minutes.

2. Meanwhile, dissolve the gelatin in water; add lemon juice and raspberries. Carefully spoon half over cream cheese layer. Chill until set, about 30 minutes.

3. Set aside the remaining gelatin mixture at room temperature. Carefully spread remaining cream cheese mixture over top of pie. Chill for 30 minutes. Top with remaining gelatin. Chill until firm.

Chocolate-Caramel Dream Pie

Frozen
Peach Pies

Frozen Peach Pies

A refreshing, peachy filling and a buttery graham cracker crust are a terrific pair. This pie can be frozen for up to three days.

—**ATHENA RUSSELL** GREENVILLE, SC

PREP: 20 MIN. • **BAKE:** 10 MIN. + FREEZING
MAKES: 2 PIES (8 SERVINGS EACH)

- 2½ cups graham cracker crumbs
- ½ cup plus 2 tablespoons butter, melted
- ¼ cup sugar
- 1 can (14 ounces) sweetened condensed milk
- ¼ cup lemon juice
- ¼ cup orange juice
- 1 package (16 ounces) frozen unsweetened sliced peaches
- 1 tablespoon grated lemon peel
- 1½ cups heavy whipping cream
  Sweetened whipped cream, optional

1. In a small bowl, combine the graham cracker crumbs, butter and sugar; press onto the bottom and up the sides of two greased 9-in. pie plates. Bake at 350° for 10-12 minutes or until lightly browned. Cool on wire racks.

2. In a blender, combine the milk, lemon juice, orange juice, peaches and lemon peel; cover and process until smooth. Transfer to a large bowl. In a large bowl, beat cream until stiff peaks form; fold into peach mixture.

3. Spoon into the crusts. Cover and freeze for at least 4 hours or until firm. Remove from the freezer 15 minutes before serving. Top with sweetened whipped cream if desired.

> ❝Yum! I'll make this again. It's very easy and has such a refreshing taste after a full meal.❞
>
> —XLSALBUMS
> FROM TASTEOFHOME.COM

Toffee Ice Cream Pie

Toffee Ice Cream Pie

I modified a recipe originally from my sister in order to save time in the kitchen, and this is the result. No doubt about it, you'll want a second serving.

—**JANELL GREISEN** SAN DIMAS, CA

PREP: 25 MIN. + FREEZING
MAKES: 8 SERVINGS

- 1 quart vanilla ice cream, softened
- 1 Heath candy bar (1.4 ounces), crushed
- 1 chocolate crumb crust (8 inches)

CHOCOLATE SAUCE

- 1 cup (6 ounces) semisweet chocolate chips
- ¼ cup butter, cubed
- 1 cup confectioners' sugar
- 1 can (5 ounces) evaporated milk
- 1 teaspoon vanilla extract

1. In a large bowl, combine ice cream and crushed candy; spread into crust. Cover and freeze until firm.

2. In a small saucepan, melt the chocolate chips and the butter over medium-low heat. Add confectioners' sugar and evaporated milk; cook and stir for 4-5 minutes or until thickened. Remove from the heat; stir in vanilla. Cut pie into slices and drizzle each with the sauce.

Grasshopper Pie

Creamy Banana-Berry Pie

Cool, creamy and topped with bananas and fresh blueberries, this pretty pie is lighter than air and is sure to melt all resistance to dessert!

—*TASTE OF HOME* TEST KITCHEN

PREP: 30 MIN. + CHILLING
MAKES: 8 SERVINGS

- 1 **sheet refrigerated pie pastry**
- ¼ **cup chopped pecans**
- 1¼ **cups cold fat-free milk**
- ½ **cup reduced-fat sour cream**
      Sugar substitute equivalent
      to ¼ cup sugar
- 1 **package (.9 ounce) sugar-free**
      instant banana pudding mix
- 2 **cups reduced-fat whipped topping**
- 1 **tablespoon lemon juice**
- 2 **medium bananas**
- ⅓ **cup fresh blueberries**

1. Unroll pastry on a lightly floured surface. Sprinkle with pecans; lightly roll pecans into pastry. Transfer to a 9-in. pie plate. Line unpricked pastry shell with a double thickness of heavy-duty foil. Bake at 450° for 8 minutes. Remove foil; bake 5 minutes longer. Cool on a wire rack.
2. In a small bowl, combine the milk, sour cream and the sugar substitute. Gradually whisk in dry pudding mix. Fold in whipped topping.
3. Place the lemon juice in a small bowl. Slice bananas into juice and stir gently to coat. Set aside ⅓ cup of bananas; spoon remaining banana slices into the crust. Top with pudding mixture, blueberries and reserved banana slices. Cover and refrigerate for 30 minutes before serving.
NOTE *This recipe was tested with Splenda no-calorie sweetener.*

FREEZE IT
Grasshopper Pie

I need only six ingredients to whip up this fluffy and refreshing treat. I usually make two minty pies for our family because we're never satisfied with just one slice. Kids will love this one!

—**LOUCINDA ZACHARIAS** SPOONER, WI

PREP: 15 MIN. + FREEZING
MAKES: 8 SERVINGS

- 2 **packages (3 ounces each)**
      cream cheese, softened
- 1 **can (14 ounces) sweetened**
      condensed milk
- 15 **drops green food coloring**
- 24 **chocolate-covered mint**
      cookies, divided
- 2 **cups whipped topping**
- 1 **chocolate crumb crust (8 inches)**

In a large bowl, beat the cream cheese until fluffy. Gradually beat in the milk until smooth. Beat in the food coloring. Coarsely crush 16 cookies; stir into the cream cheese mixture. Fold in whipped topping. Spoon into the crust. Cover and freeze overnight. Remove from the freezer 15 minutes before serving. Garnish with remaining cookies.

"It was very easy to make and it tastes delicious! I used Girl Scout Thin Mint cookies. I would definitely make this again."
—OBSESSEDWITHFOOD FROM TASTEOFHOME.COM

FREEZE IT **(5) INGREDIENTS**

Cookie Ice Cream Pie

With no baking involved in this recipe, you won't heat up your kitchen on sweltering days. Whip it up and serve to company or the neighborhood kids.

—**DEBBIE WALSH** MADISON, WI

PREP: 25 MIN. + FREEZING
MAKES: 8 SERVINGS

- 10 **Oreo cookies, crushed**
- 3 **tablespoons butter, melted**
- 14 **whole Oreo cookies**

FILLING

- ½ **gallon white chocolate raspberry truffle ice cream, softened and divided**
- ½ **cup prepared fudge topping, divided**
  Fresh raspberries, optional

1. In a small bowl, combine crushed cookies and butter; press onto bottom of a 9-in. pie plate. Stand the whole cookies up around edges, pressing lightly into crust. Freeze for 1 hour or until set.

2. For filling, spread half of ice cream over crushed cookies. Drizzle with ¼ cup of fudge topping. Freeze for 1 hour or until set. Spread remaining ice cream on top. Drizzle with the remaining fudge topping. Freeze the pie several hours or overnight.

3. Garnish with fresh raspberries if desired. Let pie stand at room temperature for 15 minutes before cutting.

**Cookie
Ice Cream
Pie**

Frozen Hawaiian Pie

BIG BATCH

Frozen Hawaiian Pie

Cool summer pies are one of Mom's specialties. This version offers pineapple, maraschino cherries and walnuts that are folded into a fluffy filling. It's an easy yet tempting no-bake dessert.

—**JENNIFER MCQUILLAN** JACKSONVILLE, FL

PREP: 10 MIN. + FREEZING
MAKES: 2 PIES (6-8 SERVINGS EACH)

- 1 can (14 ounces) sweetened condensed milk
- 1 carton (12 ounces) frozen whipped topping, thawed
- 1 can (20 ounces) crushed pineapple, drained
- ½ cup chopped walnuts
- ½ cup chopped maraschino cherries
- 2 tablespoons lemon juice
- 2 graham cracker crusts (9 inches)
  Fresh mint and additional walnuts and maraschino cherries

1. In a large bowl, combine milk and whipped topping. Fold in the pineapple, nuts, cherries and lemon juice. Pour half into each crust. Freeze until firm, about 4 hours.

2. Remove from the freezer 20 minutes before serving. Garnish with mint, additional nuts and cherries.

> ❝The recipe tasted very cool and refreshing. An extra bonus is that it makes two pies, so it's perfect for a gathering!❞
>
> —SHECOOKSALOT
> FROM TASTEOFHOME.COM

Caramel Banana Ice Cream Pie

With six ingredients and a prepared graham cracker crust, this pie is easy to make and luscious, too. Guests will enjoy the symphony of caramel, banana and toffee bits.

—APRIL TIMBOE SILOAM SPRINGS, AR

PREP: 20 MIN. + FREEZING
MAKES: 8 SERVINGS

- ¼ cup plus 1 tablespoon caramel ice cream topping, divided
- 1 graham cracker crust (9 inches)
- 1 cup cold 2% milk
- 2 packages (3.4 ounces each) instant banana cream pudding mix
- 1 quart vanilla ice cream, softened
- 1¾ cups whipped topping
- 1 English toffee candy bar (1.4 ounces), chopped

1. Spread ¼ cup caramel topping into crust. In a large bowl, beat milk and pudding mix on low speed for 2 minutes. Add ice cream; mix well.
2. Spoon into prepared crust. Top with whipped topping. Drizzle with remaining caramel topping; sprinkle with chopped candy bar.
3. Cover and freeze for 2 hours or until firm. Remove from the freezer 15 minutes before serving.

Old-Fashioned Strawberry Pie

I've been cooking since I was a girl and especially enjoy making fresh, fruity desserts like this. It's a wonderful and light dessert to follow dinner and a must when fresh berries are in season.

—ERICA COOPER ELK RIVER, MN

PREP: 30 MIN. • **COOK:** 10 MIN. + CHILLING
MAKES: 8 SERVINGS

- 1 sheet refrigerated pie pastry
- 1 package (3 ounces) cook-and-serve vanilla pudding mix
- 1½ cups water
- 1 teaspoon lemon juice
- 1 package (.3 ounce) sugar-free strawberry gelatin

Old-Fashioned Strawberry Pie

- ½ cup boiling water
- 4 cups sliced fresh strawberries
- 3 ounces reduced-fat cream cheese
- 2 cups reduced-fat whipped topping, divided
- 1 teaspoon vanilla extract
- 8 fresh strawberries

1. On a lightly floured surface, unroll the pastry. Transfer to a 9-in. pie plate. Trim pastry to ½ in. beyond edge of plate; flute edges. Line unpricked pastry with a double thickness of heavy-duty foil. Bake at 450° for 8 minutes. Remove foil; bake 5-7 minutes longer or until lightly browned. Cool on a wire rack.
2. In a small saucepan, combine pudding mix, water and lemon juice. Cook and stir over medium heat until mixture comes to a boil. Cook and stir for 1-2 minutes longer or until thickened. Remove from the heat; set aside.
3. In a large bowl, dissolve gelatin in boiling water. Gradually stir in pudding. Cover and refrigerate for 30 minutes or until thickened. Fold in sliced strawberries. Transfer to crust.
4. For topping, in another bowl, beat the cream cheese, ½ cup whipped topping and vanilla until smooth. Fold in remaining whipped topping. Cut a small hole in the corner of a pastry or plastic bag; insert a medium star tip. Fill with topping. Pipe topping around edges of pie; garnish with whole strawberries. Refrigerate for at least 1 hour.

Hazelnut Cream Pie

The key ingredient in this creamy-crunchy pie is my children's favorite chocolate-hazelnut spread. For the finishing touch, sprinkle on semisweet chips and toasted nuts.

—**SUSAN BLOCK** CUMMING, GA

PREP: 35 MIN. + CHILLING
MAKES: 10 SERVINGS

- 1 cup graham cracker crumbs
- ⅓ cup butter, melted
- ¼ cup sugar
- ¼ cup finely chopped hazelnuts, toasted
- 2 tablespoons Nutella

FILLING

- 1 package (8 ounces) cream cheese, softened
- ¾ cup Nutella
- 1 cup plus 2 tablespoons confectioners' sugar
- 4½ teaspoons 2% milk
- 1 tablespoon hazelnut liqueur
- 1 cup heavy whipping cream
- ⅔ cup miniature semisweet chocolate chips

TOPPING

- 2 tablespoons chopped hazelnuts, toasted
- 1 tablespoon miniature semisweet chocolate chips

1. In a small bowl, combine the cracker crumbs, butter, sugar and hazelnuts. Press onto the bottom and up the sides of a greased 9-in. pie plate. Bake at 350° for 10 minutes. Cool on a wire rack. In a microwave, heat Nutella until melted; stir until smooth. Spread over bottom of the crust. Refrigerate.
2. For filling, in a large bowl, beat cream cheese and Nutella until fluffy. Add the confectioners' sugar, milk and liqueur; beat until smooth. In another bowl, beat cream until soft peaks form. Gently fold into cream cheese mixture. Fold in the chocolate chips.
3. Spoon into prepared crust. Sprinkle hazelnuts and chocolate chips over top. Cover and refrigerate at least 2 hours or until chilled.

Winning Coffee Ice Cream Pie

Winning Coffee Ice Cream Pie

While coffee ice cream is great, I sometimes vary the flavor of this family favorite. It's one dreamy treat that's always high on demand for dessert.

—**VELMA BROWN** TURNER STATION, KY

PREP: 30 MIN. + FREEZING
MAKES: 8 SERVINGS

- 2 ounces unsweetened chocolate, chopped
- ¼ cup butter, cubed
- 1 can (5 ounces) evaporated milk
- ½ cup sugar
- 1 pint coffee ice cream, softened
- 1 chocolate crumb crust (8 inches)
- 1 carton (8 ounces) frozen whipped topping, thawed
- ¼ cup chopped pecans

1. In a heavy saucepan, melt chocolate and butter over low heat. Stir in milk and sugar. Bring to a boil over medium heat, stirring constantly. Cook and stir for 3-4 minutes or until thickened. Remove from the heat; cool completely.
2. Spoon ice cream into crust. Stir sauce; spread over ice cream. Top with whipped topping; sprinkle with pecans. Freeze until firm. Remove the pie from the freezer 15 minutes before serving.

Triple Chocolate Dream Pie

A creamy chocolate pie makes for a sweet, indulgent dessert. My light version lets you have this treat without the guilt. Sometimes I add a teaspoon of instant coffee granules to the sugar-cocoa mixture for a mocha pie.

—MARY ANN RING BLUFFTON, OH

PREP: 30 MIN. + CHILLING
MAKES: 8 SERVINGS

- 1½ cups graham cracker crumbs
- 2 tablespoons butter, melted
- 1 large egg white

FILLING
- ⅔ cup sugar
- ⅓ cup baking cocoa
- 3 tablespoons cornstarch
- ⅛ teaspoon salt
- 2 cups fat-free milk
- 1 large egg, beaten
- ¼ cup semisweet chocolate chips
- 1 teaspoon vanilla extract

TOPPING
- 1½ cups reduced-fat whipped topping
- 1 teaspoon grated chocolate

1. Combine the graham cracker crumbs, butter and egg white; press onto the bottom and up the sides of a greased 9-in. pie plate. Bake at 375° for 6-8 minutes or until lightly browned. Cool on a wire rack.

2. For filling, in a large saucepan, combine the sugar, cocoa, cornstarch and salt. Stir in milk until smooth. Cook and stir over medium-high heat until thickened and bubbly. Reduce heat to low; cook and stir 2 minutes longer.

3. Remove from the heat. Stir a small amount of hot mixture into egg; return all to the pan, stirring constantly. Bring to a gentle boil; cook and stir for 2 minutes. Remove from the heat; stir in chocolate chips and vanilla.

4. Pour into crust. Refrigerate for at least 2 hours or until firm. Spread whipped topping over filling; sprinkle with grated chocolate.

Coconut Chiffon Pie

My mother-in-law gave this recipe to me the first year I was married. It's a holiday must at my husband's family Christmas dinners. We call it White Christmas Chiffon and garnish it with coconut.

—KRISTINE FRY FENNIMORE, WI

PREP: 30 MIN. + CHILLING
MAKES: 6-8 SERVINGS

- 1 unbaked pastry shell (9 inches)
- 1 envelope unflavored gelatin
- ¼ cup cold water
- ½ cup sugar
- ¼ cup all-purpose flour
- ½ teaspoon salt
- 1½ cups 2% milk
- ¾ teaspoon vanilla extract
- ¼ teaspoon almond extract
- 1 cup heavy whipping cream, whipped
- 1 cup flaked coconut
  Shaved fresh coconut, optional

1. Line unpricked pastry shell with a double thickness of heavy-duty foil. Bake at 450° for 8 minutes. Remove foil; bake 5 minutes longer. Cool on a wire rack.

2. Sprinkle gelatin over cold water; let stand for 1 minute. In a small saucepan, combine the sugar, flour and salt. Gradually stir in milk until smooth. Cook and stir over medium-low heat until mixture comes to a boil; cook and stir 1 minute longer or until thickened.

3. Remove from the heat. Whisk in the gelatin mixture until dissolved. Transfer to a large bowl. Refrigerate until slightly thickened, about 30 minutes.

4. Add extracts; beat on medium speed for 1 minute. Fold in whipped cream and flaked coconut. Spread into pie crust. Refrigerate for at least 3 hours before serving. Garnish pie with shaved fresh coconut if desired.

Triple Chocolate Dream Pie

Layered
Lemon Pies

Layered Lemon Pies

My sister shared this recipe with me, and it is simply delicious. The secret to the great flavor is using fresh lemon juice.

—**NANETTE SORENSEN** TAYLORSVILLE, UT

PREP: 55 MIN. + CHILLING
MAKES: 2 PIES (10 SERVINGS EACH)

    Pastry for two single-crust pies (9 inches)
1½ **cups sugar**
  6 **tablespoons cornstarch**
  ¼ **teaspoon salt**
  2 **cups cold water**
  3 **large egg yolks, lightly beaten**
  ⅓ **cup lemon juice**
  ¼ **cup butter, cubed**
  1 **teaspoon grated lemon peel**
  1 **teaspoon lemon extract**
  3 **drops yellow food coloring, optional**
SECOND LAYER
  1 **package (8 ounces) cream cheese, softened**
  1 **cup confectioners' sugar**
1½ **cups cold 2% milk**
  2 **packages (3.4 ounces each) instant lemon pudding mix**
TOPPING
  1 **package (8 ounces) cream cheese, softened**
  1 **cup confectioners' sugar**
  1 **carton (16 ounces) frozen whipped topping, thawed**

1. Preheat the oven to 450°. Line two 9-in. pie plates with pastry; trim and flute edges. Line unpricked pastry with a double thickness of heavy-duty foil. Bake 8 minutes. Remove foil; bake 5-7 minutes longer or until golden brown. Cool on wire racks.

2. In a large saucepan, combine sugar, cornstarch and salt. Stir in water until smooth. Cook and stir over medium-high heat until thickened and bubbly. Reduce heat; cook and stir 2 minutes longer. Remove from heat.

3. Stir a small amount of hot filling into egg yolks; return all to pan, stirring constantly. Bring to a gentle boil; cook and stir 2 minutes longer. Remove from heat. Gently stir in lemon juice, butter, lemon peel, extract and food coloring if desired. Cool to room temperature without stirring. Spread lemon mixture into crusts. Refrigerate 30 minutes or until firm.

4. In a large bowl, beat cream cheese and confectioners' sugar until smooth. Gradually beat in milk. Add pudding mix; beat 2 minutes longer. Let stand 2 minutes or until soft-set. Gently spread into pies. Refrigerate for 30 minutes or until set.

5. For topping, in a large bowl, beat cream cheese and confectioners' sugar until smooth. Fold in whipped topping. Spread over tops of pies. Refrigerate until set.

Frosty Peanut Butter Pie

With only a handful of ingredients, this creamy pie promises to deliver well-deserved compliments. Whenever I bring it to get-togethers, I'm asked for the recipe.

—**CHRISTI GILLENTINE** TULSA, OK

PREP: 10 MIN. + FREEZING
MAKES: 6 SERVINGS

  4 **ounces cream cheese, softened**
  ¼ **cup peanut butter**
  ¼ **cup sugar**
  1 **teaspoon vanilla extract**
  1 **package (8 ounces) frozen whipped topping, thawed**
  1 **chocolate crumb crust (8 inches)**
  2 **teaspoons chocolate syrup**

1. In a large bowl, beat the cream cheese, peanut butter, sugar and vanilla until smooth. Fold in the whipped topping. Spoon into the crust. Drizzle with chocolate syrup. Cover and freeze for 4 hours or until set.

2. Remove the pie from the freezer 30 minutes before serving.

Frosty Peanut
Butter Pie

**BLUSHING FRUIT TARTS WITH
AMARETTO TRUFFLE SAUCE** *PAGE 294*

Classic Tarts

◇◇

CRISP CRUSTS AND CREAMY FILLINGS ARE HERE TO STEAL THE SHOW. WHETHER YOUR TOP TART IS
LOADED WITH FRUIT, CHOCOLATE, CARAMEL OR NUTS, YOU SIMPLY CAN'T GO WRONG. TAKE A BITE
OUT OF THESE TARTS TO SEE WHY!

TURTLE PRALINE TART
PAGE 295

SWEET POTATO TARTLETS
PAGE 289

CHAI TRUFFLE TART
PAGE 292

White Chocolate Cranberry Almond Tart

White Chocolate Cranberry Almond Tart

A sweet white chocolate drizzle perfectly balances the tangy cranberries in my signature holiday dessert. I also make it for local coffee houses and restaurants.
—**TRISHA KRUSE** EAGLE, ID

PREP: 55 MIN. • **BAKE:** 20 MIN. + CHILLING
MAKES: 12 SERVINGS

- ½ cup slivered almonds, toasted
- 3 tablespoons sugar
- 1⅔ cups all-purpose flour
- ¼ teaspoon salt
- ¼ cup butter, melted
- ¼ cup heavy whipping cream
- ⅔ cup white baking chips

FILLING
- 2 cups fresh or frozen cranberries
- 1 cup sugar
- ½ cup dried cranberries
- ⅓ cup orange juice
- 2 tablespoons butter

TOPPING
- ⅔ cup white baking chips
- 2 teaspoons shortening
- ⅓ cup slivered almonds, toasted

1. Preheat oven to 375°. Place almonds and sugar in a food processor; pulse until almonds are ground. Add flour and salt; pulse until blended. Transfer mixture to a small bowl; stir in melted butter and cream. Press onto bottom and up the sides of an ungreased 9-in. fluted tart pan with removable bottom.
2. Bake 15-18 minutes or until lightly browned. Remove from oven; sprinkle baking chips evenly over bottom. Cool on a wire rack.
3. In a saucepan, combine the filling ingredients; bring to a boil. Reduce the heat, simmer, uncovered, 10-15 minutes or until slightly thickened, stirring occasionally. Pour over baking chips.
4. Bake 20-25 minutes or until filling is bubbly and crust is golden brown. Cool on a wire rack. Refrigerate for 2 hours or until cold.
5. In a microwave, melt baking chips and shortening; stir until smooth. Drizzle over tart. Sprinkle with almonds.
NOTE *To toast nuts, bake in a shallow pan in a 350° oven for 5-10 minutes or cook in a skillet over low heat until lightly browned, stirring occasionally.*

BIG BATCH
Chocolate Ganache Tarts

Decadent, chocolate mousse-like filling and a flaky crust make this very special. Be sure to coat your hands well with flour when putting the dough into pastry cups.
—**LORRAINE CALAND** SHUNIAH, ON

PREP: 30 MIN. + CHILLING
BAKE: 20 MIN. + COOLING
MAKES: 2 DOZEN

- ½ cup butter, softened
- 1 package (3 ounces) cream cheese, softened
- 1 cup all-purpose flour
- ½ cup semisweet chocolate chips
- ½ cup milk chocolate chips
- ⅔ cup heavy whipping cream
  Whipped cream, fresh raspberries and confectioners' sugar, optional

1. In a small bowl, beat the butter and cream cheese until smooth; beat in flour. Drop dough by scant tablespoonfuls into greased miniature muffin cups; with well-floured hands, press dough onto bottoms and up sides of cups.
2. Bake at 325° for 20-25 minutes or until golden brown. Cool for 5 minutes before removing from pans to wire racks to cool completely.
3. Place chocolate chips in a small bowl. In a small saucepan, bring cream just to a boil. Pour over chocolate; whisk until smooth. Transfer to a small bowl; cover and refrigerate until firm.
4. Beat chocolate mixture until soft peaks form. Pipe or spoon into the tart shells. Garnish with whipped cream, raspberries and confectioners' sugar if desired.

Citrus Cream Tartlets

Citrus Cream Tartlets

Make this attractive dessert ahead of time for convenience. It's nice for company, and the flavor is refreshing after a large meal.

—**BRIAN BARGER** CHEVY CHASE, MD

PREP: 20 MIN. • **BAKE:** 15 MIN. + CHILLING
MAKES: 2 SERVINGS

- ½ **cup chopped macadamia nuts, toasted**
- 3 **tablespoons sugar**
- 2 **tablespoons all-purpose flour**
- 2 **tablespoons cold butter**
- 6 **ounces cream cheese, softened**
- ¼ **cup confectioners' sugar**
- 2 **teaspoons each orange, lemon and lime juice**
- 1 **teaspoon each grated orange, lemon and lime peel**
  Orange slices, optional

1. In a food processor, combine nuts, sugar and the flour; cover and process until blended. Add butter; blend until mixture forms coarse crumbs.

2. Press onto the bottom and up the sides of two greased 4-in. tartlet pans with removable bottoms. Bake at 350° for 13-15 minutes or until golden brown. Cool completely.

3. In a small bowl, beat cream cheese until fluffy. Add the confectioners' sugar, citrus juices and peels; beat until blended.

4. Spoon into crusts. Refrigerate for at least 1 hour. Top with orange slices if desired.

"Fabulous. Fabulous. Easy and did I say fabulous? Everyone liked it."
—FIREDANSE
FROM TASTEOFHOME.COM

Peach-Blueberry Crumble Tart

Peach-Blueberry Crumble Tart

Whether fresh out of the oven or at room temperature with a scoop of vanilla ice cream, this easy-to-prepare tart is a favorite in our home.

—JAMES SCHEND PLEASANT PRAIRIE, WI

PREP: 30 MIN. + COOLING • **BAKE:** 35 MIN.
MAKES: 12 SERVINGS

1⅓ cups all-purpose flour
¼ cup sugar
¼ teaspoon ground cinnamon
½ cup butter, melted
2 cups frozen unsweetened blueberries, thawed
2 cups frozen unsweetened sliced peaches, thawed
1 tablespoon honey

CRUMB TOPPING

¼ cup all-purpose flour
¼ cup packed brown sugar
¼ cup old-fashioned oats
¼ cup chopped pecans
⅛ teaspoon ground cloves
2 tablespoons butter, melted

1. Preheat oven to 350°. In a small bowl, mix flour, sugar and cinnamon; stir in butter just until blended. Press onto the bottom and up the sides of a 9-in. fluted tart pan with removable bottom. Bake 15-20 minutes or until lightly browned. Cool on a wire rack.

2. In a large bowl, combine blueberries, peaches and the honey; toss to coat. In a small bowl, combine first five topping ingredients; stir in butter.

3. Spoon fruit mixture into crust; sprinkle with topping. Bake at 350° for 35-40 minutes or until the topping is golden brown and the filling is bubbly. Cool on a wire rack at least 15 minutes before serving.

Chocolate Pear Hazelnut Tart

As a foreign exchange student living in France, I was homesick. My host family's grandmother asked if I'd like to help bake a tart with her, and we were instantly bonded. She made the trip unforgettable for me and inspired my passion for baking.
—**LEXI MCKEOWN** LOS ANGELES, CA

PREP: 45 MIN. + CHILLING
BAKE: 30 MIN. + COOLING
MAKES: 12 SERVINGS

- 1¼ cups all-purpose flour
- ⅓ cup ground hazelnuts
- ¼ cup packed brown sugar
  Dash salt
- ½ cup cold butter, cubed
- 3 to 5 tablespoons ice water

FILLING
- 3 large eggs, separated
- ⅓ cup butter, softened
- ⅓ cup packed brown sugar
- 2 tablespoons amaretto or ½ teaspoon almond extract
- 1 cup ground hazelnuts
- 2 tablespoons baking cocoa
- 6 canned pear halves, drained, sliced and patted dry
- 2 tablespoons honey, warmed
  Confectioners' sugar, optional

1. In a small bowl, mix flour, hazelnuts, brown sugar and salt; cut in butter until crumbly. Gradually add ice water, tossing with a fork until dough holds together when pressed. Shape into a disk; wrap in plastic wrap. Refrigerate for 30 minutes or overnight.

2. Place egg whites in a large bowl; let stand at room temperature for 30 minutes. Preheat oven to 400°. On a lightly floured surface, roll the dough to a ⅛-in.-thick circle; transfer to a 9-in. fluted tart pan with removable bottom. Trim pastry even with edge. Prick bottom of pastry with a fork. Refrigerate while preparing the filling.

3. In a large bowl, cream butter and brown sugar until blended. Beat in egg yolks and amaretto. Beat in hazelnuts and cocoa.

4. With clean beaters, beat egg whites on medium speed until stiff peaks form. Fold a third of egg whites into hazelnut mixture, then fold in remaining whites. Spread onto bottom of pastry shell. Arrange pears over top.

5. Bake tart on a lower oven rack for 30-35 minutes or until crust is golden brown. Brush pears with warm honey. Cool on a wire rack. If desired, dust with confectioners' sugar before serving.

Chocolate Pear Hazelnut Tart

HOW-TO

DIY Ground Nuts

❶ Add 1 or 2 tablespoons of flour from the recipe with nuts into the food processor. Doing this will keep your mixture from turning into nut butter.

❷ Pulse processor on and off to prevent over processing. Repeat until nuts are completely ground.

Rustic Fruit Tart

Rustic Fruit Tart

My husband, Don, and I love pie, but finishing an entire one by ourselves is a tall order. So I make these easy tarts using fruit from our red raspberry bushes. Sometimes I'll swap apples, peaches or our homegrown blueberries for the rhubarb.

—**NAOMI OLSON** HAMILTON, MI

PREP: 20 MIN. + STANDING • **BAKE:** 25 MIN.
MAKES: 2 SERVINGS

- 1 **cup all-purpose flour**
- ½ **teaspoon salt**
- ¼ **cup canola oil**
- 2 **tablespoons milk**
- 1 **cup diced fresh or frozen rhubarb, thawed**
- 1 **cup fresh or frozen raspberries, thawed**
- ½ **cup sugar**
- 2 **tablespoons quick-cooking tapioca**

GLAZE
- 6 **tablespoons confectioners' sugar**
- 1 **teaspoon water**
- ⅛ **teaspoon almond extract**

1. In a large bowl, combine flour and salt. Add oil and milk, tossing with fork until mixture forms a ball. Shape the dough into a disk; wrap in plastic wrap. Refrigerate for at least 1 hour.

2. In another bowl, combine rhubarb, raspberries, sugar and tapioca; let stand for 15 minutes. Unwrap dough and place on a parchment-lined baking sheet. Cover with waxed paper and roll the dough into an 11-in. circle. Discard the waxed paper.

3. Spoon the fruit mixture into the center of dough to within 2 in. of the edges. Fold edges of dough over fruit, leaving center uncovered. Bake at 400° for 25-30 minutes or until crust is golden brown and filling is bubbly. Remove to a wire rack. Combine glaze ingredients until smooth. Drizzle over warm tart.

NOTE *If using frozen rhubarb, measure rhubarb while still frozen, then thaw completely. Drain in a colander, but do not press liquid out.*

⑤ INGREDIENTS *BIG BATCH*

Lime Tartlets

These sweet-tart treats are perfect for parties. I like to serve them with a tiny slice of melon for color.

—**BILLIE MOSS** WALNUT CREEK, CA

PREP: 30 MIN. • **BAKE:** 10 MIN./BATCH + COOLING
MAKES: 4 DOZEN

- 2 **packages (15 ounces each) refrigerated pie pastry**
- 1 **package (8 ounces) cream cheese, softened**
- 1 **cup (8 ounces) plain yogurt**
- 3 **tablespoons confectioners' sugar**
- 1 **jar (10 ounces) lime curd, divided**
  Whipped cream and lime slices, optional

1. Preheat oven to 450°. Roll out each pastry on a lightly floured surface. Using a 2½-in. round cookie cutter, cut out 12 circles from each pastry. Press rounds onto bottoms and up sides of greased mini-muffin cups. Prick bottoms with a fork.

2. Bake 8-10 minutes or until golden brown. Cool 5 minutes before removing from pans to wire racks.

3. In a large bowl, beat cream cheese, yogurt and confectioners' sugar until smooth. Stir in ½ cup lime curd. Spoon into tart shells; top with remaining lime curd. Garnish with whipped cream and lime slices if desired.

Sweet Potato Tartlets

My family can't resist sweet potato that's been mashed, stuffed into phyllo shells and topped with marshmallows. The bite-size tarts attract kids of all ages.

—MARLA CLARK MORIARTY, NM

START TO FINISH: 30 MIN.
MAKES: 15 TARTLETS

- 1 **medium sweet potato, peeled and chopped**
- 1 **tablespoon butter**
- 1 **tablespoon maple syrup**
- ⅛ **teaspoon ground cinnamon**
- ⅛ **teaspoon ground nutmeg**
- 1 **package (1.9 ounces) frozen miniature phyllo tart shells**
- 15 **miniature marshmallows**

1. Place the sweet potato in a small saucepan; cover with water. Bring to a boil. Reduce heat; cover and simmer for 10-15 minutes or until tender. Drain.
2. In a bowl, mash sweet potato with butter, syrup, cinnamon and nutmeg. Place 1 tablespoon potato mixture in each tart shell. Place on an ungreased baking sheet. Top with marshmallows. Bake at 350° for 8-12 minutes or until marshmallows are lightly browned.

TOP TIP

Sweet Potato Secret Ingredient

Want to add an extra zing to the mashed sweet potato in Sweet Potato Tartlets? Stir in some grated orange peel! It'll nicely complement the other flavors in these treats.

Sweet Potato Tartlets

Salted Caramel & Nut Cups

Salted Caramel & Nut Cups

These indulgent cups, with four kinds of nuts, have helped to make many of my get-togethers even more special.

—ROXANNE CHAN ALBANY, CA

PREP: 30 MIN. + CHILLING
BAKE: 20 MIN. + COOLING
MAKES: 1½ DOZEN

½ cup butter, softened
3 ounces cream cheese, softened
2 tablespoons sugar
1 cup all-purpose flour
1 large egg
¼ cup hot caramel ice cream topping
¼ to ½ teaspoon ground allspice
¼ cup chopped pecans
¼ cup chopped slivered almonds
¼ cup chopped macadamia nuts
¼ cup chopped pistachios

Coarse sea salt
Sweetened whipped cream, optional

1. In a small bowl, beat the butter, cream cheese and sugar until blended. Gradually beat in flour. Refrigerate, covered, 30 minutes or until firm.
2. Preheat oven to 350°. Shape level tablespoons of dough into balls; press evenly onto bottoms and up the sides of greased mini-muffin cups.
3. In a small bowl, whisk egg, caramel topping and allspice until blended. Stir in nuts. Place about 2 teaspoons mixture in each cup.
4. Bake 20-22 minutes or until edges are golden and filling is set. Immediately sprinkle tops with salt. Cool in pans for 10 minutes. Remove to wire racks to cool. If desired, serve with whipped cream.

BIG BATCH
Fudgy Turtle Pie

Everyone needs a fudgy, luscious dessert recipe. I love to mix chocolate, caramel and crunchy candy bits in a tart pie that's ooey-gooey fabulous.

—DOLORES VACCARO PUEBLO, CO

PREP: 55 MIN. + CHILLING
MAKES: 16 SERVINGS

1½ cups chocolate wafer crumbs (32 wafers)
⅓ cup butter, melted
FILLING
20 caramels
¼ cup heavy whipping cream
2 cups chopped pecans
4 Snickers candy bars (1.86 ounces each), chopped
TOPPING
2 cups (12 ounces) semisweet chocolate chips
1 cup heavy whipping cream
Caramel ice cream topping, optional
Additional chopped Snickers candy bars, optional

1. Preheat oven to 375°. In a small bowl, mix wafer crumbs and butter. Press onto bottom and up the sides of a greased 9-in. fluted tart pan with removable bottom. Bake 8-10 minutes or until set. Cool on a wire rack.
2. For filling, in a small heavy saucepan, combine caramels and cream. Cook and stir over low heat until caramels are melted. Stir in pecans. Remove from heat; pour into crust. Top with chopped Snickers candy.
3. For topping, place chocolate chips in a small bowl. In a small saucepan, bring cream just to a boil. Pour over chocolate; stir with a whisk until smooth. Pour and spread, if necessary, over top. Refrigerate 1 hour or until set.
4. If desired, drizzle ice cream topping over individual pieces and top with additional chopped candy.

Fudgy Turtle Pie

BIG BATCH

Chai Truffle Tart

When winter descends, I long for a decadent dessert to lift spirits. This chai-flavored tart with a salty caramel sauce delights the palate.

—**CHANTAL BOURBON** MONTREAL, QC

PREP: 55 MIN. + CHILLING
MAKES: 16 SERVINGS

- 2 cups crushed pretzels
- ¼ cup packed brown sugar
- ¾ cup butter, melted
- ½ cup hot caramel ice cream topping
- 16 ounces 70% cacao dark baking chocolate, chopped
- 1 cup heavy whipping cream
- 2 tablespoons butter
- 4 chai tea bags
- 2 tablespoons baking cocoa
- 3 ounces milk chocolate, melted
- 2 tablespoons finely chopped crystallized ginger

1. Preheat the oven to 350°. In a large bowl, mix the pretzels and brown sugar; stir in butter. Press the crumbs onto bottom and up the sides of a greased 9-in. fluted tart pan with removable bottom. Bake for 12-15 minutes or until golden brown. Drizzle caramel topping over crust; cool on a wire rack.

2. Place dark chocolate in a large bowl. In a small saucepan, bring cream and butter just to a boil; remove from heat. Add tea bags; let stand 10 minutes. Discard tea bags.

3. Reheat cream mixture just to a boil. Pour over dark chocolate; let stand 5 minutes. Stir with a whisk until smooth. Pour 1½ cups ganache into prepared crust. Refrigerate, covered, 1 hour or until firm. Press plastic wrap onto the surface of remaining ganache. Refrigerate 35-40 minutes or until firm enough to shape.

4. Shape reserved ganache into sixteen 1-in. balls; roll in cocoa. Drizzle milk chocolate over tart; sprinkle with ginger. Arrange truffles as desired on tart. Refrigerate until serving.

Chai Truffle Tart

Streusel-Topped Lemon Tart

A sweet streusel topping pairs well with this citrusy tart. It's a spectacular spin on classic lemon bars. The treat appears on my menus for both family and company.

—LISA VARNER EL PASO, TX

PREP: 20 MIN. • **BAKE:** 40 MIN. + COOLING
MAKES: 12 SERVINGS

1¼ cups all-purpose flour
⅓ cup confectioners' sugar
½ teaspoon grated lemon peel
½ cup plus 2 tablespoons cold butter

FILLING

4 large eggs
1½ cups sugar
¼ cup lemon juice
¼ cup all-purpose flour
1 teaspoon baking powder
1 teaspoon grated lemon peel

TOPPING

⅓ cup all-purpose flour
⅓ cup packed brown sugar
3 tablespoons cold butter
2 tablespoons chopped pecans
 Confectioners' sugar

1. Preheat oven to 350°. In a small bowl, combine flour, confectioners' sugar and lemon peel; cut in butter until crumbly. Press onto the bottom and ½ in. up the sides of a greased 9-in. springform pan. Bake 10-15 minutes or until the crust is lightly browned. Cool on a wire rack.
2. In a bowl, beat eggs, sugar and lemon juice until thick and lemon-colored. Beat in flour, baking powder and lemon peel until blended. Pour into crust. Bake for 20-25 minutes or until set.
3. For the topping, in a small bowl, combine flour and brown sugar; cut in butter until crumbly. Stir in the pecans. Sprinkle over filling. Bake 20-25 minutes or until a toothpick inserted near the center comes out clean. Cool completely on a wire rack. Remove the sides of the pan. Dust with the confectioners' sugar. Refrigerate leftovers.

Chocolate-Nut Caramel Tart

⑤ INGREDIENTS

Chocolate-Nut Caramel Tart

With just a few ingredients and in less time than you'd think, this irresistible tart is ready to go. It's a good recipe to have in your collection for any occasion.

—KATHY SPECHT CLINTON, MT

PREP: 25 MIN. + CHILLING
MAKES: 12 SERVINGS

1 sheet refrigerated pie pastry
1 jar (13 ounces) Nutella, divided
20 caramels
⅓ cup heavy whipping cream
1¾ cups chopped macadamia nuts, toasted
 Whipped cream, optional

1. Preheat oven to 450°. Unroll the pastry into a 9-in. fluted tart pan with removable bottom. Press onto bottom and up the sides of pan; trim pastry even with edge (discard trimmed pastry or save for another use). Generously prick bottom of crust with a fork. Bake for 9-11 minutes or until golden brown. Cool completely on a wire rack.
2. Reserve 2 tablespoons Nutella for topping; spread the remaining Nutella into cooled crust. In a small saucepan, combine caramels and cream; cook over medium-low heat until blended, stirring occasionally. Remove from heat; stir in the macadamia nuts. Spread mixture evenly over Nutella.
3. In a microwave, heat the reserved Nutella until warmed; drizzle over filling. Refrigerate for 1 hour or until firm. If desired, serve tart with whipped cream.
NOTE *To toast nuts, bake in a shallow pan in a 350° oven for 5-10 minutes or cook in a skillet over low heat until lightly browned, stirring occasionally.*

Blushing Fruit Tarts with Amaretto Truffle Sauce

Dried fruits are available year-round, so they are ideal ingredients for a winter tart. I also use the dough recipe to make cutout cookies.
—DENISE POUNDS HUTCHINSON, KS

PREP: 40 MIN. + CHILLING
BAKE: 25 MIN. + COOLING
MAKES: 4 TARTS

- 2 **cups all-purpose flour**
- 3 **tablespoons sugar**
  Dash salt
- ¾ **cup unsalted butter, cubed**
- 2 **large egg yolks, beaten**
- ¼ **cup chopped almonds**
- 3 **tablespoons coarse sugar**

FILLING
- ½ **cup chopped dried apricots**
- ½ **cup dried cranberries**
- ½ **cup dried cherries**
- 1 **tablespoon sugar**
- 1 **cup amaretto, divided**
- 1¼ **cups fresh or frozen blueberries**
- 2 **teaspoons cornstarch**

SAUCE
- 1 **cup white baking chips**
- ½ **cup heavy whipping cream**
- 3 **tablespoons amaretto**

1. Place flour, sugar and salt in a food processor. Cover, pulse until blended. Add the butter; pulse until mixture resembles coarse crumbs. While processing, gradually add the egg yolks until dough forms a ball. Divide dough into five portions; wrap each in plastic wrap. Refrigerate for 30 minutes or until easy to handle.
2. Roll out four dough portions into 6-in. circles. Press into 4-in. fluted tart pans with removable bottoms. Trim edges; save scraps. Line unpricked pastry shells with a double thickness of heavy-duty foil. Fill with dried beans, uncooked rice or pie weights. Place on baking sheet.
3. Bake at 400° for 8 minutes. Remove foil and weights; bake 4 minutes longer. Cool on a wire rack. Meanwhile, crumble remaining pastry; toss with almonds and sugar. Set aside.

4. In a small saucepan, combine the apricots, cranberries, cherries, sugar and ¾ cup amaretto. Bring to a boil. Add blueberries; cook 10 minutes longer. Combine cornstarch and remaining amaretto until smooth. Gradually stir into pan. Bring to a boil; cook and stir for 2 minutes or until thickened.
5. Pour filling into crusts; sprinkle with crumbled pastry mixture. Bake at 400° for 10-15 minutes or until topping is golden brown. Cool on a wire rack.
6. Place baking chips in a small bowl. In a small saucepan, bring cream just to a boil. Pour over the chips; whisk until smooth. Stir in amaretto. Cool, stirring occasionally. Drizzle over tarts.
NOTE *Let pie weights cool before storing. Beans and rice may be reused for pie weights, but not for cooking.*

Blushing Fruit Tarts with Amaretto Truffle Sauce

Cinnamon-Pear Rustic Tart

When visiting my husband's family in Montana, I fell in love with the comforting simplicity of each dish we had, especially this pear tart my mother-in-law made.
—LEAH WALDO JAMAICA PLAIN, MA

PREP: 45 MIN. + CHILLING • **BAKE:** 45 MIN.
MAKES: 8 SERVINGS

- 2½ cups all-purpose flour
- 1 teaspoon salt
- 1 cup cold butter, cubed
- 8 to 10 tablespoons ice water

FILLING

- 2 tablespoons butter
- 8 medium ripe pears, peeled and thinly sliced
- 1½ teaspoons ground cinnamon
- ⅓ cup apple cider or juice
- ¼ cup packed brown sugar
- 1 teaspoon vanilla extract
- 1 tablespoon coarse sugar

1. In a large bowl, mix flour and salt; cut in butter until crumbly. Gradually add ice water, tossing with a fork until the dough holds together when pressed. Shape into a disk; wrap in plastic wrap. Refrigerate for 30 minutes or overnight.

2. Preheat oven to 375°. In a large skillet, heat the butter over medium-high heat. Add pears and cinnamon; cook and stir 2-3 minutes or until tender. Stir in cider and brown sugar. Bring to a boil; cook and stir 8-10 minutes or until thickened. Stir in vanilla; cool slightly.

3. On a lightly floured surface, roll dough into a 14-in. circle. Transfer to a parchment paper-lined baking sheet.

4. Spoon the filling over pastry to within 2 in. of edge. Fold pastry edge over filling, pleating as you go and leaving an opening in the center. Brush folded pastry with water; sprinkle with coarse sugar. Bake 45-50 minutes or until crust is golden and filling is bubbly. Transfer tart to a wire rack to cool.

---

(5)INGREDIENTS *BIG BATCH*
Turtle Praline Tart

I'm very proud to say this beautiful tart is my own creation. It's easy enough to make for every day, but special enough for company or a potluck.
—KATHY SPECHT CLINTON, MT

PREP: 35 MIN. + CHILLING
MAKES: 16 SERVINGS

- 1 sheet refrigerated pie pastry
- 36 caramels
- 1 cup heavy whipping cream, divided
- 3½ cups pecan halves
- ½ cup semisweet chocolate chips, melted

1. Preheat oven to 450°. Unroll pastry on a lightly floured surface. Transfer to an 11-in. fluted tart pan with removable bottom; trim edges.

2. Line the unpricked pastry shell with a double thickness of heavy-duty foil. Bake for 8 minutes. Remove foil; bake for 5-6 minutes longer or until light golden brown. Cool on a wire rack.

3. In a large saucepan, combine the caramels and ½ cup cream. Cook and stir over medium-low heat until caramels are melted. Stir in pecans. Spread the filling evenly into crust. Drizzle with melted chocolate.

4. Refrigerate 30 minutes or until set. Whip remaining cream; serve with tart.

❝I made the Turtle Praline Tart for a bake sale and it was a hit!❞
—LISASKOV
FROM TASTEOFHOME.COM

Cinnamon-Pear Rustic Tart

RHUBARB STRAWBERRY
COBBLER *PAGE 301*

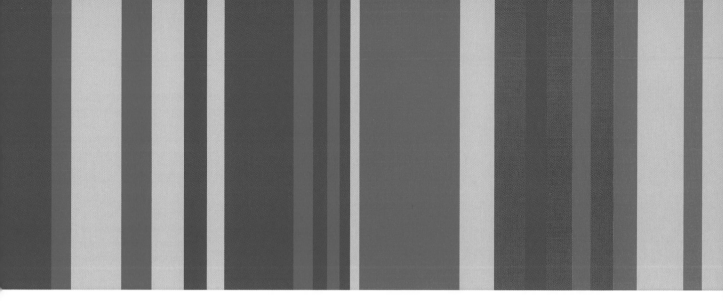

Crisps, Minis & More

LOOKING TO PUT A NEW SPIN ON A TRADITIONAL TREAT? TRY THESE CHANGE-OF-PACE DELIGHTS! FROM CRISPS AND COBBLERS TO GRUNTS AND SLUMPS, THESE RECIPES MAKE FOR A SWEET SLICE OF COMFORT ANY TIME OF THE YEAR. TRY THEM FOR SPECIAL OCCASIONS OR SIMPLY SERVE UP A LITTLE FUN AFTER WEEKNIGHT DINNERS.

SLOW-COOKED BLUEBERRY GRUNT *PAGE 300*

CARAMEL-APPLE SKILLET BUCKLE *PAGE 300*

LI'L PECAN PIES *PAGE 307*

Tropical Crisp

One bite of this sweet, juicy, crunchy fruit crisp, and you just might hear the crash of ocean waves and feel the warm sand under your toes!
—*TASTE OF HOME* TEST KITCHEN

PREP: 20 MIN. • **BAKE:** 30 MIN.
MAKES: 9 SERVINGS

1 **fresh pineapple, peeled and cubed**
4 **medium bananas, sliced**
¼ **cup packed brown sugar**
2 **tablespoons all-purpose flour**

TOPPING
⅓ **cup old-fashioned oats**
¼ **cup all-purpose flour**
2 **tablespoons flaked coconut, toasted**
2 **tablespoons brown sugar**
¼ **teaspoon ground nutmeg**
¼ **cup cold butter, cubed**

1. Preheat the oven to 350°. In a large bowl, combine pineapple and bananas. Sprinkle with the brown sugar and flour; toss to coat. Transfer to an 11x7-in. baking dish coated with cooking spray.
2. In a small bowl, mix the first five topping ingredients; cut in butter until crumbly. Sprinkle over pineapple mixture.
3. Bake 30-35 minutes or until filling is bubbly and topping is golden brown. Serve warm or at room temperature.

NOTE *To toast coconut, bake in a shallow pan in a 350° oven for 5-10 minutes or cook in a skillet over low heat until golden brown, stirring occasionally.*

Tropical Crisp

Apple Danish Pies

Prepared with an easy crescent roll crust and served in cute ramekins, these single-serving pies are fun to share with your special someone.
—**JOANNE WRIGHT** NILES, MI

PREP: 25 MIN. • **BAKE:** 20 MIN.
MAKES: 2 SERVINGS

- ⅓ cup sugar
- 1 tablespoon plus 1 teaspoon cornstarch
- ½ teaspoon ground cinnamon
- ⅛ teaspoon ground nutmeg
- 2 cups chopped peeled tart apples
- ¼ cup unsweetened apple juice
- 1 tube (4 ounces) refrigerated crescent rolls
- 1 package (3 ounces) cream cheese, softened
- 2 tablespoons confectioners' sugar
- ½ teaspoon vanilla extract

GLAZE
- ¼ cup confectioners' sugar
- 2 teaspoons 2% milk

1. In a small saucepan, combine the sugar, cornstarch, cinnamon and nutmeg. Add apples and juice; toss to coat. Bring to a boil; cook and stir for 2 minutes or until thickened. Remove from the heat.
2. Separate crescent dough into four triangles. On a lightly floured surface, roll two triangles into 5-in. circles. Place each into an 8-oz. ramekin, pressing dough onto the bottom and ½ in. up the sides.
3. In a small bowl, beat cream cheese, confectioners' sugar and vanilla. Spread over the dough in ramekins. Top with apple mixture. Roll out remaining crescent dough into 4-in. circles; place over filling. Cut slits in top.
4. Bake at 375° for 20-25 minutes or until filling is bubbly and topping is golden brown. Combine glaze ingredients; drizzle over the pies. Serve warm.

Cherry-Blackberry Crisp

BIG BATCH
Cherry-Blackberry Crisp

I've used mulberries instead of blackberries in this old family recipe. Whichever you choose, it's a mouthwatering treat.
—**WANDA ALLENSWORTH** WEBSTER CITY, IA

PREP: 20 MIN. + STANDING • **BAKE:** 55 MIN.
MAKES: 15 SERVINGS

- ⅔ cup packed brown sugar
- 2 tablespoons quick-cooking tapioca
- ½ teaspoon almond extract
- ¼ teaspoon ground cinnamon
- 4 cups frozen pitted tart cherries, thawed
- 2 cups frozen unsweetened blackberries, thawed

TOPPING
- 1½ cups all-purpose flour
- 1½ cups sugar
  Dash salt
- ⅔ cup cold butter
- 1½ cups finely chopped walnuts
  Whipped cream

1. In a large bowl, combine the brown sugar, tapioca, extract and cinnamon. Gently stir in cherries and blackberries. Allow to stand for 10 minutes. Pour into a greased 13x9-in. baking dish.
2. In another bowl, combine the flour, sugar and salt. Cut in the butter until crumbly. Add walnuts; sprinkle over fruit. Bake, uncovered, at 350° for 55-60 minutes or until topping is golden brown and filling is bubbly. Serve warm with whipped cream.

"The topping adds a nice touch to the flavor combination."
—SALLYGIRL7
FROM TASTEOFHOME.COM

Slow-Cooked Blueberry Grunt

If you love blueberries, then you can't go wrong with this easy dessert. For a special treat, serve it warm with vanilla ice cream.
—**CLEO GONSKE** REDDING, CA

PREP: 20 MIN. • **COOK:** 2½ HOURS
MAKES: 6 SERVINGS

- 4 **cups fresh or frozen blueberries**
- ¾ **cup sugar**
- ½ **cup water**
- 1 **teaspoon almond extract**

DUMPLINGS
- 2 **cups all-purpose flour**
- 4 **teaspoons baking powder**
- 1 **teaspoon sugar**
- ½ **teaspoon salt**
- 1 **tablespoon cold butter**
- 1 **tablespoon shortening**
- ¾ **cup 2% milk**
  Vanilla ice cream, optional

1. Place blueberries, sugar, water and extract in a 3-qt. slow cooker; stir to combine. Cook, covered, on high 2-3 hours or until bubbly.
2. For the dumplings, in a small bowl, whisk the flour, baking powder, sugar and salt. Cut in butter and shortening until crumbly. Add milk; stir just until a soft dough forms.
3. Drop dough by tablespoonfuls on top of hot blueberry mixture. Cook, covered, 30 minutes longer or until a toothpick inserted in the center of dumplings comes out clean. If desired, serve warm with ice cream.

Caramel-Apple Skillet Buckle

My grandma used to make a version of this for me when I was a little girl. She would make it using fresh apples from her backyard tree. I've adapted her recipe because I love the mix of apples, pecans and caramel.
—**EMILY HOBBS** SPRINGFIELD, MO

PREP: 35 MIN. • **BAKE:** 1 HOUR + STANDING
MAKES: 12 SERVINGS

- ½ **cup butter, softened**
- ¾ **cup sugar**

Caramel-Apple Skillet Buckle

- 2 **large eggs**
- 1 **teaspoon vanilla extract**
- 2 **cups all-purpose flour**
- 2½ **teaspoons baking powder**
- 1¾ **teaspoons ground cinnamon**
- ½ **teaspoon ground ginger**
- ¼ **teaspoon salt**
- 1½ **cups buttermilk**

TOPPING
- ⅔ **cup packed brown sugar**
- ½ **cup all-purpose flour**
- ¼ **cup cold butter**
- ¾ **cup finely chopped pecans**
- ½ **cup old-fashioned oats**
- 6 **cups thinly sliced peeled Gala or other sweet apples (about 6 medium)**
- 18 **caramels, unwrapped**
- 1 **tablespoon buttermilk**
  Vanilla ice cream, optional

1. Preheat oven to 350°. In a large bowl, cream butter and sugar until light and fluffy. Add eggs, one at a time, beating well after each addition. Beat in vanilla. In another bowl, whisk flour, baking powder, cinnamon, ginger and salt; add to creamed mixture alternately with buttermilk, beating well after each addition. Pour into a greased 12-in. ovenproof skillet.
2. For the topping, in a small bowl, mix brown sugar and flour; cut in butter until crumbly. Stir in pecans and oats; sprinkle over batter. Top with apples. Bake for 60-70 minutes or until apples are golden brown. Cool in pan on a wire rack.
3. In a microwave, melt caramels with buttermilk; stir until smooth. Drizzle over cake. Let stand until set. If desired, serve with ice cream.

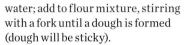

Rhubarb Strawberry Cobbler

Mom's yummy cobbler is a wonderful finale to any meal. This seasonal family favorite is chock-full of berries and rhubarb and has a thick, easy-to-make crust.

—SUSAN EMERY EVERETT, WA

PREP: 20 MIN. • **BAKE:** 40 MIN.
MAKES: 8 SERVINGS

- 1⅓ cups sugar
- ⅓ cup all-purpose flour
- 4 cups sliced fresh or frozen rhubarb, thawed (½-inch pieces)
- 2 cups halved fresh strawberries
- 2 tablespoons butter, cubed

CRUST

- 2 cups all-purpose flour
- ½ teaspoon salt
- ⅔ cup canola oil
- ⅓ cup warm water
- 1 tablespoon 2% milk
- 1 tablespoon sugar
  Vanilla ice cream, optional

1. Preheat oven to 425°. In a large bowl, mix sugar and flour. Add fruit; toss to coat. Transfer to a greased 11x7-in. baking dish. Dot with butter.
2. For crust, in a bowl, mix flour and salt. In another bowl, whisk oil and water; add to flour mixture, stirring with a fork until a dough is formed (dough will be sticky).
3. Roll dough between two pieces of waxed paper into an 11x7-in. rectangle. Remove top piece of waxed paper; invert rectangle over filling. Gently peel off waxed paper. Brush pastry with milk; sprinkle with sugar.
4. Bake 40-50 minutes or until golden brown. If desired, serve with ice cream.
NOTE *If using frozen rhubarb, measure rhubarb while still frozen, then thaw completely. Drain in a colander, but do not press liquid out.*

Rhubarb
Strawberry
Cobbler

⑤INGREDIENTS *BIG BATCH*

Chocolate Lover's Pizza

I created this after my dad said that my graham cracker crust should be topped with dark chocolate and pecans. It's easy to customize by adding your favorite chocolate and toppers. Dad thinks the whole world should know about this pizza.

—KATHY RAIRIGH MILFORD, IN

PREP: 10 MIN. • **BAKE:** 10 MIN. + CHILLING
MAKES: 16 SLICES

- 2½ cups graham cracker crumbs
- ⅔ cup butter, melted
- ½ cup sugar
- 2 packages Dove dark chocolate candies (9½ ounces each)
- ½ cup chopped pecans

1. Combine cracker crumbs, butter and sugar; press onto a greased 12-in. pizza pan.
2. Bake at 375° for 7-9 minutes or until lightly browned. Top with the chocolate candies; bake for 2-3 minutes longer or until chocolate is softened.
3. Spread chocolate over crust; sprinkle with nuts. Cool on a wire rack for 15 minutes. Refrigerate for 1-2 hours or until set.

Summer Blackberry Cobbler

Tart Cranberry Apple Crisp

I first tasted this apple crisp at a church potluck and thought it was delicious. I lightened the recipe by reducing the sugar and adding oats to replace some of the flour. I was so pleased with the results.
—**CAROLYN DIPASQUALE** MIDDLETOWN, RI

PREP: 15 MIN. • **BAKE:** 40 MIN.
MAKES: 8 SERVINGS

- 5 medium tart apples, sliced
- 1 tablespoon all-purpose flour
- 1 can (14 ounces) whole-berry cranberry sauce

TOPPING
- ¾ cup quick-cooking oats
- ⅓ cup packed brown sugar
- ¼ cup all-purpose flour
- 2 tablespoons plus 2 teaspoons wheat bran
- 2 tablespoons canola oil
- 2 tablespoons butter, melted
- ¾ teaspoon ground cinnamon
  Fat-free vanilla frozen yogurt, optional

1. In a large bowl, combine the apples and flour; toss to coat. Stir in cranberry sauce. Transfer to a 13x9-in. baking dish coated with cooking spray.
2. In a small bowl, combine first seven topping ingredients; sprinkle over apple mixture. Bake, uncovered, at 350° for 40-45 minutes or until topping is golden brown and fruit is tender. Serve with frozen yogurt if desired.

"We ate it hot from the oven and will be making it again and again. I'm considering this for Thanksgiving dessert."
—**CJBRUNICK**
FROM TASTEOFHOME.COM

Summer Blackberry Cobbler

My husband is from Alabama, so I like to treat him to classic Southern desserts. This cobbler is a must-have for us in the summer.
—**KIMBERLY DANEK PINKSON**
SAN ANSELMO, CA

PREP: 25 MIN. • **BAKE:** 25 MIN.
MAKES: 6 SERVINGS

- 5 cups fresh blackberries
- ⅓ cup turbinado (washed raw) sugar
- 2 tablespoons quick-cooking tapioca
- 1 tablespoon lemon juice
- 1½ teaspoons cornstarch or arrowroot flour
- 1 cup all-purpose flour
- ¼ cup sugar
- 1¼ teaspoons baking powder
- ¼ teaspoon salt
- ¼ teaspoon ground cinnamon
- 3 tablespoons cold butter
- ⅓ cup fat-free milk
  Vanilla ice cream, optional

1. Preheat oven to 375°. In a large bowl, combine first five ingredients. Transfer to a 2-qt. baking dish coated with cooking spray.
2. In a small bowl, combine flour, sugar, baking powder, salt and cinnamon. Cut in the butter until mixture resembles coarse crumbs. Stir in milk just until moistened. Drop by tablespoonfuls onto the blackberry mixture.
3. Bake, uncovered, 25-30 minutes or until golden brown. Serve warm, with ice cream if desired.

Personal Pear Pot Pies

Talk about cutie pies! These mini treats baked in ramekins are yummy and easy to prepare using frozen puff pastry. Top each warm dessert with a scoop of vanilla ice cream.

—BEE ENGELHART
BLOOMFIELD TOWNSHIP, MI

PREP: 30 MIN. • **BAKE:** 25 MIN.
MAKES: 4 SERVINGS

- 2 **tablespoons butter, divided**
- 2 **tablespoons sugar**
- 1 **tablespoon cornflake crumbs**
- 1 **tablespoon brown sugar**
- ¼ **teaspoon ground ginger**
- 2 **cups finely chopped peeled Anjou pears**
- 2 **cups finely chopped peeled Bartlett pears**
- 1 **tablespoon orange juice**
- ½ **sheet frozen puff pastry, thawed**
- 1 **large egg, lightly beaten Vanilla ice cream**

1. Preheat oven to 400°. Grease bottoms and sides of four 8-oz. ramekins with 1 tablespoon butter (do not butter rims). Place on a baking sheet.

2. In a small bowl, mix sugar, cornflake crumbs, brown sugar and ginger. In a large bowl, toss pears with orange juice. Add crumb mixture and toss to combine. Divide mixture among ramekins; dot with remaining butter.

3. Without unfolding, cut pastry crosswise into fourteen ¼-in. strips. Carefully unfold strips. Cut eight strips in half; cut remaining strips into thirds. Arrange over the ramekins in a lattice pattern, using four long strips and four short strips for each. Gently press ends onto ramekin rims. Brush lattices with egg.

4. Bake 25-30 minutes or until filling is bubbly and pastry is golden brown. Serve warm with ice cream.

Personal Pear Pot Pies

Nutella Hand Pies

Nutella Hand Pies

These pint-size Nutella hand pies made with puff pastry are too good to keep to yourself. Indulge with friends!
—*TASTE OF HOME* **TEST KITCHEN**

PREP: 10 MIN. • **BAKE:** 20 MIN.
MAKES: 9 SERVINGS

- 1 large egg
- 1 tablespoon water
- 1 sheet frozen puff pastry, thawed
- 3 tablespoons Nutella
- 1 to 2 teaspoons grated orange peel

ICING
- ⅓ cup confectioners' sugar
- ½ teaspoon orange juice
- ⅛ teaspoon grated orange peel
     Additional Nutella, optional

1. Preheat oven to 400°. In a small bowl, whisk egg with water.
2. Unfold puff pastry; cut into nine squares. Place 1 teaspoon Nutella in center of each; sprinkle with orange peel. Brush edges of pastry with egg mixture. Fold one corner over filling to form a triangle; press edges to seal. Transfer to an ungreased baking sheet.
3. Bake 17-20 minutes or until golden brown. Cool slightly.

4. In a small bowl, mix confectioners' sugar, orange juice and orange peel; drizzle over pies. If desired, warm additional Nutella in a microwave and drizzle over tops.

Peach Crumble Dessert

Old-fashioned, delicious and easy to make describe this yummy dessert. It's wonderful served with ice cream.
—**NANCY HORSBURGH** EVERETT, ON

PREP: 15 MIN. • **BAKE:** 35 MIN.
MAKES: 10-12 SERVINGS

- 6 cups sliced peeled ripe peaches
- ¼ cup packed brown sugar
- 3 tablespoons all-purpose flour
- 1 teaspoon lemon juice
- ½ teaspoon grated lemon peel
- ½ teaspoon ground cinnamon

TOPPING
- 1 cup all-purpose flour
- 1 cup sugar
- 1 teaspoon baking powder
- ¼ teaspoon salt
- ¼ teaspoon ground nutmeg
- 1 large egg, lightly beaten
- ½ cup butter, melted and cooled
     Vanilla ice cream, optional

1. Preheat oven to 375°. Place peaches in a greased shallow 2½-qt. baking dish. In a small bowl, combine brown sugar, flour, lemon juice, peel and cinnamon; sprinkle over the peaches.
2. Combine flour, sugar, baking powder, salt and nutmeg. Stir in egg until the mixture resembles coarse crumbs. Sprinkle over the peaches. Pour butter evenly over topping.
3. Bake 35-40 minutes. Serve with ice cream if desired.

Skillet Blueberry Slump

My mother-in-law made a slump of wild blueberries with dumplings and served it warm with a pitcher of farm cream. We've been eating slump for nearly 60 years!
—**ELEANORE EBELING** BREWSTER, MN

PREP: 25 MIN. • **BAKE:** 20 MIN.
MAKES: 6 SERVINGS

- 4 cups fresh or frozen blueberries
- ½ cup sugar
- ½ cup water
- 1 teaspoon grated lemon peel
- 1 tablespoon lemon juice
- 1 cup all-purpose flour
- 2 tablespoons sugar
- 2 teaspoons baking powder
- ½ teaspoon salt
- 1 tablespoon butter
- ½ cup 2% milk
     Vanilla ice cream

1. Preheat the oven to 400°. In a 10-in. ovenproof skillet, combine the first five ingredients; bring to a boil. Reduce heat; simmer, uncovered, 9-11 minutes or until slightly thickened, stirring occasionally.
2. Meanwhile, in a small bowl, whisk flour, sugar, baking powder and salt. Cut in butter until mixture resembles coarse crumbs. Add milk; stir just until moistened.
3. Drop batter in six portions on top of the blueberry mixture. Transfer to oven. Bake, uncovered, 17-20 minutes or until the dumplings are golden brown. Serve warm with ice cream.

Skillet Blueberry Slump

Cranberry-Apple Nut Crunch

Cranberry-Apple Nut Crunch

My mother gave me the recipe for this dessert, which I think is especially pretty and very appropriate for fall. I updated the recipe to use instant oatmeal to make it even easier.

—JOYCE SHEETS LAFAYETTE, IN

PREP: 15 MIN. • **BAKE:** 50 MIN.
MAKES: 8 SERVINGS

- 3 cups chopped peeled apples
- 2 cups fresh or frozen cranberries
- 3 tablespoons all-purpose flour
- 1 cup sugar

TOPPING

- 3 packets (1.51 ounces each) instant oatmeal with cinnamon and spice
- ¾ cup chopped pecans
- ½ cup all-purpose flour
- ½ cup packed brown sugar
- ½ cup butter, melted
  Whole cranberries for garnish
  Vanilla ice cream, optional

In a large bowl, combine the first four ingredients and mix well. Place in a 2-qt. baking dish; set aside. For the topping, combine the oatmeal, nuts, flour, sugar and butter in another bowl. Mix well; spoon evenly over fruit mixture. Bake, uncovered, at 350° for 50-60 minutes or until fruit is bubbly and tender. Garnish with cranberries. Serve warm with ice cream if desired.

TOP TIP

Cranberry Choosing

Fresh cranberries are in season from early fall through December. When buying, look for packages with shiny, bright red (light or dark) berries. Avoid berries that are bruised, shriveled or have brown spots. Ripe cranberries should bounce when dropped, which is why cranberries are sometimes called bounceberries.

Sugar Cookie Fruit Pizzas

Purchased sugar cookies create a sweet "crust" for these colorful pizzas. Make them throughout the year using a variety of fresh and canned fruits.

—MARGE HODEL ROANOKE, IL

PREP: 45 MIN. + CHILLING
MAKES: 1 DOZEN

- ½ cup sugar
- 1 tablespoon cornstarch
- ½ cup unsweetened pineapple juice
- ¼ cup water
- 2 tablespoons lemon juice
- 4 ounces cream cheese, softened
- ¼ cup confectioners' sugar
- 1¾ cups whipped topping
- 12 sugar cookies (3 inches)
- 1 cup fresh blueberries
- 1 cup chopped peeled kiwifruit
- ½ cup chopped fresh strawberries

1. For glaze, in a small saucepan, combine the sugar, cornstarch, pineapple juice, water and lemon juice until smooth. Bring to a boil; cook and stir for 2 minutes or until thickened. Transfer to a small bowl; refrigerate until cooled but not set.
2. In a small bowl, beat cream cheese and confectioners' sugar until smooth; fold in whipped topping. Spread over tops of cookies. Arrange fruit on top; drizzle with glaze. Refrigerate for 1 hour or until chilled.

Li'l Pecan Pies

I love having all the rich, traditional flavors of a full-size pecan pie in an adorable size. They are just perfect for my husband and me.

—CHRISTINE BOITOS LIVONIA, MI

PREP: 15 MIN. + CHILLING
BAKE: 35 MIN. + COOLING
MAKES: 2 SERVINGS

- ½ cup all-purpose flour
- ⅛ teaspoon salt
- 3 tablespoons shortening
- 4 teaspoons cold water

Li'l Pecan Pies

FILLING
- ⅓ cup pecan halves
- 1 large egg
- ⅓ cup packed brown sugar
- ⅓ cup corn syrup
- ½ teaspoon vanilla extract
  Whipped cream, optional

1. In a small bowl, combine flour and salt; cut in shortening until crumbly. Gradually add water, tossing with a fork until dough forms a ball. Cover and refrigerate for at least 30 minutes.

2. Divide dough in half. Roll each half into a 6-in. circle. Transfer to two 4½-in. tart pans; fit pastry into pans, trimming if necessary. Arrange pecans in shells.
3. In another small bowl, whisk egg, brown sugar, corn syrup and vanilla. Pour over pecans. Place shells on a baking sheet. Bake at 375° for 35-40 minutes or until a knife inserted near the center comes out clean. Cool on a wire rack. Top with whipped cream if desired.

COOKIES